TEST BANK

for

BARON AND BYRNE
SOCIAL PSYCHOLOGY
EIGHTH EDITION

---

prepared by

Thomas T. Jackson
Fort Hays State University

Allyn and Bacon
Boston · London · Toronto · Sydney · Tokyo · Singapore

TABLE OF CONTENTS

INTRODUCTION

EXAM CONSTRUCTION FORM

INTRODUCTION

This testbank is to accompany *Social Psychology: Understanding Human Interaction (Eighth Edition)* by Baron and Byrne. The testbank provides 2075 multiple choice questions that address the content in the various chapters of the textbook. Some of the features of this testbank are standard, yet some of the features represent what I would like to see in a testbank. A listing of the features are:

1. Each chapter has between 140 and 160 questions.
2. In an attempt to provide minimum coverage of the content addressed in the Learning Objectives (LO), with the exception of two LOs in the entire testbank each LO in each of the 14 chapters has a minimum of four questions related to issues in the LO. Some LOs have over 10 questions.
3. Each chapter in the testbank begins with a listing of the specific LOs for that chapter and then is followed by the questions. Few testbanks have the LOs listed with the chapters, which means that in order to make up an exam, the professor may need at least one other book, either the textbook or another supplement. Including the LOs in the current testbank is a convenience for the professor.
4. This testbank also has the names of the chapters listed in the Table of Contents, in addition to the chapter name being in the running head. In my experience, many testbanks list the chapter number and page number on which the chapter starts, but not the chapter name. When making up an exam, I usually remember the topics over which I want to construct the exam, but rarely the chapter numbers from which to select the material. The inclusion of the chapter names is a convenience for the professor.
4. There are no "all of the above," "none of the above," type of answers in this testbank.
5. Each multiple choice question has specific information at the left of the item. The following question illustrates this information:

1.5	An example of how common sense knowledge can be confusing comes from
c	a. unsuccessful personal encounters
LO 1	b. unsuccessful social encounters
Applied	c. contradictory proverbs
5	d. personal idiosyncracies
M	

In this item, the first line lists the chapter and number of the question (Chapter 1, item 5). The second line contains the correct answer to the question and will be a **bold** typed small letter (c in this example). I have used small letters in the information line for consistency with the small letters in the question. The third line contains the specific Learning Objective (LO 1 in this example) for the chapter. Many chapters have over 20 LOs. The fourth line contains the type of question, either Applied, Concept, Fact, or Study (Applied in this example). The fifth line contains the page number of the text on which the relevant material is presented (page 5 in this example). When the material covers two pages of the text, I have underline usually used the first page number. The sixth line contains a subjective estimate of the item difficulty (M in the example). There are three categories of difficulty, Easy (E), Medium (M), or Challenging (C). The assignment of difficulty level is based upon several considerations. The type of item (Applied, Concept, Fact, Study) was considered, with Concept and Fact questions usually being easier than Applied and Study questions. The wording and specificity of the question was also considered. Finally, I have collected limited performance data over some of the questions from previous editions of the testbanks for *Social Psychology*, and used some of that information in making the assignment of difficulty. However, the difficulty rating is still highly subjective.

6. I have also included a sheet titled, "EXAM CONSTRUCTION FORM" in the front of this testbank. This sheet is a convenient form that could be used when making up an exam. The headings for the various columns correspond to the information items at the left of each question in the testbank. This

form provides an easy way to see what LOs are being covered by the exam, the mix of types of question on the exam, what parts of the chapter have been covered by the exam, and the mix of difficulty level of questions on the exam. The last column could be used to write a brief comment about the topic of a question, or it could be used as a place to record performance data after the exam. I have found that using this form reduces my time in preparing an exam, makes it much easier for a secretary to prepare the exam from the computerized version since all the information needed is in an organized format, and provides me with an organized record of each exam.

7.   This testbank will also have a computerized version that will have many options for your use.

If you have modifications of the testbank you would like to see or suggestions for improvement of this testbank, please send this information to me at the address listed below.

I sincerely appreciate the patience, encouragement, and guidance of Beth Brooks of the Allyn and Bacon psychology production team. I also appreciate the work of Laura Ellingson in making this testbank a more consistent supplement. In order that this testbank provide some continuity with previous testbanks for this textbook, I have used many of the questions from these earlier testbanks. Accordingly, I thank the many individuals who prepared these questions.

I realize that a testbank is not a "big deal" in the grand scheme of things, but I also realize that producing one takes time and the willingness of individuals to postpone activities until the testbank is finished. In this vein, I sincerely thank my wife, Nancy, and my son, Bret, for their willingness to tolerate my endeavors.

Thomas T. Jackson, Ph.D.
Department of Psychology
Fort Hays State University
Hays, Kansas 67601
pstj@fhsuvm.fhsu.edu

SOCIAL PSYCHOLOGY (8th Edition)

Chapter_____   Form _____   Date _____

Item	Question Number	Learning Objective	Type	Page Number	Difficulty	Comments

Question Types   Difficulty
A = Applied   **F** = Fact   **E** = Easy
C = Concept   **S** = Study   **M** = Medium
                                    C = Challenging

CHAPTER 1

Learning Objectives

After studying this chapter, students should be able to:

1.   *Describe everyday experience as a basis of knowledge in social psychology, and indicate why "common sense" notions present a confusing picture of human social behavior.*

2.   *Define social psychology.*

3.   *Explain why social psychology is a "scientific field."*

4.   *Explain why the field of social psychology focuses its study on the behavior of individuals.*

5.   *Describe the five major causes of social behavior and thought: a) the actions and characteristics of others; b) cognitive processes; c) ecological variables; d) cultural context; and e) biological factors.*

6.   *Compare the approaches to social psychology in the 1908 McDougall text and the 1924 text by Floyd Allport.*

7.   *Describe the growth in social psychology through the 1930s, focusing on the contributions by Sherif and Lewin.*

8.   *Describe how the behavior of the boys who participated in Lewin's experiment was affected by whether their leader was autocratic, laissez-faire, or democratic.*

9.   *Describe contributions of the 1940s, 50s, and 60s, including emphases on groups, the authoritarian personality, and cognitive dissonance theory.*

10.   *Describe the growing influence of the cognitive perspective and the recent trend toward application in such areas as health, the legal process, and work settings.*

11.   *Explain two guesses offered by the authors regarding expected trends to the year 2000 and beyond.*

12.   *Examine historical changes regarding the assumption that the findings of social psychology are generalizable across cultures and across gender.*

13.   *Describe the basic steps involved when an investigator conducts an experiment.*

14.   *Understand the nature of independent variables and dependent variables, drawing examples from the mood/willingness to help experiment.*

15.   *Give an example illustrating how an interaction between independent variables can be demonstrated only when the study includes two or more independent variables.*

16.   *Explain why it is important that subjects be randomly assigned to groups in an experiment.*

17.   *Explain the importance of holding factors other than the independent variable constant.*

18.   *Describe two circumstances under which it is impossible to use the experimental method to investigate a particular question.*

19.   *Describe the procedures followed when the correlational method is used to examine a hypothesis.*

20.   *Describe the major drawback that plagues the correlational method, and give examples illustrating how third variables often underlie correlational findings.*

21.   *Explain how replication, meta-analysis, and converging operations help increase confidence in the validity of social psychological findings.*

22.   *Trace the steps in an investigation, from formulating a theory, to deriving a hypothesis, to testing the hypothesis, and finally to re-examining the theory.*

23.   *Understand why social psychologists sometimes deceive their research subjects.*

24.   *Describe ethical issues raised by the use of deception, and indicate how informed consent and debriefing help to decrease the dangers of deception.*

Questions

1.1
a
LO 1
Concept
5
M

Common sense is often confused with social psychology because
a. both common sense and social psychology refer to collective knowledge about social interactions
b. social psychology shows that common sense is inaccurate
c. psychology is the scientific pursuit of common sense
d. people like to apply psychology in common sense situations

1.2
c
LO 1
Applied
4
E

Which of the following situations is most relevant to social psychology?
a. an angry response to an automobile breaking down
b. learning how I.Q. is calculated
c. falling in love with an attractive stranger
d. evolutionary theory

1.3
c
LO 1
Applied
5
M

An example of how common sense knowledge can be confusing comes from
a. unsuccessful personal encounters
b. unsuccessful social encounters
c. contradictory proverbs
d. personal idiosyncracies

1.4
b
LO 1
Fact
5
M

The text's evaluation of everyday experience as a source of information regarding social behavior is that
a. it does not contain truthful statements
b. it is quite inconclusive
c. it is quite conclusive
d. it is not very insightful or informative

1.5
a
LO 1
Applied
5
M

"Opposites attract" and "Birds of a feather flock together" are examples of common sense explanations of social behavior. Why do these explanations create difficulties?
a. They both explain the same behavior.
b. Only one of them is accurate.
c. Neither one of them is accurate.
d. The behavior being explained is not relevant.

1.6
a
LO 2
Concept
6
M

Social psychology is the field that
a. seeks to understand the nature and causes of individual behavior and thought in social situations
b. seeks to understand how groups of people interact with one another
c. seeks to understand the nature and causes of individual behavior and attitudes
d. seeks to integrate knowledge about individual interactions and knowledge about group interactions

1.7
a
LO 2
Concept
6
M

The text argues that social psychology is difficult to define for two reasons. These two reasons are
a. its diversity and its rapid rate of change
b. its applied nature and its short history
c. its diversity and its short history
d. its applied nature and its rapid rate of change

1.8
c
LO 2
Concept
6
E

The text's definition of social psychology includes the phrase
a. historically based
b. technological problems
c. scientific field
d. correlational methods

1.9
a
LO 2
Concept
6
M

In the definition of social psychology, it is implied that social psychologists seek to
a. understand how we think about and interact with others
b. understand how groups interact with other groups
c. understand how groups deal with social behavior
d. understand how we function in society

1.10
d
LO 2
Applied
6
M

As a social psychologist, you would be most interested in studying
a. problem solving in humans
b. perceptual processes in humans
c. physiological responses in humans
d. aggression in humans

1.11
c
LO 3
Concept
7
E

The fundamental approach that distinguishes science from areas such as art and philosophy is the
a. subject material
b. type of people in the field
c. methods of study
d. state of development of the field

1.12
d
LO 3
Concept
7
M

Statement A: The text concludes that social psychology is not scientific when compared to such fields as chemistry and physics.
Statement B: Social psychology focuses on the behavior of individuals.
a. both statements are true
b. both statements are false
c. statement A is true; statement B is false
d. statement B is true; statement A is false

1.13
d
LO 3
Concept
7
E

Social psychologists rely upon gaining accurate and useful information through
a. casual observation
b. examining proverbs for common themes
c. applications of equity
d. basic scientific methods

1.14
b
LO 3
Concept
7
M

Social psychology can be considered a science because
a. it has existed for a long time
b. social psychologists use the scientific method
c. it has developed along scientific lines
d. the field can now be quantified

1.15
a
LO 3
Concept
7
E

The field of social psychology relies on _____ methods to gain accurate information about social behavior.
a. scientific
b. informal
c. statistical
d. historical

1.16
b
LO 3
Concept
7
M

The scientific method involves gathering systematic information about issues, and it involves
a. an attitude of aggressiveness
b. an attitude of skepticism
c. an attitude of acceptance
d. an attitude of fatalism

1.17   An attitude of skepticism that is required of the scientific method implies
a   a. that all assertions about the natural world be repeatedly tested before being accepted as accurate
LO 3   b. that assertions about the natural world can be accepted if they have been questioned
Concept   c. that assertions about the natural world be subjected to rational investigation
7   d. that all assertions about the natural world be subjected to emotional investigation
C

1.18   Both social psychology and sociology study aggression. The focus of social psychology is on
b   a. the societal factors that influence aggression
LO 4   b. the individual factors that influence aggression
Concept   c. the group factors that influence aggression
8   d. the governmental factors that influence aggression
M

1.19   Social psychology focuses on the behavior of individuals because
a   a. individuals hold the attitudes and perform the behaviors
LO 4   b. individuals are more interesting than groups
Concept   c. individuals are not as complex as groups
8   d. individuals have more functions than groups
M

1.20   It is the contention of social psychologists that the causes of behavior ultimately rest with
d   a. social expectations
LO 4   b. national expectations
Concept   c. the expectations of any defined group in society
8   d. individuals
M

1.21   Social psychology is a branch of psychology and focuses on
c   a. concepts related to group behavior
LO 4   b. concepts related to societal behavior
Fact   c. social behavior of the individual
4   d. social behavior of the group
M

1.22   Social psychology studies _____, sociology studies _____.
b   a. groups, individuals
LO 4   b. individuals, groups
Concept   c. groups, groups
8   d. individuals, individuals
E

1.23   Which of the following categories is NOT one of the five categories mentioned in your text regarding
c   factors affecting social interaction?
LO 5   a. ecological variables
Fact   b. cognitive processes
8   c. perceptual processes
M   d. biological factors

1.24   Your response to an elderly person in a grocery line illustrates
b   a. the impact of ecological variables
LO 5   b. the impact of the actions and characteristics of others
Applied   c. the impact of perceptual processes
9   d. the impact of biological factors
M

1.25
d
LO 5
Concept
9
M

The term "ecological variable" refers to the impact of _____ on human behavior.
a. personality
b. social cognition
c. cultural factors
d. the physical environment

1.26
c
LO 5
Applied
9
E

An example of how a basic cognitive process can influence the course of social interaction is
a. the use of motor skills
b. visual recognition
c. the memory of a past interaction
d. a response to a cry for help

1.27
c
LO 5
Concept
10
C

One area in which many social psychologists question the tenets of sociobiology is
a. whether or not genes are inherited
b. whether or not genes have any influence on behavior
c. whether or not genetically driven behaviors can be changed
d. whether or not mating strategies exist for maximal reproductive success

1.28
b
LO 5
Concept
11
M

Recent research on mate selection illustrates the role of genetic or evolutionary factors in human behavior. This research indicates that
a. females place greater emphasis on youth and status
b. females place greater emphasis on dominance and status
c. males place greater emphasis on status and physical attractiveness
d. males place greater emphasis on youth and dominance

1.29
c
LO 5
Applied
9
M

Which of the following is a general factor affecting social interaction?
a. role modeling
b. concept modeling
c. basic cognitive processes
d. a predisposition to interact with others

1.30
d
LO 5
Concept
10
M

Evolutionary social psychology suggests that
a. social behavior is the result of natural selection
b. social behavior is the result of inherited genetic traits
c. social behavior cannot be measured in terms of reproductive success
d. social behavior is affected by natural selection, but can be altered by other influences

1.31
c
LO 6
Fact
12
M

Social psychology first became a recognizably independent field around
a. 1810-1830
b. 1850-1870
c. 1908-1924
d. 1960-1971

1.32
a
LO 6
Fact
12
M

The earliest identified social psychologist (McDougall) assumed that social behavior was largely based upon
a. instincts
b. learned behaviors
c. a combination of instincts and learned behaviors
d. the desire to get along with others

1.33   It is suggested that the field of social psychology was basically formed by the middle of the 1920s
c   because
LO 6   a. some psychologists from that period were the first to identify themselves as social psychologists
Concept   b. human social behavior was not an area of interest to researchers before the 1920s
13   c. research literature indicates that some psychologists from that period studied some of the same
M   material as social psychologists today
       d. social psychology was not formed until the 1960s

1.34   McDougall's 1908 <u>Social Psychology</u> text assumed that social behavior stems from ____; Allport's
b   1924 <u>Social Psychology</u> text assumed that social behavior stems from ____.
LO 6   a. many different factors, instincts
Concept   b. instincts, many different factors
12   c. instincts, instincts
M   d. many different factors, many different factors

1.35   Allport's 1924 textbook emphasized
a   a. the value of experimentation
LO 6   b. the value of speculation
Concept   c. the value of emotional thought in discovery
13   d. the value of historical reasoning
M

1.36   Sherif, an early founder of social psychology, studied the nature and impact of rules indicating how
d   people ought to behave. In other words, Sherif studied
LO 7   a. cognitive dissonance
Concept   b. social cognition
13   c. ecological variables
M   d. social norms

1.37   The area of <u>conformity</u> was studied by ____ in the 1930s.
b   a. Lewin
LO 7   b. Sherif
Concept   c. Festinger
13   d. Allport
E

1.38   The area of <u>group processes</u> was studied by ____ in the 1930s.
a   a. Lewin
LO 7   b. Sherif
Concept   c. Festinger
13   d. Allport
E

1.39   Sherif (1935) studied the nature and impact of ____ and Lewin and his colleagues (1939) studied the
d   nature of ____.
LO 7   a. leadership, cognitive dissonance
Concept   b. cognitive dissonance, leadership
13   c. social cognition, cognitive dissonance
M   d. social norms, leadership

1.40   In addition to his research, Kurt Lewin also had an impact on social psychology by
b   a. his development of a research institute
LO 7   b. his training of students, many of whom went on to make significant contributions to social
Concept   psychology
13   c. his numerous books and articles defining the scope of social psychology
C   d. his higher education organizational skills

1.41
a
LO 8
Study
14
C

The research that Lewin and his colleagues conducted on leadership indicated that
a. work of the boys in the authoritarian group dropped when the leader left the room
b. work of the boys in the laissez-faire group dropped when the leader left the room
c. work of the boys in the democratic group dropped when the leader left the room
d. work of the boys in all three groups dropped when the leader left the room

1.42
a
LO 8
Study
14
C

The research that Lewin and his colleagues conducted on leadership indicated that the work of the boys in the authoritarian and democratic group was basically the same
a. when the leader was in the room
b. when the leader left the room
c. when the work was more difficult
d. when the work was relatively easy

1.43
b
LO 8
Study
14
C

The research that Lewin and his colleagues conducted on leadership indicated that
a. boys in the democratic group made more aggressive demands for attention
b. boys in the authoritarian group made more aggressive demands for attention
c. boys in the laissez-faire group made more aggressive demands for attention
d. boys in all three groups made equal aggressive demands for attention

1.44
b
LO 8
Study
14
C

The research that Lewin and his colleagues conducted on leadership indicated that
a. there were more leader-dependent actions in the democratic group
b. there were more leader-dependent actions in the authoritarian group
c. there were more leader-dependent actions in the laissez-faire group
d. there were an equal number of leader-dependent actions in all three groups

1.45
c
LO 8
Study
14
C

Lewin and his colleagues interpreted the findings of the study of leadership to suggest that overall
a. a laissez-faire style of leadership is best
b. an authoritarian style of leadership is best
c. a democratic style of leadership is best
d. all three styles of leadership are basically equal

1.46
c
LO 8
Study
15
C

Current research on leadership indicates that in times of imminent danger
a. an authoritarian style of leadership may not be best
b. a laissez-faire style of leadership may not be best
c. a democratic style of leadership may not be best
d. all three styles of leadership are basically equal

1.47
a
LO 9
Applied
15
M

The post-WWII expansion of social psychology paid attention to how
a. groups influence individuals
b. traits are passed from one generation to the next
c. individuals interact on a one-to-one basis
d. human behavior can turn violent

1.48
b
LO 9
Concept
15
M

The trait cluster that predisposes people to accept extreme political ideologies along the line of Nazism is called the
a. acceptance of violence paradigm
b. authoritarian personality
c. outgroup homogeneity cluster
d. socialist tendency cluster

1.49   Margaret knows that stealing is wrong, but she just cannot stop herself from raiding the cookie jar.
d   Her mental discomfort can be explained through
LO 9   a. correspondent tendencies
Applied   b. the less-leads-to-more effect
16   c. competing tendencies
M   d. cognitive dissonance

1.50   The theory that proposes that people strive to reduce inconsistencies between their attitudes and their
a   behaviors is called
LO 9   a. cognitive dissonance theory
Fact   b. inconsistency theory
16   c. balance theory
M   d. cognitive discrepancy theory

1.51   The less-leads-to-more effect describes how
b   a. fewer discrepancies between behavior and attitudes leads to more change
LO 9   b. giving someone a small inducement to perform a task can be more effective in attitude change
Applied   than a large inducement
16   c. people try to reduce discrepancies between similar attitudes rather than very dissimilar ones
C   d. less discrepancies between similar attitudes leads to more change

1.52   The 1960s is looked at as a time when social psychology came of age. One of the reasons for this
b   view is that
LO 9   a. the social psychologists had defined a paradigm for study
Concept   b. the social psychologists studied a tremendous number of lines of research
16   c. the social psychologists had matured enough to secure academic positions for continued research
M   d. the social psychologists had incorporated the findings of other sciences into their field

1.53   The two major trends from social psychology's recent history are
d   a. application and attraction research
LO 10   b. personality theories and attribution research
Concept   c. legal applications and health applications
16   d. application and interest in cognition
M

1.54   Statement A: While social psychologists have not yet involved themselves in such concerns, your text
b   predicts that in the future social psychologists will begin to study applied issues.
LO 10   Statement B: The new perspective, called cognitive dissonance, studies such cognitive
Concept   processes as memory and attention and how they influence our judgments about other people.
17   a. both statements are true
M   b. both statements are false
          c. statement A is true; statement B is false
          d. statement B is true; statement A is false

1.55   Personal health strategies, the legal process, and work settings are
a   a. examples of areas of application of social knowledge
LO 10   b. examples of rarely studied area of social psychology
Concept   c. examples of areas not amenable to scientific study
17   d. examples of the application of the scientific method to alter predispositions
M

1.56   Which perspective takes basic knowledge about cognitive processes and attempts to apply it to an
b   understanding of social behavior?
LO 10   a. the applied perspective
Concept   b. the cognitive perspective
16   c. the correlational perspective
M   d. the integrative perspective

1.57
a
LO 10
Applied
16
M

If an individual remembers only information consistent with an already held stereotype, this finding would indicate the role of _____ in social behavior.
a. cognition
b. affect
c. physiology
d. groups

1.58
b
LO 10
Applied
17
M

Kurt Lewin's statement that "There's nothing as practical as a good theory" supports the modern attempt to
a. apply the cognitive perspective to problems in social psychology
b. apply the findings and principles of social psychology to the solution of practical problems
c. use the scientific method to gain an understanding of social behavior
d. seek a reasonable balance between the quest for knowledge and the rights of individuals

1.59
d
LO 11
Concept
17
M

Your text predicts that all of the following will be future trends in social psychology except
a. continued growth and expansion of the cognitive perspective
b. increased interest in application
c. increased emphasis on a multicultural perspective
d. increased emphasis on the theory of cognitive dissonance

1.60
a
LO 11
Fact
18
C

The two trends that your authors expect for the year 2000 and beyond are
a. increased interest in cognition and application, and increased emphasis on multicultural perspective
b. increased interest in cognition and application, and decreased interest in social diversity
c. decreased interest in cognition and application, and increased interest in multicultural perspective
d. decreased interest in cognition and application, and increased interest in social diversity

1.61
a
LO 11
Concept
18
M

The text suggests that as the U. S. becomes more _____, social psychology will become more
a. diverse
b. mature
c. idiosyncratic
d. scientifically organized

1.62
d
LO 11
Concept
18
M

The social diversity perspective in social psychology is concerned with
a. how increased diversity affects the scientific method
b. how decreased diversity affects the scientific method
c. how increased diversity makes research more complicated
d. how social psychology reflects diversity in the U. S.

1.63
a
LO 11
Concept
18
E

The fact that there are a disproportionate number of social psychologists in the U. S. raises the problem of
a. repetition
b. replication
c. generalizability of psychological concepts to the real world
d. generalizability of psychological concepts to the rest of the world

1.64
a
LO 12
Concept
19
M

A new task of social psychology is to differentiate between
a. universal and cultural aspects of human behavior
b. theoretical and empirical viewpoints
c. theoretical and applied positions
d. theories that have been proven, and theories that have not yet been thoroughly tested

1.65   Recent research suggests that
b   a. most basic aspects of social behavior are cultural universals
LO 12   b. some basic aspects of social behavior are not cultural universals
Concept   c. individual differences always outweigh social pressure
19   d. the aspects of social behavior that we know are not accurate
M

1.66   Areas of research in social psychology currently receiving more attention include
b   a. cognitive dissonance theory
LO 12   b. multicultural perspectives
Concept   c. learning theories
19   d. physiological theories
M

1.67   An example of a social process that is different across cultures would be
c   a. a finding that prejudice does not exist in North America
LO 12   b. a finding that prejudice does not exist in Africa
Concept   c. a finding that romantic love is stronger in North America than in Africa
19   d. a finding that African children are taller than North American children
E

1.68   The reason that it is important to include both genders as participants in research studies is that
d   a. there is less control with just one gender
LO 12   b. there is more generalizability with one gender
Concept   c. the results would be meaningless if the experimenter was of the other gender
19   d. the results would not give a complete picture if there were only one gender
C

1.69   An indication that social psychologists recognize differences in behavior between genders is that
a   a. the increase from 51% to 82% of published studies using both male and female subjects
LO 12   b. the emphasis on using female tasks to investigate human behavior
Concept   c. the increase from 35% to 57% of published studies having both male and female authors
19   d. the emphasis on using male tasks to investigate human behavior
M

1.70   The main goal of experimentation in social psychology is to
a   a. find out if a factor influences social behavior
LO 13   b. find out if social behavior influences some factor
Concept   c. compare the relative strength of at least two factors of social behavior and decide which is
20   strongest
M   d. compare the relative strength of at least two factors upon social behavior and decide which is
                 strongest

1.71   The experimental method is based upon
b   a. conjecture
LO 13   b. logic
Concept   c. emotion
20   d. superstition
E

1.72   The research method generally preferred by social psychologists is the _____ method.
c   a. correlational
LO 13   b. theoretical
Fact   c. experimental
20   d. observational
E

1.73
d
LO 13
Fact
20
M

Social psychologists use many different methods in their research on social behavior. The two most frequently used methods are
a. experimental and observational
b. correlational and observational
c. observational and theoretical
d. experimental and correlational

1.74
a
LO 13
Concept
20
M

Statement A: The preferred method of social psychologists has tended to be the experimental method.
Statement B: There has been a modest increase in the use of correlational methods in social psychology in the past few years.
a. both statements are true
b. both statements are false
c. statement A is true; statement B is false
d. statement B is true; statement A is false

1.75
b
LO 13
Concept
20
M

The two basic steps to the experimental method, in sequence, are
a. measure the impact of one factor on behavior and vary the strength of another factor
b. vary the strength of one factor and measure the impact of this factor on behavior
c. vary the strength of one factor and measure the impact of another factor on behavior
d. measure the strength of one factor on behavior and measure the strength of another factor on behavior

1.76
a
LO 14
Fact
21
M

The dependent variable is defined as the variable that is
a. measured by the experimenter
b. varied by the experimenter
c. adjusted by the experimenter
d. known by the experimenter

1.77
c
LO 14
Concept
21
M

An experimenter varies the strength of one factor to determine whether this variation has an impact on the behavior being studied. The systematically varied factor is the _____ variable, while the behavior being studied is the _____ variable.
a. control, experimental
b. experimental, control
c. independent, dependent
d. dependent, independent

1.78
c
LO 14
Applied
21
M

Jane is conducting an experiment where she is trying to determine the influence of staring at a speechmaker upon how much such persons stutter. Jane sends in people to a speech class with instructions to stare for varied amounts of time at the speechmakers. The independent variable is/are the
a. speechmakers
b. people doing the staring
c. amount of time that the people stare
d. amount of stuttering that occurs

1.79
c
LO 14
Applied
21
M

Albert conducts an experiment in which he measures aggression in schoolchildren at different levels of temperature during recess. The independent and dependent variables are
a. the experiment, the levels of temperature
b. the school children, the levels of temperature
c. the levels of temperature, the level of aggression
d. the level of aggression, the time of recess

1.80   A control condition
a
LO 14   a. is an experimental condition in which the variable expected to influence behavior is absent
Fact   b. is an experimental condition in which the variable expected to influence behavior is measured
21   c. is an experimental condition in which the variable expected to influence behavior is manipulated
M   d. is an experimental condition in which the variable expected to influence behavior is confounded

1.81   In the "mood/willingness to help study" described in your text, the independent variable was
c
LO 14   a. participants' willingness to help another researcher
Applied   b. participants' willingness to give a small gift to others
21   c. participants' receipt of a small gift
M   d. participants' receipt of help from someone

1.82   The dependent variable in the "mood/willingness to help" study described in your text was
a
LO 14   a. participants' willingness to help
Concept   b. participants' receipt of small gift
21   c. participants' receipt of help
M   d. participants' giving of a small gift

1.83   When conducting experiments, social psychologists usually examine the effects of
c
LO 15   a. one independent variable at a time, because that is all that is possible
Concept   b. one independent variable at a time, although it is possible to study more than one
22   c. more than one independent variable at a time
M   d. one dependent variable at a time

1.84   When one or more independent variables affects the influence of other independent variables (as
d   measured by the dependent variable), they are said to
LO 15   a. connect
Concept   b. confound
22   c. interfere
M   d. interact

1.85   The reason that social psychologists are interested in interactions in research is because
b
LO 15   a. the effects of independent variables can be isolated
Concept   b. social behavior is influenced by different factors acting concurrently
22   c. social behavior is determined by different dependent variables acting concurrently
M   d. the effects of independent variables cannot be isolated

1.86   When an investigator includes several independent variables in an experiment to determine whether
a   the impact of one independent variable is affected by one or more other independent variables, the
LO 15   investigator is testing for
Concept   a. interactions
22   b. confounds
M   c. correlations
      d. controls

1.87   The difference between an interaction and a confound is that an interaction
b
LO 15   a. is a complete surprise
Applied   b. provides useful information
22   c. makes the results uninterpretable
M   d. complicates future research

1.88
b
LO 15
Concept
22
M

In the "mood/willingness to help" study described in your text, the results indicated that good mood increases helping only when a low degree of effort was required. This result is an example of
a. a correlation
b. an interaction
c. a confound
d. an hypothesis

1.89
a
LO 16
Fact
23
M

Two conditions that must be met for social psychology research to be considered experimentation are
a. random assignment, relevant variables other than the IV held constant
b. random assignment, presence of at least one confounding variable
c. ordered assignment, relevant variables other than the IV held constant
d. ordered assignment, presence of at least one confounding variable

1.90
d
LO 16
Concept
23
M

Two basic requirements must be met in order for a researcher to conduct a successful experiment. These two basic requirements are to
a. deceive the participants and confound the independent variables
b. randomly assign participants to the groups and confound the independent variables
c. randomly assign participants to the groups and avoid interactions
d. randomly assign participants to the groups and avoid confounding

1.91
b
LO 16
Concept
23
M

The reason that we want each subject in an experiment to have an equal chance of being exposed to each level of the independent variable is because
a. we would like to be fair to all subjects
b. we would like to evenly distribute subject characteristics over all levels of the independent variable
c. the experimenter must not know which subjects are in which conditions
d. the experimenter must know the characteristics of the subjects before the end of the experiment

1.92
c
LO 16
Concept
23
C

Why is it important that each person taking part in an experiment have an equal chance of being exposed to each level of the independent variable?
a. if not, it would be impossible to determine the level of response for each participant
b. if not, it would be impossible to determine the level of the independent variable
c. if not, it would be impossible to determine if differences in behavior were due to the independent variable or other factors
d. if not, it would be impossible to determine if differences in behavior were due to the dependent variable or other factors

1.93
c
LO 16
Concept
23
M

The procedure that ensures that participants are not assigned to an experimental condition on the basis of any individual characteristics is
a. interaction
b. informed consent
c. random assignment
d. confound control

1.94
d
LO 16
Applied
23
C

In the "mood/willingness to help" study in the text, if participants were selected based upon their class schedules, what experimental requirement would this selection process violate?
a. the requirement that there be at least two independent variables
b. the requirement that there be an independent variable and a dependent variable
c. the requirement that there be a control condition
d. the requirement that there be random assignment to conditions

1.95
d
LO 17
Concept
24
M

The opposite of confounding between variables is to
a. find statistically significant results
b. do a correlational study
c. vary several factors simultaneously while holding the dependent variable constant
d. hold constant all other factors while varying the independent variable

1.96
c
LO 17
Concept
24
M

Confounding variables are variables that operate in a way such that
a. each magnifies the effect of the other
b. each mutes the effect of the other
c. it is impossible to tell the source of any effects
d. the effects of one variable are the same as the effects of the other

1.97
a
LO 17
Concept
24
M

When confounding occurs, the results of an experiment
a. are largely uninterpretable
b. are extremely valuable
c. are useful in determining the effect of variables
d. are valuable for guiding future research

1.98
a
LO 17
Concept
24
M

If the effects of the independent variable are confused with the possible effects of a variable that is not part of the research, the two are said to
a. confound each other
b. connect each other
c. interact with each other
d. be contacted variables

1.99
b
LO 17
Concept
24
M

One way to avoid the problem of confounding variables in an experiment is to
a. get different measures of the dependent variable
b. hold non-experimental variables constant across conditions
c. get different measures of the independent variable
d. include as many independent variables as possible

1.100
c
LO 17
Applied
24
M

In the "mood/willingness to help" study in your text, suppose that an attractive experimenter conducted the gift condition and an unattractive experimenter conducted the no-gift condition, and that the results indicated more helping by participants receiving gifts. This situation is an example of
a. an interaction
b. a correlation
c. a confound
d. a connection

1.101
c
LO 18
Concept
24
M

What two factors often make the use of the experimental approach impossible?
a. variation of the factor of interest is beyond the experimenter's control and it is too powerful
b. ethical constraints and the variable is too powerful
c. variation of the factor of interest is beyond the experimenter's control and ethical constraints
d. it cannot be used in field studies and it is too powerful

1.102
a
LO 18
Concept
24
M

Sometimes an experiment cannot be conducted because the systematic variation of the variables of interest
a. are beyond the experimenter's control
b. are not of sufficient interest
c. are irrelevant to the behavior of interest
c. are not capable of measurement

1.103
c
LO 18
Concept
24
M

_____ constraints prevent us from using experimental methods to determine whether certain conditions that we could institute affect the occurrence of violence in intimate relationships.
a. Practical
b. Observational
c. Ethical
d. Correlational

1.104
d
LO 18
Concept
24
M

_____ prevents us from doing experiments on the use, by certain politicians, of specific persuasive techniques in their speeches.
a. Ethical constraints
b. Correlational limitations
c. Observational limitations
d. Lack of experimenter control

1.105
a
LO 18
Applied
24
M

Ralph wants to conduct an experiment on the occurrence of violence in close relationships. He would probably be discouraged from conducting such an experiment on _____ grounds.
a. ethical
b. practical
c. scientific
d. political

1.106
c
LO 18
Concept
24
M

Which of the following is a reason for using correlational methods to investigate some human behavior?
a. correlation indicates causation
b. experiments cannot be used in real-life situations
c. experimentation is sometimes unethical
d. appropriate statistics are not available for experiments

1.107
c
LO 19
Concept
24
M

Which of the following distinguishes the correlational method from the experimental method?
a. the correlational method uses a small sample of participants
b. the correlational method enables researchers to study cognitive activities
c. no attempt is made to systematically manipulate variables within the correlational method
d. the findings of the correlational method are more likely to be contaminated by confounds

1.108
d
LO 19
Fact
24
E

Correlations range from
a. 0 to +1.0
b. 0 to +10.0
c. -1.0 to 0
d. -1.0 to +1.0

1.109
b
LO 19
Applied
24
M

Suppose smoking and drinking alcohol are found to be correlated at .65. We can say that
a. smoking is probably unrelated to drinking
b. smoking is probably related to drinking
c. smoking causes drinking
d. drinking causes smoking

1.110
b
LO 19
Concept
24
M

Correlational methods rely on _____ to draw conclusions about social behavior
a. systematic variation of independent variables
b. naturally occurring variation in variables of interest
c. systematic variation in naturally occurring independent variables
d. association of independent with dependent variables

1.111
a
LO 19
Concept
24
E

In the "mood/willingness to help" study in your text, if no attempt was made to vary the mood of a participant, yet there was a finding that mood was related to willingness to help, the _____ method would probably have been used to get this result.
a. correlational
b. experimental
c. practical
d. relational

1.112
b
LO 19
Concept
25
M

The correlational method has several advantages, one of which is that it is
a. highly controlled
b. highly efficient
c. highly complex
d. highly speculative

1.113
d
LO 20
Concept
25
M

The major drawback of correlation studies is that they
a. are somewhat unreliable
b. are highly complex
c. are not as efficient as experimental studies
d. do not provide conclusive cause and effect relationships

1.114
d
LO 20
Concept
25
C

Which is <u>not</u> true of the correlational method?
a. it can be readily used to study behavior in real-life situations
b. it can be used to study topics that would be impractical or unethical to study experimentally
c. it can be used to study ongoing behavior without disrupting the behavior
d. it demonstrates that two variables are causally related

1.115
a
LO 20
Concept
25
M

When two variables are found to be correlated, one could cause the other, or
a. a third variable could be causing them both
b. they might not really be related
c. the independent variable may be indistinguishable from the dependent variable
d. they might both be the cause of a third variable

1.116
b
LO 20
Concept
25
M

Statement <u>A</u>: If two variables are correlated with each other, it is certain that one of them is a cause and the other is an effect.
Statement <u>B</u>: Experimental methods are always preferred over correlational methods.
a. both statements are true
b. both statements are false
c. statement A is true; statement B is false
d. statement B is true; statement A is false

1.117
c
LO 20
Concept
25
M

If we systematically vary the physical beauty of a defendant through appropriate photos to determine its effect on length a sentence by a simulated jury, we are using the _____ method; if we simply observe the relationship between the physical beauty of defendants and the length of sentence, we are using the
a. correlational, experimental
b. role playing, correlational
c. experimental, correlational
d. experimental, role playing

1.118
d
LO 20
Applied
25
M

Assume that a carefully done correlational study has found that the more crowded the living conditions in a given area, the higher the crime rate. On the basis of this study, one could conclude that
a. crowding causes crime
b. being a criminal causes the person to seek a crowded place to live
c. the poorer people are, the smaller the living quarters they can afford and the more likely they are to engage in crime
d. a correlational study does not allow one to choose among these interpretations

1.119   What does it mean to <u>replicate</u> findings from previous studies?
c
a. to show that results were due mainly to confirmation bias
LO 21
b. to fail to find the same results as previous researchers
Concept
c. to repeat research and find the same results as before
26
d. to explain previous findings in terms of a dramatically modified theory
M

1.120   Before accepting the hypothesis that being in a good mood increases helping, most researchers would
a   want to see a laboratory finding
LO 21
a. replicated in a natural field setting
Concept
b. replicated in the same laboratory
26
c. duplicated with the same variables
M
d. investigated with similar controls

1.121   Rarely do the results of social psychological research yield
b
a. barely comparable findings
LO 21
b. totally consistent findings
Concept
c. completely correlated findings
26
d. mildly connected findings
E

1.122   The two alternatives for comparing research from many experiments are
d
a. concept analysis and meta-analysis
LO 21
b. sampling procedure and sampling weights
Fact
c. sampling weights and concept analysis
26
d. meta-analysis and narrative review
M

1.123   Meta-analysis is a way of
b
a. predicting from a theory
LO 21
b. combining results across experiments
Concept
c. testing the same theory in more than one way
27
d. conducting more than one experiment at the same time
M

1.124   Meta-analysis is used as an indicator of what two points across studies?
b
a. existence and proof of the independent variables
LO 21
b. direction and size of the effects of the independent variables
Concept
c. size and proof of the effects of the independent variables
27
d. viability and usefulness of the independent variables
C

1.125   Research indicates that
a
a. meta-analysis is a better analytic tool than narrative review
LO 21
b. meta-analysis is a better analytic tool than concept analysis
Concept
c. concept analysis is a better analytic tool than meta-analysis
27
d. sampling weights are a better analytic tool than narrative review
M

1.126   The concept of <u>converging operations</u> involves
b
a. obtaining the same results in other settings that are essentially the same as the original
LO 21
b. obtaining the same results in other settings that are logically related to the original
Concept
c. obtaining the same results in other settings that are totally unrelated to the original
27
d. obtaining the same results in other settings that are contrived to appear the same as the original
M

1.127   The findings of the "mood/willingness to help" study mentioned in your text also have been when
c   found using pleasant fragrances. Obtaining two findings essentially the same in different situations
LO 21   illustrates
Applied   a. illusory correlation
27   b. extreme good fortune
C   c. converging operations
          d. meta-analysis

1.128   Theories of social psychology commonly originate
c   a. from deductive reasoning about a problem
LO 22   b. from inductive reasoning about a problem
Concept   c. from individual's current knowledge and observations
28   d. from experiments
M

1.129   Theories are different from observation in that they
c   a. precede observation
LO 22   b. are predicted by observation
Concept   c. seek to explain behavior
29   d. theories are the same as observation
M

1.130   A theory is best described as
d   a. a hypothesis
LO 22   b. a fact
Concept   c. a proof
29   d. an explanation
E

1.131   If a theory is to be useful, its predictions must be
a   a. confirmed
LO 22   b. tested
Comcept   c. testable
29   d. comparable to predictions of other competing theories
C

1.132   Statement A: One must be able to derive testable predictions from a theory for it to be a valid
c   theory.
LO 22   Statement B: If the predictions derived from a theory are not supported by research findings, the only
Concept   option is to reject the theory.
29   a. both statements are true
M   b. both statements are false
          c. statement A is true; statement B is false
          d. statement B is true; statement A is false

1.133   A testable prediction derived from a theory is called
b   a. an independent variable
LO 22   b. a hypothesis
Concept   c. a manipulation
29   d. a dependent variable
M

1.134
b
LO 22
Concept
29
M

The two essential parts of a theory are
a. its verbal and mathematical concepts
b. its basic concepts, plus statements concerning the relationship between these concepts
c. its hypotheses and its predictions
d. its logical concepts and the predictions derived from them

1.135
b
LO 22
Concept
29
M

When a hypothesis derived from a particular theory is disconfirmed
a. the researcher must reject the theory
b. the theory may need to be modified
c. confidence in the theory's accuracy is increased
d. confidence in the theory's accuracy is not affected

1.136
d
LO 22
Concept
29
C

Which list places the stages of conducting social psychological research in the order in which they usually occur?
a. research, hypothesis, theory
b. hypothesis, research, theory
c. hypothesis, theory, research
d. theory, hypothesis, research

1.137
a
LO 22
Concept
30
M

If a researcher set out to _____ a theory, he or she has violated the concept of _____.
a. prove, skepticism
b. prove, ethics
c. disprove, experimentation
d. disprove, confounding

1.138
c
LO 23
Concept
31
M

One area where social psychology experiments often differ from other scientific experiments is in the use of
a. humans as participants in the experiments
b. meta-analysis
c. deception
d. sampling weights

1.139
c
LO 23
Concept
31
M

Why do social psychologists use deception in their research?
a. They want to protect participants from the harmful effects of learning negative things about themselves.
b. They know that causal relationships between independent and dependent variables are impossible to establish without deception.
c. They believe it is not possible to obtain accurate information if subjects know the true purpose of the research.
d. They know that participants usually enjoy experiments more when deception is involved.

1.140
b
LO 23
Concept
31
M

Deception in social psychology experiments is the result of
a. not letting participants know the outcome of the experiment
b. withholding information about the purpose of the experiment from participants in the experiment
c. making predictions from correlational studies
d. failing to check on the well-being of participants in experiments

1.141
b
LO 23
Fact
31
M

According to your text, the problem raised by the prevalence of deception methodology in social psychology research is
a. a statistical problem
b. an ethical problem
c. a theoretical problem
d. a methodological problem

1.142   The type of deception most commonly used by social psychologists in their research is
a
LO 23   a. temporary deception
Concept   b. long-lasting deception
31   c. first-order deception
M   d. second-order deception

1.143   Social psychology researchers usually employ deception in their research in order to
b
LO 23   a. maintain participant alertness
Concept   b. conceal the true purpose of the experiment from the participant
31   c. reduce experimenter bias
E   d. measure physiological responses

1.144   Statement A: The majority of social psychologists have concluded that deception, no matter how
b   useful in research, must be avoided.
LO 24   Statement B: Because debriefed subjects often ruin an experiment by discussing it with future
Concept   subjects, your text concludes that it is best to not debrief subjects.
31   a. both statements are true
M   b. both statements are false
              c. statement A is true; statement B is false
              d. statement B is true; statement A is false

1.145   Informed consent in experiments involving deception is defined as subjects making a decision whether
b   or not to participate in the experiment based upon receiving
LO 24   a. information about previous experimental results
Concept   b. as full a description of the procedures as possible
31   c. a full description of the purpose of the experiment
M   d. the guarantee of a full debriefing after the experiment

1.146   The potential negative effects of deception can be lessened when subjects
b
LO 24   a. give informed consent to the deception
Concept   b. give informed consent and are debriefed
32   c. give informed consent, are debriefed, and demonstrate understanding of the experiment's purpose
C   d. give informed consent, are debriefed, and write a paper on the experiment

1.147   Research on informed consent and debriefing indicated that
a
LO 24   a. they usually reduce the dangers of deception
Study   b. they reduce the dangers of deception in a substantial minority of subjects
32   c. debriefing is superior to informed consent
M   d. informed consent is superior to debriefing

1.148   Statement A: Informed consent is obtained more often from subjects in field experiments than in
d   laboratory experiments.
LO 24   Statement B: The findings of field experiments are more often open to conflicting interpretations than
Concept   those of laboratory experiments, due to loss of experimental control in the field.
32   a. both statements are true
C   b. both statements are false
              c. statement A is true; statement B is false
              d. statement B is true; statement A is false

1.149
a
LO 24
Concept
32
M

The majority of participants who learn that they have been deceived in an experiment seem to react

a. positively
b. with resentment over having been fooled
c. negatively
d. without surprise, since the deceptions were very transparent

1.150
b
LO 24
Concept
32
C

One of the guiding principles concerning the use of deception that was mentioned in your text was

a. participants don't mind being deceived, so it is an appropriate technique with or without debriefing
b. make certain that every possible precaution is taken to protect the rights, safety, and welfare of participants
c. take special precautions to ensure that every participant is aware of the deception before the experiment begins
d. make certain that all participants have been thoroughly debriefed before the experiment begins

CHAPTER 2

Learning Objectives

After studying this chapter, students should be able to:

1.   *Explain the five basic channels through which we communicate nonverbally.*

2.   *Describe the six (or perhaps seven) basic emotions expressed in unique facial expressions.*

3.   *Describe patterns of physiological activity and self-reported emotions that occur when subjects pose particular facial expressions.*

4.   *Explain how the cross-cultural studies by Ekman and Friesen (1975) demonstrate that facial expressions of basic emotions are universal.*

5.   *Unerstand to what degree the recognition of basic facial expressions is dependent on the research methods used.*

6.   *Explain how we respond when others: a) maintain high levels of gazing; b) avoid eye contact; and c) stare at us.*

7.   *Describe how body language communicates emotion, including examples from ballet, restaurant servers, and various types of gestures.*

8.   *Describe how being touched by a waitress in the Crusco and Wetzel (1984) study affected the size of customers' tips.*

9.   *Examine gender differences and age differences in touching.*

10.   *Describe how emotional expressiveness affects occupational success and psychological adjustment, and examine the role of ambivalence in determining the impact of emotional expressiveness.*

11.   *Describe five nonverbal cues that help us to recognize that someone is lying.*

12.   *Based on Jones and Davis' theory of correspondent inference, understand the three circumstances that lead us to infer that behavior reflects underlying traits.*

13.   *Compare the ability of subjects in the Gilbert et al. (1992) study to categorize verbal behavior, characterize the speaker, and correct their judgments when listening to a degraded vs. a normal audiotape.*

14.   *Using Kelley's theory of attribution, distinguish between internal and external causes of behavior, and define the concepts of consensus, distinctiveness, and consistency.*

15.   *Compare attributions made when consensus is low, distinctiveness is low, and consistency is high with attributions made when consensus is high, distinctiveness is high, and consistency is high.*

16.   *Give examples of how past experience may keep us from engaging in careful causal attribution, and note how unexpected events and unpleasant outcomes heighten our attention to causal information.*

17.   *Explain the discounting that occurs when two possible supportive causes for a behavior are' present, and the augmenting that occurs when both a supportive and an inhibitory factor are present.*

18.   *Describe the fundamental attribution error, and compare attributions made right away with those made after the passage of time.*

19.   *Explain the actor-observer effect, and why it occurs.*

20.   *Describe self-serving bias, and compare the cognitive and motivational explanations for self-serving bias.*

21.   *Describe the self-defeating attributional pattern that often underlies depression.*

22.   *Explain how each of the following factors influences attributions about a rape: a) whether the rapist is a date or a stranger; b) whether the rater is male or female.*

23.   *Explain how Asch's early work on central traits and on the order of traits supports his assertion that forming impressions of others involves more than simply adding together individual traits.*

24.   *Understand the four factors that determine how much weight a piece of information will receive in forming an impression.*

25.   *Describe the role played by exemplars and by abstractions when we make judgments about others.*

26.   *Explain how research by Sherman and Klein (1994) supports the hypothesis that early impressions of others consist mainly of exemplars, while later impressions consist mainly of mental abstractions.*

27.   *List self-enhancement tactics and other-enhancement tactics used in impression management.*

28.   *Summarize research by Wayne and Liden (1995) documenting that impression management can "pay off" for persons using it.*

29.   *Compare French and American reactions to facial expressions and to party affiliation of political candidates.*

Questions

2.1   Facial expressions, eye contact, body movements, posture, and touching are the five basic channels of
a   a. nonverbal communication
LO 1   b. self-presentation
Fact   c. microexpressions
40   d. impression management
E

2.2   Which of the following is NOT an example of a basic channel of nonverbal communication?
d   a. facial expression
LO 1   b. posture
Concept   c. eye contact
40   d. visual acuity
E

2.3   Facial expressions, eye contact, and posture are examples of
c   a. nonverbal cues
LO 1   b. body movement characteristics
Concept   c. basic channels of nonverbal communication
40   d. perceptual mechanisms of communication
M

2.4   Roberta asks Fred the location of her car keys. Fred frowns, looks away, slouches, rubs his forehead,
a   and then says that he does not know where the keys are located. By paying attention to the _____ of
LO 1   nonverbal communication, Roberta concludes that Fred is lying.
Applied   a. basic channels
40   b. emotional expressions
M   c. irrepressible configurations
             d. overt enhancement

2.5   Which of the following is NOT one of the emotions represented by a distinct facial expression?
d   a. happiness
LO 2   b. surprise
Concept   c. anger
40   d. suspicion
M

2.6   The fact that only six emotions are represented by distinct facial expressions means that we are
a   capable of only six different emotional expressions. What is wrong with this statement?
LO 2   a. various combinations, plus variations in intensity make the number of possible emotional
Concept   expressions almost limitless
40   b. more than six emotions have their own distinct facial expressions
M   c. fewer than six emotions have their own distinct facial expressions
             d. nothing in the statement is wrong

2.7   How many basic emotions are represented by their own distinct facial expressions?
c   a. none
LO 2   b. only one
Fact   c. six
40   d. the number is immense
E

2.8   Human beings are capable of showing
c
LO 2   a. two or three basic emotions only
Fact   b. six basic emotions only
40   c. six basic emotions and their combinations
E   d. a number of emotions, but only in a specified sequence

2.9   There are six basic emotions that are uniquely expressed through facial expressions. Research
b   indicates that there may be a seventh expression that is quite basic. This seventh emotion is _____.
LO 2   a. happiness
Concept   b. contempt
40   c. surprise
M   d. disgust

2.10   When people are instructed to assume a facial expression that corresponds to a basic emotion, they
d   a. usually find it difficult to comply
LO 3   b. cannot associate the expression with any particular emotion
Concept   c. can assume the expression, but without feeling the emotion
40   d. report feeling the accompanying emotion
M

2.11   According to research, if Ralph is instructed to assume an expression of fear, Ralph is likely to
a   a. show an increased heart rate
LO 3   b. refuse to comply
Study   c. fail to register the expression properly
40   d. show a mixture of fear and aggression
M

2.12   Evidence from measures of physiological activity indicates that
b   a. there are two or three basic emotions
Lo 3   b. facial expressions are closely linked to underlying emotions
Concept   c. facial expressions are not accurate guides to underlying emotions
40   d. physiological activity is highest in unhappy people
M

2.13   The facial expression of happiness is associated with
b   a. increased heart rate
LO 3   b. decreased heart rate
Concept   c. short periods between breaths
40   d. increased skin conductance
M

2.14   Research findings indicate that the link between emotional experiences and certain facial expressions
d   is
LO 3   a. a spurious relationship
Study   b. interesting, but not significant
40   c. real but highly complex
M   d. real and very basic

2.15   Ekman and Friesen (1975) asked subjects from widely separated geographic areas to imagine emotion-
a   producing events and then to show how they would feel in each case. The subjects' facial expressions
LO 4   were
Study   a. quite similar to those expressed in other cultures
41   b. very different from those expressed in other cultures
C   c. very different for most emotions, but quite similar for some emotions
   d. confusing because most people do not express emotions facially

2.16   A smile is recognized as a sign of happiness and a frown as a sign of sadness
a   a. among all people
LO 4   b. among all people except those living in remote, isolated regions
Concept   c. only among Americans
42   d. only among closely related people
M

2.17   The ability to "read" other peoples' facial expressions seems to be
d   a. dependent on learning, since each culture has its own meaning for each expression
LO 4   b. dependent on learning, since only people who know each other are able to do it
Concept   c. uniquely associated with Americans
42   d. universal
M

2.18   In response to similar emotion-provoking situations, compare the facial expressions of people living in
b   widely separated geographic regions.
LO 4   a. since facial expressions are due mainly to learning, they are quite different in different cultures
42   b. facial expressions are universal in nature, and thus quite similar across cultures
M   c. for a few emotions there are universal facial expressions, but for most emotions the expressions are
               quite different
            d. this question is interesting, but methodologically impossible to answer

2.19   Regarding being able to recognize the facial expressions of people from widely separated geographical
c   regions, research has shown
LO 4   a. we are able to recognize expressions of people from our own region with much more accuracy
Fact   b. we are able to recognize expressions of people from other regions only after considerable
42   interaction with them
M   c. we are able to recognize expressions of people from other regions even when we have had no prior
               contact with them
            d. even within our own region, we are able to recognize the expressions of only our close friends

2.20   Russell (1994) has argued that recognition of basic facial expressions is dependent upon the
c   methodology used. The recommended methodology is
LO 5   a. to provide a list of labels of emotions to subjects
Concept   b. to provide a list of the facial expressions to subjects
42   c. to not provide a list of labels of emotions to subjects
M   d. to not provide a list of facial expressions to subjects

2.21   The fixed-choice paradigm in the investigation of facial expressions involves
b   a. providing a list of emotion labels for the subjects
LO 5   b. not providing a list of emotion labels for the subjects
Concept   c. increasing the number of choices of emotion labels
42   d. decreasing the number of choices of emotion labels
E

2.22   A recent study by Rosenberg and Ekman concerning the accuracy in recognizing facial expressions
b   found that
LO 5   a. regardless of how they made their judgments, participants were not that accurate
Study   b. regardless of how they made their judgments, participants were quite accurate
43   c. the fixed-choice paradigm resulted in greater accuracy
C   d. the free-choice paradigm resulted in greater accuracy

2.23
a
LO 5
Study
43
M

In comparing the various methods of investigation of the accuracy in recognizing facial expressions, the general conclusion seems to be that
a. there was essentially no difference between the methods, all yielding quite accurate judgments
b. there was a wide difference between the methods, with the fixed-choice being more accurate than free-choice
c. there was a wide difference between the methods, with the free-choice being more accurate than the fixed-choice
d. there was a wide difference between the methods, but the difference was due to the emotion being shown

2.24
a
LO 6
Concept
43
E

A high level of gazing from another is often interpreted as a sign of _____, avoiding eye contact as a sign of _____, and staring as a sign of _____.
a. liking, shyness, hostility
b. shyness, liking, hostility
c. liking, hostility, shyness
d. hostility, liking, shyness

2.25
d
LO 6
Concept
43
E

An avoidance of eye contact with others is sometimes interpreted as a sign of
a. liking
b. hostility
c. admiration
d. shyness

2.26
b
LO 6
Concept
43
E

If someone stares at us, we sometimes interpret that behavior as a sign of
a. liking
b. hostility
c. admiration
d. shyness

2.27
a
LO 6
Applied
43
M

Ralph notices that a stranger is gazing at him in 5 to 10 second intervals. In the absence of other information, you would expect Ralph to assume that the stranger is
a. friendly
b. older
c. shy
d. hostile

2.28
b
LO 6
Concept
43
M

Continuous gazing at another person regardless of what they do is generally perceived by the other person as
a. unusually friendly behavior
b. hostile behavior
c. the result of attraction
d. other people usually do not notice eye contact by a stranger

2.29
b
LO 6
Study
44
M

A study by Greenbaum and Rosenfield (1978) indicated that someone staring at us increased the probability that we would
a. approach and engage this person in conversation
b. leave the scene of the interaction
c. increase our own staring behavior
d. decrease our own gazing behavior

2.30   Body language is a combination of
d   a. posture and facial expression
LO 7   b. body movements and facial expression
Concept   c. emotional arousal and verbal repression
44   d. posture and body movements
M

2.31   According to research, when people are aroused or nervous, they tend to
a   a. move more than usual
LO 7   b. make more macro movements (such as shifting posture), but fewer micro movements (such as
Study   rubbing fingers together)
44   c. make more micro movements, but fewer macro movements
M   d. move less than usual

2.32   Research findings indicate that high rates of self-touching are associated with
b   a. friendliness
LO 7   b. nervousness
Study   c. self-centeredness
44   d. hostility
M

2.33   Research by Aronoff and his colleagues indicates that non-threatening characters in ballet engage in
b   significantly more
LO 7   a. still poses
Study   b. rounded poses
44   c. sharply angular poses
M   d. diagonal poses

2.34   A study by Lynn and Mynier (1993) indicated that servers received larger tips when they
d   a. stood next to the customer while taking the initial order
LO 7   b. leaned toward the customer while taking the initial order
Study   c. smiled at the customer while taking the initial order
44   d. squatted next to the customer while taking the initial order
M

2.35   Body movements that carry special meaning in a given culture are known as
a   a. emblems
LO 7   b. display movements
Fact   c. gestures
46   d. posturing
M

2.36   Emblems convey
c   a. that a person is emotionally aroused
LO 7   b. a low level of emotional arousal
Concept   c. a specific meaning within a given culture
46   d. that the person is ill-at-ease
E

2.37   The hand signal for "peace" (index and middle finger spread to form a V shape) is an example of
b   a. a cognitive marker
LO 7   b. an emblem
Applied   c. a cultural marker
46   d. a postural display
E

2.38
d
LO 7
Concept
46
M

Statement A: Emblems are the same from one culture to the next.
Statement B: While emblems are used more often in some parts of the world than others, all societies make use of emblems.
a. both statements are true
b. both statements are false
c. statement A is true; statement B is false
d. statement B is true; statement A is false

2.39
c
LO 8
Concept
46
M

Touching another person during an interaction is usually considered positive if
a. both people know each other
b. the people are of opposite sex
c. the cultural context makes touching acceptable in that situation
d. there is the potential for romantic attraction between the two people

2.40
c
LO 8
Concept
46
M

When one person touches another person gently, briefly, and on a nonsensitive part of the body
a. no effects are produced
b. negative reactions generally result
c. positive reactions generally result
d. violent reactions generally result

2.41
a
LO 8
Study
46
M

In the study by Crusco and Wetzel (1984), the smallest tips were left by customers in the
a. no-touch condition
b. condition where waitresses briefly touched customers on the hand
c. condition where waitresses touched customers on the shoulder
d. condition where older customers were briefly touched

2.42
b
LO 8
Study
46
M

In the study of tipping by Crusco and Wetzel (1984) it was found that
a. female customers left larger tips than male customers
b. touched customers left larger tips than nontouched customers
c. nontouched customers left larger tips than touched customers
d. there was no effect for touching

2.43
c
LO 8
Concept
46
E

If touching is perceived as a power play, such behavior may evoke
a. positive reactions
b. neutral reactions
c. negative reactions
d. noneffective reactions

2.44
b
LO 9
Concept
46
M

Choose the best alternative. Among young couples,
a. females touch males more often than males touch females
b. males touch females more often than females touch males
c. touching is unrelated to sex of the persons
d. cross-sex touching produces universally positive effects

2.45
b
LO 9
Applied
46
M

Ralph predicts Sam will be more likely than Sally to touch him during a conversation because Sam is a male. Ralph is likely to be correct
a. because males are more likely to engage in touching behavior than females
b. if Sam and Sally are both in their twenties
c. if Sam and Sally are both in their sixties
d. Ralph is not likely to be correct, because females engage in more touching behavior than males

2.46   According to research, the best predictor of touching behavior is
d   a. age
LO 9   b. gender
Concept   c. age or gender
46   d. the interaction between age and gender
E

2.47   The interaction between age and gender is a good predictor of
c   a. hostility
LO 9   b. use of nonverbal cues
Concept   c. touching behavior
46   d. self-presentation
M

2.48   A possible explanation for the change in touching behaviors among genders with increasing age comes
a   from a study on
LO 9   a. sex roles
Concept   b. cognitive development
46   c. the correlation between touching and verbal behavior
M   d. relationship violence

2.49   The tendency to show strong and clear nonverbal cues is known as
d   a. low self-regulation
LO 10   b. impression management
Fact   c. expression management
47   d. expressiveness
E

2.50   In looking at the relationship between expressiveness and success in certain occupations, Friedman
b   and his colleagues found automobile salesmen scoring high on expressiveness
LO 10   a. irritated more customers
Study   b. sold more automobiles
47   c. sold fewer automobiles
M   d. were liked by opposite sex customers

2.51   Emotional expressiveness is usually defined as the extent to which persons
c   a. show outward expression of inner cognitions
Lo 10   b. show outward expression of physiological reactions
Concept   c. show outward expression of inner feelings
47   d. show outward expression of ambivalent feelings
M

2.52   The relationship between emotional expressiveness and psychological adjustment is
b   a. straightforward
LO 10   b. based upon the extent to which individuals express concern over expressing their emotions
Concept   c. based upon the original level of psychological adjustment
47   d. based upon the original level of emotional expressiveness
M

2.53   A study by Katz and Campbell (1994) concerning emotional expressiveness and psychological
c   adjustment indicated that
LO 10   a. individuals high in expressiveness were better adjusted
Study   b. individuals low in expressiveness were better adjusted
48   c. individuals low in ambivalence over expressiveness were better adjusted
M   d. individuals high in ambivalence over expressiveness were better adjusted

2.54
a
LO 11
Fact
49
M

What are microexpressions?
a. fleeting facial expressions lasting a few tenths of a second
b. changes in voice pitch
c. shifts in overall patterns of eye contact
d. using inappropriate words under conditions of arousal

2.55
d
LO 11
Concept
49
M

An important tool that people use in recognizing deception in others is the examination of
a. speech
b. large scale movements
c. the time between spoken words of other people
d. microexpressions

2.56
c
LO 11
Concept
49
M

The reason that microexpressions are useful in detecting deception among others is that
a. the opposite of the expression is usually what the other person is really feeling
b. the minuscule twitches in the hands of people who are lying are not the same as the twitches that occur from nervousness
c. they reflect true emotion and are hard to suppress
d. they are a form of interchannel discrepancy

2.57
a
LO 11
Concept
49
C

Detection of deception from interchannel discrepancies arises from the fact that
a. it is hard for liars to control all of their nonverbal behaviors
b. it is hard for a person who is lying to keep making the right amount of eye contact
c. nonverbal cues in liars do not reflect what they are saying
d. nonverbal cues send different message in different situations

2.58
d
LO 11
Fact
49
M

Inconsistencies between different nonverbal cues from people who are lying are known as
a. regulatory malfunctions
b. regulatory dysfunctions
c. impression management malfunctions
d. interchannel discrepancies

2.59
b
LO 11
Concept
49
M

Which of the following is NOT characteristic of people who are lying?
a. sentence repair
b. only moderate eye contact
c. rising voice pitch
d. interchannel discrepancies

2.60
c
LO 11
Concept
49
M

What is communicated by sentence repairs?
a. the person is being honest with his audience
b. the person's behavior is under internal control
c. the person is probably telling a lie
d. the person is probably experiencing positive affect

2.61
d
LO 11
Concept
49
M

All of the following are clues telling us that someone is telling a lie except
a. sentence repairs
b. microexpressions
c. interchannel discrepancies
d. emblems

2.62   Which statement best describes the attribution process?
a
LO 12   a. the process by which we infer the causes of the behavior of others and ourselves
Concept   b. the process by which we combine information about others into unified impressions of them
50   c. the process by which we focus attention inward for cause
C   d. the process by which we seek to understand our own feelings, traits, and motives

2.63   The process by which people try to understand the underlying causes behind the behavior of others is
b   called
LO 12   a. correspondence theory
Fact   b. attribution theory
50   c. presentation theory
M   d. impression management theory

2.64   According to Jones and Davis, which of the following would help us decide that a behavior shown by
b   another person truly reflects a lasting trait possessed by that person
LO 12   a. he or she performs the behavior by force
Concept   b. the behavior produces noncommon effects
51   c. the behavior is high on social desirability
M   d. the behavior produces uncommon effects

2.65   We acquire useful information about others from behavior that has
b
LO 12   a. many reasons supporting its occurrence
Concept   b. only one distinct reason supporting its occurrence
51   c. no apparent reason supporting its occurrence
C   d. the number of reasons supporting its occurrence doesn't matter

2.66   We are more likely to reach correspondent inferences about others when their behavior
b   a. is seen to be socially desirable and to have occurred by choice
LO 12   b. is seen to be socially undesirable and to have occurred by choice
Concept   c. is seen to be socially desirable and to have occurred without choice
51   d. is seen to be socially undesirable and to have occurred without choice
C

2.67   According to the theory of correspondent inferences, which of the following behaviors is MOST likely
b   to be attributed to a trait in a person?
LO 12   a. a cashier refusing a person check
Applied   b. a TV announcer picking her teeth on the air
51   c. a salesman admiring your dog
C   d. a parent playing catch with his daughter

2.68   According to the theory of correspondent inferences, which of the following behaviors is LEAST likely
c   to be attributed to a trait in a person?
LO 12   a. an accountant taking flying lessons
Applied   b. a broadcaster squinting at the camera
51   c. a baseball player taking extra batting practice
C   d. a parent playing catch with her daughter

2.69   According to the theory of correspondent inferences, which of the following behaviors is MOST likely
a   to be attributed to a trait in a person?
LO 12   a. an accountant taking flying lessons
Applied   b. a baseball player taking extra batting practice
51   c. an accountant taking work home over the weekend
C   d. a dentist performing a root canal operation

2.70
d
LO 13
Concept
52
M

Three distinct tasks involved in Jones and Davis's theory are, in order
a. characterization, correction, categorization
b. correction, categorization, characterization
c. categorization, correction, characterization
d. categorization, characterization, correction

2.71
d
LO 13
Concept
52
E

According to research, people are less likely to correct trait inferences if the traits
a. are common
b. have common effects
c. have high social desirability
d. are hard to categorize in the first place

2.72
a
LO 13
Concept
52
C

People are less likely to correct trait inferences if the traits are hard to categorize because such traits
a. use up more conscious attentional resources
b. are hard to compare to traits that are contained within one's schema
c. are hard to fit into a given situation
d. take more time to categorize and thus are more likely to be accurate

2.73
b
LO 13
Concept
52
M

Behavior is generally harder to categorize if it is
a. low in social desirability
b. obscure
c. distinctive
d. affected by the situation

2.74
d
LO 13
Concept
53
M

Researchers have found that it is hard to correct trait inferences if the observed person's behavior
a. is strongly influenced by the environment
b. is weakly influenced by the environment
c. does not fit with previous behavior
d. is obscure

2.75
b
LO 13
Study
53
C

Gilbert and colleagues (1992) measured subjects' ratings of other peoples' tape recorded attitudes. These researchers varied the amount of distracting noise on the tape. The subjects rated the tape recorded attitudes as being most likely to reflect true attitudes
a. on the tape without the distracting noise
b. on the tape with the distracting noise
c. on both of the tapes
d. on neither of the tapes

2.76
c
LO 13
Study
53
C

The study that used tapes from the "dating game" revealed that females rated men's gender-role attitudes as being accurate if
a. the tape was of high quality, with little noise
b. the tape was of high quality, with accurate answers
c. the tape was of poor quality, with lots of noise
d. the quality of the tape had no influence

2.77
b
LO 13
Concept
53
M

When a person's behaviors are obscure, the effort we devote to answering the question ___ makes it more difficult for us to answer the question ___.
a. How?, Why?
b. What?, Why?
c. Why?, How?
d. What?, How?

2.78 People are more likely to believe that spoken attitudes reflect underlying attitudes
c
LO 13 a. if there are no accompanying nonverbal cues
Concept b. if they see interchannel inconsistencies
53   c. if they have to concentrate to understand what the attitudes are
C   d. if they have other knowledge about the person

2.79 People are more likely to believe that spoken attitudes reflect underlying attitudes when they have to
d   concentrate on understanding the spoken attitudes because
LO 13 a. people do not like to change their minds when they have put a lot of effort into a decision
Concept b. they are unsure of what the attitudes are
53   c. they cannot categorize the person's attitudes, even when they understand what they are
C   d. they do not have enough conscious attentional capacity left to engage in correction

2.80 The task we face in making a causal attribution is to determine whether a behavior is caused by
d
LO 14 a. consensus or consistency
Concept b. consistency or distinctiveness
53   c. objective or subjective causes
M   d. internal or external causes

2.81 Causal attribution is concerned with
d
LO 14 a. assigning a cause to an attitude
Fact   b. how people behave
53   c. how to detect deception
E   d. why people behave

2.82 When our attribution is influenced by the extent to which other persons react in the same manner to a
c   particular stimulus, our attribution is being affected by _____
LO 14 a. consistency
Fact   b. correspondent inference
54   c. consensus
M   d. distinctiveness

2.83 When our attribution is affected by whether the target person reacts in the same way to other,
d   different stimuli, our attribution is a product of _____
LO 14 a. consistency
Fact   b. correspondent inference
54   c. consensus
M   d. distinctiveness

2.84 When I consider the extent to which this person reacts in the same way to this same stimulus on other
a   occasions, I am basing my attribution on _____
LO 14 a. consistency
Fact   b. correspondent inference
54   c. consensus
M   d. distinctiveness

2.85 Which describes high distinctiveness?
c
LO 14 a. a person makes the same response to a wide range of stimuli
Concept b. a person reacts to a particular stimulus the same way on several occasions
54   c. a person makes a unique response to each of several different stimuli
C   d. a person reacts to a particular stimulus differently on each of several occasions

2.86
c
LO 15
Concept
54
M

We are likely to attribute another person's behavior to internal causes when consensus is _____, consistency is _____, and distinctiveness is _____
a. high, high, high
b. low, low, low
c. low, high, low
d. high, low, high

2.87
a
LO 15
Concept
54
M

We are likely to attribute another person's behavior to external causes when consensus is _____, consistency is _____, and distinctiveness is _____
a. high, high, high
b. low, low, low
c. low, high, low
d. high, low, high

2.88
a
LO 15
Applied
54
C

Imagine that one of the students in this class gets up one day and attacks the professor in an angry manner. Further, imagine that this student is in another of your classes, and does the same thing there. Finally, imagine that he attacks the professor at other times also. To what would you attribute this behavior?
a. internal factors (characteristics of the student)
b. external factors (characteristics of the professors)
c. a combination of internal and external factors
d. insanity -- no one would want to attack my professor

2.89
c
LO 15
Applied
54
M

You observe Kathryn laughing hard over a joke. All the other people around her are laughing as well. You also know that Kathryn does not laugh at many jokes. To what would you attribute this behavior?
a. Kathryn has developed a better sense of humor
b. Kathryn is trying to hide her true feelings
c. the joke must be very funny
d. Kathryn has been eating funny brownies

2.90
b
LO 15
Applied
54
M

Sue is afraid of the dog. Everyone else is also afraid of the dog. Sue is always afraid of this particular dog, but not of other dogs. What attribution follows from this information?
a. an internal attribution (about Sue)
b. an external attribution (about the dog)
c. a mixed attribution (Sue's behavior stems from internal and external causes)
d. the information given is not sufficient to make an attribution

2.91
a
LO 16
Concept
54
M

Why do people not use causal attributional processes all of the time to determine underlying causes of behavior?
a. causal attribution takes considerable cognitive effort
b. causal attribution is not very accurate
c. causal attribution does not take external factors into account
d. causal attribution is not relevant to underlying causes of behavior

2.92
c
LO 16
Concept
54
M

With regard to the amount of attributional work we do in a particular situation, it seems that
a. we usually do more than is necessary
b. we usually do more, but no less than is necessary
c. we usually do as little as possible
d. no conclusion can be reached

2.93   We are likely to jump to quick and easy conclusions about other peoples' behavior when
b   a. the behavior is unexpected and doesn't fit what we already know
LO 16   b. the behavior is expected and consistent with prior knowledge
Concept c. we are not at all sure as to why the person behaved this way
55   d. we tend to engage in careful attributional analyses most of the time
C

2.94   When a person encounters someone succeeding in a sphere of life where she has come to believe that
c   success is due mainly to talent and effort, she will likely
LO 16   a. analyze this new situation carefully to determine why the person is successful
Concept b. ignore this situation
55   c. jump to the conclusion that this person's success is due to talent and effort
M   d. avoid the "path of least resistance"

2.95   People are more likely to use techniques of causal attribution when
d   a. they have to determine whether or not a behavior is internally motivated
LO 16   b. they have to determine whether or not a behavior is externally motivated
Concept c. the solution to the cause of a behavior is relatively apparent
55   d. other techniques of attribution are not useful
M

2.96   The person who takes the "path of least resistance" would explain the fact that someone laughs at a
d   funny joke
LO 16   a. only after doing a careful attributional analysis
Applied b. on the basis of consensus information
55   c. on the basis of distinctiveness information
M   d. in terms of the joke, based on past experience about why people laugh

2.97   The careful attributional analysis described by Kelley occurs when people are confronted with
c   a. expected and pleasant events
LO 16   b. expected and unpleasant events
Concept c. unexpected and unpleasant events
55   d. unexpected and pleasant events
M

2.98   Kelley's model seems to be an accurate description of causal attribution
b   a. because it fits the data
LO 16   b. when such attribution occurs
Concept c. only when external factors are expected
55   d. only when internal factors are expected
M

2.99   _____ states that we tend to downplay the importance of any potential cause of another person's
b   behavior to the degree that other possible causes are present
LO 17   a. the augmenting principle
Concept b. the discounting principle
56   c. the ego-defensive principle
M   d. the "cognitive miser" principle

2.100   When a behavior occurs despite the presence of a factor that would be expected to inhibit it
a   a. we give added weight to whatever facilitative factor is present
LO 17   b. we discount any facilitative factor that is present
Concept c. we are unable to make an attribution
56   d. we augment the inhibitory factor
M

2.101
c
LO 17
Concept
56
M

When augmenting takes place
a. only one potential cause for the behavior is present
b. several potential facilitory causes are present
c. both facilitory and inhibitory causes are present
d. we tend to downplay the importance of the facilitory factor

2.102
b
LO 17
Concept
56
C

The decreased likelihood of attributing causality to one factor in the presence of another is called the
a. augmenting principle
b. discounting principle
c. consensus effect
d. causal theory of attribution

2.103
b
LO 17
Concept
56
M

Statement A: The discounting and augmenting principles apply mainly to situations in which we have the opportunity to observe a person's behavior in several situations and at different times.
Statement B: Kelley and colleagues concluded that the only dimension on which our causal attributions differ is the internal-external dimension.
a. both statements are true
b. both statements are false
c. statement A is true; statement B is false
d. statement A is false; statement B is true

2.104
c
LO 17
Concept
57
C

An unfortunate possible side effect of affirmative action is the
a. reluctance of businesses to comply with the law
b. inability of schools to comply with the law
c. discounting of the abilities of beneficiaries of affirmative action programs
d. augmentation of the abilities of beneficiaries of affirmative action programs

2.105
b
LO 17
Study
57
M

Research indicates that people are more likely to discount the abilities of women in companies that
a. have previously discriminated against women
b. have affirmative action programs
c. resist affirmative action programs
d. promote many women

2.106
a
LO 18
Concept
57
M

The "fundamental attribution error" refers to our tendency to
a. overestimate the role of dispositions in causing others' behavior
b. overestimate the role of situations in causing others' behavior
c. overestimate the role of situations in causing our own behavior
d. assume that we can do no wrong

2.107
b
LO 18
Applied
57
M

When we read an essay written by another person favoring a particular point of view, we assume that this person holds this view even if we are told the person was forced to write the essay. This situation illustrates
a. the self-serving bias
b. the fundamental attribution error
c. the ego-defensive bias
d. the self-presentation bias

2.108   The fundamental attribution errors refers to
a
LO 18   a. the tendency to assume internal causes for others' behavior
Fact   b. the tendency to assume external causes for others' behavior
57   c. the tendency to overestimate the strength of external causes
M   d. the tendency to overestimate the number of external causes

2.109   The fact that people are likely to assume that someone tripping on the steps is clumsy is explained by
c   the
LO 18   a. accompanying nonverbal cues
Concept   b. distinctiveness of the action
57   c. fundamental attribution error
M   d. consistency of the action

2.110   The fundamental attribution error has been used to explain why some people
d   a. are more likely to help others
LO 18   b. are better at detecting deception
Concept   c. are good at causal attribution
57   d. blame poor people for poverty
M

2.111   Which of these is an explanation of the fundamental attribution error?
b   a. when we interpret our own behavior, we do not assign sufficient weight to situational factors
LO 18   b. when we interpret others' behavior, we do not assign sufficient weight to situational factors
Concept   c. when we interpret our own behavior, we do not assign sufficient weight to dispositional factors
57   d. when we interpret others' behavior, we do not assign sufficient weight to dispositional factors
M

2.112   You witness the following scene: a student visits a professor in his office and begs him to raise a
c   grade. When the professor refuses, the student bursts into tears. The professor relents and raises the
LO 18   grade. On the basis of this incident, you conclude that the professor is a simple push-over, easily
Applied   swayed by others. This might be an example of
57   a. jumping to the right conclusions
M   b. social inference gone astray
    c. the fundamental attribution error
    d. the link between attributions and behavior

2.113   The decrease over time of the fundamental attribution error in relation to making attributions
a   about an event suggests that
LO 18   a. personal information is lost more quickly than situational information
Concept   b. older people are more accurate at making attributions than younger people
58   c. younger people are more accurate at making attributions than older people
C   d. detection of deception is a long term process

2.114   Examining newspaper accounts of presidential elections over time provides evidence that
b   a. people make the largest number of inferences about candidates immediately after an election
LO 18   b. the fundamental attribution error for a particular event tends to diminish over time
Study   c. making the fundamental attribution error is associated with voting patterns
58   d. most candidates' behavior does come from internal underlying causes
M

2.115   The actor-observer effect refers to the tendency for people to
c
LO 19   a. observe the actions of others when making attributions
Concept   b. observe the dispositions of others when making attributions
58   c. take more account of external influences when explaining their own actions compared to the
M   actions of others
          d. take more account of internal influences when explaining their own actions compared to the
             actions of others

2.116   It is hypothesized that the actor-observer effect occurs in part because
d
LO 19   a. there is self-serving bias
Concept   b. it is easier to detect deception in the self than in others
58   c. people do not attach much importance to the actions of others
M   d. external influences on our own behavior are more obvious than upon others' behavior

2.117   Karen sees Martha trip while walking down an outside flight of steps. "Clumsy person," thinks
a   Karen. Five minutes later, Karen trips on the same flight of steps. "Very icy today," thinks Karen.
LO 19   This is an illustration of the
Applied   a. actor-observer effect
58   b. self-serving bias effect
M   c. categorization principle
          d. blame avoidance principle

2.118   We tend to perceive our own behavior as stemming largely from _____; we tend to perceive the
c   behavior of others as stemming largely from _____
LO 19   a. dispositional factors, situational factors
Concept   b. dispositional factors, dispositional factors
58   c. situational factors, dispositional factors
M   d. situational factors, situational factors

2.119   Compared to how we evaluate ourselves, we generally weigh _____ factors more heavily in
a   evaluating the performances of other persons
LO 19   a. dispositional
Concept   b. situational
58   c. conscious
E   d. unconscious

2.120   The tendency to attribute positive outcomes to internal factors and negative outcomes to external
b   factors is called the
LO 20   a. fundamental attributional error
Fact   b. self-serving bias
59   c. blame avoidance principle
M   d. self-deception principle

2.121   A cognitive model for the self-serving bias suggests that we attribute successes to internal factors
c   because we
LO 20   a. are protecting self-esteem
Concept   b. are less aware of external influences on our own actions
59   c. generally expect to succeed and attribute expected outcomes to internal factors
C   d. tend to repress thoughts of failure

2.122   A motivational model for the self-serving bias suggests that we attribute success to internal factors
a   because we
LO 20   a. are boosting our self-esteem
Concept   b. are less aware of external influences on our own actions
59   c. generally expect to succeed and attribute expected outcomes to internal factors
C   d. tend to repress thoughts of failure

2.123   You and I work on a joint project, and it succeeds. In describing our relative contributions to the
b   project, you assume that your contribution is greater than mine, but I assume that my
LO 20   contribution is greater than yours. This illustrates
Applied   a. the actor-observer bias
59   b. the self-serving bias
C   c. the false consensus effect
        d. the self-centered bias

2.124   The tendency to view successes of others as externally caused is part of the ____ , while viewing
c   failures of others as internally caused is part of the ____
LO 20   a. cognitive viewpoint, social viewpoint
Concept   b. social viewpoint, cognitive viewpoint
59   c. self-serving bias, fundamental attributional error
C   d. self-esteem theory of attribution, self-serving bias

2.125   A self-defeating pattern of attributions has received attention in recent years as possibly playing a
a   role in depression. This patterns involves
LO 21   a. attributions that are the opposite pattern of the self-serving bias
Concept   b. attributions that are the same pattern of the self-serving bias
59   c. attributions in a pattern that are not related to the self-serving bias
M   d. attributions that are the same pattern as the self-enhancement bias

2.126   Depressed people make attributions that are in a pattern
c   a. similar to the self-serving bias
LO 21   b. similar to the self-enhancement bias
Concept   c. opposite to the self-serving bias
59   d. opposite to the self-enhancement bias
M

2.127   Depressed people tend to attribute
d   a. negative outcomes to external causes and positive outcomes to internal causes
LO 21   b. negative outcomes to internal causes and positive outcomes to internal causes
Concept   c. negative outcomes to external causes and positive outcomes to external causes
59   d. negative outcomes to internal causes and positive outcomes to external causes
M

2.128   A therapy that is based on changing attributions of depressed people involves
d   a. channeling negative emotion into positive emotion
LO 21   b. channeling negative emotion from depression into action
Applied   c. the client transferring depressive affect from themselves to the therapist
60   d. changing the way that depressed people make attributions about success and failure
M

2.129   If a woman is sexually assaulted, and someone says, "She was dressed in a skimpy skirt, so she
b   must have deserved it," this statement illustrates
LO 22   a. self-serving bias
Applied   b. belief in a just world
60   c. self-enhancement bias
M   d. self-defeating effect

2.130
c
LO 22
Study
60
C

Bell and colleagues recently conducted a study involving males and females rating the extent to which a female rape victim was perceived as being to blame for the assault. The results indicated
a. males and females attributed more blame to the victim if she did not know the rapist
b. males attributed more blame to the victim if she knew the rapist, but females attributed less blame to the victim if she did not know the rapist
c. males and females attributed more blame to the victim if she knew the rapist
d. males attributed more blame to the victim if she did not know the victim, but females attributed less blame to the victim if she knew the rapist

2.131
d
LO 22
Concept
61
M

Which statement summarizes the perception of rape victims that attribution theorists are working to counter?
a. the perception that she has suffered no harm
b. the perception that she is just trying to cause trouble by reporting this crime
c. the perception that she actually enjoyed the attack
d. the perception that she was somehow responsible for the attack

2.132
c
LO 22
Applied
61
M

One implication of attribution theory concerning date rape prevention is that
a. males correctly interpret female communication
b. females correctly interpret male communication
c. males often misinterpret female communication
d. females often misinterpret male communication

2.133
c
LO 23
Concept
62
M

Asch was influenced by what psychological school of thought?
a. behaviorism
b. structuralism
c. Gestalt
d. functionalism

2.134
a
LO 23
Study
63
M

Asch suggested that we do not just add all traits together to form an impression, but that we
a. perceive traits in relation to one another
b. perceive traits in relation to the emotion they create
c. perceive traits in relation to how familiar they are to us
d. perceive traits in relation to the ratio of positive to negative

2.135
b
LO 23
Study
64
M

In Asch's study on impression formation, he found that subjects did not just add traits together, put paid particular attention to
a. peripheral traits
b. central traits
c. emotional traits
d. common traits

2.136
b
LO 23
Fact
64
M

Asch defined "central traits" as those traits that
a. were located near the middle of a list of traits
b. were crucial in shaping the overall impression of a stranger
c. were crucial for making cognitive decisions about the other traits
d. were located near the middle of our cognitive structure for attitudes

2.137   The "weighted average" model of impression formation involves
b
LO 24   a. weighting all traits and then taking an average of traits
Fact   b. weighting each trait in terms of relative importance and then taking an average of traits
64   c. taking the average rating of all traits and then weighting each trait
M   d. taking the average rating of each trait and then weighting each trait

2.138   The more unusual the trait, the
c
LO 24   a. less weight given the trait in forming an overall impression
Fact   b. less weight given the trait in relation to other traits
65   c. more weight given the trait in forming an overall impression
M   d. more weight given the trait in relation to other traits

2.139   More weight is given information
d
LO 24   a. that is received last in the list
Concept   b. that is received toward the last half of the list
65   c. that is received toward the middle of the list
M   d. that is received first in the list

2.140   Which of the following is NOT one of the factors that influences the weight a piece of
c   information has on impression formation?
LO 24   a. source of the input
Concept   b. whether the information is positive or negative in nature
65   c. whether the information is simple or complex
M   d. whether the information is presented first or last

2.141   Current research on impression formation involves the way we notice, store, remember, and
a   integrate information, all processes in
LO 25   a. social cognition
Concept   b. social recognition
65   c. social attribution
M   d. social comparison

2.142   Concrete examples of behaviors that are consistent with a given trait are called
b
LO 25   a. abstractions
Fact   b. exemplars
65   c. impressions
E   d. attributions

2.143   In impression formation, "abstractions" are
d
LO 25   a. concrete examples of behaviors that are consistent with a trait
Fact   b. abstract examples of behaviors that are consistent with a trait
65   c. mental summaries that are derived from one's observation of another's behavior
M   d. mental summaries that are derived from repeated observations of another's behavior

2.144   During your first interaction with a person in the Registrar's Office of your university, this person
b   interrupted you repeatedly, made snide comments about other students, and made you repeat your last
LO 25   name for every form. Later, while discussing this person with your roommate, you recalled these
Applied   behaviors and called this person "inconsiderate." You were using _____ to form your impression.
65   a. abstractions
M   b. exemplars
       c. emotions
       d. expressions

2.145
c
LO 26
Concept
65
M

As we gain experience with others, the nature of our impressions of someone shifts
a. from simple abstractions to complex abstractions
b. from complex abstractions to simple abstractions
c. from exemplars to abstractions
d. from abstractions to exemplars

2.146
a
LO 26
Study
66
C

Sherman and Klein (1994) in their investigation of impression formation found
a. for participants who received a small amount of information, the describe task did facilitate recall of the stranger
b. for participants who received a small amount of information, the describe task did not facilitate recall of the stranger
c. for participants who received a large amount of information, the describe task did facilitate recall of the stranger
d. for both classes of participants, the describe task had no effect on recall of the stranger

2.147
d
LO 26
Study
66
M

The research by Sherman and Klein (1994) on impression formation support the view that at first, impressions of others are consistent with _____, but later, impressions are based on _____.
a. abstractions, exemplars
b. exemplars, exemplars
c. abstractions, abstractions
d. exemplars, abstractions

2.148
c
LO 26
Concept
66
C

In the research by Sherman and Klein (1994) on impression formation, the purpose of the "describe task" was to
a. activate abstractions in memory
b. activate later recall of the stranger
c. activate exemplars in memory
d. activate later impressions of the stranger

2.149
c
LO 27
Applied
67
E

When Ralph goes out on a first date with someone, he brushes his teeth carefully and puts a dab of cologne around his ears. He is engaging in
a. self-attribution
b. schema formation
c. self-enhancement
d. other-enhancement

2.150
d
LO 27
Fact
67
M

The impression management tactic of trying to induce a favorable impression in another through a specific action aimed at them is called
a. inductive impression management
b. self-enhancement
c. cognitive categorization
d. other-enhancement

2.151
c
LO 27
Applied
67
M

A common example of an other-enhancement tactic is
a. putting on your best suit
b. taking someone else to a good restaurant
c. telling someone how nice they look
d. getting good grades to please your parents

2.152
b
LO 27
Concept
67
M

Flattery is an example of the impression management tactic of _____
a. self-enhancement
b. other-enhancement
c. categorization
d. induction

2.153   Results of research by Wayne and Liden (1995) on impression management found that
a   a. the more that employees engaged in self-enhancement tactics, the more their supervisors liked
LO 28   them
Study   b. the less that employees engaged in self-enhancement tactics, the more their supervisors liked them
68   c. the more that employees engaged in other-enhancement tactics, the more their supervisors liked
C   them
         d. the more that employees engaged in other-enhancement tactics, the less their supervisors liked
            them

2.154   Results of research by Wayne and Liden (1995) on impression management found that
a   a. the more that employees engaged in other-enhancement tactics, the more their supervisors viewed
LO 28   them as similar
Study   b. the less that employees engaged in other-enhancement tactics, the more their supervisors viewed
68   them as similar
C   c. the more that employees engaged in self-enhancement tactics, the more their supervisors viewed
            them as similar
         d. the less that employees engaged in self-enhancement tactics, the more their supervisors viewed
            them as similar

2.155   The usefulness of impression management techniques is illustrated by the finding that people
c   with good impression management skills tend to
LO 28   a. be better at detecting deception
Concept b. be more immune to flattery
68   c. receive higher performance ratings
M   d. have more self-motivational skills

2.156   Research findings indicate that impression management tactics often
b   a. are crudely defined
LO 28   b. succeed in enhancing the appeal of those who use them
Concept c. fail to enhance the appeal of those who use them
69   d. are based upon insufficient evidence
M

2.157   In a study of facial expressions of political leaders, it was found that French participants
b   reacted _____ than American participants
LO 29   a. less favorably to expressions of anger/threat
Study   b. more favorably to expressions of anger/threat
69   c. less favorably to expressions of happiness/reassurance
M   d. more favorably to expressions of happiness/reassurance

2.158   French and American participants were able to distinguish between three types of facial
c   expressions
LO 29   a. with some difficulty
Study   b. depending upon the culture of the political leader
69   c. equally well
M   d. depending upon the culture of the participant

2.159   In France, viewers' political attitudes would probably _____ of their reactions to political
c   candidates than in America.
LO 29   a. be less predictive
Concept b. be equally predictive
71   c. be more predictive
C   d. be unrelated to prediction

2.160
a
LO 29
Concept
71
M

The results of studies of political leaders in different cultures indicate that
a. nonverbal cues play an important role
b. nonverbal cues do not play an important role
c. nonverbal cues do not play an important role because of the cultural context
d. nonverbal cues have not been investigated

CHAPTER 3

Learning Objectives

After studying this chapter, students should be able to:

1.   *Define the concepts of schema and prototype, and give an example illustrating each concept.*

2.   *Understand person schemas, role schemas, and scripts.*

3.   *Examine how schemas influence attention, encoding, and retrieval of information.*

4.   *Explain how the favorability of one's prototype regarding pregnant teen-agers and one's perceived similarity to these persons is related to willingness to engage in risky sexual behavior.*

5.   *Describe the basic nature of heuristics, indicating how they allow us to reduce cognitive effort and to avoid information overload.*

6.   *Describe the representativeness heuristic, and indicate how use of this heuristic sometimes leads us to commit the base-rate fallacy.*

7.   *Summarize how our judgments regarding others are affected by the availability heuristic.*

8.   *Define the false consensus effect, and indicate why it occurs.*

9.   *Describe research that demonstrates priming, automatic priming, and spontaneous trait inferences.*

10.   *Compare rational thinking and intuitive thinking when subjects had to choose one of the bowls of jelly beans in the Denes-Raj and Epstein (1994) study.*

11.   *Examine the degree to which unexpected information grabs our attention and influences later social judgments.*

12.   *Summarize research by Buehier et al. on the planning fallacy, noting subjects' thinking patterns during planning and their attributions concerning past failures.*

13.   *Describe the automatic vigilance effect, including the face-in-the-crowd effect.*

14.   *Based on the Wilson and Schooler (1991) study, indicate how "thinking too much" while rating jams or rating courses lowered the accuracy of ratings.*

15.   *Give examples of counterfactual thinking in response to negative outcomes. Secondly, examine the experience of regret over actions performed vs. actions we didn't do.*

16.   *Describe various forms of magical thinking, including the law of contagion, the law of similarity, and the possibility of inviting catastrophes by thinking about them.*

17.   *Summarize and compare the views of emotion expressed by the Cannon-Bard theory, the James-Lange theory, and Schachter's 2-factor theory.*

18.   *Describe the facial feedback hypothesis, along with research findings relevant to the hypothesis.*

19.   *Explain how did being in a happy mood affected each of the following: a) social cognition in the Mayer and Hanson (1995) study; b) creativity in the Estrada et al. (1995) study.*

20.   *Summarize research supporting the conclusion that the effects of positive and negative affect are not always simply opposite in nature.*

21.   *Describe the four ways in which cognition can influence our current feelings or moods.*

22.   *According to Forgas' (1994) affect infusion model, explain the two mechanisms through which our feelings influence social thought.*

23.   *Describe circumstances in the Forgas (1994) study where affective states influenced cognition through priming and circumstances where affective states influenced cognition through heuristics.*

24.   *Compare Japanese and Americans in terms of levels of trust and levels of assurance shown in personal relationships.*

Questions

3.1   Mental frameworks that order information related to specific events or
c   situations are called
LO 1   a. heuristics
Fact   b. memories
77   c. schemas
E   d. cognitions

3.2   Ralph is talking to Lisa at a track meet. Lisa is constantly fidgeting and
b   looking over Ralph's shoulder at someone else in the distance. Due to
LO 1   Ralph's _____ of appropriate "track meet" behavior, he does not interpret
Applied   Lisa's behavior as disinterest in him, but of nervousness of competition.
77   a. prototype
M   b. schema
               c. judgment
               d. heuristic

3.3   A prototype is a _____
a   a. mental model of the typical qualities of members of some group
LO 1   b. mental framework of specific situations or events
Fact   c. mental judgment of situations affecting our behavior
77   d. mental judgment of individuals affecting our behavior
M

3.4   Lisa is talking to Ralph at a track meet. Ralph is small, muscular, and
d   lean. Lisa asks him how he is doing in the sprints. Ralph replies that he is not in the sprints, but
LO 1   throws the javelin. Lisa has asked her question based upon a _____
Applied   a. schema
78   b. judgment
M   c. heuristic
               d. prototype

3.5   A _____ schema is a mental framework that ties certain traits and behaviors together.
b   a. role
LO 2   b. person
Fact   c. event
78   d. judgment
M

3.6   Your psychology professor knocks on your door and tries to sell you a vacuum cleaner. This
a   behavior violates your _____ schema.
LO 2   a. role
Applied   b. person
79   c. event
M   d. judgment

3.7   A script is
c   a. a global representation of a specific situation
LO 2   b. a prepared way of behaving
Fact   c. an indication of what is expected to happen in a given setting
79   d. an overview of the behaviors associated with an unusual situation
M

3.8
b
LO 2
Concept
79
C

Scripts are similar to other schemas because, once established, they
a. call attention to specific characteristics of individuals
b. save us considerable mental effort
c. provide us with usual ways of interpreting unusual behaviors
d. allow us to review specific behaviors in specific situations

3.9
a
LO 2
Applied
79
M

It is your week to visit your dentist. When you arrive at the dental office, your dentist comes into the room dressed in an string bikini. She asks you to take off your outer clothes and sit in the chair in your underwear. This dentist has violated the _____ you have about visits to the dentist.
a. script
b. prototype
c. heuristic
d. framework

3.10
b
LO 3
Fact
80
M

In which order do our cognitive processes generally occur?
a. encoding, attention, retrieval
b. attention, encoding, retrieval
c. retrieval, encoding, attention
d. attention, retrieval, encoding

3.11
c
LO 3
Concept
80
M

Whether we will notice or ignore an event that doesn't fit our schema seems to be determined by
a. how vivid the event is
b. whether the event gets encoded or not
c. the degree to which the event is unexpected
d. whether the event involves someone we know

3.12
a
LO 3
Concept
80
M

Information is more likely to grab our attention if it is
a. inconsistent with our viewpoint
b. easily available in memory
c. related to a heuristic
d. related to a schema

3.13
b
LO 3
Concept
80
M

Once a schema has been formed, information
a. inconsistent with the schema is easier to remember
b. consistent with the schema is easier to remember
c. provided later in the interaction is easier to remember
d. provided earlier in the interaction is easier to remember

3.14
c
LO 3
Applied
80
M

Lisa is starting to form an impression of Ralph by the type of answers he gives in class. She has a tendency to pay attention to the incorrect answers he has given because he has given primarily _____
a. incorrect answers in the past
b. incorrect answers very recently
c. correct answers in the past
d. correct answers very recently

3.15
d
LO 4
Study
81
C

A study by Gibbons and his colleagues (1995) investigated the relationship between prototype and behavior. The study found that
a. the more unfavorable the prototype of pregnant teenage girls and their boyfriends, the less willing participants were to engage in unprotected sex
b. the more unfavorable the prototype of pregnant teenage girls and their boyfriends, the more willing participants were to engage in unprotected sex
c. the more favorable the prototype of pregnant teenage girls and their boyfriends, the less willing participants were to engage in unprotected sex
d. the more favorable the prototype of pregnant teenage girls and their boyfriends, the more willing participants were to engage in unprotected sex

3.16
d
LO 4
Study
81
M

The participants who viewed themselves as _____ to the prototypes and who had _____ prototypes were more willing to engage in unprotected sex.
a. similar, unfavorable
b. dissimilar, unfavorable
c. dissimilar, favorable
d. similar, favorable

3.17
c
LO 4
Concept
81
E

A favorable prototype of pregnant teenage girls and their boyfriends, plus perceived similarity to these individuals was related to _____ willingness to engage in unprotected sex
a. decreased
b. depleted
c. increased
d. enhanced

3.18
b
LO 4
Concept
82
M

The findings of Gibbons and his colleagues may have important practical implications. For example, TV shows sometimes show individuals engaged in unprotected sex, while minimizing the consequences of such behavior. Such scenes may encourage
a. the development of unrealistic schemas
b. the development of favorable prototypes
c. the development of unfavorable prototypes
d. the development of realistic schemas

3.19
d
LO 5
Concept
82
M

Mental rules-of-thumb that allow individuals to make rapid decisions about social stimuli are called
a. social inference rules
b. inference schemas
c. appraisal rules
d. heuristics

3.20
d
LO 5
Concept
82
M

A heuristic is a
a. schema that permits the processing of contrary information
b. schema that helps to organize thoughts into memory
c. type of mental simulation
d. decision making rule that saves mental effort

3.21
a
LO 5
Concept
82
M

One basic fact of social life is that we
a. have limited rather than unlimited cognitive resources
b. have unlimited rather than limited cognitive resources
c. have limited demands on our cognitive resources
d. have unlimited demands on our cognitive resources

3.22
c
LO 5
Concept
82
M

A situation that demands more cognitive resources than we have available is known as
a. cognitive stress
b. cognitive overload
c. information overload
d. information stress

3.23
d
LO 5
Concept
82
M

Cognitive strategies are designed to
a. decrease our cognitive effort and increase information overload
b. increase our cognitive effort and increase information overload
c. increase our cognitive effort and decrease information overload
d. decrease our cognitive effort and decrease information overload

3.24
a
LO 6
Fact
83
M

Which describes the representativeness heuristic?
a. to determine whether someone is a lawyer, I compare his traits to the "average" lawyer
b. to determine whether someone is "conscientious," I try to recall instances of such behavior
c. to determine my impressions of someone, I combine the available bits of information to find an average
d. to determine whether someone in "conscientious," I engage in decoding

3.25
d
LO 6
Fact
83
M

The representativeness heuristic is used by people to make decisions about others
a. based on the ease of recall of salient characteristics from memory
b. based on early information that then tends to have a primacy effect
c. based on certain characteristics that they possess that are assumed to be representative of that person
d. based on their perceived similarity to members of a particular group

3.26
b
LO 6
Concept
83
M

Although often accurate, the representativeness heuristic can lead to overlooking
a. consensus effects
b. base rate information
c. availability information
d. prior schematic information

3.27
d
LO 6
Applied
83
M

Ralph is given a message to take to the chief executive of E&D Corp at an office party. Too embarrassed to ask who she is, Ralph looks for the person who seems to be the best dressed, and who seems to have the biggest aura of power about her. Ralph is using
a. the availability heuristic
b. the anchoring heuristic
c. self-schematic processing
d. the representative heuristic

3.28
b
LO 6
Applied
83
M

Participants are given base rate information as well as information either consistent or inconsistent with the "typical engineer." In deciding whether this particular person is indeed an engineer, participants will tend to use _____ information and to ignore _____ information.
a. base rate, representativeness
b. representativeness, base rate
c. extreme, more typical
d. typical, more extreme

3.29 When my evaluation of someone is influenced by how quickly I can bring relevant instances to mind,
d   or by how many relevant instances I can recall, I am using
LO 7 a. the representativeness heuristic
Fact b. base rate information
83   c. visual imagery
M   d. the availability heuristic

3.30 The heuristic that bases a decision on how easily an example of something is brought to mind is
b   called the
LO 7 a. representativeness heuristic
Fact b. availability heuristic
84   c. anchoring heuristic
M   d. mental simulation heuristic

3.31 The reason that most people think that there are more English words beginning with "k" than have
c   "k" as the third letter is because
Concept a. words beginning with "k" are more commonly used
LO 7 b. words beginning with "k" are more representative of English
84   c. it is easier to think of words that have "k" as the first letter
M   d. people tend to also think of words that begin with "c"

3.32 People's greater fear of flying than of driving can probably be best explained by the
c   a. representativeness heuristic
Applied b. vividness heuristic
LO 7 c. availability heuristic
84   d. self-fulfilling prophecy
C

3.33 "Does this student show initiative?" Since I can't readily think of an instance of such behavior, I
b   assign him a low rating. My rating is based on
LO 7 a. the representative heuristic
Applied b. the availability heuristic
84   c. base rate information
M   d. visual imagery

3.34 The false consensus effect suggests that people
b   a. tend to perceive general agreement on most topics
LO 8 b. overestimate the proportion of people that agree with them on a given topic
Concept c. tend to recall positive experiences more readily than negative ones
84   d. tend to recall negative experiences more readily than positive ones
M

3.35 An explanation of the false consensus effect is that
a   a. the belief that others are like us enhances our confidence
LO 8 b. we are motivated to perceive consensus in others
Concept c. people who are really like us tend to share the same opinions
84   d. people tend to be inaccurate at assessing others' opinions and attitudes
M

3.36 The false consensus effect is explained by the availability heuristic because
d   a. we will more easily remember attitudes if they are like those of friends
LO 8 b. we are motivated to perceive consensus to protect self-esteem
Concept c. people who are really similar to us tend to share the same attitudes
84   d. the opinions of our friends are both more like ours and easier to bring to mind than the
M   "average" opinion

3.37
b
LO 8
Applied
84
C

Consistent with the false consensus effect, researchers found that high school boys who smoked estimated that _____ percent of their fellow male students smoked, and nonsmoking boys estimated that _____ smoked.
a. 38, 52
b. 52, 38
c. 53, 52
d. 38, 38

3.38
a
LO 8
Concept
84
M

The availability heuristic explains the false consensus effect by assuming that
a. instances of agreement with oneself are easiest to recall
b. instances of agreement with oneself are seen to be more typical
c. instances of agreement with oneself usually are provided by people we like
d. instances of agreement with oneself are usually common behaviors

3.39
d
LO 9
Applied
84
M

The "medical student" syndrome is an example of
a. confirmation bias
b. theory perseverance
c. the vividness effect
d. priming

3.40
a
LO 9
Concept
85
M

When planting certain ideas or categories in people's minds causes them to use such ideas or categories to interpret subsequent events, we have an example of
a. priming
b. the vividness effect
c. confirmation bias
d. encoding

3.41
b
LO 9
Concept
85
M

Subjects who were primed with honest traits such as "honorable" tended to
a. form a more negative impression of a subsequent stimulus person
b. form a more positive impression of a subsequent stimulus person
c. view a subsequent stimulus person more objectively
d. be unaffected by the priming when they judged the stimulus person

3.42
a
LO 9
Applied
85
M

You watch a movie in which the greed of one of the leading characters is emphasized. The priming notion suggests that
a. you will be likely to notice "greed" in a person you encounter later
b. you will be unlikely to notice "greed" in a person you encounter later
c. you will be primed to intensify whatever strong characteristics are possessed by people you encounter later
d. you will be ready to see "generosity" in a person you encounter later

3.43
d
LO 9
Fact
85
M

When we receive information about others, we tend to form immediate impressions about their underlying characteristics. This tendency is called
a. heuristic management
b. automatic processing
c. subliminal modeling
d. spontaneous trait inference

3.44
a
LO 9
Concept
85
M

Spontaneously trait inferences influence future perception through
a. priming
b. representativeness
c. subliminal modeling
d. heuristic cognitions

3.45
c
LO 10
Concept
86
M

The theory suggesting that both rational thought and intuitive thought help us understand the world around us is called
a. Cognitive Dissonance Self-Theory
b. Cognitive Discovery Self-Theory
c. Cognitive-Experiential Self-Theory
d. Rational-Intuitive Self-Theory

3.46
a
LO 10
Applied
87
M

Cognitive-Experiential Self-Theory would predict that, if given the choice of picking a red jelly bean from a small bowl with 1 red and 9 white beans or a large bowl with 10 red and 90 white beans, you would probably pick
a. the large bowl
b. the small bowl
c. neither bowl because you do not like jelly beans
d. the bowl with the best odds of being correct

3.47
c
LO 10
Concept
87
M

When you are experiencing strong emotion arousal and are in a situation involving other people, you will probably rely upon _____ thought to make your decisions.
a. rational
b. emotional
c. intuitive
d. experiential

3.48
a
LO 10
Study
87
M

The study by Denes-Raj and Epstein (1994) found that many participants selected a bowl of jelly beans that
a. the odds were lower for drawing a red bean
b. the odds were higher for drawing a red bean
c. the odds were the same for drawing a red bean
d. the odds were originally higher, then decreased

3.49
b
LO 11
Applied
88
M

Which of the following statements would be most easily explained by the finding that we pay more attention to inconsistent viewpoints?
a. "The Times always prints the best news."
b. "T.V. reporters are too conservative."
c. "Most people like chocolate, don't they?"
d. "I clearly remember that Hazel voted for me."

3.50
c
LO 11
Concept
88
E

Information that is inconsistent with our viewpoint is
a. usually wrong
b. false consensus information
c. unexpected
d. more likely to be schematically processed

3.51
a
LO 11
Concept
88
M

According to theory, you would be more likely to remember an incorrect answer given by someone if they
a. had given mostly correct answers before
b. had given mostly incorrect answers before
c. seemed confident about their responses
d. answered in the same way you would have

3.52
c
LO 11
Concept
88
M

The tendency to pay more attention to unexpected information can bias recall by
a. breaking down previously existing schemas
b. decreasing the use of heuristics to process information
c. making such instances more available in memory
d. reducing confidence in one's own decision making power

3.53
b
LO 11
Applied
89
C

Which of the following headlines would probably not have an effect on our cognitive activity in any serious way?
a. "Clinton announces he is retiring from politics!"
b. "Woman gives birth to a dinosaur!"
c. "Butter is shown to be good for your health!"
d. "Ford announces a 100 mile per gallon automobile!"

3.54
c
LO 12
Fact
89
M

The tendency to make optimistic predictions concerning how long a task will take is called the
a. expectation fallacy
b. unawareness fallacy
c. planning fallacy
d. organizational fallacy

3.55
b
LO 12
Fact
89
E

The planning fallacy involves
a. making false plans before the facts are readily available
b. making optimistic predictions about how long a task will take
c. making plans concerning a task, but not completing the task
d. making plans based upon false information

3.56
a
LO 12
Concept
89
M

One of the explanations concerning the planning fallacy is that
a. individuals often enter a planning mode focused on the future and do not attend to the past
b. individuals often enter a narrative mode focused on the future and do not attend to the present
c. individuals often enter a planning mode focused on the past and do not attend to the future
d. individuals often enter a planning mode focused on the past and do not attend to the present

3.57
c
LO 12
Concept
89
M

In the planning fallacy, an individual entering the narrative mode of thought
a. focuses on how he or she has performed the task in the past
b. focuses on how he or she feels about the task
c. focuses on how he or she will perform the task
d. focuses on how he or she thinks about the task

3.58
b
LO 12
Concept
89
M

An individual who engages in the planning fallacy makes _____ attributions about the failure of past projects
a. internal
b. external
c. transient
d. role specific

3.59
c
LO 12
Study
90
M

Buehler and colleagues (1994) found that the planning fallacy did not occur when participants
a. concentrated on future projects and the relevance of such projects for the present project
b. concentrated on present projects and the relevance of such projects for the present project
c. concentrated on past projects and the relevance of such projects for the present project
d. concentrated on future projects and the relevance of such projects for future projects

3.60   Automatic vigilance refers to the tendency to
c   a. guard against shocks
LO 13   b. repress negative events
Fact   c. notice negative information about people
91   d. try to process information into an existing schema
M

3.61   Which of the following types of information about another person is most
d   likely to be remembered?
LO 13   a. facial features
Fact   b. clothing
91   c. positive statements
M   d. a frown

3.62   Which of the following people at a track meet would you be most likely to
d   spot quickly?
LO 13   a. a person who is not looking at the track
Applied b. a person with blond hair
91   c. a person who is tying his/her shoe
M   d. a person who has just been in an argument with someone

3.63   The face-in-the-crowd effect refers to the ability to pick out
b   a. positive expressions from a crowd
LO 13   b. negative expressions from a crowd
Concept c. other-directed behavior from a crowd
91   d. self-directed behavior from a crowd
M

3.64   The face-in-the-crowd effect is a feature of
c   a. the availability heuristic
LO 13   b. the representativeness heuristic
Concept c. automatic vigilance
91   d. other-directed behavior
M

3.65   An adaptive reason for noticing negative expressions more easily than others
a   is that
LO 13   a. negative expressions are more likely to imply danger
Concept b. negative expressions are relatively rare
91   c. negative expressions are evolutionary markers
M   d. negative expressions tend to stand out from a crowd

3.66   Being sensitive to negative facial expressions is consistent with the
c   principles of
LO 13   a. cultural psychology
Concept b. developmental psychology
91   c. evolutionary psychology
M   d. humanistic psychology

3.67   One interesting finding concerning the face-in-the-crowd effect is that we
a   are
LO 13   a. somewhat slower to pick out a happy face from a crowd of angry faces
Concept b. somewhat faster to pick out a happy face from a crowd of angry faces
91   c. somewhat slower to pick out a angry face from a crowd of happy faces
C   d. the facial expression does not have an effect on identification

3.68
c
LO 14
Concept
92
M

Too much cognitive activity can be a bad thing because
a. heuristics are generally more accurate anyway
b. it limits decision making ability
c. too much introspection causes decrements in performance
d. many problems do not have rational answers

3.69
a
LO 14
Concept
92
M

Research suggests that thinking about the causes of actions
a. can impair judgments
b. leads to more accurate judgments
c. leads to more satisfying judgments
d. leads to motivated skepticism

3.70
b
LO 14
Study
92
M

When participants were asked to analyze their reasons for rating certain jams in comparison to those who just rated the jams, the results indicated that
a. those who analyzed their reasons agreed more with the experts
b. those who simply rated agreed more with the experts
c. those who analyzed their reasons gave confusing ratings
d. reason analysis had nothing to do with agreement with the experts

3.71
c
LO 14
Study
92
C

A study concerning students rating college courses and indicating the likelihood they would take the course found that
a. students in the "think deeply" conditions were more likely to make effective decisions
b. students in the "rating" condition were less likely to make effective decisions
c. students in the "think deeply" conditions were less likely to make effective decisions
d. students in the "rating" condition were handicapped in making effective decisions

3.72
d
LO 14
Study
92
C

Wilson and Schooler (1991) found that asking people to think about why they made a particular judgment may not lead to more accurate judgments because
a. the representativeness heuristic (which promotes the base rate fallacy) is likely to be used
b. this limits the amount of attention that can be paid to decision making
c. it focuses their attention away from the consequences of the judgment
d. the true reasons for an action are not always the ones that come immediately to mind

3.73
c
LO 14
Applied
92
M

One suggestion from research on thinking too much is that individuals suffering from _____ might add to their problem by engaging in effortful social thought.
a. mania
b. phobia
c. depression
d. paranoia

3.74
b
LO 15
Concept
93
M

People generally think another will feel more regret over a negative outcome if
a. mental simulations are operating on a heuristic level
b. the other person rarely performs actions that could lead to that outcome
c. the other person often performs actions that could lead to that outcome
d. the other person seemed to anticipate the outcome

3.75   Counterfactual thinking is a form of
c   a. the representativeness heuristic
LO 15   b. the availability heuristic
Fact   c. mental simulation
93   d. cognitive anchoring
E

3.76   Thinking about the results of an action and alternative actions and outcomes is called
d   a. cognitive representation
LO 15   b. mental representation
Fact   c. automatic vigilance
93   d. counterfactual thinking
E

3.77   Events for which a person can easily conceive of an alternative to what actually happened are readily
d   subject to the form of thinking known as
LO 15   a. base rate fallacy
Concept b. primacy effect
93   c. false consensus effect
M   d. counterfactual thinking

3.78   Which is true regarding a woman robbed by a hitchhiker to whom she has given a ride?
a.   a. the woman who hardly ever picks up hitchhikers elicits greater sympathy
LO 15   b. the woman who often picks up hitchhikers elicits greater sympathy
Study   c. neither woman elicits much sympathy because both are perceived to have caused their own
94   problem
M   d. both women elicit considerable sympathy because both were victims of crime

3.79   Gilovich and Medvec (1994) found that participants initially expressed more regret for actions they
c   _____ perform, and later expressed more regret for actions they _____ perform.
LO 15   a. didn't, did
Study   b. didn't, didn't
94   c. did, didn't
M   d. did, did

3.80   Gilovich and Medvec (1994) suggested that one of the reasons why we may express more regret for
a   actions we did not perform is that
LO 15   a. missed opportunities may never occur again
Study   b. we were simply too afraid to act
94   c. other people acted and reaped the benefit
C   d. once an action is performed, the negative results can never be reversed

3.81   The research of Gilovich and Medvec (1994) indicate that
b   a. there is no shift in the pattern of regret over time
LO 15   b. there is a major shift in the pattern of regret over time
Study   c. counterfactual thinking is not related to the pattern of regret over time
94   d. the pattern of regret over time is related to the degree of negative result
M

3.82   When asked to describe the biggest regrets of their lives, individuals are
b   more likely to describe
LO 15   a. things they did do
Study   b. things they didn't do
95   c. things others wanted them to do
M   d. things they did with others

3.83   Thinking that involves assumptions that do not hold up to rational scrutiny is termed
c
LO 16   a. faulty reasoning
Fact   b. assumption confusion
95   c. magical thinking
M   d. counterfactual thinking

3.84   When two objects touch, they pass properties to one another and the effects last long after the
c   initial contact. This process is known as
LO 16   a. the law of similarity
Concept   b. the law of physical contact
95   c. the law of contagion
M   d. the law of proximity

3.85   The law of contagion states that
a   a. when two objects touch, they pass properties to one another
LO 16   b. when two objects touch, they are joined together
Concept   c. when two objects touch, they are repelled
95   d. when two objects touch, they are assimilated
M

3.86   Things that resemble one another share fundamental properties. This
b   statement illustrates the
LO 16   a. law of contagion
Concept   b. law of similarity
95   c. law of proximity
M   d. law of perspective

3.87   The law of similarity states that
d   a. things that resemble one another are grouped together
LO 16   b. things that have fundamental properties resemble one another
Fact   c. things that resemble other things are grouped together
95   d. things that resemble one another share fundamental properties
M

3.88   Keinan (1994) found that residents from Israel who were attacked by Iraqi missiles, in contrast to
b   residents who were not attacked,
LO 16   a. engaged in less magical thinking
Study   b. engaged in more magical thinking
96   c. engaged in less false consensus thinking
M   d. engaged in more false consensus thinking

3.89   The term that best describes mild, temporary shifts in feelings is
d   a. emotion
LO 17   b. feeling
Fact   c. effect
97   d. affect
E

3.90   The Cannon-Bard theory suggests that in the recall of emotion provoking events
b   a. cognitions precede affect
LO 17   b. affect and cognition occur simultaneously
Concept   c. affect precedes cognition
98   d. both cognitions and affect cause changes in the surrounding environment
M

3.91
c
LO 17
Applied
98
C

If you ran an experiment that showed that people experience affect about a recalled event at the same time as cognitions about the event, you would have provided evidence in favor of
a. James-Lange theory
b. Schachter's two-factor theory
c. Cannon-Bard theory
d. facial feedback theory

3.92
d
LO 17
Concept
98
M

The theory of emotion suggesting that various events simultaneously elicit both physiological reactions and the subjective reactions we label affect is the _____ theory.
a. vascular
b. Schachter two-factor
c. James-Lange
d. Cannon-Bard

3.93
c
LO 17
Concept
98
M

The theory of emotion suggesting that we become fearful because of our awareness of such physiological reactions as increased heartbeat, shortness of breath, etc. is the _____ theory.
a. vascular
b. Schachter two-factor
c. James-Lange
d. Cannon-Bard

3.94
a
LO 17
Concept
98
M

The theory that proposed that emotional sequences follow physiological arousal is the
a. James-Lange theory
b. Schachter's two-factor theory
c. Cannon-Bard theory
d. facial feedback theory

3.95
d
LO 17
Concept
99
M

Schachter's two-factor theory of emotion suggests that
a. arousal level is the key to determining cognitions
b. cognitions are the direct result of affective feelings
c. cognitions interfere with arousal level through affect
d. arousal is interpreted in different ways depending upon the situation

3.96
a
LO 17
Concept
99
M

Schachter's two-factor theory suggests that affect from arousal is moderated by
a. external cues
b. emotion
c. motivation
d. internal cues

3.97
d
LO 17
Concept
99
M

If you believe that subjective emotional states are determined by the labels we attach to our internal feelings of arousal, you most likely subscribe to the _____ theory of emotion.
a. Cannon-Bard
b. James-Lange
c. Bem self-perception
d. Schachter two-factor

3.98
c
LO 17
Concept
99
M

Evidence in favor of the James-Lange theory has been provided by the findings that
a. emotional patterns remain constant across situations
b. arousal levels are generally lower than previously expected
c. different emotions are connected with different patterns of physiological activity
d. recall of past events tends to stimulate emotion

3.99
d
LO 18
Concept
100
M

The facial feedback hypothesis is most clearly connected with
a. Cannon-Bard theory
b. Schachter's two-factor theory
c. Bem's self-perception theory
d. James-Lange theory

3.100
a
LO 18
Concept
100
C

The facial feedback hypothesis suggests that
a. feedback from the interpretation of physiological experiences drives the production of affect
b. psychological memories produce changes in facial temperature
c. attitudinal consistency is reduced under conditions of stress
d. emotional expressions influence the perceptions of others, which in turn influences your own perceptions

3.101
b
LO 18
Study
100
M

Evidence for the facial feedback hypothesis has been found from the research of McCanne and Anderson (1991), which indicated that people who were told to smile
a. generated more memories of past positive events
b. tended to report feeling happier than those told to frown
c. tended to report feeling the same emotions as those told to frown
d. were more accurate in recall of past positive events

3.102
b
LO 18
Concept
100
M

The explanation for the effects of the facial feedback hypothesis comes from the
a. Cannon-Bard theory
b. James-Lange theory
c. Schachter two-factor theory
d. Bem's self-perception theory

3.103
a
LO 19
Study
101
M

The research by Mayer and Hanson (1995) indicated that
a. changes in participant's mood over time were closely related to changes in social cognition
b. changes in participant's mood over time were not related to changes in social cognition
c. changes in participant's mood over time caused changes in social cognitions
d. changes in participant's mood over time did not cause changes in social cognitions

3.104
c
LO 19
Study
101
M

The results of the research by Mayer and Hanson (1995) support the
a. mood-cognition effect
b. mood-congruent effect
c. mood-congruent judgment effect
d. mood-cognition judgment effect

3.105
b
LO 19
Concept
101
M

Which of the following statements about affect and cognition is most accurate?
a. affect is not related to cognition
b. affect can affect cognitions
c. James-Lange theory predicts the primacy of cognition
d. cognition always precedes affect

3.106
b
LO 19
Concept
101
M

The suggestion that people in a good mood are more creative is an example of
a. Cannon-Bard theory
b. how mood influences cognition
c. a popular myth
d. a popular stereotype

3.107   Ralph was in a good mood when he read information about Lisa. What Ralph read contained equal
d   amounts of positive and negative information. If asked to write down everything he can remember
LO 19   about Lisa, Ralph will probably remember
Applied a. most of what he read because he was in a good mood
101   b. little of what he read because his good mood distracted him
C   c. more of the negative information about Lisa
         d. more of the positive information about Lisa

3.108   When asked to interview applicants whose qualifications for a job are ambiguous, participants who
c   are ____ assign higher ratings to these applicants.
LO 19   a. in a cognitive mood
Applied b. in a neutral mood
102   c. in a positive mood
M   d. in a negative mood

3.109   Baron (1987) had people conduct job interviews while in either a good or bad mood. The findings
a   indicated that
LO 19   a. interviewers in a good mood evaluated the applicants more positively
Study   b. interviewers in a good mood evaluated the applicants more negatively
102   c. interviewers in a bad mood evaluated the applicants more negatively
M   d. interviewer's mood did not influence the evaluations

3.110   Lisa has just finished viewing a happy film and is experiencing positive mood. How is her positive
b   mood likely to influence her judgments and views immediately after the film?
LO 19   a. her judgments and views will not be changed
Applied b. her judgments and views will change in a positive direction
102   c. her judgments and views will change in a negative direction
M   d. her judgments and views will change depending upon her personality

3.111   When Estrada and colleagues (1995) presented physicians with three words and then asked them
b   to provide an associate to these words, more correct associations were provided by physicians
LO 19   a. experiencing negative affect
Study   b. experiencing positive affect
102   c. experiencing neutral affect
C   d. experiencing cognitive blockage

3.112   Research by Estrada and colleagues (1995) provides evidence to support the conclusion that positive
c   affect
LO 19   a. causes people to generate narrow memory categories
Study   b. causes people to be less creative
102   c. causes people to be more creative
M   d. has a weaker and more temporary effect than negative affect

3.113   Compared to the effects produced by positive affect, research has found that negative affect
a   a. exerts a weaker and less consistent effect on cognition
LO 20   b. exerts a stronger and more consistent effect on cognition
Concept c. exerts an equally strong, though opposite effect on cognition
103   d. has no effect on cognition
M

3.114   Current research indicates that the effects produced by positive and negative affect on cognition
b   a. are always opposite in nature
LO 20   b. are not always opposite in nature
Study   c. depend upon the external environment
103   d. depend upon the internal state of the individual
M

3.115
a
LO 20
Study
103
C

Goldstein and Strube (1994) found that unless they are quite intense,
a. positive affect and negative affect may be independent of each other in their influence on cognition
b. positive affect and negative affect produce consistent effects on cognition
c. positive affect and negative affect produce countering effects on cognition
d. positive affect and negative affect are positively correlated in their influence on cognition

3.116
b
LO 20
Applied
103
C

Individuals in a negative mood are _____ from a primary task they are performing than are individuals in a positive mood.
a. more easily distracted
b. less easily distracted
c. equally distracted
d. negatively distracted

3.117
c
LO 21
Concept
103
M

An example of a theory where cognition precedes affect is the
a. Cannon-Bard theory
b. James-Lange theory
c. Schachter two-factor theory
d. Bem self-perception theory

3.118
d
LO 21
Concept
103
M

In Schachter's two-factor theory
a. mood depends on the type of arousal experienced
b. affect precedes cognition
c. affect precedes arousal
d. cognitions are used to interpret arousal

3.119
b
LO 21
Applied
103
C

Two drivers on a highway are cut off by a third driver. The first driver is startled but shrugs, thinking that "that other driver was careless, but I don't think he noticed me." The second driver is furious, thinking that "that other driver deliberately tried to run me off the road." This scenario is an illustration of
a. Cannon-Bard theory of emotion
b. how cognition influences affect
c. how affect influences cognition
d. how affect influences arousal

3.120
d
LO 21
Concept
103
M

Sometimes the activation of schemas containing a strong affective component exerts powerful effects upon our current feelings. This situation is an example of the fact that
a. information consistent with a schema is easier to notice and remember
b. information inconsistent with a schema is easier to notice and remember
c. affect influences cognition
d. cognition influences affect

3.121
d
LO 21
Concept
103
M

If we label an individual as belonging to some group, the activated stereotype may exert a strong effect upon our feelings. This situation is an example of the fact that
a. information consistent with a schema is easier to notice and remember
b. information inconsistent with a schema is easier to notice and remember
c. affect influences cognition
d. cognition influences affect

3.122
d
LO 21
Applied
103
M

Ralph is standing in a waiting line when another person bumps against him. Is Ralph likely to react with anger?
a. no
b. yes
c. there is no way of knowing
d. it depends on how the bumping is interpreted

3.123   When participants were told to expect funny cartoons, the cartoons were rated to be
b   a. less funny
LO 21   b. funnier
Study   c. less exciting
103   d. more intense
C

3.124   The findings that expectancies can influence affect are supported when
c   a. people have superior memory for events they enjoyed
LO 21   b. people become happier when they remember pleasant experiences
Concept c. people who expect to enjoy a candy bar enjoy it more than those who have no prior opinion
104   d. people who expect to enjoy something tend to think about it more than those who do not
M

3.125   Forgas (1995) proposed that affect influences social thought through two major mechanisms. This
b   proposal is called the
LO 22   a. Affective Influence Model
Concept b. Affective Infusion Model
104   c. Affective Inclusion Model
C   d. Affective Inversion Model

3.126   According to the Affective Infusion Model, the two mechanisms through which affect influences social
c   thought are
LO 22   a. cohesion and attachment
Concept b. affect and cognition
104   c. prime and heuristic cue
M   d. expectancy level and interpretation

3.127   In the Affective Infusion Model, affects serves to _____ similar or related cognitive categories.
a   a. prime
LO 22   b. enhance
Concept c. catalog
104   d. alter
M

3.128   Affect may influence cognition by acting as a _____.
b   a. category operative
LO 22   b. heuristic cue
Concept c. cognitive representation
104   c. discriminative stimulus
M

3.129   In the Affective Infusion Model, _____ works in situations where we engage in _____ thought.
c   a. affect-as-information, substantive
LO 22   b. affect-as-information, transitive
Concept c. priming, substantive
104   d. priming, transitive
M

3.130   In the Affective Infusion Model, _____ works in situations where we engage in _____ thought.
b   a. affect-as-information, transitive
LO 22   b. affect-as-information, heuristic
Concept c. priming, transitive
104   d. priming, heuristic
M

3.131
a
LO 22
Applied
104
C

You are in a good mood and make the following statement, "I am favorable toward it." This situation illustrates the mechanism of
a. affect-as-information
b. prime
c. substantive thought
d. transitive thought

3.132
b
LO 22
Concept
104
M

The affect influences cognition mechanism that asks us to examine our feelings and respond accordingly is known as
a. prime
b. affect-as-information
c. cognitive association
d. affective association

3.133
a
LO 23
Study
104
C

Forgas (1994) predicted that individuals would be more likely to engage in substantive processing about serious conflicts; therefore the effects of mood
a. would be stronger for such conflicts
b. would be stronger for trivial conflicts
c. would be strong for both type of conflicts
d. would have no effects on either type of conflict

3.134
d
LO 23
Study
104
M

Forgas (1994) predicted that _____ would be stronger for _____ conflicts
a. priming, trivial
b. affect-as-information, trivial
c. affect-as-information, serious
d. priming, serious

3.135
b
LO 23
Study
104
M

In the research on the Affective Infusion Model, Forgas (1994) found that people in a sad mood
a. were less likely to blame themselves for serious conflicts than those in a happy mood
b. were more likely to blame themselves for serious conflicts than those in a happy mood
c. were equally likely to blame themselves for serious conflicts as those in a happy mood
d. were unconcerned with serious conflicts as compared to those in a happy mood

3.136
d
LO 23
Study
104
M

In the research on the Affective Infusion Model, Forgas (1994) found that trivial conflicts indicated that
a. people in a positive mood were more likely to blame themselves for the conflict
b. people in a negative mood were more likely to blame themselves for the conflict
c. people in a positive mood were less likely to blame themselves for the conflict
d. mood had little impact on blame for the conflict

3.137
c
LO 24
Study
106
M

In several studies on cultural differences of trust, it was found that
a. Japanese were more trusting than Americans
b. Japanese were more accepting of trust than Americans
c. Americans were more trusting than Japanese
d. Americans and Japanese were equally trusting

3.138
a
LO 24
Study
106
M

In several studies on cultural differences of trust and assurance, it was found that
a. Japanese were higher in assurance than Americans
b. Americans were higher in assurance than Japanese
c. Japanese were lower in assurance than Americans
d. Americans and Japanese were equal in assurance

3.139   In a study on cultural issues surrounding trust, Americans rated _____ as more important than did
b   Japanese.
LO 24   a. one's social group
Study   b. one's personal reputation
106   c. one's personal interactions
M   d. one's level of assurance

3.140   Americans, more so than Japanese, have a tendency to assume that other persons
a   a. are likely to behave in an honest manner and out of good intentions
LO 24   b. are likely to behave in an dishonest manner and out of bad intentions
Concept   c. are likely to behave in a manner that is coercive
106   d. are likely to behave in a manner to capitalize on weakness
M

CHAPTER 4

Learning Objectives

After studying this chapter, students should be able to:

1. *Examine the textbook's definition of "attitude" and note reasons why attitudes are important.*

2. *Describe evidence to support the idea that attitudes can be formed via classical conditioning, including subliminal conditioning and conditioning of arm flexion vs. arm extension movements.*

3. *Explain how particular attitudes can be strengthened or weakened via instrumental conditioning and also through modeling.*

4. *Explain how the social comparison process accounted for the attitudes Canadians formed toward the fictitious Camarians.*

5. *Examine attitude similarity among identical and nonidentical twins, and describe the significance and validity of these results.*

6. *Describe the attitude-behavior inconsistency observed in the LaPiere (1934) study.*

7. *Consider how the following aspects of the situation are related to whether people will act on their attitudes: a) norms; b) time pressures; and c) having chosen to enter attitudinally-relevant situations.*

8. *Consider how these aspects of attitudes are related to whether people will act on the attitudes: a) formed by direct experience; b) strong; c) important; d) serves self-interest; e) fosters social identification; f) possesses value relevance; g) accessible; and h) has specificity.*

9. *Explain why attitudes held by low self-monitors more accurately predict their behavior than attitudes held by high self-monitors.*

10. *According to the theory of planned behavior, describe the three factors that determine whether persons with the opportunity to engage in careful thought will act consistently with their intentions.*

11. *Consider how attitudes influence behavior when the person must act quickly and spontaneously.*

12. *Summarize the traditional approach to persuasion, and know the eight classic research findings reviewed by the textbook.*

13. *Contrast persuasion that takes place on the central route vs. the peripheral route, according to the elaboration likelihood model.*

14. *Explain how the persuasion process is influenced by the relevance of a message and by the presence of a distraction.*

15. *Descibe three ways attitude change on the central route has been shown to be more lasting than attitude change on the peripheral route.*

16. *Examine the idea that attitudes can serve different functions for the person holding them.*

17. *Describe how reciprocity produces "public" attitude change.*

18. *Explain when a positively-framed message is more influential, and when a negatively-framed message is more influential.*

19.   *Understand how "reactance" explains the fact that we often show negative attitude change when faced with hard-sell persuasion attempts.*

20.   *Describe why we are better able to resist persuasive messages when they are preceded by forewarning of persuasive intent.*

21.   *Describe the roles played by selective avoidance and selective exposure in helping us resist persuasion.*

22.   *Define cognitive dissonance, and describe three strategies people can use to get rid of dissonance.*

23.   *Explain how research by Elliot and Devine (1994) supports the view that dissonance is unpleasant and that the discomfort of dissonance often motivates attitude change.*

24.   *Explain when subjects use trivialization as the mode to reduce their dissonance, and when they actually change their attitudes toward the attitudinal issue.*

25.   *Describe the attitude change that occurs following forced compliance.*

26.   *Indicate why the less-leads-to-more effect occurs, and know the three circumstances that must exist for this effect to happen.*

27.   *Describe how the hypocrisy procedure was used to get subjects to engage in safe sex.*

28.   *Summarize the relationship between economic attitudes held by individuals and the rate of economic growth and gross national product of nations.*

Questions

4.1
a
LO 1
Concept
112
E

Social thought and social behavior are both influenced by
a. attitudes
b. research procedures
c. behavioral constraints
d. self-schematic conceptualizations

4.2
c
LO 1
Fact
112
M

Attitudes consist of associations between
a. behaviors and evaluations
b. objects and object behaviors
c. attitude objects and evaluations of those objects
d. attitude concepts and personal theories about others

4.3
d
LO 1
Fact
112
M

According to the definition of attitudes, attitudes are linked to
a. the self
b. the situation
c. schemas
d. evaluations

4.4
b
LO 1
Concept
112
M

Attitudes influence current thought through
a. perception
b. memory
c. personal theories about future thought
d. verbal and nonverbal cues

4.5
a
LO 1
Concept
112
M

Attitudes often function as _____ in terms of influencing social thought.
a. schemas
b. guides
c. concepts
d. evaluations

4.6
a
LO 2
Concept
114
M

The process through which we acquire attitudes from the observation of others is called
a. social learning
b. cognitive development
c. acquisition strategy
d. social cognition

4.7
d
LO 2
Concept
114
M

Social learning is related to attitudes through
a. the testing in society of spontaneously generated attitudes
b. the testing in society of operantly acquired attitudes
c. the association of two or more stimuli
d. learning of attitudes through observing others

4.8
d
LO 2
Applied
114
M

Professor Jones always smiles broadly when he hands back your social psychology test with a big "A" across the front. After a semester, you begin to feel pleased whenever you see Professor Jones smile. This process is known as
a. semantic association
b. social learning
c. attitude acquisition
d. classical conditioning

4.9
b
LO 2
Concept
114
M

The type of learning that is based on association of two or more stimuli is called
a. social learning
b. classical conditioning
c. operant learning
d. instrumental conditioning

4.10
c
LO 2
Concept
114
M

Classical conditioning suggests that people can learn to
a. form evaluations only in the presence of others
b. form evaluations through spontaneous experiences
c. dislike stimuli to which they are initially neutral
d. use memory in the process of forming attitudes

4.11
b
LO 2
Concept
115
M

Classical conditioning works because the participant eventually
a. forms an attitude about the stimuli that are presented
b. associates the two stimuli that are presented
c. uses memory to retrieve evaluations of previous cues
d. learns to avoid painful experiences

4.12
c
LO 2
Concept
115
M

A subliminal presentation is a presentation that
a. means something other than what the subject thinks
b. can lead to a response that cannot be predicted by the experimenter
c. is below the threshold of conscious awareness of its content
d. is common in deception experiments

4.13
c
LO 2
Concept
115
M

When shown a subliminal, aversive stimulus before a neutral one, most people eventually
a. ignore the neutral stimulus
b. ignore the negative stimulus
c. show negative feelings toward the neutral stimulus
d. show negative feelings toward the negative stimulus

4.14
c
LO 2
Applied
115
E

According to the experimental evidence on subliminal classical conditioning, the best time to place a subliminal advertisement for a product would be during a
a. scary film
b. documentary
c. comedy
d. romantic film

4.15
b
LO 2
Study
116
M

In their study on arm muscle movements and attitudes, Cacioppo and colleagues (1993) found that
a. arm flexion induced negative reactions
b. arm flexion induced positive reactions
c. arm extension induced positive reactions
d. arm muscle movement was unrelated to positive or negative reaction

4.16
c
LO 2
Concept
116
C

One of the explanations for the finding of Cacioppo and colleagues (1993) that arm flexion induced positive attitudes is that
a. we pull things we like toward us, thereby extending of arm muscles
b. we push things we don't like away from us, thereby flexing our arm muscles
c. we pull things we like toward us, thereby flexing our arm muscles
d. arm muscle movement is not related to positive attitudes

4.17
a
LO 3
Fact
116
M

Instrumental conditioning occurs when
a. behavior alters in response to an outcome
b. two stimuli are paired together in memory
c. a person learns to associate two stimuli that occur together
d. one's own attitude evaluation matches the evaluations of others

4.18
a
LO 3
Concept
116
C

In one learning process, behaviors that are followed by positive outcomes are strengthened and behaviors that are followed by negative outcomes are weakened. The learning process described is
a. instrumental conditioning
b. social learning
c. modeling
d. classical conditioning

4.19
b
LO 3
Concept
117
C

The process by which one raises or lowers the production of a given behavior based on the outcomes associated with that behavior is called
a. classical conditioning
b. instrumental conditioning
c. social learning
d. affect based behavior

4.20
a
LO 3
Concept
117
M

According to the process of instrumental conditioning, behavior will be displayed more often by an individual if
a. it is reinforced
b. it is preceded by a pleasant stimulus
c. is preceded by a pleasant subliminal stimulus
d. the individual sees a role model perform the action

4.21
b
LO 3
Applied
117
M

When children's attitudes are strengthened by a parent's reinforcement for the expression of "correct" views, the process involved is
a. classical conditioning
b. instrumental conditioning
c. observational conditioning
d. modeling

4.22
d
LO 3
Concept
117
M

When children learn attitudes merely by observing the examples displayed by their parent's behavior, the specific learning process involved is
a. classical conditioning
b. instrumental conditioning
c. observational conditioning
d. modeling

4.23
d
LO 3
Applied
117
M

When Ralph sees his father shaving, he covers his own face with shaving cream. This behavior is an example of
a. instrumental conditioning
b. classical conditioning
c. observational conditioning
d. modeling

4.24   Modeling indicates that children are more likely to act according to
c   a. their own preferences
LO 3   b. random influences
Concept   c. the actions of others
117   d. nonrandom influences
E

4.25   Social comparison is a process through which we
b   a. compare the views of others to our own views
LO 4   b. compare the views we hold to the views of others
Fact   c. compare the views we hold to the views of another society
117   d. compare the views we hold to the views of authorities
M

4.26   The process by which we compare ourselves to others to assess our views is called
d   a. social processing
LO 4   b. social evaluation
Concept   c. social reality
117   d. social comparison
E

4.27   Maio and colleagues (1994) found that Canadians who received positive information about a
b   fictitious group called Camarians
LO 4   a. expressed more negative attitudes toward the group
Study   b. expressed more positive attitudes toward the group
118   c. expressed more neutral attitudes toward the group
M   d. expressed neither neutral nor positive attitudes toward the group

4.28   If given favorable information about a fictitious group called Camarians, Canadian participants
c   a. were less likely to allow the group to immigrate to Canada
LO 4   b. were less likely to allow the group to leave Canada
Concept   c. were more likely to allow the group to immigrate to Canada
118   d. were more likely to allow the group to leave Canada
M

4.29   If genetic influences in attitude acquisition exist, one would expect to find that the attitudes of
b   identical twins correlate _____ when compared to those of nonidentical twins.
LO 5   a. the same
Concept   b. more highly
118   c. less highly
M   d. neutrally

4.30   Research has found that identical twins have attitudes that are more highly correlated on the average
a   than nonidentical twins, indicating that there is
LO 5   a. a genetic component to attitude acquisition
Concept   b. more social learning in twin populations
118   c. greater than average similarity in the environments of identical twins
M   d. greater than average similarity in the environments of twins

4.31   Hershberger and colleagues (1994), in their study of twins living in Sweden, found that
c   a. identical twins had less similar attitudes toward their jobs than nonidentical twins
LO 5   b. nonidentical twins had more similar attitudes toward their jobs than identical twins
Study   c. identical twins had more similar attitudes toward their jobs than nonidentical twins
118   d. there was no correlation between genetics and attitudes
M

4.32 b LO 5 Applied 118 M	Mindy has a identical twin sister, Lisa, who has been separated from her for many years. Mindy recently was reunited with her and was very surprised to find a. that they had few attitudes in common b. that they had many attitudes in common c. that Lisa was not as attractive as he remembered d. that they both had to learn the attitudes of the other
4.33 c LO 5 Concept 119 M	One possible explanation for the finding regarding attitudes and twins is that a. genetic factors directly influence attitudes b. genetic factors influence comparison processes c. genetic factors influence general dispositions d. genetic factors influence cognitive structures
4.34 c LO 6 Study 121 M	In his classical study, LaPiere (1934) toured the U.S. with a young Chinese couple to determine whether restaurants, etc. would refuse service. The study found that the couple was a. usually refused service, which was consistent with the strong and openly expressed prejudice of the 1930s b. seldom refused service, which was consistent with the self-reported policy of these establishments c. seldom refused service, which was inconsistent with the self-reported policy of these establishments d. sometimes refused service, and the refusal was usually consistent with the written policy of these establishments
4.35 a LO 6 Study 121 M	After returning from his trip across the U.S. with a Chinese couple, LaPiere (1934) wrote to all the places he had visited and found that a. the overwhelming majority of the places reported they would not serve Chinese b. the overwhelming majority of the places reported they would serve Chinese c. the overwhelming majority of the places reported they had no policy regarding Chinese d. the overwhelming majority of the places reported they needed two weeks advance notice
4.36 c LO 6 Study 122 M	LaPiere (1934) suggested that social psychologists should study a. verbally reported attitudes, not actual behaviors b. verbally reported attitudes, and actual behaviors c. actual behavior, not verbally reported attitudes d. the gap between actual behavior and verbally reported attitudes
4.37 b LO 6 Concept 122 C	LaPiere's research with the Chinese couple pointed out the a. concordance between reported attitudes and actual behavior b. sizable gap between reported attitudes and actual behavior c. difficulty of studying reported attitudes and actual behavior d. difficulty of predicting reported attitudes from actual behavior
4.38 c LO 7 Applied 122 M	Ralph feels he cannot express his negative attitude regarding the way students dress because a. doing so would call attention to himself b. doing so would make him appear to be conservative c. doing so would go against the norms of the situation d. doing so would be against his political leanings

4.39   _____ have an influence on the relationship between attitudes and behavior.
d   a. Attitudinal constraints
LO 7   b. Behavioral constraints
Fact   c. Dispositional constraints
122   d. Situational constraints
M

4.40   Rules indicating how people are supposed to behave in certain situations are called
a   a. norms
LO 7   b. laws
Fact   c. expectancies
122   d. policies
E

4.41   The attitude-behavior link tends to be stronger in situations in which the
b   a. time pressure is low
LO 7   b. time pressure is high
Concept   c. time pressure is neutral
122   d. time pressure is nonexistent
M

4.42   When individuals are under great time pressure and have to act very quickly, they tend to
c   a. fall back upon early behavior
LO 7   b. consider all alternatives
Concept   c. fall back upon established attitudes
122   d. fall back upon new attitudes
M

4.43   People tend to prefer situations that allow them
d   a. to confront issues inconsistent with their attitudes
LO 7   b. to confront behaviors that are inconsistent with their attitudes
Concept   c. to carefully consider all alternatives
122   d. to maintain a match between attitudes and behavior
M

4.44   DeBono and Snyder (1995) investigated the relationship between attitudes and behaviors toward
b   affirmative action. They found that students who held positive attitudes toward this policy
LO 7   a. were less willing to volunteer for a study dealing with affirmative action
Study   b. were more willing to volunteer for a study dealing with affirmative action
123   c. were less willing to volunteer for a study dealing with religious issues
C   d. were more willing to volunteer for a study dealing with religious issues

4.45   In a study regarding level of participation in situations supporting one's attitudes, DeBono
a   and Snyder (1995) found that
LO 7   a. quick responses were related to high level of participation
Study   b. slow responses were related to a high level of participation
123   c. quick responses were related to a low level of participation
C   d. speed of response and level of participation were not related

4.46   The strongest attitudes for an individual are usually acquired through
b   a. social learning
LO 8   b. direct experience
Concept   c. parental influence
123   d. peer influence
M

4.47
c
LO 8
Concept
124
M

Based on what we know about attitude strength, we expect the attitudes that best predict behavior to be formed through
a. specificity
b. social learning
c. direct experience
d. instrumental conditioning

4.48
d
LO 8
Concept
124
M

An attitude is a better predictor of behavior when the attitude is
a. based on little information
b. derived from indirect experience
c. global in nature
d. formed through direct, personal experience

4.49
d
LO 8
Concept
124
M

The importance of an issue to a person refers to the
a. degree of familiarity that the issue has to the person
b. breadth and strength of the attitudes the person holds about the issue
c. perceived interest of the issue to other people
d. effect that it has upon the person's life

4.50
c
LO 8
Concept
124
C

The importance of an issue tends to
a. increase processing depth concerning the issue
b. lead to direct experiences
c. strengthen attitudes about the issue
d. decrease attitude specificity

4.51
b
LO 8
Concept
124
M

One of the factors that plays a key role in determining attitude importance is how much impact the attitude has on the individual. This factor is called
a. social identification
b. self-interest
c. value relevance
d. attitude comparison

4.52
c
LO 8
Concept
124
C

The greater the extent to which an attitude is held by groups with which an individual identifies, the
a. greater the value relevance
b. greater the self-interest
c. greater the social identification
d. greater the social relevance

4.53
a
LO 8
Fact
125
M

Value relevance is one of the three factors that plays a key role in determining attitude importance. It is defined as
a. the closeness with which an attitude is connected to an individual's personal values
b. the ability of an individual to connect an attitude to a specific value
c. the correlation of one's values with the values of society
d. the relationship of society's values to a person's attitudes

4.54
b
LO 8
Concept
125
M

Research on attitude importance indicates that what makes an attitude important is its
a. relationship to crucial cultural needs
b. relationship to basic social and individual needs and values
c. relationship to highly valued societal needs
d. relationship to widely known and accepted values

4.55   Attitude accessibility is at least partly determined by
a   a. associative strength of the object-evaluation link
LO 8   b. the type of memory that a person has
Concept   c. whether or not the attitude has an evaluative component
125   d. the presence of an attitude object
M

4.56   Attitude accessibility is an important concept because it
c   a. predicts which attitudes will be stronger than others
LO 8   b. explains the evaluative component of attitudes
Concept   c. links many ideas about attitudes
125   d. links attitudes with affect
M

4.57   One characteristic of attitudes that predicts how strongly they are related to behavior is
b   a. evaluation
LO 8   b. specificity
Concept   c. acquisition strategy
126   d. its place in the attitude network
M

4.58   Very specific attitudes tend to be
c   a. rigid
LO 8   b. strongly evaluative
Concept   c. strongly related to behavior
126   d. factually based
E

4.59   Attitudes are more likely to predict behavior if they are
d   a. evaluative
LO 8   b. wide-ranging
Concept   c. broad
126   d. specific
E

4.60   It appears as if attitudes are a better predictor of behavior for _____.
c   a. high self-monitoring people
LO 9   b. high self-focused people
Concept   c. low self-monitoring people
126   d. low self-focused people
M

4.61   A person who is high in self-monitoring will probably
b   a. focus attention inward and use attitudes as guides to behavior
LO 9   b. focus attention outward and use what others are doing as guides to behavior
Concept   c. focus attention inward and use what others are doing as guides to behavior
126   d. focus attention outward and use attitudes as guides to behavior
C

4.62   The dimension of self-monitoring involves the degree to which individuals monitor
a   a. their behavior as appropriate for a specific social setting
LO 9   b. their behavior as appropriate to represent a particular social value
Fact   c. their behavior as appropriate for involvement in important issues
126   d. their behavior as appropriate for resolving conflicts
M

4.63
c
LO 9
Concept
126
M

The attitude-behavior link is weaker for individuals
a. low in self-monitoring
b. average in self-monitoring
c. high in self-monitoring
d. removed from self-monitoring

4.64
b
LO 10
Concept
126
M

The _____ suggests that the best predictor of a behavior is the strength of the intention regarding that behavior.
a. theory of cognitive dissonance
b. theory of planned behavior
c. theory of attitudinal value
d. theory of attitude intentionality

4.65
d
LO 10
Concept
127
M

The best single predictor of an individual's behavior is
a. his or her attitude about that behavior
b. his or her feeling about that behavior
c. his or her thoughts about that behavior
d. his or her intentions about that behavior

4.66
c
LO 10
Concept
127
C

Which of the following three factors does NOT play a role in influencing intentions?
a. attitude toward the behavior
b. subjective norms toward the behavior
c. cognitions regarding the behavior
d. perceived behavioral control over the behavior

4.67
a
LO 10
Applied
127
M

Ralph thinks that his family will hate the idea of him wearing a nose ornament. His intention to get his body pierced is weakened because of
a. subjective norms
b. perceived behavioral control
c. his attitudes toward the piercing
d. cognitive interpretation

4.68
b
LO 10
Applied
127
M

Lisa wants to take birth control pills, but she finds out that her friends are against this behavior, and finds out that she will have to make regular appointments with her physician in order to get a perscription. According to the theory of planned behavior, her intention to take the pills should be
a. strengthened
b. weakened
c. unaltered
d. deferred

4.69
b
LO 11
Concept
127
M

The presence of an attitude object will often
a. overwhelm the evaluative aspect of attitudes
b. activate the accompanying attitude
c. counteract conditioned responses
d. decrease attitude accessibility

4.70
c
LO 11
Concept
127
M

Fazio's _____ suggests that when an event activates an attitude at the same time it also activates our knowledge about various social norms is also activated. These two factors then influence our behavior.
a. cognitive dissonance model
b. theory of planned behavior
c. attitude-to-behavior process model
d. theory of heuristics

4.71
a
LO 11
Applied
127
M

When a panhandler asks you for money on the street, you will activate two factors before responding. These two factors are
a. an attitude and knowledge about appropriate behavior
b. an emotion and stereotyped behavior
c. a cognition about panhandlers and emotion about the behavior
d. a cognition about panhandlers and a cognition about the behavior

4.72
c
LO 11
Concept
127
C

When we must act quickly and spontaneously, we tend to
a. activate an attitude and an emotion at the same time before responding
b. activate a cognition and an emotion at the same time before responding
c. activate an attitude and knowledge about the behavior at the same time before responding
d. activate a behavior and knowledge about the behavior at the same time before responding

4.73
b
LO 12
Concept
129
M

The technique of the two-sided approach to persuasion involves
a. changing attitudes through persuasion and examples
b. acknowledging good points on each side of an issue
c. intensive negotiation and persuasion
d. pretending to have one attitude, then changing in the middle of a communication

4.74
c
LO 12
Concept
129
E

The two-sided approach to communication is most effective with a
a. heckler
b. sales pitch
c. hostile audience
d. negative message

4.75
c
LO 12
Concept
129
M

In general, the best rate of speech for enhancing persuasion is
a. slower than average
b. average
c. faster than average
d. the same pace as the audience

4.76
b
LO 12
Concept
129
M

According to the classic Yale persuasion research, persons low in _____ are more easily persuaded than persons high on this characteristic.
a. need for social approval
b. self-esteem
c. intelligence
d. self-monitoring

4.77
b
LO 12
Concept
129
M

Which of the following is NOT a finding reported by the persuasion researchers at Yale?
a. experts are more persuasive than nonexperts
b. people who speak slowly are more persuasive than people who speak rapidly
c. persuasion can be enhanced by fear-arousing messages
d. it is sometimes easier to persuade a person who is distracted from a message than one paying full attention

4.78
b
LO 12
Applied
129
M

A gun manufacturer delivers a speech against stricter gun control legislation, but his arguments have little impact on the audience. The reason his speech has so little impact is probably
a. the speaker is not an expert on guns
b. the audience recognizes the speaker's intent to manipulate
c. the speaker is too specific on the issues involved
d. the audience has weak attitudes on the issue of guns

4.79
c
LO 12
Applied
129
M

Lisa is a very attractive individual. She has a job on TV selling soap and is very successful. Research indicates that even if she did not know her product line, we would expect her to be successful. What research findings are applicable to Lisa's situation?
a. she knows her product line
b. she is selling an inexpensive line of soap
c. she is attractive
d. she has a soothing speaking voice

4.80
a
LO 12
Concept
129
M

Basing a persuasive communication on an emotion such as fear is most effective when
a. the communication provides specific recommendations about how a change in attitude or behavior will prevent the negative consequences
b. the emotion elicited is very strong regarding the specific behavior
c. the emotion elicited is very mild regarding the specific behavior
d. the communication is combined with an appeal to "better natures"

4.81
d
LO 13
Concept
131
M

Which approach to attitude change focuses on understanding what people think about when they are exposed to persuasive appeals and on how their thoughts determine the extent of attitude change?
a. the traditional Yale approach
b. the social learning approach
c. the heuristic model
d. the cognitive response analysis model

4.82
b
LO 13
Concept
131
M

The approach to understanding persuasion that tries to find out what people think when they are exposed to persuasive efforts is known as the
a. traditional approach
b. elaboration likelihood model
c. cognitive approach
d. social learning model

4.83
b
LO 13
Concept
131
M

In dealing with persuasive attempts, cognitive activities that focus on the rationality of an argument are characteristic of the
a. traditional approach to persuasion
b. central route of the ELM
c. peripheral route of the ELM
d. cognitive accessibility model

4.84
c
LO 13
Applied
131
M

While listening halfheartedly to a commercial, Ralph hears an admired physician suggest that aspirin taken daily promotes good health. Ralph accepts this idea solely because this physician has been correct before. In this example, Ralph is using
a. self-monitoring
b. attributions
c. the peripheral route
d. the central route

4.85
d
LO 13
Concept
131
M

When persuasion is based on careful and thoughtful consideration of the content of a persuasive message, people are using
a. the peripheral route
b. the elaborative route
c. the heuristic route
d. the central route

4.86   The central and peripheral routes of cognition are characteristic of the
a   a. elaboration likelihood model
LO 13   b. social learning model
Concept   c. traditional approach to persuasion
131   d. classical conditioning approach to learning
M

4.87   Research reports that a person who is distracted from a message is more likely to be persuaded by
d   that message. The ELM explains this by suggesting that
LO 14   a. distractions take up most of the person's peripheral processing ability
Applied   b. distractions serve as cues for rewards and punishments concerning being persuaded
132   c. a distracting attitude make the source more likable
C   d. distractions prevent people from engaging in central route processing of information

4.88   According to the ELM, people who are highly involved in an issue will be most strongly
c   influenced by the
LO 14   a. attractiveness of the source
Concept   b. expertise of the source
132   c. strength of the arguments
C   d. sheer number of arguments

4.89   People are more likely to be influenced by peripheral cues such as the appearance of the
c   communicator when the issues are
LO 14   a. complex and sophisticated
Concept   b. highly relevant to the individual
132   c. not relevant to the individual
M   d. highly emotional

4.90   The ELM predicts that if weak arguments are added to strong arguments in a persuasive appeal,
b   these weak arguments may
LO 14   a. increase the amount of persuasion
Concept   b. decrease the amount of persuasion
132   c. not affect the amount of persuasion
M   d. eliminate cognitive appraisal of the arguments

4.91   Attitudes changed through the _____ seem to last longer than attitudes changed through the _____.
c   a. peripheral route, central route
LO 15   b. peripheral route, critical route
Concept   c. central route, peripheral route
133   d. central route, critical route
M

4.92   Attitudes changed through the _____ are more resistant to later change attempts than attitudes
d   changed through the _____.
LO 15   a. central route, critical route
Concept   b. peripheral route, central route
133   c. peripheral route, critical route
M   d. central route, peripheral route

4.93   Attitudes changed through the ____ are more closely related to behavior than attitudes changed
b   through the ____.
LO 15   a. peripheral route, central route
Concept   b. central route, peripheral route
133   c. peripheral route, critical route
M   d. critical route, peripheral route

4.94 c LO 15 Concept 133 C	In contrast to change due to peripheral route processing, attitudes changed due to central route processing represent a. a response to a current situation b. a momentary shift of attitude position, then a return to the original position c. a reorganization of the cognitive structure related to the issue d. a strengthening of the cognitive structure related to the arguments presented related to the issue
4.95 a LO 16 Fact 133 M	Characteristics of attitudes include a. knowledge functions b. objectification c. self-awareness d. self-monitoring
4.96 c LO 16 Concept 133 M	Organization of knowledge and maintenance of self-esteem are potential functions of a. learning models b. persuasion tactics c. attitudes d. self-identification
4.97 b LO 16 Applied 133 E	Most clothing advertisements from upscale tailors focus on the image qualities of their clothing, because expensive clothing activates attitudes with a. utilitarian functions b. social identity functions c. usefulness functions d. esteem functions
4.98 a LO 16 Concept 134 M	Persuasive messages that focus on the functions that attitudes serve may be processed _____, and exert greater impact than those that do not. a. more carefully b. more emotionally c. more socially d. more peripherally
4.99 d LO 17 Concept 134 M	We are more likely to be persuaded by an individual who has previously yielded to our persuasion due to the effect of a. sensory gratification b. esteem gratification c. image functions in attitude change d. reciprocity
4.100 a LO 17 Study 134 M	Participants in a study on attitude change and reciprocity were more easily persuaded to change an attitude due to a confederate when a. they thought they had previously changed an attitude of the confederate b. the confederate was the same sex as the participant c. the confederate was the opposite sex to the participant d. the persuasion was presented in a negotiative framework
4.101 b LO 17 Study 134 M	According to research, _____ attitudes are more likely to change in the face of persuasion from an individual who has exhibited reciprocity. a. private b. public c. high involvement d. low involvement

4.102 Ralph got Lisa to agree to go to a movie he particularly wanted to see, but that she definitely did not
c want to see. Based upon the principle of ____, the odds seem fairly good that Lisa can now get
LO 17 Ralph to tell her he likes the ballet more than he expected, and that he wouldn't mind attending.
Applied a. cognitive dissonance
134 b. self-esteem maintenance
M c. reciprocity
   d. framing

4.103 Negative framing is more effective with individuals who have
c a. actual:ideal discrepancies
LO 18 b. actual:real discrepancies
Concept c. actual:ought discrepancies
134 d. actual:unreal discrepancies
M

4.104 The "bad-news" approach is known as ____, while the "good news" approach is known as ____.
b a. negative framing, positive presentation
LO 18 b. negative framing, positive framing
Fact c. negative presentation, positive framing
135 d. negative presentation, positive presentation
E

4.105 In 1994, Tykocinski and colleagues found that participants who had actual:ideal discrepancies were
b affected more by ____ messages.
LO 18 a. positively framed
Study b. negatively framed
135 c. neutrally framed
M d. emotionally framed

4.106 A positively framed message that emphasized the benefits of eating breakfast was more effective for
b participants who had an ____ discrepancy.
LO 18 a. actual:ideal
Study b. actual:ought
135 c. actual:real
M d. actual:unreal

4.107 You have been trying to convince Ralph to stay away from the Booper Bungee Jump for the last
c three days. Eventually, Ralph says, "I've had enough of this. I'm going there today!" This is an
LO 19 example of
Applied a. ignorance
137 b. reciprocity
M c. reactance
   d. hostility

4.108 Reactance is most likely to occur when attempts to persuade are seen as
c a. motivated by greed
LO 19 b. image oriented
Concept c. attempts to limit personal freedom
137 d. source trait oriented
M

4.109 The unpleasant, negative reaction that occurs when we perceive that someone is trying to limit our
d personal freedom is called
LO 19 a. dissonance
Fact b. framing
137 c. discrepancy
E d. reactance

4.110
c
LO 19
Concept
137
M

An attitude shift in the direction opposite to that advocated by a persuasive argument is called
a. attitude-discrepancy resolution
b. cognitive dissonance resolution
c. negative attitude change
d. reverse incentive effect

4.111
d
LO 19
Concept
137
M

Negative attitude change often occurs
a. when dissonance is aroused
b. in response to strong fear appeals
c. when information is inconsistent with our prior beliefs
d. under conditions that arouse reactance

4.112
a
LO 19
Concept
137
C

When presented with a strong, "hard-sell" attempt to influence us, reactance suggests that
a. we will shift away from the view being presented
b. we will identify with the influencing agent
c. we will have dissonance aroused
d. we will shift more strongly toward the view being presented

4.113
d
LO 19
Applied
137
M

You tell me that I have no choice but to change my opinions. I tell you to stuff it in your ear, and exactly the opposite. This is an example of
a. selective avoidance
b. forewarning
c. dissonance
d. reactance

4.114
d
LO 20
Applied
137
M

Which of the following persuasive attempts is most likely to suffer from the effects of forewarning?
a. a professor warning you to study for a test
b. a driving instructor's lesson
c. a TV news broadcast
d. a car salesman's speech

4.115
b
LO 20
Concept
137
M

Sales speeches are particularly vulnerable to the effects of
a. typecasting
b. forewarning
c. heuristic judgments
d. reactance

4.116
a
LO 20
Concept
137
E

Forewarning protects against persuasion by leading to our forming
a. advance counterarguments
b. reactance
c. reciprocity
d. counteracting source traits

4.117
c
LO 20
Concept
137
E

Advance knowledge that we are to be the target of a persuasive appeal is called
a. reactance
b. dissonance
c. forewarning
d. vigilance

4.118   Forewarning about a speaker's intent
d   a. does not help us to resist influence attempts
LO 20   b. makes us more likely to be influenced by the speaker's arguments
Concept c. helps us resist influence attempts, but only if the issue is unimportant to us
137   d. helps us to resist influence attempts because we formulate counterarguments
M

4.119   Forewarning people before exposing them to a persuasive communication
d   a. distracts them and makes them susceptible to influence
LO 20   b. generally has no effect on their susceptibility to influence
Concept c. reduces their comprehension of the message
137   d. makes them resistant to influence
M

4.120   Failing to read newspaper editorials that contain contrary viewpoints to our own is an example of
b   a. heuristic exposure
LO 21   b. selective avoidance
Concept c. selection heuristic
137   d. reactance formation
E

4.121   Selective exposure consists of
c   a. attempts to resist overbearing sources while accepting reciprocating sources
LO 21   b. attempt to categorize persuasive attempts based on the characteristics of the communication
Concept   rather than the source
137   c. attempts to find consistent viewpoints while avoiding inconsistent viewpoints
M   d. attempts to find inconsistent viewpoints while avoiding consistent viewpoints

4.122   The tendency for people to direct their attention away from information that challenges existing
b   attitudes is known as
LO 21   a. selective exposure
Concept b. selective avoidance
137   c. forewarning
M   d. discounting

4.123   Our tendency to "tune out" information that contradicts our attitudes and "tune in" to information
d   consistent with them constitutes the two sides of
LO 21   a. discounting
Concept b. attitude accessibility
137   c. self-monitoring
M   d. selective exposure

4.124   Negative feelings arising from inconsistent attitudes are known as
a   a. cognitive dissonance
LO 22   b. reactance
Fact   c. source effect
138   d. negative self-schematic conceptualization
M

4.125   Which of the following situations is most likely to cause cognitive dissonance?
c   a. a person who has just cheated on a test convincing himself that is does not matter
LO 22   b. a person who is low in self-monitoring being persuaded by a salesperson
Concept c. a person who perceives himself as honest who has just cheated on an exam
138   d. a person who is high in self-monitoring being persuaded by a salesperson
M

4.126
b
LO 22
Concept
138
M

Cognitive dissonance can be viewed as
a. a heuristic
b. a motivational state
c. something that causes resistance to persuasion
d. an accessibility factor

4.127
d
LO 22
Concept
138
M

Attitudes can change to fit inconsistent behaviors if
a. reactance occurs
b. the attitude is image oriented
c. the person does not feel responsible for the behavior
d. cognitive dissonance occurs

4.128
a
LO 22
Concept
139
M

Which of the following will serve to reduce dissonance?
a. change attitudes and/or behavior to make them more consistent
b. get new information that further contradicts the inconsistent attitude or behavior
c. maximize the importance of the conflict
d. engage in attitude discrepant behavior

4.129
a
LO 22
Concept
139
M

Which of the following will serve to reduce your dissonance?
a. convince yourself that the inconsistency is actually unimportant
b. change your attitude so it is now inconsistent with your behavior
c. acquire new information that further contradicts the inconsistent attitude or behavior
d. maximize the importance of the inconsistency

4.130
d
LO 22
Concept
139
M

Seeking out information that will support a particular behavior or changing the way one thinks about a particular behavior are both ways to reduce
a. reliance on heuristics
b. persuadability
c. openness to experience
d. cognitive dissonance

4.131
a
LO 22
Concept
139
M

Attempts to reduce cognitive dissonance are generally guided by
a. the least effortful available method
b. minimizing the importance of the inconsistency between inconsistent attitudes and behaviors
c. changing the inconsistent attitude
d. changing the inconsistent behavior

4.132
b
LO 23
Study
140
C

Elliot and Devine (1994) found the highest level of discomfort occurred in participants who were asked to rate their feelings _____ regarding tuition increase.
a. immediately after reporting on their attitudes
b. immediately after writing a counterattitudinal essay
c. immediately after writing a proattitudinal essay
d. immediately before writing a counterattitudinal essay

4.133
c
LO 23
Study
140
M

Research by Elliot and Devine (1994) supports the view that cognitive dissonance is
a. an emotional state
b. a cognitive state
c. an unpleasant state
d. a thoughtful state

4.134   The group of participants in the study by Elliot and Devine (1994) that showed the lowest level of
d   discomfort was the group that
LO 23   a. wrote the essay, rated their feelings, reported their attitudes
Study   b. wrote a proattitudinal essay
141   c. rated their feelings, wrote the essay, reported their attitudes
C   d. wrote the essay, reported their attitude, rated their feelings

4.135   The explanation for the essay, attitude, feelings group of participants in the Elliot and Devine (1994)
a   study reporting a low level of discomfort was that this group
LO 23   a. had apparently changed their attitudes
Study   b. had not understood the experimental task
141   c. had to write a proattitudinal essay
M   d. had already formed attitudes that were incapable of change

4.136   One low effortful strategy to reduce dissonance involves perceiving the attitudes or behaviors
c   involved as relatively unimportant. This strategy is called
LO 24   a. minimalization
Concept b. miniaturization
140   c. trivialization
M   d. conditionalization

4.137   Simon and her colleagues (1995) found that participants were _____ to engage in _____ if they
b   first expressed their attitude.
LO 24   a. more likely, trivialization
Study   b. less likely, trivialization
141   c. more likely, minimalization
C   d. less likely, minimalization

4.138   Individuals are more likely to use trivialization as a means for reducing dissonance when changing
c   attitudes was made relatively _____
LO 24   a. easy
Concept b. salient
141   c. difficult
M   d. comprehensive

4.139   The overall conclusion from several studies indicates that once a person selects the easiest or most
a   convenient form of dissonance reduction, that person tends
LO 24   a. to ignore all other alternatives
Concept b. to evaluate all other alternatives
141   c. to ignore alternatives that are not obviously relevant
M   d. to evaluate alternatives only in terms of salience

4.140   Sometimes we get caught in situations where circumstances force us to say things we don't really
d   believe. This is an example of
LO 25   a. role playing
Concept b. following the peripheral route
142   c. attitudinal ambivalence
M   d. forced compliance

4.141   A forced compliance situation increases the probability that you will
a   a. change your attitude to be consistent with your behavior
LO 25   b. change your behavior to be consistent with your attitude
Concept c. continue in the inconsistent situation
142   d. resist change when you are forced to comply
C

4.142
b
LO 25
Applied
142
M

Ralph sees Lisa and asks her what she thinks about the his new car. Lisa has just read a report that presents information about the unreliability of this particular model. However, Lisa does not want to hurt Ralph's feelings, so she says, "I love your car. It is beautiful!" Lisa has just experienced a
a. classical conditioning paradigm
b. forced compliance situation
c. reactance situation
d. consistency of attitude situation

4.143
c
LO 25
Fact
142
C

Forced compliance involves situations in which
a. individuals are reinforced for doing something inconsistent with their attitudes
b. individuals are not allowed to do something inconsistent with their attitudes
c. individuals do something inconsistent with their attitudes
d. individuals force themselves to do something consistent with their attitudes

4.144
d
LO 26
Fact
142
M

The "less leads to more" effect occurs in experiments using the
a. effort justification technique
b. superattitudinal procedure
c. selective avoidance procedure
d. forced compliance procedure

4.145
a
LO 26
Study
143
M

Which subjects in the Festinger and Carlsmith (1959) experiment ended up being the most positive about the dull, boring task they had performed earlier?
a. those paid $1 to say it was fun and exciting
b. those paid $20 to say it was fun and exciting
c. those who simply performed the dull, boring task
d. all subjects ended up seeing the task as equally bad

4.146
b
LO 26
Applied
143
M

If students were to write an attitude-discrepant essay, greater attitude chance toward their essay would be expected if they
a. were told they had no choice but to write the essay
b. were told that the decision to write the essay was up to them
c. were offered a large reward for writing the essay
d. felt no sense of responsibility for bad consequences produced by the essay

4.147
c
LO 26
Applied
143
C

Which of the following is a condition that makes the "less leads to more" effect likely to occur?
a. people feel they had no choice but to perform the attitude-discrepant behavior
b. people view as a bribe the payment they receive for attitude-discrepant behavior
c. people feel personally responsible for both the chosen course of action and negative consequences it produces
d. people feel no personal sense of responsibility for the chosen action or its negative consequences

4.148
b
LO 27
Concept
144
M

Research indicates that a way to use cognitive dissonance to induce compliance with socially desirable goals is to induce feelings of
a. reactance
b. hypocrisy
c. inconsistency between attitudes
c. inconsistency between behaviors

4.149
d
LO 27
Concept
144
M

Hypocrisy works to induce compliance by
a. reducing cognitive dissonance
b. increasing reactance
c. providing a socially acceptable heuristic as a framework for decision making
d. reminding people of the desirability of an action and that they are not performing that action

4.150   Stone and his colleagues (1994) predicted and found that participants in the _____ condition would
c   express the greatest intentions of engaging in safe sex and purchasing condoms.
LO 27   a. commitment
Study   b. mindfulness
144   c. hypocrisy
M   d. information only

4.151   Inducing individuals to make a public commitment to some course of action, and reminding them
d   that they have failed to live up to this commitment describes the process of _____.
LO 27   a. reactance
Fact   b. willfulness
144   c. cognitive dissonance
E   d. hypocrisy

4.152   A study by Furnham and colleagues (1994) found that, across all countries, _____ were a significant
b   predictor of economic growth.
LO 28   a. attitudes about the importance of money
Study   b. attitudes toward competitiveness
146   c. attitudes toward work
C   d. attitudes toward saving money

4.153   A study by Furnham and colleagues (1994) found that, across all countries, _____ were a significant
a   predictor of gross domestic product.
LO 28   a. attitudes about the importance of money
Study   b. attitudes toward competitiveness
146   c. attitudes toward work
C   d. attitudes toward saving money

4.154   What explanation is given for the relationship between attitudes and economic growth indicators?
b   a. attitudes toward economic growth lead to the acquisition of additional personal wealth
LO 28   b. attitudes toward economic growth lead to behaviors that contribute to their country's wealth
Concept c. attitudes toward economic growth lead to behaviors that are socially acceptable
146   d. attitudes and economic growth are not related
M

4.155   Furnham and colleagues (1994) found that individuals from _____ scored lowest on most of the
d   attitudes related to economic growth.
LO 28   a. North American countries
Study   b. South American countries
146   c. Asian countries
C   d. European countries

CHAPTER 5

Learning Objectives

After studying this chapter, students should be able to:

1. Describe the self-concept, including specific content as well as overall structure.

2. Describe the self-reference effect, and understand the two ways in which recall of self-relevant information is facilitated.

3. Explain the three major components of sexual self-schema, and how they affect self-reported sexual attitudes and sexual behavior.

4. Compare the concepts of present self and future self, and summarize the advantages of holding varied and complex future-self schemas.

5. Summarize factors that can produce changes in our self-concept, including aging, unemployment, combat, and interpersonal relationships.

6. Compare role-specific self-concepts and general self-concepts.

7. Examine the concept of self-esteem, including high vs. low self esteem, global self esteem, discrepancy between self and ideal self, and the impact of common vs. rare components.

8. Describe circumstances in which social comparisons lead to increases in self-esteem, and also circumstances in which social comparisons lead to decreases in self-esteem.

9. Define the three motives that underlie self-evaluation, and summarize ways in which people achieve self-enhancement.

10. Examine consequences of low self-esteem, including the lowering of serotonin levels and the impact on perceptions of task performance.

11. Understand the self-ideal discrepancy is important, and how the therapy developed by Carl Rogers deals with self-ideal discrepancy.

12. Explain which is a better predictor of depression, consistently low self-esteem or variable self-esteem.

13. Describe the circumstances that increase self-focusing, and the effects created when we become self-focused.

14. Describe high and low self-monitors and indicate the various ways in which the behavior of high and low self-monitors is different.

15. Define self-efficacy, noting that it tends to be situation-specific and does not usually generalize.

16. Explain how self-efficacy is related to physical endurance and success on academic tasks among students and professors.

17. Examine the role of self-efficacy in social situations, and compare the impact of harm-looming vs. self-efficacy in helping participants cope with a fear-inducing stimulus.

18. Summarize the development of gender identity by examining parents' reactions to newborns, gender awareness among two-year-olds, and gender consistency among older children.

19. Give examples of sex-typing that occurs as children learn gender appropriate stereotypes.

20.   *Describe the Bem Sex Role Inventory and the assumptions underlying it, and indicate characteristics of persons who are sex-typed, sex reversed, androgynous, and undifferentiated.*

21.   *Summarize advantages that accrue to individuals who are androgynous, and problems often associated with strong adherence to traditional sex roles.*

22.   *Compare gender role behaviors of men and women within the home.*

23.   *Examine gender-related effects in the workplace, focusing on expectancies and motivation, occupational restrictions, communication styles, leadership styles, and reactions to successful women.*

24.   *Give examples from children's stories, movies, television and computers where cultural support is provided for traditional gender roles, along with examples demonstrating movement away from traditional gender roles.*

25.   *Describe and explain sex differences in willingness to deprive self in order to help others and in the tendency to dominate and control others.*

26.   *Consider ways in which concern with their own appearance impacts women and causes biases in their self-perceptions.*

27.   *Compare Asian and Caucasian women with regard to concern about weight.*

Questions

5.1
c
LO 1
Concept
152
E

Self-concept is primarily acquired through
a. developmental maturation
b. parental guidance
c. social interaction
d. peer guidance

5.2
a
LO 1
Fact
152
M

The self-concept is defined as
a. an organized collection of beliefs and feelings about oneself
b. an organized collection of introspective findings about oneself
c. an organized collection of beliefs about what others think of oneself
d. an organized collection of behaviors that define oneself

5.3
d
LO 1
Applied
152
M

Which of the following situations is likely to be the most important in contributing to one's self-concept?
a. reading your first book
b. reaching the age where true introspection can begin
c. learning how to perform a new task
d. playing with other children in elementary school

5.4
c
LO 1
Study
154
E

In a study to investigate the components of self-concept, Rentsch and Heffner (1994) found that _____ were used to identify individuals.
a. two different categories
b. six different categories
c. eight different categories
d. twelve different categories

5.5
c
LO 1
Study
154
C

One of the categories discovered by Rentsch and Heffner (1994) that was used to identify an individual's self-concept was
a. interpersonal interactions
b. cognitive abilities
c. social differentiation
d. social identification

5.6
b
LO 2
Fact
154
C

The self-reference effect refers to
a. the tendency to process information in terms of how it affects the self
b. the tendency to process information more readily when it is related to the self
c. the tendency to split self-relevant information into positive and negative consequences
d. the tendency to forget negative self-relevant experiences

5.7
c
LO 2
Applied
154
M

Your first name is Bret. You are interested in, and can remember and cite portions of, the writings of Bret Hart, even though you have never met the individual. This situation describes
a. the self-esteem effect
b. the self-concept effect
c. the self-reference effect
d. the self-awareness effect

5.8
a
LO 2
Concept
155
M

Self-relevance may be connected to elaborative processing because
a. people are more likely to try to think about references to themselves
b. self-relevance is a primary schema
c. self-relevance is not related to categorical processing
d. self-relevance is not related to self-enhancement

5.9   According to research, a process that aids memory of items that have clear relationships among
a   them is
LO 2   a. categorical processing
Study   b. self-maintenance
155   c. elaborative processing
M   d. concept processing

5.10   Categorical processing aids the self-reference effect because
d   a. categorical processing leads to elaboration
LO 2   b. it takes more cognitive effort to process self-relevant information than other information
Concept c. self-relevance forms a major category of classification
M   d. self-relevant information is more easily categorized than other information

5.11   The cognitive generalizations about the sexual aspects of oneself that originate in past experience,
b   are manifested in current experience, influence the processing of sexual information, and guide
LO 3   sexual behavior is the definition of
Fact   a. sexual self-ideal
156   b. sexual self-schema
C   c. sexual self-enhancement
         d. sexual self-concept

5.12   Research by Andersen and Cyranowski (1994) indicated that women who differ in sexual self-schema
b   also respond differently to sexual cues
LO 3   a. emotionally, attitudinally, affectionately
Study   b. emotionally, attitudinally, behaviorally
156   c. affectionately, emotionally, behaviorally
M   d. emotionally, categorically, behaviorally

5.13   Research emphasizes the importance of further research on the _____ of sexual self as a central
c   aspect of the self-concept.
LO 3   a. emotional representations
Study   b. behavioral representations
156   c. cognitive representations
M   d. ideal representations

5.14   Three major components of the sexual self-schema have been proposed. These components are
a   a. passionate-romantic, open-direct, embarrassed-conservative
LO 3   b. passionate-romantic, open-closed, liberal-conservative
Fact   c. affectionate-romantic, open-direct, embarrassed-conservative
157   d. idealist-romantic, open-closed, embarrassed-conservative
C

5.15   Concepts of how we might change in the future are called
c   a. potentialities
LO 4   b. self-referenced concepts
Fact   c. possible selves
156   d. self-schematic conceptualizations
M

5.16   The working self-concept is
b   a. less accurate than most self-concepts
LO 4   b. the self-concept of oneself that exists in the present, and that is open to change
Concept c. another term for elaboration likelihood of the self
156   d. the goal oriented self-concept
M

5.17
c
LO 4
Concept
156
C

Self initiated major changes in lifestyle may be brought about as a consequence of
a. the dominance of positive possible selves
b. the dominance of negative possible selves
c. differing alternative possible selves
d. present oriented possible selves

5.18
d
LO 4
Concept
156
E

Possible selves affect motivation to reach future
a. schemas
b. choices
c. experiences
d. goals

5.19
d
LO 4
Concept
157
C

Which of the following individuals is most likely to respond emotionally to failure feedback about the likelihood of achieving a career goal?
a. a person with a complex elaboration likelihood schema
b. a person with a simple elaboration likelihood schema
c. a person with few categories for failure
d. a person with few possible selves

5.20
a
LO 4
Concept
157
M

The emotionally of a person's response to failure feedback is negatively affected by the _____ of possible selves available, and the _____ of the possible self-concept.
a. number, complexity
b. complexity, number
c. number, number
d. complexity, self-relevance

5.21
b
LO 4
Applied
158
M

After experiencing an intervention program over a four-week period, Mexican American children changed from expressing primarily gender stereotypes about occupations to expressing interest in _____.
a. self-relevant types of occupations
b. many different types of occupations
c. only those occupations that had been presented at the intervention program
d. occupations that were culturally oriented

5.22
c
LO 5
Applied
159
M

Ralph has been employed at one company for 5 years. Because of downsizing, this company released Ralph. The resulting new _____ has had a tremendous impact on Ralph's self-concept.
a. status identity
b. cultural identity
c. social identity
d. emotional identify

5.23
a
LO 5
Concept
159
M

Entering a new occupation can lead to changes in an individual's _____.
a. self-concept
b. self-definition
c. self-assessment
d. self-enhancement

5.24
b
LO 5
Study
160
M

McNulty and Swann (1994) found that the self can be altered by
a. cognitions of others
b. reactions of others
c. attitudes of others
d. emotions of others

5.25   There seems to be an _____ between the perceptions of self and the perceptions of others in
c   defining the self-concept.
LO 5   a. emotional effect
Concept b. attitudinal effect
160   c. interactive effect
M   d. evaluative effect

5.26   A _____ involves consistency of self-concept across roles.
a   a. general self-concept
LO 6   b. role-specific self-concept
Fact   c. idealized self-concept
160   d. interpersonal self-concept
M

5.27   A _____ involves differences of self-concept across roles.
b   a. general self-concept
LO 6   b. role-specific self-concept
Fact   c. idealized self-concept
160   d. interpersonal self-concept
M

5.28   Lisa is a daughter, which is her _____. She is also an emotional daughter, which is her _____.
c   a. general self-concept, role-specific self-concept
LO 6   b. general self-concept, idealized self-concept
Concept c. role-specific self-concept, general self-concept
160   d. role-specific self-concept, idealized self-concept
C

5.29   Roberts and Donahue (1994) found that women reported self-concepts that differed to some extent
d   in different interpersonal situations. This self-concept is called a
LO 6   a. general self-concept
Study   b. idealized self-concept
161   c. interpersonal self-concept
C   d. role-specific self-concept

5.30   Self-esteem refers to the
b   a. desire to be liked by others
LO 7   b. positive or negative evaluation of the self by oneself
Fact   c. evaluations of others about the self
160   d. amount of positive emotion that one is experiencing at the moment
M

5.31   Ralph feels helpless at his job, feels that he cannot control his workday, and feels that he is useless,
c   worthless, and inept. These characteristics would probably mean that Ralph has
LO 7   a. high locus of control
Applied b. high self-insight
160   c. low self-esteem
M   d. negative possible selves

5.32   Your global self-esteem is made up of a combination of the
a   a. relative number and relative intensity of self-evaluations
LO 7   b. relative strength and relative emotionality of self-evaluations
Concept c. relative cultural strength and relative interpersonal perception of self-evaluations
160   d. relative strength and relative accessibility of self-evaluations
C

5.33
d
LO 7
Concept
160
M

The discrepancy between the self and the ideal self refers to
a. the total difference between our most positive and negative possible selves
b. the perceived total difference between our most positive and negative possible selves
c. the perceived average difference between our most positive and negative possible selves
d. the gap between the self-perceived ideal and the actual self

5.34
c
LO 7
Concept
161
M

The greater the discrepancy between a person's self and the ideal self, the _____ the self-esteem.
a. higher
b. more organized
c. lower
d. less organized

5.35
d
LO 7
Concept
161
M

Which of the following is related to large self/ideal-self discrepancy gaps?
a. the desire to get an "A" on an exam
b. the goal of getting an "A" on an exam
c. the goal of becoming more physically fit
d. the goal of being the first person to find a cure for the common cold

5.36
b
LO 7
Applied
161
M

Lisa has the perception that her liked characteristics (e.g., good cook) are quite common, and her unliked characteristics (e.g., good writer) are quite rare. Lisa would be a candidate for
a. very high self-esteem
b. very low self-esteem
c. average self-esteem
d. confounded self-esteem

5.37
a
LO 8
Concept
162
M

In social comparison processes, when you compare yourself to others who have some inadequacy, your self-esteem _____.
a. increases
b. decreases
c. is refocused
d. is recalibrated

5.38
a
LO 8
Concept
162
C

The contrast effect in self-esteem/social comparison processes means that
a. you have compared yourself with someone who has some inadequacy, and your self-esteem increases
b. you have found a contrast between your abilities and your expectations, and your self-esteem increases
c. you have compared your self-esteem with another person's self-esteem, and your self-esteem decreases
d. you have compared yourself with someone who has some similar quality, and your self-esteem decreases

5.39
a
LO 8
Concept
162
M

If you compare yourself to someone to whom you feel close and you perceive something very good about that person, your self-esteem may _____.
a. increase
b. decrease
c. be refocused
d. be recalibrated

5.40   The assimilation effect in self-esteem/social comparison processes mean that
d
LO 8   a. you have found an assimilation between your abilities and your expectations and your self-esteem
Concept   increases
162   b. you have assimilated your self-esteem with another person's self-esteem, and your self-esteem
C   decreases
         c. you have assimilated yourself with someone who has some similar quality and your self-esteem
         decreases
         d. you have compared yourself to someone with whom you are close, perceive something good
         about them, and your self-esteem increases

5.41   Self-esteem can be raised by identifying with a group because _____ can compensate for problems
b   involving _____.
LO 8   a. personal identity, social identity
Concept   b. social identity, personal identity
162   c. social identity, self-concept
M   d. self-concept, social identity

5.42   Bat-Chava (1994) found that deaf adults expressed higher self-esteem if they
d   a. identified with hearing adults
LO 8   b. identified with hearing teachers
Study   c. identified with hearing parents
162   d. identified with deaf individuals
M

5.43   Sedikides (1993) suggests three motives for evaluating oneself. Which of the following is NOT one
c   of those self-evaluation motives?
LO 9   a. self-assessment
Study   b. self-enhancement
162   c. self-effacement
M   d. self-verification

5.44   Of the three motives for self-evaluation, which one is the most often sought by research participants?
b   a. self-effacement
LO 9   b. self-enhancement
Concept   c. self-verification
162   d. self-assessment
M

5.45   Seeking accurate self-knowledge, whether positive or negative defines _____.
b   a. self-enhancement
LO 9   b. self-verification
Fact   c. self-assessment
162   d. self-effacement
M

5.46   Individuals low in self-esteem seek which type of motive for self-evaluation?
a   a. self-enhancement, but only when it is not risky to seek such information
LO 9   b. self-assessment, but only when it is not risky to seek such information
Concept   c. self-assessment, but only when it is risky to seek such information
163   d. self-verification, but only when it is risky to seek such information
C

5.47
c
LO 9
Applied
163
M

Ralph did not do well on a standardized exam he took, even though he usually does quite well on exams. He made a point of asking his friends how they scored on the exam. From this information, you would predict that Ralph has
a. a lot of courage
b. low self-esteem
c. high self-esteem
d. a lot of gall

5.48
b
LO 9
Applied
163
M

Lisa uses the coping strategy of maintaining a positive view of oneself by focusing on the shortcomings of others. Lisa is
a. a "pain" to her friends
b. high in self-esteem
c. low in self-esteem
d. always disappointed by her performance

5.49
c
LO 10
Concept
163
M

Negative self-evaluation is associated with
a. unrealistic social concern
b. increased social assessment
c. less adequate social skills
d. unrealistic self-verification

5.50
b
LO 10
Study
163
M

_____ levels of the biochemical serotonin is associated with _____ social success in male monkeys.
a. high, low
b. high, high
c. low, low
d. low, high

5.51
a
LO 10
Study
164
M

The card sorting task used by Martin and Murberger (1994) found that participants' perceptions of task performance were more positive for _____ students.
a. high self-esteem
b. low self-esteem
c. high self-enhancement
d. low self-enhancement

5.52
b
LO 10
Study
164
M

Both groups of participants in the card sorting task used by Martin and Murberger (1994) perceived their performance to be worse in the _____.
a. easy goal condition
b. hard goal condition
c. RED card condition
d. low self-esteem condition

5.53
d
LO 11
Concept
165
M

Carl Rogers emphasized that _____ is the most important aspect of each person's world.
a. family support
b. appropriate regard
c. appropriate behavior
d. the self

5.54
b
LO 11
Concept
165
M

The self-ideal discrepancy is important because it is an indicator of
a. positive regard for the individual
b. maladjustment of the individual
c. self-perception of the individual
d. self-enhancement of the individual

5.55   The _____ therapy of Carl Rogers creates a positive atmosphere in which the client is free to change.
a   a. client-centered
LO 11   b. change-centered
Fact   c. therapist-directed
165   d. self-directed
M

5.56   The effectiveness of the therapy of Carl Rogers has been investigated, with the results of one study
c   indicating that those clients showing _____ had the greatest decrease in _____.
LO 11   a. definite improvement, self-perception scores
Study   b. little improvement, self-ideal discrepancy
166   c. definite improvement, self-ideal discrepancy
C   d. little improvement, self-perception scores

5.57   Individuals whose self-esteem fluctuates up and down are most likely to become
b   a. elated
LO 12   b. depressed
Concept   c. disoriented
166   d. anxious
E

5.58   Low self-esteem is to _____ as variable self-esteem is to _____.
d   a. depression, depression
LO 12   b. negative emotions, depression
Fact   c. negative emotions, negative emotions
166   d. depression, negative emotions
M

5.59   When Ralph receives an "A" on an exam, he feels great and proud of himself for being so successful.
c   When Ralph cannot balance his checkbook, he feels defeated, worthless, and stupid. Ralph is a
LO 12   prime candidate for _____.
Applied   a. self-assessment therapy
166   b. anxiety
M   c. depression
              d. self-perception therapy

5.60   The research of Butler and colleagues (1994) indicate which of the following is the best predictor
b   of depression?
LO 12   a. high self-esteem
Study   b. variable self-esteem
166   c. low self-esteem
M   d. moderate self-esteem

5.61   Self-focusing refers to
a   a. the extent to which attention is directed toward oneself
LO 13   b. the degree to which a person relies on his or her own judgment
Fact   c. a measure of self-enhancement
167   d. the presence of a sense of self
E

5.62   Self-focusing is linked to the quality of an individual's
b   a. cognitions about others
LO 13   b. memory
Concept   c. method of processing situations
167   d. method of elaboration
M

5.63 c LO 13 Study 167 M	According to research, self-focusing tends to a. be greater in males b. be greater in females c. increase with age d. decrease with age

5.64 c LO 13 Concept 168 M	Mood changes based on memories are characteristic of people high in a. number of possible selves b. self-esteem c. self-focusing d. self-discrepancy

5.65 d LO 13 Concept 168 M	The relationship between mood and self-focusing appears to be that a. mood affects self-focusing b. self-focusing affects mood c. mood and self-focusing have to be stimulated by an external factor d. mood and self-focusing affect each other

5.66 a LO 13 Concept 168 M	Although people often engage in self-focusing behavior a. self-focusing is not always conscious b. self-focusing is rarest in Western cultures c. self-focusing is usually brief d. self-focusing usually has small effects on behavior

5.67 c LO 14 Fact 168 M	The degree to which individuals regulate their behavior based on the situation is referred to as a. self-efficacy b. self-esteem c. self-monitoring d. self-concept

5.68 d LO 14 Concept 169 M	Self-monitoring theory holds that individuals who are high in self-monitoring behavior act so as to a. increase their self-esteem b. increase their self-efficacy c. simplify their self-concept d. receive positive evaluations from others

5.69 d LO 14 Concept 169 M	Responsiveness to others' opinions or to particular situations are characteristics of a. self-awareness b. self-esteem c. self-efficacy d. self-monitoring

5.70 a LO 14 Concept 169 M	Measures of self-monitoring tend to assess whether or not the respondent a. looks for internal versus external cues for behavior b. looks for ways to increase self-esteem from situational sources c. varies behavior rapidly d. varies behavior randomly

5.71   Low self-monitors are more likely than high self-monitors to respond to advertisements directed at
b   a. product image
LO 14   b. product quality
Concept c. product consistency
171   d. products aimed at enhancing self-esteem
M

5.72   A person high in _____ is most likely to be overconfident regarding the accuracy of her decision.
c   a. self-esteem
LO 14   b. self-efficacy
Concept c. self-monitoring
171   d. self-focusing
M

5.73   When Ralph talks about himself and his accomplishments, he tends to use the first person (I, me
d   mine). Ralph would be classified as
LO 14   a. a person high in self-monitoring
Applied b. a person high in self-esteem
171   c. a person low in self-esteem
C   d. a person low in self-monitoring

5.74   High self-monitors are more likely to select a sports companion based on _____ than low self-monitors.
b   a. friendliness
LO 14   b. ability
Concept c. attractiveness
171   d. their liking for that person
M

5.75   According to research, high self-monitors tend to be committed to _____, while low self-monitors
d   tend to be committed to _____.
LO 14   a. people, friends
Study   b. individuals, situations
171   c. images, situations
C   d. situations, individuals

5.76   Howells (1993) found that individuals high in self-monitoring had more _____ personality
b   characteristics than individuals low in self-monitoring.
LO 14   a. negative
Study   b. positive
172   c. neutral
C   d. variable

5.77   People who are well adjusted tend to be
b   a. high self-monitors
LO 14   b. medium self-monitors
Concept c. low self-monitors
172   d. variable in self-monitoring
M

5.78   Your evaluation of your ability to perform a task is called
b   a. self-efficiency
LO 15   b. self-efficacy
Fact   c. self-esteem
172   d. self-reliance
E

5.79
a
LO 15
Concept
173
M

An aspect of self-efficacy that differentiates it from self-esteem is its
a. situational specificity
b. reliance upon internal motivation
c. reliance upon external motivation
d. reliance upon social skills

5.80
b
LO 15
Concept
173
M

According to self-efficacy theory, success at one task
a. reduces negative self-efficacy
b. does not generally lead to higher self-efficacy about other tasks
c. raises overall feelings of self-efficacy
d. increases the chances of success at another task

5.81
c
LO 15
Applied
173
C

Lisa does not have a lot of confidence that she can deal with an tornado, but does feel quite confident about her ability to change the tire on her car. This scenario describes the lack of ____ of self-monitoring.
a. reliability
b. specificity
c. generality
d. effectiveness

5.82
b
LO 16
Concept
173
M

High self-efficacy generally leads to improved task performance
a. if the individual is skilled at the task
b. independently of ability
c. only if the task is not difficult
d. only if the task is complete

5.83
c
LO 16
Concept
173
M

Endogenous opioids are a form of
a. self-esteem enhancer
b. self-efficacy enhancer
c. painkiller
d. bandurin

5.84
d
LO 16
Concept
173
C

Self-efficacy is related to expectancies in that
a. people with high self-efficacy tend to have low expectancies
b. people with high self-efficacy tend to have many possible selves
c. people high in self-efficacy tend to have developed self-schemas
d. people high in self-efficacy tend to outperform expectancies

5.85
a
LO 16
Applied
173
M

Ralph is trying out for the mathematics competition team for his university. He knows that currently he is the third best mathematician, but he also has carefully evaluated his past performance and knows that he can significantly improve his performance. Ralph has ____.
a. high self-efficacy
b. low self-efficacy
c. variable self-efficacy
d. medium self-efficacy

5.86
a
LO 17
Concept
173
M

People with high self-efficacy for a situation are more likely than people with low self-efficacy to
a. externalize the causes of negative feedback
b. take the blame for failure
c. have high self-discrepancies
d. internalize the causes of negative feedback

5.87   Self-efficacy can be raised through favorable
b
LO 17   a. self-discrepancies
Concept   b. evaluations by others
173   c. self-esteem comparisons
M   d. internalizations of failure feedback

5.88   According to Bandura, the relationship between successful therapy and self-efficacy is that
c
LO 17   a. therapy replaces self-efficacy
Study   b. therapy reduces reliance on self-efficacy to protect self-esteem
174   c. therapy increases self-efficacy
M   d. therapy provides an effective role model

5.89   One model of fear is the _____ model, which describes fear as a function of closeness of the feared
c   object and whether it is moving.
LO 17   a. self-efficacy
Fact   b. moving-threat
174   c. harm-looming
M   d. moving-closeness

5.90   In a study by Riskind and Maddux (1993), it was found that the highest fear was shown by participants
a   who had _____ self-efficacy in the condition in which the tarantula was _____.
LO 17   a. low, toward the viewer
Study   b. low, away from the viewer
175   c. high, toward the viewer
C   d. high, away from the viewer

5.91   The study by Riskind and Maddux (1993) found that regardless of self-efficacy, less fear was
c   expressed in the conditions in which the tarantulas were either still or moving away from the viewer.
LO 17   This result supports the _____ model of fear.
Study   a. self-efficacy
175   b. moving-threat
M   c. harm-looming
               d. moving-closeness

5.92   Biological differentiation between males and females is defined as
d   a. masculinity and femininity
LO 18   b. gender
Fact   c. androgyny and typing
175   d. sex
E

5.93   Gender is used to refer to discussions about male and female
a   a. roles
LO 18   b. biology
Concept   c. sexuality
175   d. similarities
E

5.94   Gender identity refers to
b   a. an individual's biological sex
LO 18   b. the sex with which individuals associate themselves
Concept   c. the sex assigned by an adult to a child
176   d. the dominant gender of one's peers
M

5.95
d
LO 18
Applied
176
M

When Lisa was a child, she had no real awareness of sex or gender. We can speculate that Lisa was probably younger than
a. five years old
b. four years old
c. three years old
d. two years old

5.96
d
LO 18
Fact
176
E

The realization that gender is a basic attribute of a person is referred to as
a. sex constancy
b. developmental realism
c. sex awareness
d. gender consistency

5.97
a
LO 19
Fact
177
E

The acquisition of attributes associated with being a male or female in a culture is referred to as
a. sex typing
b. gender identification
c. sex perception
d. gender recognition

5.98
a
LO 19
Study
177
M

According to Bem's gender schema theory, sex typed behavior is influenced by
a. stereotypes
b. categorical processing
c. possible selves
d. self-discrepancies

5.99
b
LO 19
Concept
177
M

An example of sex typing is the association of
a. masculinity and femininity
b. males and assertiveness
c. males and submissiveness
d. females and assertiveness

5.100
c
LO 19
Applied
178
M

When Lisa was younger, she liked to play with toy cars and tool kits. Her parents had no problems with these behaviors and permitted her to do so. These behaviors would be a violation of the prevailing ____.
a. gender specificity
b. gender typology
c. gender stereotype
d. gender classification

5.101
d
LO 20
Fact
179
E

Acceptance of characteristics of both genders is defined as
a. sex typing
b. gender typing
c. role normality
d. androgyny

5.102
d
LO 20
Fact
180
M

The Bem Sex Role Inventory (BSRI) measures
a. the degree of sex typing in males
b. the degree of sex typing in females
c. how likely a male or a female is to act like a member of the opposite sex
d. the degree of adherence to typical masculine or feminine roles

5.103
a
LO 20
Concept
180
C

In the development of the Bem Sex Role Inventory (BSRI), masculinity was defined in terms of attributes associated with _____, while femininity was defined in terms of attributes associated with _____.
a. instrumental orientation, expressive orientation
b. expressive orientation, instrumental orientation
c. aggressive orientation, assertive orientation
d. assertive orientation, passive orientation

5.104
d
LO 20
Applied
180
M

Ralph responds to the BSRI as a masculine male, and Lisa responds as a feminine female. Both of these individuals would be classified as
a. sex-reversed
b. androgynous
c. undifferentiated
d. sex-typed

5.105
a
LO 20
Study
180
E

Based on research with the BSRI, about _____ of males and the same percent of females adhere to the sex-typed classification.
a. 30%
b. 40%
c. 50%
d. 60%

5.106
c
LO 21
Concept
181
M

Many research findings concerning gender types are consistent with the proposition that
a. masculinity is good
b. femininity is good
c. androgyny is good
d. undifferentiated is good

5.107
b
LO 21
Concept
181
M

Aggression and violence are associated with the _____ role.
a. traditional masculine
b. extreme masculine
c. masculine
d. undifferentiated

5.108
c
LO 21
Concept
182
M

Among adolescent males, _____ is associated with having multiple sexual partners.
a. high self-esteem
b. high self-efficacy
c. high masculinity
d. high androgyny

5.109
a
LO 21
Applied
182
M

Lisa has just broken up with her boyfriend, and she is depressed about the situation. Lisa is probably _____.
a. high in androgyny
b. high in self-esteem
c. high in self-efficacy
d. high in femininity

5.110
c
LO 22
Concept
182
E

If a man is classified as androgynous, he will probably do _____ housework than a female.
a. more
b. the same amount of
c. less
d. no

5.111
b
LO 22
Concept
182
M

What men and women do within the home is still influenced by _____, regardless of their classification on the BSRI.
a. gender efficacies
b. gender roles
c. gender expectancies
d. gender patterns

5.112
a
LO 22
Applied
182
E

Ralph paints the garage, and Lisa cooks the meals. Both of them are responding according to their
a. gender roles
b. gender expectancies
c. gender patterns
d. gender efficacies

5.113
b
LO 22
Concept
182
M

Regardless on one's classification on the BSRI, gender roles seem to be more powerful when it comes to
a. completing tasks in the workplace
b. doing work in the home
c. helping others in the neighborhood
d. supervising others

5.114
c
LO 23
Study
183
M

Moore (1994) speculated that one reason women are more likely than men to believe that they deserve a lower salary is that they have been taught to evaluate themselves in a
a. more cooperative manner
b. less aggressive way
c. less egotistical way
d. more assertive manner

5.115
d
LO 23
Concept
183
M

Leadership styles emphasizing connection and interaction are more typical of
a. gender-typed people
b. androgynous people
c. men
d. women

5.116
a
LO 23
Applied
183
M

In the O.J. Simpson trial, the description of Marcia Clark's change of hairstyle is an example of women being _____ when they have succeeded in a traditional masculine field.
a. patronized
b. characterized
c. ostracized
d. legalized

5.117
c
LO 23
Concept
183
M

When a higher percentage of women enter a traditionally masculine occupation, that occupation is then viewed as
a. an easy occupation
b. a more prestigious occupation
c. a less prestigious occupation
d. an unacceptable occupation

5.118
c
LO 24
Concept
183
M

Women are traditionally cast in submissive positions in
a. the U.S. constitution
b. the role of homemaker
c. Judeo-Christian religions
d. the role of bringing up the children

5.119   Traditional children's books often stereotype females through
d
LO 24   a. showing them only in dresses/skirts
Concept   b. giving them small roles in stories
183   c. depicting them as evil
M   d. placing them in submissive roles

5.120   Cooper and colleagues (1990) found that elementary school students reacted with stress to
a   computer software that depicted ____.
LO 24   a. stereotypical opposite-gender roles
Study   b. stereotypical same-gender roles
184   c. nonstereotypical opposite-gender roles
C   d. nonstereotypical same-gender roles

5.121   Evidence that gender-role stereotypes may be diminishing comes from the finding that
b   a. women are paid more than they were in the 1950s
LO 24   b. people generally find it easier than before to conceptualize women in traditionally male roles
Concept   c. most men feel comfortable with the idea of a female boss
184   d. crimes against women are diminishing
M

5.122   In the entertainment industry, there seems to be no overwhelming concern about
c   a. gender violence
LO 24   b. gender enhancement
Applied   c. gender equality
184   d. gender effectiveness
M

5.123   Males outnumber females in computer courses, in enrollment in computer camps, and in expressed
a   interest in computer science. Your textbook authors speculate that one reason might be that
LO 24   a. most educational software is based on male stereotypes
Concept   b. males are more suited to mathematics than females
184   c. females do not have the same access to computers as males
M   d. educational computer software is organized in such a manner as to bore females

5.124   In explaining differences in behavior between women and men, one needs to understand first
c   whether the differences arise from biology or
LO 25   a. role typing
Concept   b. stereotyping
185   c. learning
M   d. culture

5.125   Martin and Parker (1995) found that undergraduates believed that social and biological factors play
b   a role in gender differences, but that ____ was the more important determinant.
LO 25   a. biology
Study   b. socialization
185   c. emotion
E   d. categorization

5.126   The difference between men and women that is most likely to have a biological foundation is the
b   observed difference in
LO 25   a. friendliness
Concept   b. aggression
186   c. monetary earnings
E   d. assertiveness

5.127
d
LO 25
Concept
186
M

The evolutionary explanation for the differences in aggression in men and women centers on
a. the production of testosterone
b. sex role stereotypes
c. gender role stereotypes
d. male strategies for reproductive success

5.128
c
LO 25
Concept
186
M

In men, having a traditionally dominant and controlling occupation is associated with
a. chromosomes
b. the sex chromosome
c. testosterone level
d. fetal androgens

5.129
b
LO 25
Concept
186
M

Most of the studies investigating the effects of the female hormone estrogen have concentrated on
a. behavioral consequences
b. physical consequences
c. emotional consequences
d. chromosomal consequences

5.130
a
LO 26
Concept
186
M

It is suggested that women's generally greater preoccupation with weight is a result of
a. learned expectancies
b. biology through hormonal differences
c. female strategies for reproductive success
d. male strategies for reproductive success

5.131
d
LO 26
Concept
186
M

When an overweight female is rejected for a date, she has a tendency to
a. blame circumstances
b. blame the male
c. blame luck
d. blame herself

5.132
c
LO 26
Concept
187
M

Appearance anxiety for young males is usually expressed in terms of
a. great dissatisfaction with being overweight
b. mild dissatisfaction with being overweight
c. mild dissatisfaction about not having a muscular body
d. great dissatisfaction about not being slim

5.133
b
LO 26
Concept
187
M

As females age, they are perceived as _____, in contrast to males.
a. more feminine
b. less feminine
c. equally feminine
d. less nurturant

5.134
d
LO 26
Concept
187
M

One consequence of our society's emphasis on physical attractiveness of women is that women
a. often become bored with the discussion and isolate themselves
b. often challenge men to meet the same level of attractiveness
c. often attribute such emphasis to the historical times in which they live
d. often become vulnerable and upset when appearance is an issue

5.135   Women respond with _____, according to self-report and physiological assessment, as compared to
a   men.
LO 26   a. greater emotional intensity
Concept   b. greater cognitive complexity
188   c. greater physical variability
M   d. greater emotional variability

5.136   Within the United Kingdom and North America, African American and Asian women have _____ than
b   Caucasian women.
LO 27   a. a greater variety of eating disorders
Concept   b. fewer eating disorders overall
188   c. more eating disorders overall
M   d. more common eating disorders

5.137   Wardle and colleagues (1993) found that a greater number of _____ females were actively trying to
c   loose weight.
LO 27   a. Asian
Study   b. Black
189   c. White
E   d. Indian

5.138   Among females having access to scales, _____ females report weighing themselves less often than
d   _____ females.
LO 27   a. Asian, Black
Study   b. Black, White
189   c. White, Asian
M   d. Asian, White

5.139   Wardle and her colleagues (1993) found that among all women studied, both groups agreed that
a   a. men prefer a slim woman
LO 27   b. men prefer a blonde woman
Study   c. women prefer a slim man
189   d. women prefer a blonde man
M

5.140   One hypothesis to support the cultural differences in female concern about weight is that
b   a. Black males reject overweight females to a greater extent than do Asian males
LO 27   b. White males reject overweight females to a greater extent than do Asian males
Concept   c. Asian males reject overweight females to a greater extent than do White males
189   d. Asian males reject overweight females to a greater extent than to Black males
C

CHAPTER 6

Learning Objectives

After studying this chapter, students should be able to:

1. *Understand the meaning of "prejudice," "discrimination," and "stereotype." Explain how prejudice functions like other attitudes.*

2. *Indicate the link between the cognitive and affective components of prejudice and the labor saving aspect of stereotypes.*

3. *Outline the procedures of the Macrae et al. (1993, 1994) studies in which stereotype labels freed up the cognitive apparatus for another task.*

4. *Tell what has happened to overt expressions of prejudice. Differentiate "old fashioned racism" and "modern racism" and give some belief statements that reflect the latter.*

5. *Describe tokenism and its effects on the "tokens" and relate it to reverse discrimination.*

6. *Outline the procedure of the famous Sherif and colleagues summer camp study. Explain how antagonism between groups of boys was created, how it was resolved and the limitations of the study.*

7. *Examine the frustration-aggression hypothesis. Explain how displaced aggression in relation to economic conditions relates to lynching between 1882 and 1930. Describe the pluses and minuses of the Hovland and Sears study of lynching.*

8. *Taking the social learning view, describe how children acquire prejudice. Tell if the media depiction of minorities has become more positive or remained negative (or something in between).*

9. *Indicate how in-group and out-group members are perceived with reference to the "ultimate attribution error" as applied to the Hong Kong study. Explain why we identify with groups.*

10. *Explain how stereotypes make it easy to describe a group. Understand how we deal with information that is consistent and inconsistent with stereotypes we hold.*

11. *Describe the procedure of the Jussim and colleagues study using "rock musician" and "child abuser" targets (and gays). Explain what happens when affect and then cognition is held constant.*

12. *Outline the procedure of the Bodenhausen et al. study of cheating and assault suspects and stereotype labels. Explain what happened to guilt ratings when stereotypes were activated and subjects were in a good mood.*

13. *Define "illusory correlation." Explain how the concept plays a role in crime rate estimation. Explain why infrequent events/stimuli stand out in memory.*

14. *Indicate the difference between "out-group homogeneity" and "in-group differentiation." Explain for whom the "they all look alike" effect is stronger*

15. *Describe how experience, actual level of heterogeneity and individuality influence this effect. Contrast Lee's and Ottati's American and Chinese subjects on these two dimensions.*

16. *Indicate why parents communicate prejudice to their children despite the observation that it makes them suffer (how?) and hampers their viability in today's world (why?).*

17. *List the advantages of intergroup contact, the conditions that must prevail if it is to have positive effects and research results supporting prejudice reduction via contact.*

18.   *Explain how Gaertner and colleagues indicate we can "recategorize" and thereby confirm the "common ingroup identity model".*

19.   *Describe how knowledge about the success of a target counters stereotypes about that target. Explain how these mechanisms relate to affirmative action.*

20.   *Examine the "rebound" effect associated with stereotype suppression in the Macrae et al. study with the "skinhead" target.*

21.   *Relate "sexism" to "gender stereotypes" by contrasting the stereotypes of males and females and by discussing the accuracy of perceived differences between males and females, gender differences in expectations, women's self-confidence and reactions to female leaders.*

22.   *Indicate the circumstances under which women leaders are evaluated lower, according to Eagly and colleagues. Relate the "glass ceiling" to male executives' efforts that keep women down.*

23.   *List the kinds of "developmental opportunities" that women are denied. Describe how Van Velsor and Hughes explain women's lack of advancement, despite the observation that they had as many developmental opportunities as men.*

24.   *Define sexual harassment in terms of what happened to Teresa Harris. Explain when "sexual harassment" is not sexual?*

25.   *Outline the stereotypes of the elderly. Describe how these stereotypes can become self-fulfilling prophesies. Indicate how Levy and Langer showed that culture can moderate the effects of stereotypes about the elderly.*

Questions

done

✓ 6.1
a
LO 1
Concept
195
M

Prejudice is defined as
a. a type of attitude toward people, based on their membership in some group
b. a type of behavior toward people, based on their membership in some group
c. a type of attitude toward society in general
d. a type of behavior typical of people with restrictive schemata

✓ 6.2
b
LO 1
Fact
195
M

Prejudice is associated with _____, while discrimination is associated with _____.
a. attributes, schemata
b. attitudes, behavior
c: attributes, behavior
d. attitudes, schemata

✓ 6.3
c
LO 1
Concept
195
M

Negative actions directed toward members of a social group are defined as
a. prejudice
b. hate crimes
c. discrimination
d. outgroup homogenization

6.4
b
LO 1
Concept
195
M

A schema is a
a. type of mental prejudice
b. type of mental organizational framework
c. type of mental discrimination
d. type of mental task

6.5
a
LO 1
Applied
195
M

Ralph believes that women are bad at math tasks. He tends to notice when a woman fails at a math-oriented task, but rarely notices success. He is also good at bringing the failures to mind. Ralph is using a prejudicial
a. schema
b. outgroup category
c. discrimination category
d. inverse discrimination category

6.6
d
LO 2
Concept
196
M

The affective component of prejudice involves
a. the negative behaviors of prejudiced people in the presence of disliked groups
b. the empathic behaviors of prejudiced people in the presence of disliked groups
c. the pathological behaviors of prejudiced people in the presence of disliked groups
d. the negative emotions of prejudiced people in the presence of disliked groups

6.7
a
LO 2
Fact
196
E

In thinking about prejudice, most people tend to focus on which component of prejudice?
a. affective
b. cognitive
c. behavioral
d. organizational

6.8   It is sometimes thought that prejudice is at least partially an outcome of
b
LO 2   a. using unrehearsed schemata because of limited processing capacity
Concept   b. using mental shortcuts in evaluating people because of limited processing capacity
196   c. limited memory for unfamiliar stimuli
M   d. limited processing capacity leading to limited stimulation

6.9   Stereotypes involve
a
LO 2   a. beliefs and expectations about a particular group
Fact   b. negative emotions experienced in the presence of members of specific groups
196   c. any mental process that is involved in the evaluation of people
C   d. negative behavioral tendencies with respect to the persons who are the object of prejudice

6.10   Macrae and colleagues (1994) asked participants to simultaneously perform two unrelated tasks.
c   These tasks were:
LO 3   a. an impression formation task and a visual discrimination task
Study   b. an impression formation task and a personality measurement task
196   c. an impression formation task and an unrelated listening task
C   d. an impression formation task and an attitude measurement task

6.11   Macrae and colleagues (1994) gave some participants names of strangers and also labels about the
c   strangers. The purpose of giving this information was
LO 3   a. to confuse half of the participants
Study   b. to generate impression formation in half of the participants
196   c. to activate stereotypes in half of the participants
C   d. to give half of the participants an advantage in identifying the strangers

6.12   Performance increased on both tasks in the Macrae et al. (1994) study due to the
d
LO 3   a. cognitive ability of the participants
Study   b. activation of discrimination
197   c. activation of prejudice
C   d. activation of stereotypes

6.13   The findings of Macrae and colleagues (1994) suggest that stereotypes
a
LO 3   a. do save precious cognitive resources
Study   b. do increase negative emotions
197   c. do confuse participants on complex cognitive tasks
M   d. do increase cognitive effort

6.14   Even when people are not aware of their presence, stereotypes still serve as an
b
LO 3   a. a impression formation tactic
Concept   b. an energy-saving tactic
197   c. an affective-cognitive evaluation tactic
C   d. an attitude formation tactic

6.15   Discrimination refers to
c
LO 4   a. any kind of bias or inclination toward anything
Fact   b. positive attitudes of a special kind
197   c. negative attitudes directed toward members of some distinct social group
M   d. an attitude toward members of a group that leads possessors of that attitude to evaluate members
        based on group membership

6.16
c
LO 4
Concept
198
M

Subtle forms of discrimination
a. no longer are displayed by people
b. are evidenced mostly in Black people
c. permit users to conceal underlying negative views
d. are detectable only with use of a polygraph (lie detector)

6.17
c
LO 4
Concept
198
M

Which of the following is a form of subtle discrimination?
a. suggesting that a particular group is unhealthy
b. suggesting that a particular group is attractive
c. excessively praising a minimal accomplishment
d. excessively denigrating a person's looks

6.18
d
LO 4
Applied
199
C

Which of the following statements does NOT represent the major components of subtle racism?
a. "There is no longer a problem with discrimination against Indians."
b. "All we see lately are Hispanics clamoring for "their share of the pie."
c. "Asians are always getting special favors in the legislature for their activities."
d. "Blacks have more problems than other minorities, and they seek services"

6.19
b
LO 4
Fact
198
E

Some researchers contend that old-fashioned racism has been replaced with
a. new racism
b. modern racism
c. functional racism
d. social racism

6.20
a
LO 4
Study
199
C

Swim and colleagues (1995) have gathered data that indicate the new form of racism focuses on three major components. These components are:
a. denial, antagonism, resentment
b. antagonism, anger, hostility
c. anger, hostility, resentment
d. hostility, antagonism, denial

6.21
b
LO 5
Fact
199
M

Allowing members of a specific group to participate in an activity or event solely to avoid charges of discrimination is called
a. reverse discrimination
b. tokenism
c. visibility discrimination
d. participatory discrimination

6.22
d
LO 5
Fact
199
M

Tokenism refers to
a. refusing to accept even a token gesture of friendship from an object of prejudice
b. being merely occasionally unfriendly to objects of prejudice
c. passing out "tokens" - small rewards or praise - to other people willing to display discrimination
d. hiring a person solely as a token member of a racial or ethnic group, rather than on the basis of qualifications

6.23
b
LO 5
Study
199
M

Researchers (e.g., Chacko, 1982) have asked women holding managerial-level jobs about their feelings toward their work. In some cases, these researchers found
a. the women's sex made no difference
b. the women who felt they were hired because of their sex were upset
c. the women who felt they were hired because of their ability were upset
d. the women's ability made no difference

6.24   Heilman and colleagues (1992) found that "affirmative action hirees" were perceived as _____ by
b   persons reviewing their applications than applicants not identified in this manner.
LO 5   a. more competent
Study   b. less competent
199   c. more desirable
M   d. less desirable

6.25   Tokenism is damaging because
a   a. it gives an excuse for bigoted people to deny prejudice
LO 5   b. only unqualified people are promoted
Concept   c. general job performance by victims suffers
200   d. the gains are only superficial, not financial
M

6.26   People who engage in tokenism seem to be saying
d   a. "can't you see how I hate these people"
LO 5   b. "see how little I'm willing to do for these people"
Applied   c. "these people are willing to accept anything"
200   d. "don't bother me, haven't I done enough for these people already"
M

6.27   Lisa was hired at a manufacturing firm over some individuals who seemed to be more qualified.
a   Later in the first week, Lisa found out that the firm had hired her because she was female, and that
LO 5   she was the "token" female. At first, Lisa was very upset about this, but later she started thinking
Applied   about her ability to secure another job. This situation is an illustration of the effect of tokenism on
200   a. the self-esteem of the token
M   b. the functionality of prejudice
                  c. the emotionality of the token
                  d. the cognition of the token

6.28   Treating members of a group favorably based on their membership in the group is called
b   a. tokenism
LO 5   b. reverse discrimination
Fact   c. inverse discrimination
200   d. prejudice
E

6.29   Persons who show reverse discrimination
a   a. harbor at least residual prejudice
LO 5   b. have no trace of prejudice
Concept   c. have nothing to hide
200   d. are fully aware of what they are doing
M

6.30   Minority persons or women who are objects of reverse discrimination
c   a. gain nothing
LO 5   b. often suffer stress-related physical illness
Concept   c. may be hurt in the long run
200   d. are unaffected by reverse discrimination
M

6.31   If a teacher grades a minority child more leniently than other children (Fajardo, 1985)
c   a. the minority child will surely succeed
LO 5   b. the other children will surely do more poorly as a result
Concept   c. the minority child may show inflated opinions of his/her skills
200   d. both kinds of children will benefit
M

6.32
d
LO 5
Concept
200
M

One problem with reverse discrimination is that
a. exposure to people who do not discriminate may seem like prejudice
b. reverse discrimination leads to low self-esteem on the part of those who are discriminating
c. reverse discrimination is usually too obvious to be useful
d. reverse discrimination can lead to a false sense of ability that is later shattered

6.33
b
LO 5
Study
201
C

Martin and Parker (1995) asked young persons to indicate the extent to which differences between various social groups stem from various sources, and found that these individuals reported
a. views that were shallow, naive, and lacking sophistication concerning obvious prejudice
b. views that were sophisticated and relatively free from obvious prejudice
c. views that were sophisticated, yet subtle in maintaining high levels of prejudice
d. views that indicated that obvious prejudice was still a part of their everyday life

6.34
b
LO 6
Fact
202
E

The explanation of prejudice that says that prejudice arises from competition for scare resources is known as
a. natural selection
b. realistic conflict
c. evolutionary discrimination
d. evolved discrimination

6.35
a
LO 6
Fact
202
E

Realistic conflict theory suggests that
a. prejudice is the result of competition for resources
b. prejudice is the result of evolved discrimination
c. prejudice is the result of outgroup homogenization
d. prejudice is the result of chance

6.36
b
LO 6
Fact
202
E

Realistic conflict theory
a. fails to explain prejudice
b. refers to competition over valued commodities
c. is in fact unrealistic
d. refers to discrimination but not to prejudice

6.37
c
LO 6
Study
202
M

Studies that suggest that persistent competition leads to negative portrayals of competitors is evidence for
a. natural selection
b. evolutionary discrimination
c. realistic conflict theory
d. equity theory

6.38
c
LO 6
Study
203
M

The Robber's Cave experiment (Sherif et al., 1961) provided evidence that
a. there is a natural tendency toward prejudice
b. there is a natural tendency away from prejudice
c. conflict leads to prejudice
d. resources tend to be scarce

6.39
d
LO 6
Concept
203
M

Increasing the amount of conflict between groups prejudiced against one another
a. increases communication
b. decreases prejudice
c. has no effect on prejudice
d. increases prejudice

6.40   Sherif et al. (1961) managed to reduce prejudice among his summer campers by
d   a. separating them
LO 6   b. bringing them into conflict
Study   c. bringing them into contact
203   d. setting up superordinate goals
M

6.41   Ralph and Lisa car-pool to work to save money and reduce pollution. This cooperation is an
c   example of a
LO 6   a. selection mechanism
Applied   b. thrift mechanism
203   c. superordinate goal
M   .   d. compunction

6.42   What were some of the activities that got the conflicting groups together in the Robber's Cave
c   experiment
LO 6   a. building an outdoor movie theater
Study   b. waxing the new camp truck
203   c. jointly restoring the water supply
M   d. taking turns helping an injured boy get around camp

6.43   What were some of the problems of the Robber's Cave experiment?
d   a. half of the boys were white and half were black
LO 6   b. the study took one year
Study   c. the camp had too much of a DisneyLand atmosphere
203   d. the study took place over a short period of time
M

6.44   The research of Hovland and Sears (1940) concerning lynchings and economic conditions was based
b   upon the
LO 7   a. displaced aggression hypothesis
Study   b. frustration-aggression hypothesis
204   c. racial aggression hypothesis
M   d. economic-aggression hypothesis

6.45   The frustration-aggression hypothesis suggests that
a   a. aggression is the result of frustration
LO 7   b. frustration is the result of aggression
Concept   c. frustration and aggression have an impact on economic difficulties
204   d. aggression and frustration have an impact on racial economics
M

6.46   The result of the inability of farmers to act against the economic conditions causing their
c   frustration led to
LO 7   a. aggressive frustration
Concept   b. aggressive competition
204   c. displaced aggression
M   d. displaced frustration

6.47   The results of the Hovland and Sears (1940) study on the relationship between lynchings and
b   economic conditions in the South indicated
LO 7   a. a positive correlation between lynchings and economic conditions
Study   b. a negative correlation between lynchings and economic conditions
205   c. a neutral correlation between lynchings and economic conditions
C   d. a illusory correlation between lynchings and economic conditions

6.48
a
LO 7
Concept
204
C

Recent interpretation of the results of the Hovland and Sears (1940) study on the relationship between economic conditions and lynchings would emphasize _____ rather than _____.
a. increased prejudice, displaced aggression
b. increased aggression, displaced prejudice
c. increased aggression, increased prejudice
d. increased prejudice, increased aggression

6.49
c
LO 7
Concept
205
M

The Hovland and Sears (1940) study showed that important social problems can be investigated through the use of
a. investigative reporting
b. hypothesis generation
c. archival data
d. sophisticated research methods

6.50
c
LO 8
Concept
205
M

According to the social learning view of prejudice
a. prejudice is a byproduct of the survival instinct
b. people divide up the world into categories to reduce cognitive effort
c. children learn prejudice from parents and peers
d. prejudice results from lack of contact

6.51
a
LO 8
Concept
205
M

According to the social learning view of prejudice, children continue to express prejudice because
a. they are directly rewarded for doing so
b. those who do not generally lose resources
c. of the driving force of compunction
d. children remember what they learn at an early age

6.52
c
LO 8
Fact
205
E

The view that children pick up prejudices from their parents and peers because they are rewarded for expressing them is called
a. tokenism
b. compunction
c. social learning
d. compulsion

6.53
b
LO 8
Applied
205
M

Lisa is washing the dishes and asks her brother to help by drying them. Her brother says that dishes are women's work, which makes their father smile. Her brother sees the smile and walks away. This scenario is an example of a prejudice from
a. compunction
b. social learning
c. social assimilation
d. social discrimination

6.54
b
LO 8
Concept
205
E

Rules that suggest what actions are or are not appropriate in a given group are called
a. social compunctions
b. social norms
c. social tokens
d. social attributions

6.55
c
LO 8
Concept
206
M

How is the media implicated in the teaching of prejudice?
a. minorities appear as role models in the media
b. minorities appear unrealistically often in the media
c. minorities appear in low-status and comic roles in the media
d. minorities appear in unrealistically high status roles in the media

6.56
b
LO 8
Study
207
C

Weigel and colleagues (1995) found that the appearance of African Americans in TV programming had ____ significantly between 1978 and 1989, and the cross-racial interactions were ____ than within-race interactions.
a. increased, more intense
b. increased, less intense
c. decreased, more intense
d. decreased, less intense

6.57
b
LO 9
Fact
207
E

The process of dividing the world into distinct groups is known as
a. prejudice
b. social categorization
c. tokenism
d. compunction

6.58
b
LO 9
Fact
207
E

Race, religion, occupation, and income level are examples of
a. tokens
b. social categories
c. conflict categories
d. homogeneities

6.59
c
LO 9
Concept
207
M

Ingroups and outgroups are terms associated with
a. tokenism
b. compunction
c. social categorization
d. superordination

6.60
a
LO 9
Concept
207
M

In the "us vs. them" orientation
a. "us" are viewed in highly favorable terms
b. "us" and "them" are seen as complementary rather than antagonistic
c. "us" and "them" are seen as merely dissimilar not antagonistic
d. "them" are viewed in neutral terms

6.61
a
LO 9
Concept
207
M

The relation of social categorization to prejudice is that
a. the ingroup is viewed in positive terms while the outgroup is viewed in negative terms
b. the outgroup is viewed in positive terms while the ingroup is viewed in negative terms
c. the ingroup and outgroup compete for scarce resources
d. the ingroup will allow a few members of the outgroup in as tokens

6.62
c
LO 9
Concept
207
M

In social categorization, we are more likely to take account of external circumstances for members of the
a. selected group
b. ignored group
c. ingroup
d. outgroup

6.63
b
LO 9
Concept
207
M

A suggested reason for the existence of social categorization is that
a. groups survive if they develop competitive instincts
b. people enhance their self-esteem by identifying with particular groups
c. people enhance their processing capacity by identifying with particular groups
d. social categorization helps people recognize other people

6.64 d LO 9 Concept 207 M	Identification with a particular group enhances self-esteem to the extent that one can a. gather more resources b. display more token "outsiders" c. enhance one's compunction d. view one's own group as superior
6.65 a LO 9 Study 207 C	According to Tajfel and colleagues (1982) a. membership in a social group can serve to enhance an individual's self-esteem b. membership in a given social group is evaluated absolutely, not relative to other social groups c. different groups avoid competition that might indicate one group is superior to the other d. different groups move in the direction of integration, collapsing into one group
6.66 d LO 9 Fact 207 C	The tendency to make more favorable and flattering attributions about members of one's own group is called a. illusory attribution error b. facilitory attribution error c. positive attribution error d. ultimate attribution error
6.67 b LO 10 Concept 208 M	The existence of stereotypes demonstrates that prejudice has a. been spread by the media sources b. cognitive as well as affective sources c. always existed, and always will d. an affective rather than cognitive basis
6.68 a LO 10 Fact 208 M	A stereotype is a. a cognitive framework consisting of knowledge and belief about specific social groups b. a pattern of action that shows discrimination c. the assumption that your group is superior to others d. a pattern of prejudices that shows discrimination
6.69 c LO 10 Fact 208 M	A generalization of perceived typical or modal characteristics of a particular social group to all members of that group is called a. schema b. outgroup prejudice c. stereotype d. trait assumption
6.70 b LO 10 Concept 209 M	Stereotypes foster prejudice because a. resource competition leads people to discriminate against others b. information that is inconsistent with the stereotype is harder to retain c. stereotypes encourage discrimination d. stereotypes encourage tokenism
6.71 d LO 10 Concept 209 M	Activation of stereotypes is a. largely automatic b. dependent upon the personality of the individual c. dependent upon the degree of compulsion separation d. dependent upon the available cognitive resources

6.72
b
LO 10
Concept
209
M

What does a stereotype do to those individuals who possess one?
a. it makes them more positively inclined to minorities and women
b. it makes them notice only information consistent with the stereotype
c. it makes them avoid any kind of information about minorities and women
d. it makes them more egalitarian

6.73
a
LO 10
Concept
209
M

Stereotypes tend to be
a. self-confirming
b. self-contradictory
c. self-effacing
d. self-obligating

6.74
b
LO 11
Study
210
M

Jussim and colleagues (1995) asked participants to indicate feelings and beliefs about rock musicians and child abusers. The results of this study indicated
a. that rock musicians were comparable to child abusers
b. that rock musicians were rated higher than child abusers
c. that rock musicians were rated lower than child abusers
d. that rock musicians were rated neutral, and child abusers were rated negatively

6.75
d
LO 11
Study
210
C

Jussim and colleagues (1995) statistically held feelings constant when they were comparing ratings to rock musicians and child abusers. Why did they do so?
a. there was to much variation in the feelings scores to give accurate information
b. if stereotypes were to operate, feelings had to be constant so cognitions could vary
c. if stereotypes had influence through cognitions, feelings could not interfere with the measurements
d. if stereotypes operated through feelings, holding feelings constant would reduce the impact of the stereotype

6.76
d
LO 11
Study
210
M

The results of Jussim and colleagues (1995) indicate that stereotypes operate
a. more through cognitions than feelings
b. more through cognitions than attributions
c. more through feelings than cognitions
d. more through feelings than attributions

6.77
a
LO 11
Study
210
C

Jussim had participants rate homosexuals and heterosexuals and then held feelings constant in the overall analysis. The results indicated that _____, indicating that stereotypes operate through _____.
a. stereotypes disappear, feelings
b. stereotypes disappear, cognitions
c. stereotypes activated, feelings
d. stereotypes activated, cognitions

6.78
b
LO 12
Study
211
C

Bodenhausen and colleagues (1994) found that putting participants in a good mood when they were making evaluations for disciplinary hearings for students
a. decreased the use of stereotypes
b. increased the use of stereotypes
c. had no effect on the use of stereotypes
d. modified the content of the stereotype

6.79
b
LO 12
Study
211
C

Bodenhausen and colleagues (1994) had undergraduates evaluate disciplinary hearings and assign guilt ratings. The results indicated that putting participants in a good mood activated stereotypes, which resulted in
a. decreased guilt ratings
b. increased guilt ratings
c. neutral guilt ratings
d. no difference between good mood and neutral mood groups in guilt ratings

6.80
c
LO 12
Study
211
C

The results of the Bodenhausen and colleague (1994) study indicated that being in a good mood activated a stereotype, which in turn resulted in higher guilt ratings. Bodenhausen et al. suggest that the results are due to
a. the inability of the participants to engage in hard cognitive work
b. the inability of the participants to engage in hard emotional work
c. the lack of motivation of the participants to engage in hard cognitive work
d. the lack of motivation of the participants to engage in hard emotional work

6.81
d
LO 12
Concept
211
M

Being in a good mood does not reduce our _____, but reduces our _____.
a. motivation to do hard cognitive work, incentive for doing hard cognitive work
b. incentive to do hard cognitive work, motivation for doing hard cognitive work
c. motivation to do hard cognitive work, capacity for doing hard cognitive work
d. capacity to do hard cognitive work, motivation for doing hard cognitive work

6.82
a
LO 13
Fact
212
E

An illusory correlation is
a. the tendency to perceive a stronger relationship between two variables than actually exists
b. a stereotype about illusory groups
c. a stereotype about artificial groups
d. a stereotype about random outgroups

6.83
a
LO 13
Applied
212
M

If 10% of Group A (200 members) are found to be criminals, and 10% of Group B (10,000 members) are found to be criminals, evidence suggests that you will form less favorable impressions of
a. Group A
b. Group B
c. you will have a equally unfavorable impression of both groups
d. you will form illusory correlations linking the two groups

6.84
c
LO 13
Concept
212
M

When two or more relatively infrequent events occur together, we tend to perceive
a. that the two events happen more often than they actually do
b. that the two events happen less often than they actually do
c. that the two events are linked in some way
d. that the more important event is cause by the less important event

6.85
b
LO 13
Concept
212
M

Illusory correlations lead people to perceive a _____ link between crime and race.
a. lower than actual
b. higher than actual
c. relatively accurate
d. moderately modifiable

6.86
c
LO 13
Concept
212
M

Which statement reflects illusory correlations?
a. r = .99
b. "White persons are more likely to commit crimes."
c. rare events are seen as correlated
d. r = .00

6.87   The idea that infrequent events are readily noticed and then encoded more extensively in memory
a   is the foundation for
LO 13   a. the distinctiveness-based interpretation of illusory correlations
Concept   b. the overestimate-based interpretation of illusory correlations
213   c. the stereotype-based interpretation of illusory correlations
C   d. the attribution-based interpretation of illusory correlations

6.88   A modification of the distinctiveness-based interpretation of illusory correlations indicates that
d   a. information has to be distinctive when first encountered
LO 13   b. information has to be familiar when first encountered
Concept   c. information does not have to be familiar when first encountered, but must become distinctive
213   at a later time
C   d. information does not have to be distinctive when first encountered, but must become distinctive
                at a later time

6.89   The phrase "outgroup homogeneity" refers to
c   a. the perception that people who leave your group are somehow inferior
LO 14   b. the perception that people who leave your group are somehow different
Concept   c. the perception that members of a group not your own are relatively similar to one another
213   d. the perception that members of a group not your own are similar to your group
M

6.90   The perception that members of one's own group are much more varied than any other group is
d   called the
LO 14   a. ingroup homogeneity hypothesis
Concept   b. alternates matching hypothesis
213   c. outgroup homogeneity hypothesis
M   d. ingroup homogeneity hypothesis

6.91   The phrase "You can't trust anyone over thirty" is an example of the
b   a. illusory correlations theory
LO 13   b. illusion of outgroup homogeneity
Applied   c. illusion of outgroup differentiation
213   d. illusion of mistrust
E

6.92   Ralph realizes that some fraternities are prone to invite in only certain types of people, but is proud
a   of what he considers to be his fraternity's diversity. This situation is an example of the
LO 14   a. ingroup differentiation hypothesis
Applied   b. prejudice against similar groups
213   c. outgroup homogeneity effect
M   d. illusory correlations effect

6.93   An example of the cross-racial facial identification effect occurs when
c   a. members of one race only invite selected people from another race to join them
LO 14   b. members of one race think that they are more cohesive than members of other races
Concept   c. members of one race have low accuracy in recognizing strangers from another race when
213   compared to their accuracy in recognizing strangers from their own race
M   d. members of one race exclude members of another race from an activity

6.94   Research by Lee and Ottati (1993) found that both Americans and Chinese perceive _____ among
d   _____.
LO 15   a. moderate heterogeneity, Americans
Study   b. less heterogeneity, Americans
214   c. greater heterogeneity, Chinese
M   d. greater heterogeneity, Americans

6.95
b
LO 15
Study
214
M

The _____ Chinese participants had with Americans, the _____ the tendency to rate Americans as heterogeneous.
a. less contact, stronger
b. greater contact, stronger
c. less contact, weaker
d. greater contact, weaker

6.96
c
LO 15
Study
214
M

When American participants had greater contact with Chinese
a. the tendency to rate Chinese as heterogeneous increased
b. the tendency to rate Chinese as heterogeneous decreased
c. the tendency to rate Chinese as heterogeneous was not increased
d. the tendency to rate Chinese as heterogeneous was not decreased

6.97
b
LO 15
Study
214
M

The more Americans reported positive evaluations of Chinese people, _____ the Americans perceived for these people.
a. the less the degree of heterogeneity
b. the greater the degree of heterogeneity
c. the less the degree of homogeneity
d. the greater the degree of homogeneity

6.98
a
LO 16
Concept
216
E

The majority of evidence suggests that prejudice is
a. learned
b. innate
c. learned, but only from adult models such as parents
d. learned, but only from peer models such as friends

6.99
d
LO 16
Concept
216
M

One useful technique for reducing prejudice is to
a. allow children to play with one another naturally
b. tell the parents that they are prejudiced in order to change their behavior
c. cognitive intuitive processing
d. discourage child role models from expressing prejudicial beliefs or behaviors

6.100
c
LO 16
Concept
216
M

A difficulty in changing the behavior of children's role models is that
a. it is hard to identify children's role models
b. few role models are easily identified as prejudiced
c. few role models believe that they are prejudiced
d. few role models are the source of prejudice

6.101
c
LO 16
Concept
216
M

Growing evidence shows that prejudice is
a. not found in many people
b. a major force interpersonal interactions
c. harmful to prejudiced people as well as their targets
d. contingent upon the prejudice you receive

6.102
b
LO 16
Concept
216
M

A source of harm for prejudiced people is
a. loss of perceived credibility
b. stress from unrealistic worries about the perceived ill intentions of the outgroup
c. relative isolation that they experience
d. creation of inaccurate stereotypes

6.103
a
LO 16
Concept
216
C

A motivating factor for people to try and reduce their prejudice is that
a. prejudice is harmful to prejudiced people as well as their victims
b. the consequences of prejudice are harmful to society
c. prejudiced people provide bad role models for their children
d. the victims of prejudice are harmed

6.104
d
LO 17
Concept
217
M

The contact hypothesis suggests that
a. social contact between groups is rare
b. contact between groups is common
c. as contact between groups increases, so does prejudice
d. as contact between groups increases, prejudice decreases

6.105
d
LO 17
Concept
217
C

One reason that the contact hypothesis would be expected to work is that
a. increased contact confirms stereotypes about the outgroup through selective processing
b. decreased contact could counter the illusion of outgroup homogeneity
c. increased contact decreases the stress of novel situations
d. increased contact could counter the illusion of outgroup homogeneity

6.106
b
LO 17
Concept
217
M

The idea that large amounts of disconfirming evidence will alter a stereotype supports the
a. illusion of outgroup homogeneity
b. contact hypothesis
c. ingroup differentiation hypothesis
d. Markus-Bem schema theory

6.107
d
LO 17
Concept
217
C

Which of the following is NOT supportive of the contact hypothesis?
a. the idea that large amounts of disconfirming evidence alters stereotypes
b. increased contact can counter the illusion of outgroup homogeneity
c. increased contact leads to increased perceptions of similarity
d. decreased contact can counter the illusion of outgroup homogeneity

6.108
a
LO 17
Concept
217
M

Evidence has been found in favor of the contact hypothesis, but the interacting groups must
a. be similar in social, economic, or task-related status
b. initiate contact themselves
c. have some prior desire to meet each other
d. show some prior desire to reduce prejudice

6.109
a
LO 17
Concept
217
C

The contact hypothesis becomes much more effective if
a. the interacting groups have to cooperate
b. the interacting groups do not have a history of mutual prejudice
c. group members act cohesively
d. group members have respect for the members of the other group

6.110
d
LO 17
Concept
217
C

The contact hypothesis becomes much more effective if
a. the interacting groups do not have a history of mutual prejudice
b. the interacting groups have a history of mutual prejudice
c. group members act cohesively
d. contact is informal and individual

6.111
a
LO 17
Concept
217
M

Which of the following conditions increases the value of intergroup contact in reducing prejudice?
a. the norms of the interaction event must favor equality
b. the groups must have high internal cohesion
c. the groups must be of differing status
d. the groups should not display the ingroup differentiation effect

6.112
d
LO 17
Applied
217
M

If Ralph is prejudice against Hispanics, but is placed in a job situation where he has to work with Hispanics, you would expect Ralph to show
a. more prejudice immediately
b. more prejudice over time
c. less prejudice immediately
d. less prejudice over time

6.113
a
LO 18
Fact
218
M

The process of shifting group boundaries under certain situations is known as
a. recategorization
b. the flexibility principle
c. essential fluidity
d. social definition

6.114
b
LO 18
Fact
218
M

Recategorization is
a. placing people who were "us" into the "them" category
b. shifting from regarding certain people as "them" to regarding these people as "us"
c. declaring oneself no longer a member of the bigoted category
d. shifting oneself from the "us" to the "them" category

6.115
b
LO 18
Concept
218
C

The common ingroup identity model is described as
a. when individuals from different social groups interact, they identify with their particular group
b. when individuals from different social groups come to view themselves as a single social identity, their views toward each other become more positive
c. when individuals from the same social group come to view themselves as a single social identity, their views toward each other become more positive
d. when individuals form different social groups come to view themselves as a single social identity, their group self-esteem is enhanced

6.116
d
LO 18
Concept
218
M

Research suggests that when people view themselves as members of a group rather than as individuals
a. general levels of prejudice are decreased
b. "us" and "them" boundaries become more fluid
c. within group cooperation is decreased
d. increased positive contacts are facilitated

6.117
b
LO 18
Concept
219
M

Weakening "us-them" boundaries leads to
a. decreased cooperation
b. reduced prejudice
c. lower self-concepts
d. fluctuating boundaries

6.118   Gaertner and colleagues (1993), in conducting a study on a multicultural high school in the United
a   States, found that
LO 18   a. the more cooperative interactions with individuals from other groups, the weaker the "us-them"
Study   boundaries
219   b. the more interaction with individuals from other groups, the stronger the "us-them" boundaries
C   c. the more interactions with members of the same group, the stronger the "us-them" boundaries
          d. the longer lasting the individual interactions with individuals from other groups, the weaker the
              "us-them" boundaries

6.119   The tendency to think of others in terms of their group membership is an example of
b   a. individualistic thinking
LO 19   b. category-driven processing
Fact   c. attribute-driven processing
219   d. a selfish schema
E

6.120   Stereotyping is a form of
d   a. stress avoidance
LO 19   b. ingroup differentiation
Fact   c. attribute-driven processing
219   d. category-driven processing
E

6.121   One way to reduce the impact of stereotypes is to
c   a. attack the validity of prejudiced role models for children
LO 19   b. encourage more efficient schematic processing
Concept   c. encourage people to think carefully about people
219   d. encourage category-driven processing
M

6.122   Conditions that tip the balance toward attribute-driven processing rather than category-driven
a   processing include which of the following?
LO 19   a. creating conditions that make an individual's fate dependent on a stranger's performance
Concept   b. forcing individuals to pay attention to others' ethnic and/or racial background when making
219   decisions about them
C   c. relaxing the accuracy standards that individuals invoke when attempting to assess strangers
          d. using distractors so that individuals are caused not to focus on the personal attributes of a
              stranger they are trying to assess

6.123   Ralph would have told you that women could not do math problems, until $30.00 was offered for
c   the most accurate guess at how well a sample of women would do on a set of math problems.
LO 19   Ralph did not make use of a stereotype because
Applied   a. the evidence was overwhelming in the other direction
219   b. the reward induced him to use category-driven processing instead
C   c. there was a reason to think carefully about the individual women
          d. efficient schematic processing was necessary

6.124   Inferences based on outcomes are inferences about characteristics that are
d   a. based on your own actions
LO 19   b. based on the actions of others
Concept   c. based on your perceptions about the actions of others
219   d. based on the result of an action, rather than the action itself
M

6.125
c
LO 19
Concept
220
M

Inferences based on outcomes may lead to a weakening of stereotypes if
a. people use outcome-based inferences enough
b. the actions run counter to a prevailing stereotype
c. the action outcomes run counter to a prevailing stereotype
d. the actions reduce organized schematic processing

6.126
b
LO 19
Concept
220
M

Affirmative action programs may decrease stereotypes about disadvantaged groups because they
a. give disadvantaged adults good role models
b. improve the action outcomes for that group
c. increase the quality of role models from disadvantaged groups for disadvantaged children of the next generation
d. are effective in making people feel that they are contributing members of society

6.127
a
LO 20
Concept
220
C

The rebound effect in the operation of stereotypes indicates that
a. thought suppression of a stereotype may work temporarily, but the stereotypes come back much stronger at a later date
b. thought suppression of a stereotype may work temporarily, but when the stereotype is purposely activated, it comes back at a stronger level
c. stereotypes operate at many different levels, going from strong to weak to strong
d. thought suppression works with the cognitive component of a stereotype, but then it comes back stronger as an emotion

6.128
b
LO 20
Study
221
C

In a study to investigate the effect of thought suppression on later stereotypes, Macrae and colleagues (1994) found that
a. thought suppression was effective in eliminating the stereotypic thinking
b. thought suppression decreased stereotypic thinking for the first evaluation, and also decreased stereotypic thinking for the second evaluation
c. thought suppression decreased stereotypic thinking for the first evaluation, but in the second evaluation stereotypic thinking returned at a higher level
d. thought suppression did not decrease stereotypic thinking in the first evaluation, but did decrease stereotypic thinking in the second evaluation

6.129
b
LO 20
Study
222
M

Macrae and colleagues (1994), in a study of the effects of thought suppression on stereotypes and behavior, found that participants who were instructed to use thought suppression
a. sat closer to the clothing of a skinhead when given the opportunity
b. sat farther away to the clothing of a skinhead when given the opportunity
c. selected a seat directly opposite the clothing of a skinhead when given the opportunity
d. selected a seat directly in back of the clothing of a skinhead when given the opportunity

6.130
c
LO 20
Study
222
C

The implications from the research of Macrae and colleagues (1994) are
a. active efforts to suppress stereotypic thinking is an effective tactic
b. active efforts to suppress stereotypic thinking leads to cognitive overload and increased stereotypic thinking
c. active efforts to suppress stereotypic thinking may sometimes backfire and lead to increased stereotypic thinking
d. active efforts to suppress stereotypic thinking is not an effective tactic since suppression cannot be done

6.131
d
LO 21
Fact
223
E

In many cultures, the traits of decisiveness, confidence, and ambition are seen as most representative of
a. adults
b. females
c. children
d. males

6.132   Available evidence suggests that
d   a. the majority of stereotypes are based on sex, not gender
LO 21   b. many stereotypes have a "kernel of truth" at their base
Study   c. stereotypes are not used when one has enough available attention for fully processing an
223   individual's characteristics
M   d. stereotypes vastly overstate the number and size of male-female differences

6.133   In many countries, legal discrimination against women has been replaced by
d   a. overt discrimination
LO 21   b. official discrimination
Concept   c. institutional discrimination
224   d. subtle discrimination
M

6.134   Research suggests that women are at a disadvantage in job situations by
b   a. not having suitable traits
LO 21   b. having lower career expectations
Concept   c. having high affiliative needs
224   d. not being able to act aggressively
M

6.135   Why do women hold lower job expectations?
c   a. males decide that certain fields of study have the most value to them, regardless of how valuable
LO 21   the fields are in the real world
Concept   b. the sexes interpret such status phrases as "price of one's auto" very differently
224   c. females place less emphasis on work and monetary outcomes than do males
M   d. females base their judgments on value of facts, but males base their judgments on experience

6.136   In at least some situations, females are _____ than men, and this difference is noticed, which
a   contributes to the fact that women have not achieved equality with men in the work setting.
LO 21   a. less confident
Concept   b. more aggressive
224   c. less reliant
E   d. prone to absence

6.137   In studies that ask males and females to estimate their starting and peak salaries, it has been found
d   that
LO 21   a. males and females didn't differ in estimates of their starting salaries
Concept   b. males and females didn't differ in their ratings of the importance of starting salaries
224   c. males expected that others would have lower starting salaries than themselves
M   d. females expected starting and peak salaries to be lower than did males

6.138   Studies have indicated that leadership by females is often viewed with negative affect because it
c   a. is viewed as luck
LO 22   b. is unpopular within role behavior
Concept   c. contradicts popular gender stereotypes
225   d. is opposed by many females as well as males
M

6.139   Even though subordinates say basically the same thing to male and female leaders, they demonstrate
b   more negative
LO 22   a. nonverbal behaviors toward females
Concept   b. nonverbal behaviors toward males
225   c. stereotypes toward females
M   d. stereotypes toward males

6.140
d
LO 22
Study
225
M

Butler and Geis (1990) found that when males evaluated female leaders who adopted stereotypically masculine leadership styles, the males
a. rated the females as significantly higher in leadership skills
b. rated the females as significantly more emotional in leadership skills
c. rated the females as significantly more cognitive in leadership skills
d. rated the females as significantly lower in leadership skills

6.141
c
LO 22
Concept
225
M

Barriers based on attitudinal or organizational bias that prevent qualified females from advancing to top-level positions illustrate the
a. glass barrier effect
b. glass door effect
c. glass ceiling effect
d. glass wall effect

6.142
a
LO 23
Study
226
M

Van Velsor and Hughes (1990) found that women
a. had as many career developmental opportunities than men
b. had fewer career developmental opportunities than men
c. had more career developmental opportunities than men
d. had significantly fewer career developmental opportunities than men

6.143
a
LO 23
Study
226
M

Van Velsor and Hughes (1990) found that women, in contrast to men
a. had fewer career developmental opportunities that involved visibility and responsibility
b. had more career developmental opportunities that involved visibility and responsibility
c. had more career developmental opportunities that involved job transitions
d. had fewer career developmental opportunities in which they encountered obstacles

6.144
b
LO 23
Study
226
M

Van Velsor and Hughes (1990) found that women, in contrast to men
a. reported encountering fewer obstacles in their job
b. reported encountering more obstacles in their job
c. reported encountering fewer developmental opportunities
d. reported encountering more developmental opportunities

6.145
d
LO 23
Concept
226
M

The glass ceiling is considered to be
a. an obvious barrier to male-female achievement
b. an obvious barrier to female achievement
c. a subtle barrier to male-female achievement
d. a subtle barrier to female achievement

6.146
b
LO 24
Fact
226
E

Unwelcome sexual advances, requests for sexual favors, and other verbal or physical conduct of a sexual nature defines
a. sexual aggression
b. sexual harassment
c. sexual intent
d. sexual assertiveness

6.147
a
LO 24
Concept
227
M

Sexual harassment is not limited to the behaviors experienced by Teresa Harris, but include any actions that create
a. a hostile environment
b. an embarrassing environment
c. an assertive environment
d. a sexual environment

6.148   In one study of sexual harassment in the workplace, it was found that ____ of employed women
c   indicated being a victim of at least one incidence of sexual harassment, while ____ of employed
LO 24   men indicated being a victim of such behavior.
Study   a. 50%, 50%
227   b. 73%, 7%
M   c. 31%, 7%
         d. 92%, 12%

6.149   Sexual harassment can be viewed primarily as discrimination against women because
d   a. the definition of harassment is in terms of women
LO 24   b. women first brought the concept of sexual harassment to the public eye
Concept c. women also can harass women
227   d. women are more frequently the victims
M

6.150   Which of the following is NOT one of the steps or policies suggested by Bohren (1993) to reduce the
c   incidence of sexual harassment in the workplace?
LO 24   a. keep the workplace free of sexually offensive materials
Study   b. develop a clear policy prohibiting sexual harassment
228   c. consider the individual supervisor-subordinate situation when defining sexual harassment
M   d. set up clear grievance procedures with respect to sexual harassment

6.151   The stereotype of the "elderly" is
a   a. largely negative
LO 25   b. largely positive
Fact   c. largely neutral
228   d. largely immaterial
E

6.152   The implication by the research of Levy and Langer (1994) is that stereotypes can influence physical
c   well-being through
LO 25   a. emotional commitments
Study   b. attitudinal commitments
228   c. cognitive commitments
M   d. behavioral commitments

6.153   According to ____, if the prevailing stereotype is that older people will show a decline in cognitive
d   abilities, the older peopleprobably will show the decline.
LO 25   a. emotional commitments
Concept b. attitudinal commitments
228   c. behavioral commitments
M   d. cognitive commitments

6.154   Levy and Langer (1994) found that the worst memory performance was among ____, which has a
c   ____ of aging.
LO 25   a. Chinese, negative stereotype
Study   b. Chinese, positive stereotype
228   c. American, negative stereotype
M   d. American, positive stereotype

6.155   The results of the 1994 study by Levy and Langer suggest the ____ impact of stereotypes.
a   a. self-confirming
LO 25   b. self-enhancing
Study   c. self-assessing
228   d. self-facilitating
M

CHAPTER 7

Learning Objectives

After studying this chapter, students should be able to:

1. Examine the relationship between repeated exposure and interpersonal attraction, including subliminal repeated exposure.

2. Describe how propinquity affects: a) friendship formation in dormitories and in other residential environments; b) who one marries.

3. Explain the advantage of manipulating proximity to determine its effects on attraction, and describe what studies have found regarding seating patterns and friendship formation in classrooms.

4. Summarize research demonstrating that when a person does something arousing positive or negative affect, he or she is liked or disliked accordingly.

5. Summarize research demonstrating that when a person is simply a. ociated with positive or negative affect, he or she is liked or disliked accordingly.

6. Explain how the affect-centered model of attraction accounts for the central role played by affective responses in determining who is liked and who is disliked.

7. Summarize research that describes our affective reaction to a stigmatized person and also our reaction to someone simply associated with a stigmatized person.

8. Describe the need for affiliation as a trait, comparing explicit and implicit affiliation needs, and be familiar with Hill's four motives underlying affiliation.

9. Give examples of situations that produce an affiliation need in us.

10. Understand the three basic hypotheses derived from Festinger's social comparison theory.

11. Describe how physical attractiveness is related to the following: a) perceived desirability as a date; b) reproductive success; c) stereotyping; d) reactions to and by infants; e) appearance anxiety; and f) attribution of negative attributes.

12. Explain how Cunningham (1986) determined that males like "childlike" and "mature" features. How did Langlois and Roggman (1990) determine that people like "average" faces?

13. Describe the "contrast effect" in physical attractiveness ratings, along with the effects of knowing others' ratings and the effects of closing time.

14. Examine stereotypes that exist for endomorphs, mesomorphs, and ectomorphs.

15. Examine the negative stereotypes that are found for overweight persons, and indicate how people are affected by these stereotypes.

16. Explain how perceptions of people are influenced by the following: a) youthful-appearing adult; b) behavioral cues; c) male dominance vs. sensitivity; d) food habits; e) wearing glasses; f) first names.

17. Describe research findings supporting the hypothesis that similar attitudes lead to attraction. Compare this hypothesis to the alternate notion that initial attraction is followed by later similarity.

18. Understand the fact that the basis of the similarity-attraction effect seems to be the proportion of similar attitudes expressed, regardless of total number of topics.

19.   *Explain the role of similar vs. dissimilar attitudes in creating the similarity-attraction effect, according to Rosenbaum's repulsion hypothesis. Describe the basis for rejecting the repulsion hypothesis.*

20.   *Examine the false consensus effect, and indicate its relationship to Rosenbaum's repulsion hypothesis.*

21.   *Describe how each of the following explains the similarity-attraction effect: a) balance theory; b) social comparison theory; and c) Rushton's evolution-based genetic explanation.*

22.   *Give examples of various dimensions on which people are attracted to matched partners, and indicate how we respond to obvious mismatches in physical attractiveness.*

23.   *Describe how our behavior toward an individual is affected by the receipt of a positive evaluation from him/her.*

24.   *Describe whether the usual linear relationship between similarity and attraction was found in all five of the cultures studied. Exlain how students in Japan and Texas were different from those in Hawaii, India, and Mexico.*

Questions

7.1   How much we like or dislike another person describes
b   a. interpersonal attitudes
LO 1   b. interpersonal attraction
Fact   c. interpersonal conflict
234   d. interpersonal evaluation
E

7.2   Proximity refers to
b   a. the psychological distance between two individuals
LO 1   b. the physical distance between two individuals
Fact   c. the distance two individuals are willing to stand apart in public
234   d. the distance each individual uses to separate himself or herself from others
M

7.3   Propinquity refers to
a   a. the fact that physical proximity is a determining factor in making acquaintances
LO 1   b. the driving factor in proximation theory
Concept   c. the driving factor in romantic attraction
236   d. the theory that physical proximity to an individual leads to dislike ("too much of a good thing")
M

7.4   Infants are more likely to smile at a picture of
c   a. someone who shares specific features with them, such as eye color
LO 1   b. a composite individual
Concept   c. someone they have seen before
236   d. someone who is genetically related to them
M

7.5   The theory of repeated exposure (Zajonc, 1968) suggests that
c   a. repeated exposure to a neutral object leads to re-evaluation of the object
LO 1   b. repeated exposure to a neutral object leads to more neutral feelings toward the object
Concept   c. repeated exposure to a neutral object leads to greater positive feelings toward the object
236   d. repeated exposure to a neutral object leads to decreased positive feelings about the object
M

7.6   Classroom students more favorably evaluated a woman who attended class 15 times over a woman
d   who attended class 5 times. This finding is support for
LO 1   a. numerical effects
Study   b. repeated associations
236   c. repeated affiliations
M   d. repeated exposure

7.7   Repeated exposure can lead to negative exposure if
b   a. propinquity effects are not present
LO 1   b. the stimulus originally evokes negative emotions
Concept   c. the need for affiliation is low
237   d. the repeated exposure occurs randomly
M

7.8
b
LO 1
Applied
237
M

Ralph listened to a new song and did not like it at all. Unfortunately for Ralph, this song was used by a company as its new advertising jingle, and the song was played over and over, so Ralph was repeatedly exposed to the song. You would expect Ralph to
a. increase his liking for the song
b. decrease his liking for the song
c. turn off the radio
d. become neutral in his evaluation of the song

7.9
c
LO 1
Study
237
M

Bornstein and D'Agostino (1992) found that repeated exposure to a stimulus an individual was unaware of led to
a. increased positive ratings of the stimulus
b. decreased positive ratings of the stimulus
c. even stronger increased positive ratings of the stimulus
d. even stronger decreased positive ratings of the stimulus

7.10
b
LO 2
Concept
238
M

Choice of dating partners among undergraduates was in part a function of
a. the age of the dating partners
b. the distance between residences of the dating partners
c. the height of the dating partners
d. the extracurricular interests of the dating partners

7.11
d
LO 2
Study
238
M

Bossard (1932) obtained marriage records for 5000 people in Philadelphia in 1931. Addresses of brides and grooms showed that
a. less than a third previously lived within 20 blocks of each other
b. less than a half previously lived within 20 blocks of each other
c. about half previously lived within 20 blocks of each other
d. more than half lived within 20 blocks of each other

7.12
c
LO 2
Study
238
M

Bossard's results, showing that married couples tended to live relatively near each other prior to marriage are support for the importance of
a. need for affiliation
b. need for association
c. propinquity
d. proximate theory

7.13
a
LO 2
Concept
238
M

One of the difficulties of the studies that look at the marriage patterns of cities (e.g., Bossard, 1932) is that
a. the studies are correlational
b. the studies are using archival data
c. the studies are using restricted age ranges
d. the studies are biased in terms of marriage potential

7.14
b
LO 3
Concept
239
M

What is the most important scientific advantage that dormitory studies of propinquity would have over a study of marriage patterns in cities?
a. college age samples
b. random assignment of subjects to conditions
c. easily gathered data
d. greater control over subjects

7.15
a
LO 3
Applied
239
M

With your knowledge of propinquity, you return to your old high school and discover that many pairs of friends among the students have last names beginning with the same letter. Your best hypothesis is that
a. the principal has instituted an alphabetical seating chart
b. chance encounters must be rare in this high school
c. romantic attachment must be regulated by parents
d. no explanation is possible without additional information

7.16
a
LO 3
Applied
239
M

Lisa was new on campus and wanted to start meeting other students, so she started
a. sitting in the middle of each class
b. sharing her homework with students who were behind in their classes
c. talking as much as possible in class
d. looking for lonely people with whom to converse

7.17
c
LO 3
Concept
239
M

Students assigned to the middle seat of a row are much more likely to become acquainted with
a. the students in front of them
b. the students in back of them
c. the students on both sides of them
d. the students who leave the room when they do

7.18
d
LO 4
Applied
240
M

In the student cafeteria, Ralph finally gets a chance to talk to a female student he has really been wanting to meet. The best opening line for him would be
a. something dominant
b. something submissive
c. something cute or flippant
d. something direct

7.19
a
LO 4
Study
240
M

Kleinke and colleagues (1986) found that the opening line, "Bet I can outdrink you" by males in a bar was
a. least preferred by females
b. most preferred by females
c. least preferred by males
d. most preferred by males

7.20
d
LO 4
Study
240
E

Research in the laboratory by Kleinke and Dean (1990) found that the most positive response was toward a person saying something
a. cute or flippant
b. dominant
c. innocuous
d. simple and direct

7.21
c
LO 4
Study
240
M

Research on opening lines in a bar found that individuals using _____ with an opposite sex stranger were liked most.
a. a cute or flippant opening line
b. an innocuous opening line
c. a direct opening line
d. an assertive opening line

7.22
b
LO 5
Concept
241
M

According to a classical conditioning model of attraction, if you saw a funny film with someone, you would
a. like the film more
b. like the person more
c. think that the person was funny
d. respond to the person as you normally would

7.23
d
LO 5
Concept
241
M

What is the effect of having a subject hear good news just before encountering a stranger?
a. unless the news is specifically about the stranger, it produces no effect
b. hearing good news, by itself, does not affect the stranger's liking
c. the stranger is liked less because he seems negative when contrasted with the good news
d. the stranger is liked more

7.24   Which statement best describes an assumption underlying the relationship of affect arousal and
c   associated liking or disliking of a person?
LO 5   a. when we perform behaviors that affect someone positively, we like that person
Concept   b. when we perform behaviors that affect someone negatively, we dislike that person
241   c. we like people who reward us and dislike people who punish us
C   d. positive or negative feelings, no matter how aroused, become associated with whatever person
               happens to be present

7.25   In an experiment designed to examine the impact of current mood or emotions on liking for a
a   stranger, May and Hamilton (1980) had female subjects rate males shown in photos while various
LO 5   types of music played. The results indicated
Study   a. the presence of pleasant rock music increased liking for the strangers
242   b. the presence of avant-garde classical music increased liking for the strangers
C   c. the presence of pleasant rock music reduced liking for the strangers
           d. liking for the strangers was highest when no music was present

7.26   The theoretical model that proposes that evaluations are based on emotions, including emotions
b   elicited by cognitions is called
LO 6   a. the affect-cognition model
Concept   b. the affect-centered model
243   c. the affect-evaluation model
M   d. the affect-elicitation model

7.27   The affect-centered model of attraction emphasizes the role of _____ on _____.
c   a. affect, cognition
LO 6   b. cognition, affect
Concept   c. affect, attraction
243   d. cognition, attraction
M

7.28   Rozin and colleagues (1986) studied people's reactions to a laundered shirt. They found
b   a. the quality of the shirt itself determined how it was rated
LO 6   b. people rated the shirt to be better when it had been worn by a liked person
Study   c. people rated the shirt to be better when it had been worn by a disliked person
243   d. blue shirts were rated better than white shirts
M

7.29   Which of the following best explains the fact that people prefer a laundered shirt previously worn
d   by a liked person over one worn by a disliked person?
LO 6   a. the matching hypothesis
Concept   b. the MUM effect
243   c. the propinquity effect
M   d. the affect-centered model

7.30   Any characteristic of a person that someone perceives negatively is called a
c   a. stereotype
LO 7   b. schema
Fact   c. stigma
244   d. schism
E

7.31   A person who is perceived as having a stigma tends to activate
a   a. a negative stereotype
LO 7   b. a negative schema
Concept   c. a positive schism
244   d. a positive scenario
M

7.32
b
LO 7
Study
244
M

The research of Rodin and Price (1995) supported which of the following statements?
a. "once damaged goods" can be repaired
b. "once damaged goods" are less valued than "never damaged goods"
c. "once damaged goods" have more historical value than "never damaged goods"
d. "once damaged goods" are more valued than "never damaged goods"

7.33
c
LO 7
Study
245
M

The old slogan, "You are known by the company you keep" is similar to the findings of the _____ research by Neuberg and colleagues (1994).
a. stigma by information
b. stigma by stereotype
c. stigma by association
d. stigma by schema

7.34
c
LO 7
Study
245
M

The research by Neuberg and colleagues (1994) found that undergraduates responded _____ to the homosexual target and responded _____ to the heterosexual target with whom he was conversing.
a. positively, negatively
b. positively, positively
c. negatively, negatively
d. negatively, positively

7.35
c
LO 8
Concept
246
C

Individuals high in explicit affiliative motivation were _____, while individuals high in implicit motivation were more likely to _____.
a. very sociable and interacted with many people, not be very sociable or interact with people
b. not very sociable and did not interact with many people, be very sociable and interact with many people
c. very sociable and interacted with many people, interact in two person situations
d. likely to interact with just two people, interact with many people

7.36
b
LO 8
Concept
246
M

The amount of time any individual needs to spend with others is a function of
a. attractiveness
b. need for affiliation
c. need for association
d. overt characteristics

7.37
d
LO 8
Study
246
M

Hill (1987) suggests four basic motives for affiliation. They are
a. social comparison, positive stimulation, emotional support, propinquity
b. propinquity, positive stimulation, emotional support, attention
c. social comparison, consensual validation, emotional support, attention
d. social comparison, positive stimulation, emotional support, attention

7.38
d
LO 8
Study
246
M

According to Hill (1987), a high score on the social support comparison dimension indicates
a. a high likelihood of affiliative behavior in situations of praise/blame
b. low affiliative tendencies
c. unhealthy affiliative tendencies
d. a high likelihood of affiliative behavior in situations of uncertainty

7.39
b
LO 8
Concept
246
M

Social comparison, positive stimulation, emotional support, and attention are all factors that constitute aspects of
a. life history
b. need for affiliation
c. friendship motivation
d. need for affection

7.40   Ralph has just spent several hours in the library studying for a big exam. This situation is typical for
c   what type of affiliation need?
LO 9   a. attention
Applied   b. social comparison
247   c. positive stimulation
M   d. emotional support

7.41   Lisa has a knack for taking every opportunity to make the class laugh. The type of affiliation need
a   being exhibited is
LO 9   a. attention
Applied   b. social comparison
247   c. positive stimulation
M   d. emotional support

7.42   Ralph's professor returned an exam in class one day. Ralph received one of the lowest grades in the
d   class. What affiliation need would typically arise in this situation?
LO 9   a. attention
Applied   b. social comparison
247   c. positive stimulation
M   d. emotional support

7.43   In class one day, the professor in Lisa's class returned a set of exams. The professor gave no
b   information about the mean score, the range of scores, or the grades for the class. Lisa is now in
LO 9   a situation in which the affiliation need of _____ might arise.
Applied   a. attention
247   b. social comparison
M   c. positive stimulation
          d. emotional support

7.44   Festinger (1954) proposed three theoretical assumptions of
d   a. social efficacy
LO 10   b. social attentiveness
Study   c. social assertiveness
248   d. social comparison
M

7.45   Festinger (1954) hypothesized that humans have a basic drive to
a   a. evaluate their opinions and abilities
LO 10   b. evaluate their self-esteem
Study   c. evaluate their self-efficacy
248   d. evaluate their conceptions
M

7.46   One of the hypotheses of Festinger (1954) was that if _____ was not available, then an individual
b   would use _____.
LO 10   a. an objective comparison, self comparison
Study   b. an objective comparison, a subjective comparison
248   c. a subjective comparison, an objective comparison
M   d. a subjective comparison, self-comparison

7.47   Festinger (1954), in one of his theoretical assumptions of social comparison, stated that we
c   a. prefer to make comparisons with people who are less qualified than ourselves
LO 10   b. prefer to make comparisons with people who are more qualified than ourselves
Study   c. prefer to make comparisons with people who are similar to ourselves
249   d. prefer to make comparisons with people who are not similar to ourselves
M

7.48
b
LO 11
Concept
249
M

Females tend to be _____ males to the appearance of the opposite sex
a. more responsive than
b. less responsive than
c. about as responsive as
d. more non-judgmental than

7.49
a
LO 11
Concept
249
E

Handsome men are generally perceived as
a. more masculine
b. less masculine
c. more anxious
d. more helpful

7.50
d
LO 11
Concept
250
M

Which of the following ratings go together in ratings of attractive women?
a. anxiety, happiness, interesting person
b. anxiety, affiliation needs, well adjusted
c. vanity, affiliation needs, happiness
d. vanity, well adjusted, interesting person

7.51
b
LO 11
Concept
250
M

What do research findings suggest with regard to the effects of physical attractiveness on how people are perceived?
a. We tend to attribute negative qualities to physically attractive people
b. We tend to attribute positive qualities to physically attractive people
c. We think that physically attractive people are not different than average
d. We ignore physical attractiveness

7.52
b
LO 11
Concept
250
M

Are there any behavioral and personality differences between unattractive and attractive people?
a. No, differences are based totally on cultural biases and don't reflect actual qualities
b. Yes, physically attractive individuals possess greater interpersonal skills
c. Yes, physically attractive individuals possess less interpersonal skills
d. The question has not yet been adequately answered

7.53
c
LO 11
Study
251
C

Langlois and colleagues (1990) found that one-year old children
a. expressed more negative affect, yet played more with a person in an unattractive face mask
b. expressed more positive affect, and also played more with a person in an unattractive face mask
c. expressed more positive affect, and also played more with a person in an attractive face mask
d. expression more negative affect, and also played more with a person in an attractive face mask

7.54
c
LO 11
Concept
251
M

Appearance anxiety is defined as
a. apprehension about evaluating other people
b. apprehension about the appearance of other people
c. apprehension about one's own appearance
d. apprehension about the state of the world

7.55
c
LO 11
Concept
251
M

Given that appearance anxiety is positively associated with social anxiety, you would expect someone who is uncomfortable talking in groups to be
a. masculine
b. feminine
c. overly worried about their appearance
d. unlikely to help others

7.56   Attractiveness among those running for political office
b   a. is a bonus for females but not for males
LO 11   b. is a bonus for males but not for females
Concept   c. is a bonus for both
251   d. is a bonus neither
M

7.57   Which of the following is true regarding the effect of physical attractiveness on political candidates?
c   a. both male and female candidates are helped by being physically attractive
LO 11   b. only female candidates are helped by being physically attractive
Concept   c. only male candidates are helped by being physically attractive
251   d. candidates of neither sex are helped by being physically attractive
C

7.58   Cunningham (1986) had male undergraduates look at photographs of women and then rate their
c   attractiveness. The ratings indicated that
LO 12   a. men rated women who looked sophisticated as the most attractive
Study   b. men rated women who had large eyes as the most unattractive
252   c. men rated women who had either childlike features or had mature features as the most
M   attractive
            d. men rated women who had blond hair as the most attractive

7.59   It may be an advantage for women to have childlike characteristics when these characteristics consist
c   of
LO 12   a. speech patterns
Concept   b. facial features, because personality traits are attributed to such women
252   c. facial features, because males perceive childlike features to be attractive
M   d. facial features, because stable traits are difficult to change

7.60   When researchers claim that most people feel that "average" people are the most attractive, they are
b   claiming that
LO 12   a. this constitutes evidence for the matching hypothesis
Concept   b. average sized features are most attractive
253   c. people like to be with people of average intelligence
M   d. there is evidence against the matching hypothesis

7.61   Langlois and Roggman (1990) had participants make attractiveness ratings of photos _____, and
a   found that participants rated the _____.
LO 12   a. generated by a computer, average face higher in attractiveness
Study   b. from high school yearbooks, average face higher in attractiveness
253   c. generated by a computer, stunning face higher in attractiveness
M   d. from high school yearbooks, stunning face higher in attractiveness

7.62   Why would the average of multiple faces be rated as more attractive by male undergraduates?
b   a. the average face avoids the stereotypes of any extreme face
LO 12   b. the average face is perceived as more familiar than any actual face
Concept   c. the average face elicits a self-comparison from the participant
253   d. the average face is perceived as a whole, whereas the extreme face is perceived in parts
C

7.63   Before going out on his date, Ralph watched a portion of a TV show in which there were many attractive
c   women. When he picked up his date, for some reason she did not seem as attractive as she had in the
LO 13   past. This situation illustrates the operation of
Applied   a. the conflict effect
254   b. the dating-rating effect
M   c. the contrast effect
            d. the assessment effect

7.64
b
LO 13
Study
254
C

Undergraduate participants were given photos of opposite sex individuals and asked to rate their attractiveness. They were also given information about how same-sex peers had rated the photos. The results indicated that
a. women paid no attention to the peer ratings when they rated men
b. women paid attention to the peer ratings when they rated men
c. men paid attention to the peer ratings when they rated women
d. neither sex paid attention to the peer ratings when they rated the opposite sex

7.65
d
LO 13
Study
254
M

In an interesting field study, Gladue and Delaney (1990) asked patrons to rate same and opposite sex fellow drinkers three times during the evening. At closing time, the ratings for the ____ had ____ .
a. same sex, increased
b. opposite sex, decreased
c. same sex, decreased
d. opposite sex, increased

7.66
b
LO 13
Concept
254
M

The text explains the fact that perceived attractiveness of bar patrons changes as closing time approaches in terms of
a. the perceivers' drunkenness
b. the scarcity of available partners
c. the perceived person's drunkenness
d. the perceived person's needs

7.67
b
LO 14
Fact
254
E

Somatotypes are
a. personality divisions
b. types of physiques
c. tall, slender individuals
d. muscular individuals

7.68
b
LO 14
Fact
254
M

The correct somatotype match for muscular people, thin people, and round people is
a. mesomorph, endomorph, ectomorph
b. mesomorph, ectomorph, endomorph
c. ectomorph, mesomorph, endomorph
d. endomorph, mesomorph, ectomorph

7.69
c
LO 14
Fact
254
E

The label used for a person with a muscular body type is
a. endomorph
b. ectomorph
c. mesomorph
d. somatotype

7.70
d
LO 14
Concept
255
M

Perceptions of endomorphs as slow and sloppy are
a. examples of cognitive disregard
b. examples of obnoxious personality
c. examples of learned helplessness
d. reactions to stereotypes

7.71
c
LO 14
Study
255
M

Ryckman and colleagues (1995) found subtypes within each somatotype. Among ectomorphs,
a. female "brains" were perceived unfavorably
b. female fashion models were perceived favorably
c. male scholars were perceived favorably
d. males who had AIDS were perceived favorably

7.72   Obesity is associated with
a
LO 15   a. negative evaluation
Fact   b. practicing cognitive disregard
256   c. achievement motivation
M   d. dominant behavior

7.73   Ralph is 5.5 feet tall and weighs 250 lbs. Ralph is often uncomfortable meeting new people. A
d   reasonable explanation for this is
LO 15   a. that Ralph has low need for affiliation
Applied   b. that Ralph rarely has to meet new people
256   c. that Ralph is practicing cognitive disregard
M   d. that Ralph is negatively evaluated because of his weight

7.74   Lisa is 5.5 feet tall and weighs 250 lbs. Lisa is often uncomfortable meeting new people, even over
b   the phone. The best explanation available is
LO 15   a. that Lisa is negatively evaluated because of her weight
Applied   b. that Lisa is negatively evaluated because of her weight, which has led to low social skills
256   c. that Lisa has been negatively evaluated because of her weight, which has led to Lisa practicing
M   cognitive disregard
        d. that Lisa has been negatively evaluated because of her weight, which has led to her conversing
           in an overly friendly way

7.75   Recent research (Miller et al., 1995) has indicated that when obese women were compared on
a   several social variables (e.g., social anxiety, social competence),
LO 15   a. obesity was unrelated to these variables
Study   b. obesity was highly related to these variables
256   c. nonobese women were rated very high on these variables
M   d. nonobese women were rated very low on these variables

7.76   Adults who look or sound very young
b
LO 16   a. are perceived in positive stereotypical ways
Concept   b. are perceived in negative stereotypical ways
256   c. are perceived as being overly manipulative
M   d. are perceived as being weakly motivated

7.77   Regardless of a person's gender or age, a _____ is perceived in a _____ way.
c   a. person who whistles, positive
LO 16   b. person who often laughs, negative
Concept   c. person who has a youthful gait, positive
257   d. person who has a defined hairstyle, negative
M

7.78   It has been commonly found that males who act in a dominant fashion are more liked. Females who
b   act in a dominant fashion are
LO 16   a. more preferred than deferential females
Concept   b. less preferred than deferential females
257   c. less affiliative than deferential females
C   d. more affiliative than deferential females

7.79   With regard to our preference for dominant as compared to submissive individuals, research has
b   found
LO 16   a. we like others who have the opposite trait from our own
Concept   b. relatively dominant males are preferred to relatively submissive ones
257   c. relatively submissive males are preferred to relatively dominant ones
C   d. no preference for either dominant or submissive individuals

7.80
d
LO 16
Concept
257
M

Both men and women are liked if they express _____, but not liked if they express _____.
a. goal dominant style, goal acquisition style
b. goal cohesiveness, interpersonal cohesiveness
c. goal approach, goal avoidance
d. goal competitiveness, interpersonal competitiveness

7.81
c
LO 16
Study
257
C

Participants in a study by Stein and Nemeroff (1995) rated as morally superior those men or women who ate
a. a variety of foods (including selections from the various food groups)
b. a limited variety of foods (mainly eating from one food group)
c. good foods (e.g., salads, oranges, chicken)
d. culturally appropriate foods (e.g., rice, greens, fried chicken)

7.82
b
LO 16
Study
257
M

Research by Hasart and Hutchinson (1993) found that men and women who wear eyeglasses are perceived as _____.
a. more attractive
b. less attractive
c. more likeable
d. less likeable

7.83
c
LO 16
Study
257
M

Mehrabian and Piercy (1993) found that men with a short nickname were perceived _____ than men with a long given name.
a. less positively
b. less negatively
c. more positively
d. basically neutrally

7.84
b
LO 17
Fact
259
E

The extent to which individuals share the same attitudes about a series of topics is known as
a. attitude cohesion
b. attitude similarity
c. cognitive cohesion
d. cognitive similarity

7.85
c
LO 17
Concept
260
E

People are more likely to become friends with others who have
a. interesting attitudes
b. unusual attitudes
c. similar attitudes
d. a variety of attitudes

7.86
c
LO 17
Concept
259
M

The primary difficulty with the early research on attitude similarity and attraction was that
a. the researchers could never get a large enough sample
b. the subjects were limited in the ages they represented
c. the studies were correlational in nature, not experimental
d. the lack of power in the experimental design prevented making any conclusions

7.87
c
LO 17
Concept
259
M

The correlational data on the similarity-attraction association demonstrates that
a. similarity caused pairs of individuals to like one another
b. when two people like one another, they tend to become more similar
c. either a or b may be true, but the correlational approach does not allow a determination
d. there is no similarity-attraction relationship

7.88
a
LO 17
Study
260
M

Newcomb (1956) conducted a study in which male transfer students lived rent free in a cooperative housing unit. The results of this research indicated that, in the beginning, attraction was determined by
a. proximity
b. similar attitudes
c. cohesiveness
d. superordinate goals

7.89
b
LO 17
Study
260
M

Newcomb (1956) conducted a study in which male transfer students lived rent free in a cooperative housing unit. The results of the research indicated that, before the end of 15 weeks of living together, attraction was determined by
a. proximity
b. similar attitudes
c. cohesiveness
d. superordinate goals

7.90
d
LO 17
Study
260
C

The significance of Newcomb's (1956) study on the relationship between attitudes and attraction was that
a. it established that attraction could be measured in a field setting
b. it established that attitudes could be manipulated in a controlled situation
c. it established that attitude similarity and attraction were related
d. it established that attraction is partially based on the attitudes people hold when they first meet

7.91
c
LO 18
Concept
260
M

Which of the following statements captures the similarity-attraction relationship?
a. people are attracted to one another first and then acquire similar attitudes later
b. people are attracted to one another first and then assess for similar attitudes later
c. the greater the similarity, the greater the attraction
d. the greater the attraction, the greater the similarity

7.92
c
LO 18
Concept
260
M

When forming opinions of another person, individuals respond to
a. the number of similar attitudes
b. the number of dissimilar attitudes
c. the proportion of similar attitudes
d. dissimilar attitudes, not similar ones

7.93
d
LO 18
Concept
260
M

Which of the following is true?
a. studies have shown that the <u>number</u> of shared attitudes is important in determining attraction, but not the <u>proportion</u> of shared attitudes
b. research finds that people who like one another are no more similar in attitudes than randomly matched pairs
c. there is little support for the similarity-attraction hypothesis
d. we tend to assume that people we like agree with us

7.94
c
LO 18
Study
260
C

According to the conclusions of Byrne and Nelson (1969), which stranger is liked best?
a. the one with 0 similar attitudes and 10 dissimilar attitudes
b. the one with 10 similar attitudes and 10 dissimilar attitudes
c. the one with 15 similar attitudes and 8 dissimilar attitudes
d. the one with 10 similar attitudes and 8 dissimilar attitudes

7.95
a
LO 18
Applied
260
M

Lisa has similar attitudes to you on 3 of 5 dimensions while Ralph has similar attitudes to you on 4 of 8 dimensions. For whom do you expect to feel more liking?
a. Lisa
b. Ralph
c. both, because you will remember the similar attitudes
d. neither, because you will remember the dissimilar attitudes

7.96
c
LO 18
Study
260
C

Byrne and Nelson (1969) found what type of relationship between proportion of similar attitudes and attraction?
a. a curvilinear function
b. a correlational function
c. a linear function
d. an inverted U shape relationship

7.97
b
LO 18
Concept
260
C

According to the work done by Byrne, the statement concerning the similarity-attraction relationship should read
a. the greater the number of similar attitudes, the greater the attraction
b. the greater the proportion of similar attitudes, the greater the attraction
c. the greater the attraction, the greater the number of similar attitudes
d. the greater the attraction, the greater the proportion of similar attitudes

7.98
d
LO 18
Concept
260
M

Research has found that the association between attitude similarity and liking among individuals is
a. culturally specific
b. found across few cultures
c. found in Western cultures only
d. found across many cultures

7.99
d
LO 19
Concept
261
M

Rosenbaum's repulsion hypothesis proposes that
a. similar attitudes have a positive effect on attraction
b. dissimilar attitudes have a positive effect on attraction
c. similar attitudes have a negative effect on attraction
d. dissimilar attitudes have a negative effect on attraction

7.100
b
LO 19
Concept
261
C

Rosenbaum's repulsion hypothesis proposes that
a. similar attitudes have a positive effect on attraction
b. dissimilar attitudes have a negative effect on attraction
c. similar attitudes have a negative effect on attraction
d. similar attitudes have a positive effect on attraction and dissimilar attitudes have a negative effect on attraction

7.101
c
LO 19
Fact
261
M

The repulsion hypothesis states that
a. the proportion of similar attitudes determines liking
b. the number of similar attitudes determines liking
c. only dissimilar attitudes determine liking
d. the number of total attitudes determines liking

7.102
d
LO 19
Concept
261
M

According to the repulsion hypothesis, people initially respond to other people with
a. apathy
b. ambivalence
c. distrust
d. liking

7.103   Although it is true that increasing the number of dissimilar attitudes of a hypothetical person in an
c   experiment decreases liking, this arrangement does not invalidate the attitude similarity hypothesis
LO 19   because
Applied a. false consensus effects confound the experimental condition
261   b. it is impossible to know about the attitudes of the subjects
C   c. increasing the proportion of dissimilar attitudes also decreases the proportion of similar attitudes
         d. proportion of attitudes is unrelated to liking

7.104   Increasing the number of similar attitudes while holding the number of dissimilar attitudes constant
a   results in
LO 19   a. increased liking
Concept b. decreased liking
261   c. the repulsion effect
C   d. the matching hypothesis

7.105   According to research by Smeaton, Byrne, and Murnen (1989), which stranger is liked best?
c   a. the one who expresses no attitudes similar to us and 8 dissimilar ones
LO 19   b. the one who expresses 28 attitudes similar to us and 8 dissimilar ones
Study   c. the one who expresses 62 attitudes similar to us and 8 dissimilar ones
261   d. as predicted by the repulsion hypothesis, all of these strangers are liked equally
M

7.106   If we are shown an attractive student's picture and given no information about his opinions, we
a   attribute to him
LO 20   a. opinions similar to our own
Fact   b. opinions different from our own
261   c. neutral opinions
M   d. a lack of knowledge on issues

7.107   An implication of the false consensus effect is that ____
b   a. agreement is surprising, disagreement is expected
LO 20   b. agreement is expected, disagreement is surprising
Concept c. agreement is surprising, disagreement is surprising
262   d. agreement is expected, disagreement is expected
C

7.108   In the false consensus effect, why can disagreement can have the greater effect?
a   a. agreement is expected, and disagreement stands out
LO 20   b. agreement is expected, and disagreement is diluted
Concept c. agreement is not expected, and disagreement stands out
262   d. agreement is not expected, and disagreement does not stand out
M

7.109   Ralph thinks that he holds a minority view on a topic, and he expects most other people to disagree
d   with him. He is very surprised to find out that Lisa agrees with him. This situation would be an
LO 20   illustration of the
Applied a. proportion hypothesis
262   b. false cohesion effect
M   c. repulsion hypothesis
         d. false consensus effect

7.110   Your textbook points out that the similarity-attraction relationship resembles the history of the
a   Titanic in reverse;
LO 20   a. many are sure it will sink, but it remains afloat
Concept b. many are sure it will float, but it sinks
263   c. many are sure it will sink, and it sinks
M   d. many are sure it will float, and it remains afloat

7.111
c
LO 21
Applied
263
M

Lisa is expounding on the merits of a free market in her BUS 101 class. Ralph nods in agreement, and surprisingly, so does the exchange student from Mongolia. You would expect that Lisa
a. feels increased liking for Ralph only
b. feels increased liking for the Mongolian only
c. feels increased liking for both
d. feels decreased liking for the Mongolian

7.112
c
LO 21
263
M

According to balance theory, people who dislike each other
a. will have the same attitudes
b. will expect to have the same attitudes
c. will not care whether they agree or disagree
d. will not know about attitude similarity

7.113
a
LO 21
Concept
263
M

When two people like each other and agree, there is _____; when two people like each other and disagree, three is _____; when two people do not like each other, there is _____.
a. balance; imbalance; nonbalance
b. balance; nonbalance; imbalance
c. nonbalance; imbalance; balance
d. imbalance; nonbalance; balance

7.114
a
LO 21
Concept
263
M

When two people like each other and agree, there is _____
a. balance
b. nonbalance
c. imbalance
d. unbalance

7.115
c
LO 21
Concept
263
M

When two people like each other and disagree, there is _____
a. balance
b. nonbalance
c. imbalance
d. unbalance

7.116
b
LO 21
Concept
263
M

When two people do not like each other, there is
a. balance
b. nonbalance
c. imbalance
d. unbalance

7.117
a
LO 21
Applied
263
M

Suppose that during a conversation with one of your best friends, you discover that he/she dislikes social psychology and your professor. You, on the other hand, like both of these things very much. Under these conditions, your relationship with your friend can be described as
a. imbalanced
b. nonbalanced
c. balanced
d. unbalanced

7.118
b
LO 21
Concept
263
M

Consensual validation says that similar attitudes will lead to liking because
a. people use the matching hypothesis
b. agreement is considered evidence for being right
c. attitudes are linked to self-esteem
d. attitudes are linked to mental health

7.119   A biological explanation for the relationship between attitude similarity and attraction is that
a
LO 21   a. people with similar attitudes probably share some of the same genes
Concept   b. people with similar attitudes are also similarly attractive
263   c. consensual validation has been found to operate among non-human primates
M   d. there is no biological explanation for the relationship

7.120   While long-term male friends were compared with respect to similarity on 10 genetically determined
b   blood characteristics, it was found that friends were
LO 21   a. similar on fewer of these factors than random pairs of males
Concept   b. similar on more of these factors than random pairs of males
263   c. similar on the same number of these factors as random pairs of males
C   d. not able to be compared because of confounding caused by environmental similarity

7.121   Which viewpoint predicts greater genetic similarity between pairs of friends than between
c   randomly-paired individuals?
LO 21   a. balance theory
Concept   b. consensual validation
263   c. evolution-based genetic explanation
M   d. repulsion hypothesis

7.122   The matching hypothesis states that
a   a. people seek people who are similar in physical attractiveness
LO 22   b. people seek the most attractive people they can get
Fact   c. people seek people who are slightly less attractive than themselves
263   d. people seek to match themselves against other people
M

7.123   According to research, an average looking person is most likely to seek a relationship with
c   a. a more attractive person
LO 22   b. a less attractive person
Concept   c. another average looking person
263   d. a person with a high need for affiliation
M

7.124   The matching hypothesis has been found to occur in
b   a. competing relationships
LO 22   b. same sex friendships
Concept   c. children
263   d. the matching hypothesis has not been shown in any long lasting relationship
M

7.125   Studies of college freshmen roommates in dormitories have found that the more attractive roommate
a   a. felt more dissatisfied with the situation than the other roommate
LO 22   b. felt less satisfied with the situation than the other roommate
Study   c. felt the same amount of dissatisfaction as the other roommate
264   d. attractiveness did not influence roommate ratings
M

7.126   Ralph and Sam are assigned as roommates next door to you in your freshman dorm. Ralph is clearly
a   the more attractive of the two. You expect
LO 22   a. Ralph to be dissatisfied with the assignment
Applied   b. Sam to be dissatisfied with the assignment
264   c. both to be dissatisfied with the assignment
C   d. neither to be dissatisfied with the assignment

7.127 Dissatisfaction felt by attractive roommates toward unattractive roommates centers on
b
LO 22 a. academic life
Concept b. social life
264 c. cleanliness
M d. relative helplessness

7.128 A characteristic in which people are attracted to people who are similar to them is
d
LO 22 a. dominance/submissiveness
Fact b. willingness to engage in self-disclosure
264 c. competitiveness
M d. self-concept

7.129 A characteristic in which people are attracted to people who are similar to them is
d
LO 22 a. dominance/submissiveness
Fact b. willingness to engage in self-disclosure
264 c. competitiveness
M d. whether each is a "morning" or an "evening" person

7.130 A characteristic on which people are attracted to people who are similar to them is
d
LO 22 a. dominance/submissiveness
Fact b. willingness to engage in self-disclosure
264 c. competitiveness
M d. whether and how much they smoke and/or drink

7.131 Which of the following phrases is the most accurate concerning the similarity-attraction relationship?
b
LO 22 a. opposites attract
Applied b. birds of a feather flock together
264 c. two many cooks spoil the broth
C d. a bird in the hand is worth two in the bush

7.132 If we receive a positive evaluation from someone, we tend to like this person. The term used to
a describe this is
LO 23 a. reciprocity
Concept b. reinforcement-affect
264 c. matching
M d. propinquity

7.133 We respond negatively to
a
LO 23 a. negative evaluations from others
Concept b. positive evaluations from others that are inaccurate
264 c. positive evaluations from others that represent flattery
M d. neutral evaluations from strangers

7.134 How do people respond to positive evaluations from others that are inaccurate or represent obvious
c attempts at flattery?
LO 23 a. they respond quite negatively
Concept b. they reject them and thus they have no impact
264 c. they respond positively
M d. they laugh at them before dismissing them

7.135
c
LO 23
Study
265
C

When participants in the Curtis and Miller (1986) experiment were led to believe they were disliked by a fellow participant, how did they respond?
a. they tried to be self-disclosing so the partner would like them
b. they made more eye contact than usual so the partner would like them
c. they expressed disliking for the partner
d. eye contact and self-disclosure went up

7.136
d
LO 23
Study
265
C

When participants in the Curtis and Miller (1986) experiment were led to believe they were disliked by a fellow participant, how did they respond?
a. they expressed no particular feelings, either positive or negative
b. they showed behavioral signs of disliking, although self-report statements were not affected
c. self-reports indicating disliking, but behavioral measures showed no indication of disliking
d. behavioral signs indicated disliking, and self-report measures also indicated disliking

7.137
a
LO 24
Study
266
C

In a cross-cultural study of attraction and proportion of similar attitudes, the results indicated that
a. attraction increased as proportion of similar attitudes increased
b. attraction increased as proportion of similar attitudes increased, but only for participants from Hawaii
c. attraction decreased as proportion of similar attitudes increased for participants from Japan
d. attraction increased slightly as proportion of similar attitudes increased, especially for participants from India

7.138
b
LO 24
Study
266
C

The results of the Byrne and colleagues (1971) study of cross-cultural aspects of similarity and attraction found that
a. the five samples did not respond in a linear fashion
b. the five samples did respond in the linear fashion
c. the five samples responded in an inverted U shaped fashion
d. the five samples responded idiosyncratically

7.139
a
LO 24
Study
266
C

The major difference in the Byrne and colleagues (1971) study of cross-cultural aspects of similarity and attraction found that
a. students from Japan and Texas were relatively less attracted to a stranger
b. students from Japan and Texas were relatively more attracted to a stranger
c. students from Hawaii and India were relatively less attracted to a stranger
d. students from Mexico were relatively less attracted to a stranger

7.140
b
LO 24
Study
266
M

One possible explanation given by your authors for the fact that people from Japan and Texas were relatively less attracted to a stranger was that
a. Mexico, Hawaii, and India have a history of barely tolerating outsiders
b. Japan and Texas have a history of barely tolerating outsiders
c. Japan and Texas evaluate strangers very closely
d. Japan and Texas has stricter rules of engagement

CHAPTER 8

Learning Objectives

After studying this chapter, students should be able to:

1. Understand the difference between secure, avoidant and ambivalent attachment styles, and explain how behaviors differ among infants and adults with differing styles.

2. Outline how discipline during childhood affects relationships in adulthood. Explain what happens to parent-child relationships at puberty. Define the two factors Jeffries felt lie behind love of parents. Describe the effects of cohesion among the Chinese.

3. Discuss the life-course of sibling relations. Explain what the upside of negative sibling relations during childhood. Consider the two familiar factors that govern childhood relationships. Explain how attachment styles affect relations at childhood and at adolescence.

4. Indicate how gender and parting (graduation) affect close relations. Consider the two dimensions and four styles offered by Bartholomew. Relate the earlier to this newer attachment schema.

5. Contrast "alone" and "lonely." Describe the "lonely" pattern and relate it to the false consensus effect. Define the two factors that are associated with teen loneliness.

6. Contrast socially skilled and unskilled. Outline the college student loneliness pattern. Describe the self-perception and interaction pattern of the socially unskilled.

7. Describe the cognitive therapy and modeling (social skills training) strategies for "curing" loneliness. List the varieties of romantic relations and discuss how the experiences and partner selection practices differ for secure and insecure persons.

B. Contrast friendships with dating and restricted with unrestricted sociosexual orientation regarding major goals. Discuss abuse and termination of relations involving it.

9. Understand unrequited love and passionate romantic love. Explain the function of gazing. Compare the proportions of secure, ambivalent, and avoidant adult romantic lovers with the proportions of these styles in childhood.

10. Historically, discuss how bonding relates to success at "passing on one's genes." Understand the three conditions of passionate love arousal, and discuss the supposed role of skin color in mate selection and how do life-time celibates and gay/lesbian people contradict evolutionary rules?

11. State the role of mistaken emotions. Contrast companionate and passionate love. List and define the Hendricks' six love styles; provide example behaviors as well. Discuss how friendship relates to love. Understand relations among the corners of the love triangle.

12. Describe changes wrought by the sexual revolution. Describe the role of ethnicity and gender in partner selection and attitudes.

13. Discuss the teen pregnancy legacy of the free love period. Describe the herpes and AIDS epidemics. Track behavioral changes accompanying the spreads of HIV/AIDS. Discuss how premarital sex affects marriage and psychological health.

14. Consider people's marriage aspirations as well as the prevailing presence of fathers and blended families. Discuss the role of similarity during the course of courtship and marriage.

15. Describe the implications of settling for less than the perfect match. Discuss how similarity relates to happiness in marriage. Define the four states of early marriage uncovered by Johnson.

16.   *Contrast Johnson's four states of early marriage on marital satisfaction and parenthood. Look at intercourse frequency among partners whose relationships vary in length and commitment. Relate the decline in passionate love to relationship satisfaction and having children.*

17.   *Discuss how the marriage/happiness relationship has changed. Explain the current state of marriage, statistically speaking. Examine clashes of marital partners' personal interests, opinions and coping strategies.*

18.   *Relate self-descriptions to marital satisfaction. Contrast the genders on sources of marital upset. List marital issues upon which conflicts can develop and changes in perceptions of partners' attributes.*

19.   *Explain how relationship satisfaction relates to the expression of affect. Understand the two active and two passive responses to marital conflict and how they relate to self-esteem.*

20.   *Name the three factors that relate to reconciliation. Describe the role of attachment styles in satisfaction and abuse. Contrast collectivism and individualism.*

21.   *Contrast individualistic and collectivistic societies on the importance of romance, the role of partner evaluations, and maintenance of intimacy.*

Questions

8.1
d
LO 1
Fact
272
E

Which of the following is not included in the definition of "close relationships?"
a. friends
b. romantic partners
c. marital partners
d. business partners

8.2
c
LO 1
Fact
272
M

"Interdependence" exists when two people
a. cannot do without each other
b. have thoroughly complementary traits
c. frequently influence one another's lives for many different kinds of activities over an extended period of time
d. frequently disrupt one another's lives for many different kinds of activities over an extended period of time

8.3
b
LO 1
Applied
272
M

Ralph and Lisa engage in many joint activities and strongly influence each other's lives. They may be said to be
a. mutually bonded
b. interdependent
c. sexually attracted
d. siblings

8.4
d
LO 1
Concept
274
M

Bowlby (1982) suggested that the way a mother interacts with her child defines one of three types of attachment style. Which one of the following is NOT one of those styles?
a. secure
b. avoidant
c. ambivalent
d. assertive

8.5
a
LO 1
Fact
274
M

Attachment style can be defined as
a. an infant's degree of security in mother-infant interactions
b. a mother's degree of commitment in mother-infant interactions
c. an infant's degree of understanding in mother-child interactions
d. a mother's degree of warmth in mother-child interactions

8.6
c
LO 1
Fact
274
M

According to Goldsmith and Harman (1994), sensitive, responsive parenting during the child's first year leads to
a. warm attachment
b. ambivalent attachment
c. secure attachment
d. trusting attachment

8.7
c
LO 1
Concept
275
M

If a mother has visual contact with an infant who actively avoids visual contact, such behavior would be classified as
a. high security
b. medium security
c. low security
d. neutral security

8.8
b
LO 1
Study
275
C

Becker and Becker (1994) found that when a mother is separated from the infant, the
_____ pattern includes rejecting the mother when she returns and showing restraint
in her absence.
a. ambivalent attachment
b. avoidant attachment
c. secure attachment
d. assertive attachment

8.9
a
LO 1
Concept
275
M

There is some evidence that the _____ tend to be hostile and distant in social
relationships and resist seeking adult help.
a. insecure avoidant attachment children
b. insecure ambivalent attachment children
c. secure attachment children
d. assertive attachment children

8.10
c
LO 1
Study
275
M

Hazan and Schaver (1990) hypothesize that when an adult enters a relationship, the
_____ formed in infancy determines the nature of that relationship.
a. interaction style
b. assertiveness style
c. attachment style
d. confidence style

8.11
d
LO 1
Concept
276
C

Which of the following characterizes the securely attached type of attachment?
a. parents who were loving but unavailable because of circumstances beyond their
   control
b. rejecting parents
c. parents who were sometimes loving and sometimes rejecting
d. parents who were consistently loving and warm

8.12
b
LO 1
Concept
276
C

Which of the following characterizes the avoidant type of attachment?
a. parents who were loving but unavailable because of circumstances beyond their
   control
b. rejecting parents
c. parents who were sometimes loving and sometimes rejecting
d. parents who were consistently loving and warm

8.13
c
LO 2
Study
276
M

According to O'Leary (1995), parents who are excessively lenient in discipline could
be providing a foundation for _____ in children.
a. lazy behavior
b. unreliable behavior
c. delinquent behavior
d. apathetic behavior

8.14
a
LO 2
Study
276
M

Research indicates that as _____ arrives, typical parent-child relationships become
_____ pleasant.
a. puberty, less
b. childhood, more
c. puberty, more
d. adulthood, less

8.15
d
LO 2
Concept
276
M

The two components of "love for parents" in Jeffries' model are
a. attention and value
b. admiration and virtue
c. availability and value
d. attraction and virtue

8.16　　　　　According to research, love for parents is associated with
c
LO 2　　　　　a. high affiliative needs
Study　　　　 b. high associative needs
276　　　　　 c. high self-esteem
M　　　　　　 d. good health

8.17　　　　　Which of the following are parts of Jeffries' two components of loving your parents?
c
LO 2　　　　　a. trust and health
Concept　　　 b. emotional closeness and affiliative fulfillment
276　　　　　 c. companionship and intimacy
M　　　　　　 d. admiration and health

8.18　　　　　In Jeffries' two component theory of love toward one's parents, temperance means
b
LO 2　　　　　a. undergoing beneficial hardship
Concept　　　 b. controlling disruptive emotions
276　　　　　 c. relying on integrity
M　　　　　　 d. fulfilling obligations, such as avoiding alcohol

8.19　　　　　Research indicates that most siblings
b
LO 3　　　　　a. get closer during adolescence
Study　　　　 b. grow apart during adolescence
277　　　　　 c. grow apart during middle age
M　　　　　　 d. remain friends over their entire lifespan

8.20　　　　　An English study of middle school children found that bullies had
c
LO 3　　　　　a. larger than average heads
Study　　　　 b. increased anger in competitive situations
278　　　　　 c. low cohesion among siblings
M　　　　　　 d. decreased fear of ambiguous situations

8.21　　　　　Two children are likely to become friends if which of the following three factors are present?
a
LO 3　　　　　a. proximity, positive affect, similarity
Concept　　　 b. pleasant surroundings, excitement, knowledge of each other
279　　　　　 c. positive affect, knowledge of each other, lack of parental interference
C　　　　　　 d. similarity, pleasant surroundings, lack of parental interference

8.22　　　　　Preschoolers with secure attachment to their mothers and fathers are more likely to
b
LO 3　　　　　a. interact with teachers on an adult basis
Concept　　　 b. interact positively with their peers and engage in interactive play
279　　　　　 c. interact with their siblings in a competitive manner
M　　　　　　 d. interact with their peers in a compliant manner

8.23　　　　　In 10-year-old children, those with _____ attachment had more _____.
c
LO 3　　　　　a. insecure avoidant, neutral friendships
Concept　　　 b. insecure ambivalent, positive friendships
280　　　　　 c. secure, close friendships
E　　　　　　 d. assertive, distant friendships

8.24   The three stage model of preadolescent friendship and effects of attachment style consists of which of the
a   following three stages?
LO 3   a. behavior prior to friendship formation, connectedness, creative relatedness
Concept b. behavior prior to friendship formation, evaluation of relationship, modification of relationship
281   c. evaluation of relationship, modification of relationship, assessment of relationship
C   d. evaluation of relationship, modification of relationship, re-evaluation of relationship

8.25   Fredrickson (1995) report that _____ have more _____
b   a. women, social relationships than men
LO 4   b. women, close relationships than men
Study   c. men, close relationships than women
280   d. men, social relationships than women
M

8.26   Relationships that involve self-disclosure, trust, physical contact, and support are called
d   a. close relationships
LO 4   b. social relationships
Fact   c. satisfying relationships
280   d. intimate relationships
E

8.27   Bartholomew and colleagues (1991) formulated a model of adult attachment that contains two
b   underlying dimensions. These dimensions are
LO 4   a. the type of attachment as a child and degree of assertiveness
Study   b. a person's sense of self-worth and the perception of others as trustworthy or unreliable
282   c. the self-concept of the individual and level of social skills
C   d. the self-esteem of a person and the extent of social interaction

8.28   According to Bartholomew and colleagues (1991), an attachment pattern characterized by negative
c   self view, belief that others are loving and trustworthy, and distress when emotional needs are not
LO 4   met is called
Study   a. secure attachment pattern
282   b. dismissing attachment pattern
M   c. preoccupied attachment pattern
        d. fearful attachment pattern

8.29   According to Bartholomew and colleagues (1991), an attachment pattern characterized as avoiding
b   genuine closeness, positive self-image independence, and egocentricism is called
LO 4   a. secure attachment pattern
Study   b. dismissing attachment pattern
282   c. preoccupied attachment pattern
M   d. fearful attachment pattern

8.30   In models of close relationships, loneliness is defined as
b   a. the feelings that occur when leaving a relationship
LO 5   b. the unfilled desire to enter a close relationship
Fact   c. the absence of a long term partner
283   d. a situation of solitude
E

8.31   Scores on the UCLA Loneliness Scale are associated with all but one of the following. Which one
a   is the exception?
LO 5   a. frustration
Fact   b. depression
283   c. anxiety
M   d. dissatisfaction

8.32   Loneliness has been found to correlate with
a   a. shyness
LO 5   b. calmness
Fact   c. sexual apathy
283   d. psychoticism
E

8.33   Lonely individuals are often
d   a. genuinely liked by others
LO 5   b. poor in physical health
Concept   c. motivated to increase their need level for affiliation
283   d. disliked by others
M

8.34   Which one of the following is NOT characteristic of individuals who are lonely?
c   a. tend to spend time in solitary activity
LO 5   b. has a low level of trust in other individuals
Concept   c. believe that others share their attitudes and beliefs (false consensus effect)
283   d. have other negative emotions
C

8.35   If the false consensus effect was operative, how should lonely people rate other people?
c   a. unlike themselves, not lonely
LO 5   b. randomly, these people are unsure of their ratings
Concept   c. like themselves, lonely
283   d. it is impossible to predict, the outcome depends on the attachment type
C

8.36   All of the following are true of lonely but not nonlonely people except one. Which one is the
c   exception?
LO 5   a. lonely people often eat dinner alone
Applied   b. lonely people tend to engage in few social activities
283   c. lonely people have periods of solitude
M   d. lonely people have few dates

8.37   When during the development of an individual is it most likely that loneliness will reach its peak?
a   a. adolescence
LO 5   b. early childhood
Fact   c. middle school years
284   d. early elementary school years
M

8.38   When social situations become especially frightening and an individual totally avoids such situations
d   to protect himself or herself, the situation is called
LO 5   a. loneliness
Concept   b. withdrawal syndrome
284   c. contact anxiety
M   d. social phobia

8.39   In extreme cases, a lonely and fearful adolescent may decide that life is _____.
c   a. embarrassing
LO 5   b. humiliating
Concept   c. hopeless
284   d. frustrating
E

8.40   A main reason for loneliness is
b   a. obnoxious personality
LO 6   b. failure to learn appropriate social skills during childhood
Fact   c. extreme fear of social interactions
284   d. failure to develop the ability to converse on an equal basis with other people
M

8.41   Loneliness in adult life is associated with
d   a. marriage
LO 6   b. companionate love
Concept   c. absence of siblings
284   d. lack of social skills as a child
E

8.42   Low interest in the disclosures of others is characteristic of
c   a. hopelessness
LO 6   b. helplessness
Concept   c. poor social skills
284   d. vanity
E

8.43   Socially unskilled individuals often believe that they have
d   a. been treated irresponsibly by others
LO 6   b. poor physical health
Concept   c. poor financial health
284   d. little control over their lives
M

8.44   Langston and Cantor (1989) proposed that socially skilled college students looked at new social
b   situations as ____, while socially unskilled college students looked at the same situation as ____.
LO 6   a. an interesting exercise, an uninteresting exercise
Study   b. a challenge, a threat
284   c. another experience, another challenge
C   d. a social influence opportunity, a coercive experience

8.45   In a new social situation, socially skilled individuals behave in ____, while socially unskilled
a   individuals behave in ____.
LO 6   a. an open and informative manner, a restrained and conservative manner
Applied   b. a restrained and conservative manner, an open and informative manner
284   c. a conservative self-disclosing manner, a liberal self-disclosing manner
M   d. an uninterested manner, a interested manner

8.46   Which of the following is one of the ways to effectively treat loneliness?
d   a. gestalt therapy
LO 7   b. rational emotive therapy
Concept   c. existential therapy
285   d. social skills therapy
M

8.47   Which of the following is a successful technique used to treat loneliness?
c   a. music therapy
LO 7   b. shock therapy
Concept   c. cognitive therapy
285   d. flooding
M

8.48
a
LO 7
Concept
285
M

Which of the following is NOT a successful technique used to treat loneliness?
a. music therapy
b. cognitive therapy
c. social skills therapy
d. systematic desensitization

8.49
c
LO 7
Concept
286
C

Cognitive therapy works in treating loneliness by
a. making the client think that his or her thoughts are ridiculous
b. getting the client together with many other people with similar problems
c. altering the self-schema of the client in regard to social situations
d. forcing the client to interact with other people

8.50
b
LO 7
Concept
286
M

Changing harmful self-perceptions and perceptions about others to treat loneliness is done by
a. social skills therapists
b. cognitive therapists
c. behaviorists
d. radical behaviorists

8.51
b
LO 7
Applied
286
M

Ralph enters treatment because of chronic feelings of loneliness and isolation. The therapist concentrates on altering Ralph's perceptions of himself as dull-witted and uninteresting. The therapist is probably oriented toward
a. social skills therapy
b. cognitive therapy
c. behaviorism
d. radical behaviorism

8.52
d
LO 7
Concept
286
M

Cognitive therapy will not be successful unless changes in cognition are accompanied by changes in
a. thought
b. self-schema
c. self-perception
d. behavior

8.53
c
LO 7
Concept
286
M

Practice of socially appropriate behavior in a non-threatening situation is part of
a. companionate therapy
b. analytic therapy
c. social skills training
d. flooding techniques

8.54
a
LO 7
Concept
286
M

The use of drugs to treat extreme social anxiety results in
a. rapid behavior change
b. medication anxiety
c. cognitive enhancement change
d. self-assessment change

8.55
c
LO 7
Applied
286
C

It has been suggested that the use of drugs to treat loneliness is most effective when
a. the problem is minor, and rapid behavior change is desired
b. the problem is minor, and the drugs are used with cognitive therapy
c. the problem is severe, and the drugs are used with cognitive therapy
d. the problem is severe, and rapid behavior change is desired

8.56   One of the defining characteristics of romantic relationships is
b   a. commitment on the part of the involved individuals
LO 7   b. some degree of physical intimacy
Fact   c. recognition by social peers
287   d. lack of involvement with other individuals
M

8.57   Keelan and colleagues (1994) found that undergraduates with ____
c   a. an avoidant attachment style were involved in many casual romantic relationships
LO 7   b. an ambivalent attachment style expressed more satisfaction with casual relationships than
Study   romantic relationships
287   c. a secure attachment style expressed more satisfaction and commitment to the romantic
C   relationship
        d. an assertive attachment style expressed more satisfaction with the romantic relationship

8.58   Brennan and Shaver (1995) found that, among undergraduates involved in a romantic relationship,
a   a. there was a tendency to select someone with a matching attachment style
LO 7   b. there was a tendency to select someone with a different attachment style
Study   c. there was a tendency to select someone with a secure attachment style
287   d. there was a tendency to select someone with a romantic attachment style
C

8.59   Swann and colleagues (1994) indicate that among individuals who are involved in the early stages of close
c   relationships, the preference is for a partner who can
LO 8   a. provide validation of one's self-concept
Study   b. provide accurate self-assessment information
288   c. provide positivity feedback
C   d. provide mirror-concept feedback

8.60   Sociosexuality is defined as the
c   a. degree of sociability that an individual needs for sex
LO 8   b. degree of similarity that two people have to have to each other to have sex
Fact   c. degree of emotional closeness that an individual needs to have with another person to have sex
288   with that person
M   d. index of genetic similarity that two sexual partners possess

8.61   Ralph and Lisa are considering whether or not to have sex. Lisa has been willing to have sex from
a   the moment of their first encounter. Lisa is said to have
LO 8   a. an unrestricted sociosexual orientation
Applied b. an unrestricted sociosexual appetitive
288   c. a restricted sociosexual orientation
M   d. a sociosexually high orientation

8.62   Ralph and Lisa are considering whether or not to have sex. Lisa wants to wait until they feel closer
c   to one another. Lisa is said to have
LO 8   a. an unrestricted sociosexual orientation
Applied b. an unrestricted sociosexual appetitive
288   c. a restricted sociosexual orientation
M   d. a sociosexually low orientation

8.63   Which of the following is NOT an indication of sociosexual restriction-unrestriction?
d   a. number of sex partners in the last year
LO 8   b. number of sex partners expected in the last year
Concept c. number of fantasies about people other than current sexual partner
288   d. number of close relationships
M

8.64
b
LO 8
Concept
288
M

Sociosexual restriction is unrelated to all of the following EXCEPT
a. sex drive
b. amount of love/closeness in a relationship
c. sexual attraction
d. sex guilt and anxiety

8.65
c
LO 8
Concept
288
M

One behavior that occurs in dating that is rare in friendships is
a. habitual lateness
b. verbal confrontation
c. physical abuse
d. inattentiveness

8.66
a
LO 8
Fact
290
M

Passionate love is defined as
a. intense emotional response to another person
b. intense cognitive response to another person
c. intense assessment of another person
d. intense interest in another person

8.67
b
LO 8
Concept
290
M

Many relationships are based on propinquity and/or similarity. Passionate love seems to be
dependent upon
a. cognitive reactions
b. expectations and observable cues
c. physiological arousal
d. personality changes

8.68
c
LO 8
Study
290
M

A major difference between friendship and love revolves around similarity and propinquity. Research
results show
a. neither is important for love or friendship
b. both are equally important for love and friendship
c. the two factors are more important for friendship than love
d. the two factors are more important for love than friendship

8.69
c
LO 9
Applied
291
M

Ralph is in love with Lisa, but Lisa does not share his affection. Ralph is in a state of
a. confusion
b. emotional assessment
c. unrequited love
d. self-enhancement

8.70
c
LO 9
Concept
292
M

What does gazing into an opposite sexed person's eyes do to one's feelings about that person?
a. nothing
b. mutual gazing generates hostility
c. one feels passionate love for that person
d. one feels increasing boredom after an initial period of attraction

8.71
c
LO 9
Concept
292
M

One reason that love is found throughout the world may be based on its association with _____.
a. emotional style
b. cognitive style
c. attachment style
d. interaction style

8.72
a
LO 9
Study
292
C

Hazan and Shaver (1987) found that the percent of adults indicating one of the three attachment styles in a romantic relationship was
a. approximately the same as the percent of those attachment styles in infant-mother relationships
b. much greater for secure than for the two insecure attachment styles in infant-mother relationships
c. much greater for insecure than for secure attachment style in infant-mother relationships
d. much lower for insecure than for secure attachment style in infant-mother relationships

8.73
b
LO 10
Study
292
C

According to the evolutionary model by Buss
a. love is in the genes of only some of us
b. loving behavior survived in our genetic makeup because it led to selection of mates who could reproduce and nurture offspring
c. loving behavior has evolved from a primitive, solely sexual state to the current more emotional condition due to changes in DNA structure
d. love is in the genes of all of us

8.74
b
LO 10
Study
292
C

Which of the following represents a genetically determined orientation or trait of females in regard to reproductive strategy, according to Buss?
a. females evaluate males who can reproduce
b. females are attracted by male love acts that display his resources
c. females evaluate males on the basis of youth, health, and handsomeness
d. females are attracted by male love acts that signal reproductive capability

8.75
d
LO 10
Study
292
C

According to Buss, which of the following represents a genetically determined orientation or trait of males in regard to reproductive strategy?
a. males evaluate females on the basis of having sufficient resources for protecting his offspring
b. males seek females who can accumulate resources
c. males are attracted by female love acts that display her resources
d. males are attracted by female love acts that signal reproductive capacity

8.76
b
LO 10
Concept
293
M

How do males and females differ in age ranges that are most preferred in a partner?
a. they don't: both prefer someone almost exactly their own age
b. males prefer females younger than themselves
c. females prefer someone younger than themselves
d. both prefer someone younger than themselves

8.77
c
LO 10
Study
293
C

Hatfield and Walster (1981) have proposed that, for most individuals, passionate love is aroused if the following three conditions are present
a. opportunity to engage in sex, strong emotional arousal, culturally approved behaviors
b. contact with appropriate person, opportunity to engage in sex, strong emotional arousal
c. exposure to romantic role models, contact with appropriate person, strong emotional arousal
d. culturally approved behaviors, contact with appropriate person, strong emotional arousal

8.78
d
LO 10
Study
293
C

Hatfield and Walster's (1981) third requirement for passionate relationships (strong emotional arousal) is based upon which theory?
a. Milgram's obedience studies
b. Kendrick and Keefe's age preference theory
c. the Relationship Closeness Inventory
d. Schachter's two factor theory of emotion

8.79
d
LO 10
Study
293
M

Research shows that because of the increased odds of passing their kind of genes on to future generations, people would prefer to mate with a partner who has
a. similar religious orientations
b. similar attachment orientations
c. similar self-esteem level
d. similar physical skin color

8.80	_____ contradict evolutionary rules of mate selection
c	a. Young couples
LO 10	b. Heterosexual couples
Concept	c. Homosexual couples
293	d. Active couples
E	

8.81	The type of love that involves close friendship, mutual attraction, and reciprocal liking and respect
b	is called
LO 11	a. passionate love
Fact	b. companionate love
294	c. cooperative love
E	d. possessive love

8.82	Which describes companionate love?
c	a. short lived
LO 11	b. intense, overwhelming emotional state
Fact	c. deep friendship that involves caring about the other person
294	d. ambivalence
M	

8.83	Ralph and Lisa meet at an amusement park through mutual friends. Friends at first, they become
c	romantically involved later on, and eventually settle together on a basis of mutual attraction and
LO 11	respect. The best description for their type of love is
Applied	a. passionate love
294	b. compassionate love
M	c. companionate love
	d. game playing love

8.84	Which of the following is among Hendrick and Hendrick's (1993) six types of love?
d	a. hapless love
LO 11	b. aimless love
Study	c. longing love
297	d. possessive love
M	

8.85	Which of the following is among Hendrick and Hendrick's (1993) six types of love?
c	a. hapless love
LO 11	b. aimless love
Study	c. passionate love
297	d. obsessive love
M	

8.86	Which of the following is NOT among Hendrick and Hendrick's (1993) six types of love?
a	a. heartless love
LO 11	b. friendship love
Study	c. logical love
297	d. selfless love
M	

8.87	The least satisfactory type of love is _____, because it is associated with unhappy relationships.
c	a. logical love
LO 11	b. passionate love
Concept	c. game-playing love
297	d. possessive love
M	

8.88   Women tend to score higher than men in
b
LO 11   a. passionate love
Study   b. logical love
297   c. game-playing love
M   d. selfless love

8.89   Men tend to score higher than women in
a
LO 11   a. passionate love
Study   b. logical love
297   c. possessive love
M   d. friendship love

8.90   Intimacy, passion, and decision/commitment are components of the
a
LO 11   a. triangular model of love
Fact   b. logical theory of love
297   c. companionate model of love
M   d. romance-attraction theory of love

8.91   Which of the following is among the three sides of Sternberg's triangle of love?
d
LO 11   a. self-sacrifice
Fact   b. investment
297   c. absorption
M   d. passion

8.92   In Sternberg's triangular model of love, intimacy refers most closely to which of the following?
b
LO 11   a. sexual contact
Fact   b. concern with the other's welfare and happiness
297   c. spiritual sharing and participation
C   d. amount of time spent together

8.93   The long-term, short-term aspect of relationships is reflected in what part of Sternberg's triangular
a   model of love?
LO 11   a. decision/commitment
Concept   b. intimacy
297   c. abasement
M   d. passion

8.94   Which of the following was NOT involved in the sexual revolution?
c
LO 12   a. acceptance of premarital sexual intercourse
Fact   b. a greater tolerance of sexual practices in general
297   c. fear of sexual disease
M   d. a disappearance of sex differences in sexual experience

8.95   Sex attitudes in Western culture in the last half of the 20th century have steadily gone in the
c   direction of
LO 12   a. tolerance for premarital sex for males only
Concept   b. tolerance for premarital sex for females only
298   c. tolerance for premarital sex for both
M   d. premarital sex is still generally disapproved

8.96
d
LO 12
Concept
298
M

The apparent paradox that before 1950 most men engaged in premarital sex while most women did not is explained by the presence of
a. masturbation
b. homosexual activity
c. pornography
d. prostitution

8.97
b
LO 12
Study
298
M

According to research, differences between males and females in premarital sexuality have now
a. widened
b. disappeared
c. reappeared
d. not really changed from the 1950s

8.98
a
LO 12
Concept
299
E

Who prefers arousing sexual activity to love and intimacy?
a. males
b. females
c. neither sex
d. it depends on the age of the individuals

8.99
b
LO 12
Concept
299
E

The belief that emotional involvement should be a prerequisite for sex is more common among
a. males
b. females
c. a majority of both sexes believe in emotional involvement
d. a majority of both sexes do not believe in emotional involvement

8.100
c
LO 12
Study
299
M

The finding that women want their partners to express more intimacy is consistent with the finding that
a. women rate passionate love as more important than men do
b. women rate logical love as more important than men do
c. women rate compassion as more important than men do
d. men are less likely to believe in emotional involvement as a prerequisite for sex

8.101
c
LO 13
Concept
300
M

Given that males and females accepted the norm of the sexual revolution that one should be sexually active, how did they feel when they did become active?
a. males showed no signs of conflict or concern
b. females showed no signs of conflict or concern
c. females felt exploited by males
d. males had no reservations about their new freedom

8.102
c
LO 13
Concept
301
M

Which one of the following does NOT represent the negative aftermath of the sexual revolution?
a. sexually experienced people are seen as poor marriage risks
b. increased sexual activity was accompanied by low contraception use
c. men have come to see themselves as sexual inferiors to women
d. unwanted teen pregnancies have increased

8.103
c
LO 13
Study
301
M

According to data from the 1970s and 1980s, those individuals with the greatest amount of sexual experience
a. had the longest lasting sexual relationships
b. had the least interest in pornography
c. were often perceived as unsuitable marriage partners
d. had the least amount of sexual satisfaction

8.104   Data from the 1970s ad 1980s suggest that permissive sexuality produced a belief that
a   a. only abnormal people in a relationship abstained from sex
LO 13   b. premarital sex was wrong
Study   c. nobody should be coerced into a sexual relationship
301   d. unrestricted sociosexuality was wrong
M

8.105   Which one of the following is NOT among the sexual diseases that have come into existence and/or
a   increased in likelihood since the sexual revolution?
LO 13   a. jaundice of the urinary tract
Fact   b. AIDS
301   c. gonorrhea
M   d. chlamydia

8.106   Available data indicate that the majority of teenage pregnancies result in
a   a. abortion
LO 13   b. teenage marriage
Study   c. the mother keeping the child
301   d. the child being put up for adoption
M

8.107   Acquired Immune Deficiency Syndrome (AIDS) can be successfully treated with
d   a. antibodies
LO 13   b. anti-carcinogens
Fact   c. carcinogens
301   d. nothing currently available
E

8.108   The largest trend toward safer sexual practices due to fear of AIDS has been found in
c   a. younger people
LO 13   b. older people
Fact   c. high risk groups
301   d. college educated people
M

8.109   Current studies indicate that fear of AIDS has
b   a. made young heterosexuals practice safer sex
LO 13   b. made little behavioral impact on young heterosexuals
Study   c. increased sex guilt in young males
301   d. decreased the proportion of sexually active adolescents
M

8.110   Which of the following statements about premarital intercourse is most accurate?
c   a. premarital intercourse increases the chances of a couple marrying
LO 13   b. premarital intercourse decreases the changes of a couple marrying
Concept   c. premarital intercourse has no relationship to whether or not a couple will marry
302   d. premarital intercourse is associated with belief in game-playing love
M

8.111   Success of a marriage is _____ the sexual history of the marriage partners.
c   a. positively related to
LO 13   b. negatively related to
Concept   c. unrelated to
302   d. a function of
M

8.112   According to research, the primary interpersonal goal of most young people is
c
                    a. to maximize the number of sexual partners
LO 14   b. to minimize the number of sexual partners
Study   c. to marry
302   d. to have a meaningful relationship with siblings
E

8.113   Which of the following statements is true about families?
d
                    a. single parent families now outnumber two parent families
LO 14   b. more children live with a single parent than with two parents
Concept   c. less than a third of all couples get divorced
303   d. most families with children are two parent families
M

8.114   Spouses show which of the following characteristics?
a
                    a. greater than chance attitude similarity
LO 14   b. less than chance attitude similarity
Concept   c. increased amount of attitude similarity over time
303   d. decreased amount of attitude similarity over time
M

8.115   Research has found that married couples are NOT similar along which of the following dimensions?
d
                    a. attitudes
LO 14   b. values
Study   c. interests
303   d. sleep habits
E

8.116   Caspi and colleagues (1992) after investigating couples over a 20 year span found that similarity was
d
                    characteristic of those who married, and similarity
LO 15   a. increased over time
Study   b. decreased over time
303   c. was not relevant after 20 years
C   d. neither increased nor decreased over time

8.117   Terman (1935) found that happiness
a
                    a. was associated with degree of similarity
LO 15   b. was not associated with degree of similarity
Study   c. was associated with cohesiveness
304   d. was not associated with cohesiveness
M

8.118   Which of the following is NOT a type of relationship from Johnson et al. (1992)?
a
                    a. passionate
LO 15   b. symmetric
Fact   c. parallel
304   d. reversed
M

8.119   The most common type of marriage along the dimensions of Johnson et al. (1992) is
b
                    a. differentiated
LO 15   b. symmetric
Fact   c. parallel
304   d. reversed
M

8.120   The type of relationship where spouses engage in the least typical gender divisions of household
d   labor is
LO 15   a. differentiated
Fact   b. symmetric
304   c. parallel
M   d. reversed

8.121   The type of relationship in which spouses engage in traditional divisions of work and labor is
c   a. differentiated
LO 15   b. symmetric
Fact   c. parallel
304   d. reversed
M

8.122   The type of relationship in which men and women work, but in which the man tends to be more
a   involved in his work is
LO 15   a. differentiated
Fact   b. symmetric
304   c. parallel
M   d. reversed

8.123   Spouses who hold relatively egalitarian beliefs about sex roles and household labor are in which
b   type of relationship?
LO 15   a. differentiated
Fact   b. symmetric
304   c. parallel
M   d. reversed

8.124   Children are least common in which type of spousal relationship?
b   a. differentiated
LO 15   b. symmetric
Fact   c. parallel
304   d. reversed
M

8.125   The greatest decline in rates of sexual intercourse tend to occur over which time in a marriage?
a   a. the first few years
LO 16   b. middle age
Fact   c. old age
306   d. rates of sexual intercourse stay relatively constant
M

8.126   Which has been associated with satisfaction in marriage?
b   a. number of children
LO 16   b. frequency of sexual interactions
Study   c. physical health
306   d. age of marriage partners
M

8.127   Male satisfaction with a marriage is
b   a. highly related to passionate love
LO 16   b. not related to passionate love
Concept c. highly related to logical love
306   d. not related to companionate love
M

8.128
c
LO 16
Concept
306
M

Feelings of _____ decrease with parenthood.
a. companionate love
b. logical love
c. passionate love
d. selfless love

8.129
b
LO 17
Concept
306
M

The difference in happiness between married and unmarried people has _____ compared to in the past.
a. grown larger
b. become smaller
c. stayed about the same
d. both married and unmarried people report being less happy now than in the past

8.130
a
LO 17
Concept
306
M

One major reason given for the relative happiness of single men now as compared to the past is
a. the relatively large amount of sexual freedom
b. the relatively lower amount of sexual freedom
c. greater earning capacity
d. increased cure rate for STDs

8.131
c
LO 17
Concept
306
C

One major reason given for the decreased happiness of married women now as compared to the past is
a. the relatively large choice of romantic partners
b. increased cure rate for STDs
c. the relative increase in economic freedom and career choice
d. the relative large amount of sexual freedom

8.132
b
LO 17
Concept
306
M

Both men and women are happier in a marriage if they
a. have frequent sex
b. feel able to control the assignment of household chores
c. have between two and four children
d. have passionate as well as companionate love

8.133
c
LO 17
Concept
306
M

An example of a universal problem with a long term relationship is the conflict between
a. the desire for intimacy and the desire for closeness
b. the desire for intimacy and the desire for honesty
c. the desire for independence and the desire for closeness
d. the need to be honest and the need to be close

8.134
b
LO 17
Concept
307
C

Marriage partners whose _____ are more satisfied with the marriage.
a. stress coping styles are dissimilar
b. stress coping styles are similar
c. stress coping styles are complementary
d. stress coping styles are cohesive

8.135
a
LO 18
Concept
308
M

Women who describe themselves as _____ report marital satisfaction.
a. feminine or expressive
b. instrumental or expressive
c. feminine or unexpressive
d. instrumental or unexpressive

8.136
b
LO 18
Concept
308
M

A male becomes most jealous when his partner
a. becomes emotionally committed to someone else
b. is sexually unfaithful
c. becomes less protective
d. expresses emotion to someone else

8.137
c
LO 18
Concept
308
M

Partners who are _____ are happiest in their marriage
a. able to control their anger
b. able to deal with their boredom
c. able to express their emotions
d. able to discuss their differences

8.138
d
LO 18
Applied
308
M

When they were dating, Lisa was very compulsive about the arrangement of her things. Ralph
tended to be disorganized. Both of them thought these characteristics were cute. After marriage,
these characteristics stopped being cute and became a major source of conflict. Ralph and Lisa are
experiencing the role that _____ plays in a marriage.
a. inexperience
b. compulsiveness
c. cohesiveness
d. dissimilarity

8.139
b
LO 19
Concept
308
M

Which one of the factors discussed in the text causes relationships to deteriorate?
a. conflicts in extracurricular activities
b. boredom
c. changes in reciprocal evaluations
d. flirtation with members of the opposite sex

8.140
b
LO 19
Concept
308
M

What is apt to increase over the years of a marriage?
a. number of sexual interactions
b. reciprocal negative evaluations
c. time spent on mutual hobbies
d. arguments about children

8.141
d
LO 19
Concept
308
M

What is apt to decline over the years of a marriage?
a. financial resources
b. desire to travel together
c. the need to have someone to talk to
d. the expression of positive feelings about one another

8.142
b
LO 19
Concept
308
M

According to Rusbult and Zembrodt (1983), loyalty and neglect are terms that describe
a. active responses to an unhappy partnership
b. passive responses to an unhappy relationship
c. the equivalents of the intimacy and deterioration stages of Levinger
d. complementary poles along a relationship dimension

8.143
a
LO 19
Study
309
C

According to Rusbult and Zembrodt (1983), the two active responses to perceived deterioration in
a relationship are
a. exit and voice
b. exit and loyalty
c. voice and loyalty
d. loyalty and neglect

8.144
d
LO 19
Concept
309
M

The term used to describe the response to a deteriorating relationship by undertaking actions designed to improve the relationship is
a. exit
b. loyalty
c. neglect
d. voice

8.145
c
LO 19
Applied
310
M

Which strategies do low self-esteem partners tend to adopt when their relationships begin to deteriorate?
a. active voice
b. passive loyalty
c. passive neglect
d. active exit

8.146
c
LO 19
Concept
310
M

Active and passive responses to unhappy relationships are associated with differences in
a. companionate love
b. passionate love
c. self-esteem
d. logical love

8.147
a
LO 20
Concept
310
C

A deteriorating relationship may be maintained if three factors are present. Which of the following is NOT one of those factors?
a. a history of strong, mutual sexual gratification
b. a high level of satisfaction for each partner
c. the past investment of time and effort to build the relationship
d. the absence of alternative partners

8.148
b
LO 20
Concept
310
M

What can cause a partner to reevaluate dissatisfaction with a relationship?
a. declining sexual interest
b. lack of alternatives
c. fear of the unknown
d. family ties

8.149
d
LO 20
Concept
310
M

The dependence model of break-ups proposes that
a. dependent people go from relationship to relationship
b. sex roles in a relationship are related to the individuals' degrees of dependence on that relationship
c. break-ups are precipitated by the breakdown of the dependent partner
d. the decision to continue a relationship is related to an individual's degree of dependence on that relationship

8.150
c
LO 20
Concept
310
M

Individuals with _____ form long-lasting, committed, satisfying relationships.
a. an insecure ambivalent attachment style
b. an insecure avoidant attachment style
c. a secure attachment style
d. a secure assessment attachment style

8.151
a
LO 20
Fact
310
M

According to statistics, divorced males are _____ likely to remarry than divorced females.
a. more
b. less
c. divorced males and females do not differ in remarriage rate
d. both groups are unlikely to remarry

8.152
c
LO 21
Study
311
C

According to Dion and Dion (1993), romantic love is more of an important consideration in
a. collectivistic rather than individualistic societies
b. individualistic rather than personalistic
c. individualistic rather than collectivistic
d. collectivistic rather than personalistic

8.153
b
LO 21
Study
312
C

Psychological intimacy is more basic to marital satisfaction and personal well-being in
a. collectivistic rather than individualistic societies
b. individualistic rather than collectivistic
c. individualistic rather than personalistic
d. collectivistic rather than personalistic

8.154
d
LO 21
Fact
312
E

An example of an individualistic society would be
a. China
b. Pakistan
c. India
d. Canada

8.155
a
LO 21
Study
312
M

Dion and Dion (1993) suggest that one reason for the high divorce rate is the
a. intimacy vs interdependence conflict
b. intimacy vs communication conflict
c. personal vs collective conflict
d. dependence vs interdependence conflict

CHAPTER 9

Learning Objectives

After studying this chapter, students should be able to:

1.   *Define "social influence," "norms," "conformity," "obedience," and "compliance." Contrast written and unwritten norms. Discuss the result of wholesale disregard of norms, and how norms have changed.*

2.   *Detail the classic Asch studies of conformity. Indicate the result of breaking the unanimity among false judges.*

3.   *Understand the difference between public compliance and private acceptance. Discuss cohesiveness and, when it is high, how it will affect one's views that are different from the group. Tell what Crandall found when investigating strength of sorority friendships and binge eating.*

4.   *Explain why people get suspicious when the number of group members agreeing on issues increases beyond 3-4. Contrast descriptive and injunctive norms, and explain how the Reno group investigated these norm types in the bag dropping study.*

5.   *Identify two needs that determine our level of conformity along with certain cognitive processes. Contrast normative with informational social influence. Give the story interpretations of people who did and did not go along with others' risky advice given to a potential music student.*

6.   *Consider how individuation places limits on conformity for the purpose of gaining others' favor. Describe Daubman's research with people high or low on desire for control.*

7.   *Give a contemporary example of a minority inserting influence on the majority. Outline three conditions making minorities successful influence agents.*

8.   *Explain how Cialdini learned from real-life compliance experts. Outline six basic principles for gaining compliance.*

9.   *Explain the Freedman study involving phone requests to homemakers, and their rates of compliance.*

10.   *Explain throwing the "low ball". Discuss "bait and switch".*

11.   *Understand reciprocity and give examples. Explain the "that's not all" strategy and how reciprocity is involved.*

12.   *Describe what social ploy lies behind the "foot in the mouth" method.*

13.   *Relate "scarce commodity" to "playing hard to get." Indicate how the "deadline techniques" is used in sales.*

14.   *List the six complaint categories uncovered by Alicke and colleagues. Discuss the most and least common reasons for complaining, and explain the role of gender.*

15.   *Indicate why "can you spare some change?" is less effective than "can you spare 34 cents?"*

16.   *Define "obedience" and give examples. Explain why it is a matter of extraordinary seriousness. Outline the basic components of Milgram's experiments.*

17.   *Explain the effects of switching to an unprestigious setting, a foreign site, or pleas for release on the part of the shock victim in Milgram's studies. Discuss participants' reactions to the experiments. Describe the role of responsibility in obedience.*

18.   *Explain how the symbols of authority affect obedience level.   Indicate why gradual escalation increases obedience.   List the four kinds of knowledge that impart resistance to destructive obedience.*

19.   *Understand gender differences in proneness to social influence.   Suggest reasons why earlier and later studies of gender differences in submission to social influence yielded different results.*

20.   *Describe how Eagly showed that gender differences in status account for differences in susceptibility to social influence.*

21.   *Give Graziano's and colleagues' procedures showing that physical attractiveness judgments constitute one area where the genders do differ in proneness to social influence.*

22.   *Explain the gender difference in physical attractiveness judgments.*

Questions

9.1   Social influence is
d
LO 1
Fact
318
E

a. being influenced by others
b. the influence of society on us
c. influencing how society operates and determining how it will operate in the future
d. attempts to change the attitudes, behaviors, and perceptions of others

9.2   Conformity occurs when
a
LO 1
Concept
319
M

a. individuals change their behavior in order to fit existing norms
b. individuals adhere to conventions of a society such as wearing clothes
c. individuals influence each other
d. individuals mimic each other

9.3   Compliance is
b
LO 1
Fact
319
M

a. changing behavior in response to direct commands from others
b. changing behavior in response to direct requests from others
c. changing behavior as a result of simple observation of the behavior of others
d. changing behavior to adhere to widely accepted beliefs or standards

9.4   Obedience is
a
LO 1
Fact
319
M

a. changing behavior in response to direct commands from others
b. changing behavior in response to direct requests from others
c. changing behavior as a result of simple observation of the behavior of others
d. changing behavior to adhere to widely accepted beliefs or standards

9.5   A "social norm" is a
c
LO 1
Fact
319
E

a. written rule
b. law that has legal status in court
c. spoken and unspoken rules concerning how we ought to behave
d. the same as a taboo

9.6   Which of the following is an example of an explicit norm?
b
LO 1
Applied
319
E

a. standards of dress
b. laws
c. unwritten rules of a game
d. styles of speech

9.7   Ralph stands when the national anthem is played. His behavior is an example of a
b
LO 1
Applied
319
M

a. compliance tactic
b. social norm
c. written rule
d. temporary trend

9.8   The one common characteristic of all social norms is
d
LO 1
Concept
319
M

a. they are obeyed more by adults than children
b. they all work through voluntary compliance
c. they are obeyed more by children than adults
d. most people obey them most of the time

9.9   One result of most people NOT obeying social norms most of the time is that
a
LO 1 a. social chaos might result
Concept b. people would feel good about themselves because of the increased independence
320 c. people would be able to accomplish more because of relaxed restrictions
M   d. society would benefit because of the relaxed restrictions

9.10   The dilemma faced by subjects in Asch's experiments was related to
d
LO 2 a. compliance
Concept b. obedience
321 c. saving face
M   d. conformity pressure

9.11   In the Asch studies of conformity, subjects
d
LO 2 a. judged the movement of a point of light presented in darkness
Study b. chose from among variations of a dart game
321 c. manipulated some switches that guided a toy car
M   d. attempted to match some comparison lines to a standard line

9.12   With the Asch method
d
LO 2 a. confederates make false judgment on every trial
Study b. confederates never make false judgments
321 c. all subjects always go along with the confederates' judgments
E   d. confederates make false judgments on certain trials

9.13   Subjects in Asch's conformity experiments who stuck to the answers that they though were correct
d   in the face of others' disagreements were
LO 2 a. found to be high in self-monitoring behavior
Study b. found to be low in social skills
321 c. classed as noncompliant
C   d. resisting conformity pressure

9.14   From Asch (1951), it was found that many more people
c
LO 2 a. resisted conformity pressure
Study b. recognized conformity pressure
321 c. were influenced by conformity pressure at least some of the time
C   d. did not pay attention to other people in decision making

9.15   Asch (1951) found that
c
LO 2 a. most subjects resisted conformity pressure all of the time
Study b. most subjects were influenced by conformity pressure almost all of the time
321 c. most subjects yielded to conformity pressures, but not all of the time
M   d. the control group made almost as many errors as the experimental group

9.16   In the Asch studies, what percent of subjects went along with false judgments at least one time?
c
LO 2 a. 24%
Study b. 53%
321 c. 76%
E   d. 92%

9.17
a
LO 2
Study
322
C

In Asch's studies, he found that one way to reduce conformity was to
a. break group unanimity
b. have subjects speak their answers out loud
c. pass around a sheet of paper containing the answers of the other participants
d. change the task

9.18
b
LO 3
Study
322
M

How did Asch arrange to lower conformity?
a. he allowed subjects to speak their judgments out loud
b. he had subjects write their judgments on paper
c. he had subjects pass a sheet of paper around containing the answers of the other participants
d. he publicly announced each subject's judgments

9.19
a
LO 3
Fact
323
M

Public compliance is
a. doing or saying what others around us say or do
b. doing or saying the opposite of what others around us say or do
c. going along with others inwardly, but not outwardly
d. saying out loud what we believe inwardly

9.20
d
LO 3
Fact
323
M

Private acceptance is
a. doing or saying what others around us say or do
b. doing or saying the opposite of what others around us say or do
c. going along with others inwardly, but not outwardly
d. saying out loud what others say, and believing it inwardly

9.21
b
LO 3
Concept
323
C

The difference between saying what others say, and coming to believe what they believe is the difference between
a. normative and informational influence
b. public compliance and private acceptance
c. impression and personal management
d. surface and conceptual obedience

9.22
c
LO 3
Concept
323
M

The degree of attraction to the group or persons exerting influence upon you is called
a. compliance
b. colinearity
c. cohesiveness
d. co-option

9.23
b
LO 3
Concept
323
M

Cohesiveness influences conformity in that
a. we are more likely to yield to influence from larger groups
b. we are more likely to yield to influence from people that we like
c. we are more likely to yield to influence in the absence of social support
d. we are more likely to yield to influence in the face of threats

9.24
d
LO 3
Concept
324
M

Friends are more willing to accept influence from friends because
a. they have had chances to see that their friends have been right in the past
b. they tend to forget the times when their friends have been wrong in the past
c. they tend to discount the times when their friends were wrong in the past
d. they like their friends better than the average person

9.25   Crandall (1988) used sorority sisters in a study. What was the predicted outcome of the study?
c   a. voting behavior would be unaffected by friendships
LO 3   b. sexual behavior would conform to norms of friends
Study c. during the course of the study, subjects would become more like friends with respect to binge
324   eating
C   d. whether substance abuse would be high or low would depend upon friendship patterns during
          the course of the study

9.26   If Ralph rejects a stranger's advice to brush his teeth every day, but begins to do so when advised
b   to do so by his friend Lisa, Ralph is reacting to conformity pressure through
LO 3   a. physiological well-being
Applied b. cohesiveness
324   c. compliance
M   d. colinearity

9.27   Which of the following was found by Asch to influence the amount of conformity pressure exerted
a   upon an individual?
LO 4   a. group size
Study b. outcome responsibility
324   c. gain/loss expectancies
M   d. gender

9.28   Which of the following influences the amount of conformity pressure exerted by a group on an
c   individual?
LO 4   a. decision outcome responsibility
Concept b. decision outcome importance
324   c. suspicions of collusion
M   d. suspicions of cohesiveness

9.29   Group size affects perceived conformity pressure in that, generally, the _____ the group, the _____
a   pressure is exerted.
LO 4   a. larger, more
Concept b. more compliant, less
324   c. smaller, more
M   d. more cohesive, less

9.30   Group size stops increasing the amount of conformity pressure upon an individual if that individual
b   suspects
LO 4   a. hostility
Concept b. collusion
324   c. no responsibility for the outcome
M   d. no gain from the outcome

9.31   The size of the group that applies pressure to conform is
d   a. irrelevant
LO 4   b. important through an indefinite group size
Concept c. unimportant
324   d. important through group size 3-4
M

9.32   Why is there a limit to the effect of group size on conformity?
a   a. members in large groups suspect collusion among other members
LO 4   b. large groups always contain people who don't go along
Concept c. large groups are always poorly organized
324   d. members can't believe that all the other members of a large group understand the issues
M

9.33
a
LO 4
Fact
324
M

A descriptive norm is
a. what is generally seen as effective or adaptive behavior in a situation
b. what is approved or disapproved behavior in a situation
c. what is socially enhanced behavior in a situation
d. what is individually assessed behavior in a situation

9.34
b
LO 4
Fact
325
M

A injunctive norm is
a. what is generally seen as effective or adaptive behavior in a situation
b. what is approved or disapproved behavior in a situation
c. what is socially enhanced behavior in a situation
d. what is individually assessed behavior in a situation

9.35
b
LO 4
Study
326
C

Reno and colleagues (1991), in their study of littering found that
a. descriptive norms reduced littering in both a clean and a dirty environment
b. injunctive norms reduced littering in both a clean and a dirty environment
c. descriptive norms decreased littering in a dirty environment only
d. injunctive norms decreased littering in a clean environment only

9.36
d
LO 4
Applied
326
C

Reno and colleagues (1993) suggest that in social situations where many people do not behave in a socially beneficial way, activating _____ may be more beneficial.
a. cohesion norms
b. collusion norms
c. descriptive norms
d. injunctive norms

9.37
d
LO 5
Fact
327
M

Normative social influence is
a. redefining norms so that one's social influence is increased
b. formalizing unwritten or implicit social norms
c. using other persons as sources of knowledge
d. altering behavior to meet the expectations of others

9.38
c
LO 5
Concept
327
M

Normative social influence occurs when we
a. conform because we want to be right
b. conform due to inherited genetic patterns
c. conform in order to be liked
d. are similar to other group members

9.39
c
LO 5
Fact
327
M

Informational social influence is
a. redefining norms so that one's social influence is increased
b. formalizing unwritten or implicit social norms
c. using other persons as sources of knowledge
d. altering behavior to meet the expectations of others

9.40
a
LO 5
Concept
327
M

Informational social influence occurs when we
a. conform because we want to be right
b. conform due to inherited genetic patterns
c. conform in order to be liked
d. are similar to other group members

9.41   Buehler and Griffin (1994), in their study of conformity of responses for advice giving, found that
d   a. only those individuals who conformed adjusted their interpretation of the story in order to justify
LO 5   their decision
Study   b. only those individuals who did not conform adjusted their interpretation of the story in order
328   to justify their decision
C   c. neither conforming or not conforming had any impact on adjustment of interpretation of stories
        d. those individuals who conformed or who did not conform adjusted their interpretations of the
            story in order to justify their decision

9.42   Part of the power to resist conformity pressure comes in the possession of a desire for
d   a. approval from many groups
LO 6   b. personification
Concept c. reality
329   d. individuation
E

9.43   Individuation helps one to
a   a. maintain a unique identity
LO 6   b. cope with reality
Concept c. disagree and still be liked
329   d. not care whether one is liked or not
M

9.44   Why are individuals sometimes resistant to conformity pressures?
b   a. they all have a bit of rebellion in them
LO 6   b. they desire to maintain a felling of uniqueness or individuality
Concept c. they follow the rule to resist at least some of the time
329   d. they realize that the group is incorrect a certain percent of the time, and they unconsciously
M   approximate that percentage

9.45   Part of the desire to resist conformity comes from the desire for
c   a. approval from many groups
LO 6   b. personification
Concept c. perceived control over one's actions
329   d. reality
M

9.46   According to research, those low in need for personal control are _____ likely to conform.
b   a. less
LO 6   b. more
Concept c. more, but only under stress
330   d. it is rare for need for control to conflict with conformity pressures
M

9.47   Daubman (1993), in his study on personal control, found that
b   a. persons high in personal control felt good about receiving help
LO 6   b. persons low in personal control felt good about receiving help
Study   c. persons low in personal control felt bad about receiving help
330   d. personal control had really no impact on how persons felt after the completed the task
C

9.48   The research by Daubman (1993) lends support to the contention that
a   a. persons high in personal control tend to perceive influence attempts by others as threatening
LO 6   b. persons low in personal control tend to perceive influence attempts by others as threatening
Concept c. persons high in personal control tend to be receptive to help from others
330   d. persons low in personal control tend to be resistive to help from others
C

9.49
c
LO 7
Concept
331
M

Concerning minorities
a. they are always the influencee rather than the influencer
b. they have little influence, by definition
c. under certain circumstances, they have more influence than majorities
d. actually, and paradoxically, they have more influence than majorities

9.50
a
LO 7
Concept
331
C

Which of the following is NOT one of the principles that people in the minority must follow in order to be influential?
a. they must be careful to be variable in their point of view
b. they must not be rigid or dogmatic
c. they must endorse a point of view that is in step with the times
d. they must be consistent in expressing their point of view

9.51
c
LO 7
Concept
331
M

Which of the following increases the likelihood that minority influence will take place?
a. the minority should be rigid and dogmatic when expressing their views
b. the minority should avoid positions consistent with current social trends
c. the minority should be consistent in their expressed views
d. the minority should be a variable minority

9.52
d
LO 7
Applied
331
C

Even if minorities do not have as much influence as majorities, what positive outcomes might they produce?
a. minorities cause others to reach quick decisions without wasting a lot of thought
b. minorities cause others to like each other more
c. minorities cause others to like "rebels" more
d. minorities cause others to develop solutions that they might otherwise overlook

9.53
c
LO 7
Applied
331
C

Even if minorities do not have as much influence as majorities, what positive outcomes might they produce?
a. minorities cause others to waste little time in the decision process
b. minorities cause others to compete more reasonably
c. minorities cause others to develop more creative solutions
d. minorities cause others to develop solutions that "go against the grain"

9.54
a
LO 7
Applied
331
M

Even if a minority cannot change a majority view, dissent is still valuable because it can
a. encourage deeper thought by the majority
b. show where the blame for adverse consequences lies
c. make the majority more certain of its position
d. increase external attributions for results

9.55
c
LO 7
Study
332
C

Baker and Petty (1994), using the ELM to investigate attention paid to messages from majority or minority found
a. messages from the majority had more attention paid to them
b. messages from the minority had less attention paid to them
c. messages from an imbalanced source and message have more attention paid to them
d. messages from a balanced source and message have more attention paid to them

9.56
c
LO 7
Study
332
C

Baker and Petty (1994) found that participants gave careful scrutiny to those messages that came from
a. a minority source expressing a minority opinion
b. a majority source expressing a majority opinion
c. a majority source expressing a minority opinion or a minority source expressing a majority opinion
d. a majority source, regardless of whether the opinion was majority or minority

9.57   The type of influence exerted in the form of direct requests is called
c
LO 8   a. conformity pressure
          b. entry level influence
Fact   c. compliance
332   d. obedience
E

9.58   Compliance is
c
LO 8   a. yielding to the orders of an authority figure
          b. giving up one's own point of view for that of the group
Fact   c. expressing one's wishes in the hope that they will be granted
332   d. giving up one's sense of uniqueness and desire to control circumstances
M

9.59   Which of the following is NOT one of the principles of gaining compliance that were suggested by
d   Cialdini (1994)?
LO 8   a. authority
Study   b. friendship/liking
333   c. commitment/consistency
M   d. helpfulness

9.60   Which of the following is NOT one of the principles of gaining compliance that were suggested by
c   Cialdini (1994)?
LO 8   a. reciprocity
Study   b. social validation
333   c. self-enhancement
M   d. scarcity

9.61   Ingratiation is
b
LO 9   a. getting others to like us so that we may do them a favor
          b. getting others to like us so that we may make requests of them
Fact   c. gaining the confidence of others so that harm can be done to them
334   d. limited to the technique of "flattery"
M

9.62   Which of the following are among the "impression management" methods of ingratiation?
a   a. making oneself attractive
LO 9   b. pointing out that one is unique
Applied c. bragging about one's accomplishments
334   d. concealing one's true self
M

9.63   Improving one's grooming to increase the likelihood of gaining compliance is an example of
b   a. self-esteem
LO 9   b. self-enhancement
Concept c. self-regulation
334   d. other-enhancement
E

9.64   Making a small request before a large request is called the
c   a. two stage compliance theory
LO 9   b. door in the face approach
Fact   c. foot in the door approach
334   d. multiple request approach
M

9.65
c
LO 9
Study
334
C

When Freedman and Frazer (1966) phoned homemakers with a simple request then asked to search their houses,
a. no recipient of the call granted the search request
b. all recipients of the call granted the search request
c. more recipients of the call granted the search request than homemakers given the search request alone
d. fewer recipients of the call granted the search request than homemakers given the search request alone

9.66
b
LO 9
Study
334
M

The experimenter who asked people to allow a crew into their house after agreeing to answer some questions about their soap preferences was using the
a. two stage compliance approach
b. foot in the door approach
c. door in the face approach
d. multiple request approach

9.67
b
LO 9
Concept
335
C

One explanation of the foot in the door phenomenon is that after complying with a small request
a. people are too embarrassed to say no
b. people agree in order to be consistent
c. people feel obligated to the requester
d. people feel flattered at being asked to help

9.68
b
LO 10
Fact
335
M

Low balling is
a. the opposite of foot in the door
b. when the cost of something is given as much lower than expected by a person then raised after the person "buys it"
c. when a large request is followed by a small request
d. when the cost of something is unreasonably higher than expected by a person and then is lowered after the person "buys it"

9.69
c
LO 10
Applied
335
C

Ralph has agreed to purchase a new Mustang for $18,000. However, just before he gets ready to sign the contract, the salesman tells Ralph that the sales manager will not approve the amount allowed for his trade-in, and that the contract will have to be higher, probably around $19,000. Ralph has just been the victim of
a. the foot in the door technique
b. the door in the face technique
c. the low ball technique
d. the reversing the tables technique

9.70
c
LO 10
Applied
335
C

Which of the following is an example of the bait and switch technique?
a. signing a contract, and after some thought, backing out
b. making an initial large request for a donation and then following it with another request for an even larger donation
c. getting a person to commit to sign a contract for a standard refrigerator and then inform him that a mistake has been make and this model only comes with an icemaker, which will increase the price
d. getting an initial small donation for an organization and then following that donation with a request for a larger donation

9.71
a
LO 10
Concept
335
C

According to the commitment explanation of low balling
a. a person becomes cognitively committed to granting a request then is hesitant to change that commitment
b. after granting a request, a person becomes committed to granting no further requests
c. before becoming committed to an initial request, the target carefully examines what he is being asked to grant
d. after thinking about it, the person does not want to be embarrassed by denying the request

9.72   Following a large request with a small request is known as the
b   a. foot in the door approach
LO 11   b. door in the face approach
Fact   c. delayed request approach
336   d. two stage compliance approach
M

9.73   Cialdini and colleagues (1975) asked some subjects to be unpaid counselors to delinquents for two
b   years. When turned down, then asked them to take the delinquents to the zoo one time. They
LO 11   found
Study   a. more people complied with the zoo request when it was presented in a hurry
336   b. more people complied with the zoo request preceded by the counselor request than those asked
C   only about the zoo
                c. more people complied with the zoo request when it was presented alone
                d. more people complied with the counselor request when it was presented alone

9.74   According to the notion of reciprocal concessions
b   a. if a person complies with a small request, she has the right to refuse a subsequent large request
LO 11   b. if a requester backs down from a large request to a small one, the target of the request may feel
Concept   compelled to grant the second request
336   c. if the target of a request refuses an initial large request, he may feel that he will look bad if he
C   refuses a subsequent small request
                d. if a target of an initial small request grants the same, she may feel committed to a subsequent
                large request

9.75   Which of the following is an explanation of the door in the face?
d   a. self-perception
LO 11   b. unfulfilled obligation
Concept   c. commitment
336   d. reciprocal concessions
M

9.76   When an auto dealer offers you an extra option as a "closer" for a deal, the dealer is using
d   a. the doubled compliance technique
LO 11   b. the covert request technique
Applied   c. the integration technique
337   d. the that's not all technique
M

9.77   Which is the most effective in making sales?
a   a. the that's not all technique
LO 11   b. an indication that the price is a bargain
Applied   c. a multiple range of products
337   d. a no argument, no haggling price
M

9.78   It is suggested that the that's not all technique works due to the
c   a. benefit of multiple purchase options
LO 11   b. norm of commitment
Concept   c. norm of reciprocity
337   d. norm of unfilled obligation
M

9.79
b
LO 11
Concept
337
M

What should we bear in mind when confronted with the that's not all technique?
a. the requester is almost always lying
b. the requester had the final offer, including bonus, in mind all the time
c. the requester is watching our reactions and will add a bonus only if he or she feels it will work
d. the requester is looking for pigeons and is analyzing our behavior to determine if we "have feathers"

9.80
b
LO 12
Fact
337
M

The foot in the mouth technique involves
a. having someone make a mistake and then a request
b. the establishment of a relationship and then a request
c. getting a verbal commitment and then a request for specific behavior
d. getting someone to say something embarrassing and then follow with a request

9.81
a
LO 12
Study
337
M

Aune and Basil (1994) stopped students on a campus and asked students to make a donation. The results indicated
a. more students complied if they had been asked if they were students first and then a request was made for a donation
b. more students complied if they had not been first asked if they were students
c. more students complied if they were first asked where they were going and then asked for a donation
d. asking if they were students had no effect on donations

9.82
d
LO 12
Applied
337
M

Ralph had been stopped by a person asking for a donation. The requester first asked if he was a student. Ralph replied that he was, and the requester said that he was also a student. The requester then asked for a donation. Because of the _____, Ralph will probably donate.
a. foot in the door technique
b. door in the face technique
c. low-ball technique
d. foot in the mouth technique

9.83
a
LO 12
Applied
337
E

Lisa has just experienced the foot in the mouth technique. What would a requester have to first establish before this technique would work?
a. a relationship
b. a conflict
c. a concession
d. a manipulation

9.84
c
LO 13
Fact
338
E

The compliance technique of suggesting that a person or object is scarce is called
a. low balling
b. door in the face
c. playing hard to get
d. deadline

9.85
c
LO 13
Study
338
M

Williams and colleagues (1993) asked recruiters to rate applications for jobs. They found
a. candidates who had two other job offers were rated highest, regardless of grades
b. candidates who had the highest grades were rated highest, regardless of other job offers
c. candidates who had the highest grades and had two other job offers were rated highest
d. candidates who had the highest grades but no job offers were rated highest

9.86   The compliance technique of suggesting that there is a limited time to obtain some item is called
d   a. low balling
LO 13   b. playing hard to get
Fact   c. door in the face
338   d. deadline
E

9.87   Lisa saw in the paper that a department store was having a "Closeout of Winter Dresses" sale. If she
d   goes to that sale and buys something, she will be a victim of
LO 13   a. low balling technique
Applied   b. playing hard to get technique
338   c. door in the face technique
M   d. deadline technique

9.88   Complaints fall into which of the following categories?
c   a. global, physical, emotional
LO 14   b. obligations, emotional, global
Fact   c. global, obligations, physical
339   d. physical, global, categorical
M

9.89   The statement "I'll probably fail my test" is a complaint about
b   a. obligation expectancies
LO 14   b. achievement expectancies
Applied   c. specific expectancies
339   d. global expectancies
M

9.90   The most common reason given for complaining is to
a   a. vent frustration
LO 14   b. seek sympathy
Study   c. exert conformity pressure
339   d. seek advice
M

9.91   Complaints are more successful in changing behavior if they are
c   a. accompanied by a request
LO 14   b. accompanied by praise
Concept   c. direct
339   d. indirect
M

9.92   In responding to complaints by friends, females tend to be
c   a. less able to help
LO 14   b. less tolerant
Concept   c. more supportive
340   d. more conscientious in recognizing complaints
M

9.93   Accuracy in reporting the complaints of others is most characteristic of
b   a. men
LO 14   b. women
Concept   c. parents
340   d. romantic partners
M

9.94
b
LO 14
Study
340
C

Rind (1996), in a study on the relationship between mood and helping, found that guests in a hotel gave
a. smaller tips when the weather was described as cold rather than warm
b. larger tips when the weather was described as sunny rather than rainy
c. larger tips when the weather was described as warm rather than sunny
d. smaller tips when the weather was described as cold rather than sunny

9.95
a
LO 14
Concept
340
M

Putting someone in a good mood
a. increases their tendency to comply
b. increases their tendency to evaluate
c. increases their tendency to conform
d. increases their tendency to obey

9.96
c
LO 15
Fact
341
M

A technique for gaining compliance that focuses on preventing people from engaging in automatic refusal is called
a. the foot in the door technique
b. the door in the mouth technique
c. the pique technique
d. the door in the face technique

9.97
d
LO 15
Study
341
C

In a study by Santos and colleagues (1994), female panhandlers asked passersby for money. In two conditions, they asked for "17 cents" or "37 cents." In both cases, there was more compliance. This study was investigating the effectiveness of
a. the door in the face technique
b. the deadline technique
c. the foot in the door technique
d. the pique technique

9.98
a
LO 15
Concept
341
C

Why is the pique technique called what it is?
a. the technique arouses (piques) someone's attention by making an unusual request
b. the technique involves making a sharp (pique) request of someone
c. the technique involves keeps someone in suspense (pique) until the request is made
d. the technique irritates (piques) someone until the request is made

9.99
c
LO 15
Applied
341
C

Ralph was walking down the street and was asked for money by a panhandler, and as he has always done, he refused. Another panhandler came up to Ralph and asked for "exactly $1.37." Ralph immediately starting wondering why that amount and wound up giving money ($1.37). Ralph was influenced by a very smart panhandler who was using the
a. door in the face technique
b. foot in the door technique
c. pique technique
d. cognitive technique

9.100
b
LO 16
Fact
342
E

Gaining compliance through giving orders is
a. reward-punishment
b. an obedience tactic
c. classical conditioning
d. operant conditioning

9.101
c
LO 16
Study
342
M

Milgram (1963) studied obedience through determining whether
a. participants would attend his experiments whether or not he paid them
b. participants would cooperate with other subjects
c. participants would shock other participants
d. participants would compete with other participants

9.102
a
LO 16
Study
342
M

Which of the following were tested for the degree of obedience in Milgram's study?
a. the person giving the shocks
b. the person getting the shocks
c. the person controlling the procedure
d. the person assisting with the study

9.103
a
LO 16
Study
343
M

What kind of apparatus did Milgram use in his experiments?
a. a elaborate panel containing numerous switches capable of delivering shocks ranging from 15 to 450 volts
b. a point of light presented in total darkness that appeared to move but was attributed more movement by an authority figure
c. a simple choice dilemma device with which subjects competed by moving toy solders
d. a kind of "one-upmanship" machine that allowed a subject to select a level of shock to deliver to another subject based on what that other person had chosen to deliver

9.104
c
LO 16
Study
343
C

Which of the following is an accurate description of the experimental procedure used to study obedience by Stanley Milgram?
a. the teacher and learner were both actual subjects
b. whenever the learner made an error, the teacher was to deliver a constant, moderate shock to the learner
c. subjects thought that they were delivering a shock to a learner, but were actually were not
d. the real purpose of the experiment was to study how well someone can learn material when threatened with shock after making errors

9.105
d
LO 16
Study
343
M

What did the experimenter in the Milgram studies do when subjects protested that they did not want to go on?
a. he allowed them to quit
b. he ignored their protests and went back to his task-scoring procedure
c. he attempted to reason with them
d. he said that they had no choice, they had to continue

9.106
b
LO 16
Study
343
M

In the course of Milgram's study, it was noted that
a. many of the subjects refused to comply with the experimenter
b. many of the subjects complied reluctantly
c. many of the subjects actually insisted on continuing the shocks
d. many of the subjects did not realize that they were really giving shocks

9.107
c
LO 16
Study
344
M

The percent of subjects in Milgram's study who fully complied with the experimenter's orders was
a. 10%
b. 35%
c. 65%
d. 95%

9.108
b
LO 16
Study
344
M

One lesson to be learned from the Milgram studies is that
a. many people have an unexpected stubborn streak
b. many people will follow orders even if they do not like them
c. many people can be easily fooled
d. many people are more sadistic than they appear

9.109
a
LO 17
Study
345
C

Which of the following is true regarding the original experiments on obedience by Milgram?
a. the experimenter pressured the subjects to continue the experiment even when the learner pounded on the wall
b. the subjects were always told that since they were the ones pushing the switches, they were responsible for the learner's welfare
c. strong shocks were actually delivered to the learner
d. when the experiment was moved from the Yale campus to a rundown office building in a nearby city, the level of obedience was sharply reduced

9.110
d
LO 17
Study
346
M

One reason that the effects of Milgram's studies may have been limited was that
a. it was conducted in a prestigious location
b. the accomplice who received the shock did not ask to be released
c. the subject was separated from the accomplice who received the shock
d. Milgram's effects were replicated when all of the above conditions were changed

9.111
b
LO 17
Concept
346
M

Milgram's results are generally taken to show that
a. people can be sadistic
b. situational pressures can overwhelm personality
c. males are more aggressive than females
d. females are more aggressive than males

9.112
d
LO 17
Study
346
M

Which of the following reduced obedience in the Milgram studies to 30%?
a. the learner complained of headaches
b. conducting the experiment away from prestigious Yale University
c. pounding on a wall by the learner
d. having to actually place the learner's hand on a shock plate

9.113
b
LO 17
Fact
346
E

The Milgram obedience study was NOT conducted in which of the following countries?
a. U.S.A.
b. China
c. Australia
d. West Germany

9.114
a
LO 17
Concept
346
C

One reason that the subjects in Milgram's experiments obeyed the experimenter is that
a. the experimenter relieved them of responsibility for the outcome
b. many of the subjects had military experience
c. many of the subjects lacked military experience
d. many of the subjects had an external locus of control

9.115
b
LO 18
Concept
346
M

Badges, insignia, etc. are helpful in gaining obedience because they
a. remind people of their childhood
b. are constant reminders of who has authority
c. are characteristic of violent people
d. are a form of covert request

9.116   A possible reason why the Nazi party was so successful in getting obedience for horrific tasks was
c   that
LO 18   a. party leaders were ingratiating
Applied b. party leaders used tactics of consultation
347   c. they began their persecution gradually
C   d. no one thought that what he or she was doing was wrong

9.117   Exposing people to disobedient models in situations of destructive obedience may help people
a   a. realize that unquestioning obedience can be inappropriate
LO 18   b. feel that they are not alone in resisting
Concept c. vicariously experience relief from disobedience
347   d. disobedient models are not helpful in reducing destructive obedience
M

9.118   Reminding people that they are responsible for the outcome of their actions
b   a. increases destructive obedience
LO 18   b. reduces destructive obedience
Concept c. has no effect
347   d. stops people from viewing their obedience as destructive
M

9.119   If commands are issued gradually, what dilemma is generated?
a   a. Where should I draw the line?
LO 18   b. When should he or she stop?
Applied c. What will witnesses think of me?
347   d. What would others do in a similar situation?
M

9.120   What happened in one study when subjects were reminded that they would be responsible for the
b   victim's well-being?
LO 18   a. they continued to shock the victim
Concept b. they showed lower levels of shock than when not given the reminder
347   c. they complained more to the experimenter
C   d. they expressed more concern for the victim

9.121   Which of the following lowers harmful behavior by subjects in the Milgram-type experiment?
d   a. cries by the victim
LO 18   b. pounding on the wall by the victim
Concept c. having to increase the shock level when mistakes are made
347   d. the presence of a disobedient model
C

9.122   Which of the following would significantly lower harmful obedience?
a   a. questioning the expertise and motives of the authority figures
LO 18   b. protests by the victim
Concept c. viewing the victim receive the shocks
347   d. having them receive feedback from the victim
M

9.123   Which of the following would significantly lower harmful obedience by people?
c   a. knowing that obedience was rare
LO 18   b. empathy for the victims of obedience
Concept c. simply knowing that authority figures can command blind obedience
347   d. having to relay an order to carry out harmful behavior
M

9.124
b
LO 18
Applied
348
M

Examples of successful resistance to strong authority are
a. Milgram's subjects
b. many current Eastern European governments
c. people who are not fooled by sales talk
d. people who are entrepreneurial

9.125
b
LO 18
Applied
348
M

Which of the following world leaders was and is a model of disobedience to authority?
a. Nicolai Cesesceau
b. Boris Yeltsin
c. Pancho Villa
d. Ngo Dinh Diem

9.126
c
LO 19
Study
349
M

According to the early studies of conformity, who seemed to conform more than their counterparts?
a. males compared to females
b. blacks compared to whites
c. females compared to males
d. whites compared to blacks

9.127
d
LO 19
Study
349
C

Sistrunk and McDavid (1971) found which of the following when they varied the content of conformity items?
a. females conformed more than males
b. there was no sex difference in conformity for any items
c. males conformed more than females
d. males conformed more than females on items that were more familiar to females

9.128
b
LO 19
Concept
349
E

A common view of women is that they are more
a. intelligent
b. submissive
c. domineering
d. career oriented

9.129
c
LO 19
Concept
349
M

Data indicate that women are presently _____ submissive than men
a. more
b. less
c. no more or less
d. more eagerly

9.130
c
LO 19
Concept
349
C

One reason why women used to show more conformity than males in experimental situations is that
a. women used to conform more than men
b. males were always the authority figures in experiments
c. the tasks and materials in early experiments tended to be less familiar to women
d. women did not used to show more conformity than men

9.131
d
LO 19
Applied
349
C

Ralph and Sam are subjects in a conformity experiment involving delivering shocks to another individual. Sam is an electrical engineer, Ralph is an entry level sales representative. Who do you expect to show the most obedience?
a. Sam, because he works in a more "traditional" field
b. Sam, because he works in a higher status job
c. Ralph, because he is probably younger
d. Ralph, because he is probably less familiar with the materials

9.132
b
LO 19
Applied
349
C

Lisa and Ralph are subjects in an experiment involving delivering shocks to another individual. Lisa is an electrical engineer, and Ralph is an entry level sales representative. Who do you expect will show the most obedience?
a. Lisa, because she works in a more "traditional" field
b. Ralph, because he probably has less familiarity with the materials
c. Lisa, because she is female
d. Ralph, because he is male

9.133
a
LO 20
Study
349
M

Participants in a study by Eagly and Wood (1982) read a story about one person who influenced another. Most people thought that the influencer was
a. male
b. female
c. old
d. young

9.134
c
LO 20
Concept
349
M

A reason for the belief that females are more likely to conform in a given situation is that
a. females are used to conforming
b. females tend to be more familiar with test materials
c. females tend to be viewed as lower in status
d. females have to conform more often

9.135
d
LO 20
Concept
349
M

Conformity has been linked with which of the following conditions?
a. masculinity
b. femininity
c. androgyny
d. low status

9.136
c
LO 20
Study
349
C

Which of the following were among the procedures of Eagly and Wood's (1982) study of status and sex in determining predictions of conformity?
a. all subjects read a story with a female communicating to a female
b. all subjects read a story with a female communicating to a male
c. half of the subjects read a story that included status information
d. half of the subjects read a story with a person of undisclosed gender communicating to another such person

9.137
a
LO 21
Concept
349
M

Which of the following is an area in which there appears to be gender differences in susceptibility to social influence?
a. physical attractiveness
b. problem solving
c. line comparison
d. evaluation of stories

9.138
d
LO 21
Study
349
C

Research by Graziano and colleagues (1993) on ratings of physical attractiveness found that
a. males' judgments of female attractiveness were influenced by ratings of others
b. females' judgments of female attractiveness were influenced by ratings of others
c. males' judgments of male attractiveness were influenced by ratings of others
d. female' judgments of male attractiveness were influenced by ratings of others

9.139
b
LO 22
Study
349
C

Graziano and colleagues (1993) suggest that the reason for gender differences in judging of physical attractiveness is due to
a. males using primarily observable physical characteristics to make judgments
b. females using observable physical characteristics plus information about behavioral dispositions
c. males using information about behavioral characteristics
d. females using primarily observable physical characteristics

9.140
a
LO 22
Study
350
C

The explanation that Graziano and colleagues (1993) gave for gender differences in judgments of physical attractiveness is related to the
a. evolutionary perspective
b. social perspective
c. individual perspective
d. biological perspective

CHAPTER 10

Learning Objectives

After studying this chapter, students should be able to:

1.   *Describe cases where someone helped or failed to help in an emergency. Describe the Kitty Genovese case, and give the procedure and results of the Darley and Latane "seizure study."*

2.   *Define the "bystander effect." Understand the first step in the procession to helping. Describe the procedure and results of Batson's "seminary student study."*

3.   *Give the second step leading to eventual help. Explain how possibly "looking silly" inhibits assessing a situation as an emergency. Use "pluralistic ignorance" to explain the "smoke study."*

4.   *Outline the third and fourth steps leading to help and define "diffusion of responsibility." Explain the fifth step.*

5.   *List social interactions that are "nobody's business." Explain what the Christy/Voigt survey revealed about intervention by witnesses of abuse.*

6.   *Explain the finding on survey respondents and the bystander effect. Outline what did and did not relate to intervention by witnesses of abuse.*

7.   *List dispositions that relate to actual helping. Indicate the difference between "altruism" and "egoism."*

8.   *Indicate three traits of empathic people. Discuss how gender relates to empathy. Say what part of empathy is genetic, and give the three characteristics that Knight and colleagues found to jointly affect helping in children.*

9.   *List and define the five traits in the personality cluster of persons who help.*

10.   *Tell how Lassie inspired helping. Outline the "wrong number technique" used to determine whether gays would be helped as much as "straights."*

11.   *Explain whether dependency eclipses similarity as a determinant of helping. Discuss the role that police officers' gender plays in writing citations. Describe the effect of judging the victim responsible for her or his calamity.*

12.   *Explain how the gender of the typical perpetrator and victim of rape explain reactions to such attacks. Discuss cognitive mechanisms that help us avoid fear of victimization.*

13.   *Tell what leads up to helping a distant victim. Indicate the attributions and fears that lessens help to AIDS victims.*

14.   *Indicate who is reluctant to ask for help, and explain why any person is reluctant to ask for help, except, possibly, from a stranger. Describe the role of requester's traits and manner of asking for help in receiving help.*

15.   *In U.S. society, describe what negative trait is seen in requesters of help. Discuss some other attributions that may be aimed at requesters of help.*

16.   *Discuss the two most general reasons why we help. Explain what kinds of manipulations researchers have used to study mood and helping. Discuss when a good mood inhibits helping.*

17.   *List conditions under which negative mood inhibits helping or promotes it. Outline how subjects' level of empathy interacted with ease of getting out of the experiment in confirming Batson's theory.*

18.   *Explain when people avoid empathy-producing information. Contrast Batson's position with that of "negative state relief." Explain what Cialdini and colleagues found when they separated sadness from empathy.*

19.   *Describe the "empathic joy" hypothesis. Explain what Smith and colleagues found when subjects got feedback about the effect of their help. Discuss the "helper's high."*

20.   *Describe the genetic hypothesis regarding helping. Indicate what this theory predicts about who will receive help.*

21.   *Explain three standards that relate to helping (Reykowski). Indicate how he and colleagues studied these standards in a cross-cultural study.*

Questions

10.1   Actions that provide a benefit to others while not having any obvious benefits to oneself are called
d   a. positive reinforcers
LO 1   b. positive model behaviors
Fact   c. genetically recessive behaviors
356   d. prosocial behaviors
E

10.2   The definition of prosocial behavior stipulates that the behavior must
b   a. be easy to perform
LO 1   b. have no obvious benefits for the helper
Fact   c. help society in general
356   d. help someone specific
M

10.3   In the Genovese case
d   a. Kitty Genovese helped someone who was being mugged
LO 1   b. Kitty Genovese stood by and watched someone get mugged
Fact   c. Kitty Genovese was saved from a mugger by a passerby
358   d. Kitty Genovese was murdered in the sight of witnesses
M

10.4   Popular opinion suggests that people do not help others because
a   a. they are apathetic
LO 1   b. they are afraid to help
Concept c. they are embarrassed to help
358   d. they do not recognize emergencies
M

10.5   The concept that each member of a collection of people at the scene of an emergency will feel that
c   he or she does not have the responsibility to intervene is known as
LO 1   a. spreading the blame
Concept b. inhibited altruism
358   c. diffusion of responsibility
M   d. negative self-schematic conceptualization

10.6   According to the principle of diffusion of responsibility, you would expect members of a large group
b   to be
LO 1   a. more likely to help in an emergency
Concept b. less likely to help in an emergency
358   c. more likely to recognize an emergency
M   d. less likely to avoid an emergency

10.7   The experiment conducted by Latane and Darley involving the student with the faked seizure
d   provided evidence in favor of which explanation?
LO 1   a. that people readily aid strangers
Study   b. that people will aid friends before strangers
359   c. bystanders tend to be apathetic
M   d. diffusion of responsibility

10.8   What were the results of the seizure study?
d   a. no one helped
LO 1   b. the fewer the people present, the less the helping
Study   c. the greatest helping occurred when the subject and one other person were present with the
359   victim
M   d. even when helping occurred, there was a delay

10.9
a
LO 1
Study
359
M

Results of the "seizure" study indicated that
a. the fewer people present, the more the helping
b. sex of the subject had an important effect on helping
c. the greater the magnitude of the seizure, the more the helping
d. the more people present, the more the helping

10.10
c
LO 2
Fact
359
E

When people are aware of an emergency, but fail to help, this is known as the
a. stranger effect
b. genetic protection theory
c. bystander effect
d. altruistic effect

10.11
b
LO 2
Concept
359
C

Increasing the number of people at the scene of an emergency tends to
a. increase the number of signals that a person in an emergency puts out
b. increase the delay time in receiving aid from any particular individual
c. decrease the number of signals that a person in an emergency puts out
d. imply that the number of people at an emergency has no effect on behavior at the emergency

10.12
c
LO 2
Concept
360
M

Which statement best describes the decision making model of helping behavior developed by Latane and Darley?
a. whether we perform prosocial behavior depends on whether we have been primed to do so
b. fallacies in our thinking make it difficult for us to make rational decisions regarding prosocial behavior
c. the person confronted by an emergency situation must make five crucial decisions before helping
d. diffusion of responsibility is the reason that helping is inhibited in groups

10.13
d
LO 2
Concept
360
M

In the bystander intervention process, the first decision made by the potential bystander is
a. deciding how to help
b. assuming responsibility to help
c. interpreting the situation as an emergency
d. noticing the emergency

10.14
b
LO 2
Concept
360
M

Which of the following is a cognitive decision point about whether or not to offer help in an emergency?
a. parental teaching to help others
b. perceiving that an emergency exists
c. knowledge of the existence of emergencies
d. deciding to divide attention correctly

10.15
a
LO 2
Concept
360
M

To test whether or not people tend to notice emergency situations, it would be a good idea to
a. control for the availability of the subject's attention
b. control for the magnitude of the emergency
c. give each subject a time consuming task during the emergency
d. give each subject a time consuming task before the emergency

10.16
b
LO 2
Study
362
M

In the Good Samaritan study, seminary students varied in the amount of help that they offered to an (apparently) unconscious man as a function of
a. their major
b. the amount of time they had to spare
c. their age
d. their gender

10.17   The Good Samaritan study is an example of how
c   a. people help others based on their religious training
LO 2   b. intervention is often limited by not knowing what to do
Study   c. time pressures influence perception
362   d. it is rare for people to help strangers
M

10.18   Darley and Batson (1973) told seminary students that they were to present a talk on an assigned
c   topic in a nearby campus building. Students who encountered a "victim" enroute to giving their
LO 2   talks were most like to stop and help this person if
Study   a. their assigned topic was the Good Samaritan parable
362   b. their assigned topic was jobs enjoyed by seminary students
M   c. they thought they had extra time to reach the location of the talk
            d. they thought they were right on schedule for reaching the location of the talk

10.19   In the bystander intervention process, the second decision made by the potential bystander is
c   a. deciding how to help
LO 3   b. assuming responsibility to help
Fact   c. interpreting the situation as an emergency
362   d. noticing the emergency
M

10.20   In order for help to be given, perception that a situation exists must be followed by
d   a. a course of action
LO 3   b. a plan of action
Fact   c. the presence of a small group of bystanders
362   d. perception that the situation is an emergency
M

10.21   People often fail to help in an emergency because they
a   a. do not recognize that the situation is an emergency
LO 3   b. are not related to the victim
Concept   c. believe that in the U.S., it is their own fault when people get into trouble
362   d. can imagine themselves in the same situation
M

10.22   People often fail to help in an emergency because they
b   a. believe that in the U.S., people should help themselves
LO 3   b. would feel embarrassed to offer help if they were wrong about the situation being an emergency
Concept   c. can too easily imagine themselves in the same situation
362   d. are not related to the victim
M

10.23   One reason that potential helpers hold back in ambiguous situations is because
c   a. they are constrained by time
LO 3   b. they usually have plenty of time to make a decision
Concept   c. they are waiting for more information
362   d. they are not sure of the situation
M

10.24   Due to the nature of the potential outcomes surrounding helping and not helping in emergencies,
a   most people are prone to pay special attention to cues indicating that
LO 3   a. there is no emergency
Concept   b. helping would be easy
363   c. helping would be time consuming
M   d. the emergency is immediate

10.25
d
LO 3
Concept
363
M

Social comparison is relevant to emergency situations when
a. the emergency is clearly apparent
b. the emergency seems serious
c. there are no time pressures
d. there are several people present at the scene of the emergency

10.26
b
LO 3
Applied
363
M

According to research about the conditions under which people are most likely to receive help from others, you would be most likely to get help if
a. you twisted your ankle on Wall Street
b. you fell in the park on a Sunday afternoon in summer
c. you passed out on a park bench on Friday afternoon
d. you were attacked by muggers in a car park

10.27
d
LO 3
Concept
363
M

Helping responses are inhibited in U.S. culture because we are
a. taught to avoid giving help
b. not able to interpret ambiguous situations
c. taught to be apathetic
d. taught to appear calm in emergencies

10.28
c
LO 3
Concept
363
M

The bystander effect is especially likely to occur in situations where
a. it is clear what is happening, and the solutions is also very clear
b. the persons who witness the emergency are trained and thus know what to do
c. there is ambiguity as to what is going on and what should be done
d. someone assumes responsibility for helping

10.29
c
LO 3
Fact
363
M

The concept that bystanders interpret others' apparent calmness as unconcern is called
a. social comparison
b. self comparison
c. pluralistic ignorance
d. social pretence

10.30
a
LO 3
Concept
363
M

What term is used to describe the situation when everyone pretends to be calm and then uses the apparent calmness of the group members as an indication that an emergency situation is not serious?
a. pluralistic ignorance
b. dysfunctional modeling
c. faulty empathy
d. subliminal communication

10.31
a
LO 3
Study
363
M

If you are completing an experimental task in a room, and smoke starts coming through the door, you are most likely to report it if
a. you are alone
b. there are others in the room
c. you are in a hurry to finish your task
d. no one else seems willing to report it

10.32
b
LO 3
Concept
364
C

Which of the following are NOT factors that inhibit helping due to the presence of others?
a. fear of making a fool of oneself
b. consumption of alcohol
c. when the others present are strangers
d. when the others present are not helping

10.33   The consumption of alcohol has been shown to
d   a. increase the fear of social blunders among bystanders
LO 3   b. inhibit helping among bystanders
Concept   c. improve the quality of helping offered by bystanders
364   d. increase the rate of helping among bystanders
C

10.34   In the bystander intervention process, the third decision made by the potential bystander is
b   a. deciding how to help
LO 4   b. assuming responsibility to help
Fact   c. interpreting the situation as an emergency
364   d. noticing the emergency
M

10.35   In the bystander intervention process, the fourth decision made by the potential bystander is
a   a. deciding how to help
LO 4   b. assuming responsibility to help
Fact   c. interpreting the situation as an emergency
364   d. noticing the emergency
M

10.36   Beyond perceiving a situation to be an emergency, it is necessary for a person to
d   a. have experienced the emergency themselves
LO 4   b. to have seen others in the emergency before
Concept   c. assume responsibility for the situation
364   d. assume that he or she is responsible for offering aid
M

10.37   When an emergency happens in a situation where there is a recognized leader
c   a. it is the duty of the leader to act
LO 4   b. other people will fail to perceive an emergency
Concept   c. people assume that the leader will take responsibility
364   d. a new leader is likely to emerge to deal with the emergency
M

10.38   In studies of bystander intervention, people seem to feel
c   a. more guilt in the presence of others
LO 4   b. more responsibility in the presence of others
Concept   c. less responsibility in the presence of others
364   d. less social comparison pressure in the presence of others
M

10.39   Beyond perceiving an emergency and deciding to take responsibility, it is necessary to
a   a. know how to help the victim
LO 4   b. consult with others
Concept   c. make sure that the situation really is an emergency
364   d. ascertain that the victim wants to be helped
E

10.40   A bystander with the capability to help in an emergency is
b   a. likely to help only if he or she is alone
LO 4   b. likely to help even in the presence of other strangers
Concept   c. likely to help in the presence of others if he or she is perceived to be a leader by others
365   d. no more likely to help than any other bystander
M

10.41
a
LO 4
Concept
365
M

In which of the decisions made by a potential intervener is the competence of the bystander a crucial factor?
a. deciding how to help
b. assuming responsibility to help
c. interpreting the situation as an emergency
d. noticing the emergency

10.42
a
LO 4
Concept
365
M

Ralph has asked himself the following question in an emergency: "Do I posses the skills to do what needs to be done?" Ralph is considering which of following crucial decisions regarding whether to help or not?
a. deciding how to help
b. assuming responsibility to help
c. interpreting the situation as an emergency
d. noticing the emergency

10.43
d
LO 4
Study
365
M

Research by Cramer et al. (1988) found that registered nurses were
a. no more likely than college students to offer assistance to an accident victim
b. less likely than college students to offer assistance to an accident victim
c. more likely than college students to offer assistance to an accident victim but only in the alone condition
d. more likely than college students to offer assistance to an accident victim when another bystander was present

10.44
d
LO 4
Concept
365
M

At which decision stage do potential helpers weigh the costs of helping versus the costs of not helping before making their decision?
a. deciding how to help
b. assuming responsibility to help
c. interpreting the situation as an emergency
d. deciding whether to help

10.45
a
LO 4
Concept
365
M

Deciding whether or not to help a victim in an emergency is influenced by
a. potential costs of helping
b. inverted altruism
c. respondent altruism
d. behavioral mechanisms

10.46
a
LO 5
Applied
365
C

Lisa hears two individuals quarreling in the next apartment. She doesn't know whether or not to intervene. This situation is an example of a situation that is
a. nobody's business
b. the bystander's responsibility
c. ripe for helping
d. highly confusing

10.47
c
LO 5
Concept
365
M

Most individuals feel that an interaction between lovers or spouses is
a. the responsibility of an outsider
b. the responsibility of the courts
c. not the responsibility of an outsider
d. not the responsibility of an acquaintance

10.48
a
LO 5
Applied
366
C

Which of the following interactions would NOT be considered "nobody's business?"
a. a mother hitting her child so hard that blood comes out of the child's mouth
b. a mother spanking her child in public
c. a young child being taken from the shopping mall by two older children
d. two individuals shouting at one another in the next apartment

10.49   Shotland and Strau (1976) found three times as much intervention in situations perceived to be
a   interactions
LO 5   a. between strangers
Study   b. between marriage partners
366   c. between siblings
M   d. between mother and child

10.50   On a questionnaire designed to measure response to child abuse, Christy and Voigt (1994) found
c   that _____ witnessed an instance of child abuse.
LO 6   a. approximately 5%
Study   b. approximately 20%
366   c. approximately 50%
M   d. approximately 80%

10.51   One of the findings from the questionnaire study concerning child abuse (Christy & Voigt, 1994) was
d   that
LO 6   a. witnessing child abuse was not common, and intervention was avoided
Study   b. witnessing child abuse was not common, but intervention was necessary
366   c. witnessing child abuse was very common, and intervention was necessary
C   d. witnessing child abuse was fairly common, but intervention was usually avoided

10.52   Which of the following characteristics was NOT associated with intervention in child abuse situations,
a   according to Christy and Voigt (1994)?
LO 6   a. marital status
Study   b. personal experience with abuse
366   c. being a parent
C   d. feeling responsible

10.53   Which of the following characteristics was associated with intervention in child abuse situations,
b   according to Christy and Voigt (1994)?
LO 6   a. education
Study   b. personal experience with abuse
366   c. gender
C   d. socioeconomic status

10.54   Ralph is rushing downtown in an effort to complete his holiday shopping. He slips and falls on the
b   ice. Of the dozen people who saw Ralph fall, one person helps him up. Which of the following
LO 7   prosocial condition applied to the helper?
Applied a. the helper is going in the same direction as Ralph
367   b. the helper has just had a couple of beers
M   c. the helper is a college student
        d. the helper is expecting a reward

10.55   Dispositional factors that are associated with helping behaviors are included in the
d   a. empathic personality
LO 7   b. extroverted personality
Concept c. understanding personality
367   d. altruistic personality
M

10.56   Altruistic individuals tend to have higher self ratings of
c   a. helping competence
LO 7   b. altruism
Concept c. empathy
367   d. belief in a deity
M

10.57
a
LO 7
Concept
367
M
High need for approval is characteristic of
a. altruistic individuals
b. conservative individuals
c. liberal individuals
d. individuals who witness emergencies

10.58
b
LO 7
Concept
367
M
Need for approval
a. is found mainly in children
b. is a strong tendency to win praise and acceptance from others
c. is a tendency to heap approval on others in the hope of personal gain
d. is typical of most people

10.59
c
LO 7
Fact
367
M
Empathy refers to
a. the ability to be highly objective in analyzing another person's situation
b. the tendency to have little sympathy for another person's situation
c. the ability to feel concern over the welfare of others
d. simply being aware of another person's problems

10.60
b
LO 7
Fact
367
E
A vicarious emotional reaction that mirrors that of another person is a feeling of
a. helping behavior
b. empathy
c. state helping
d. trait helping

10.61
c
LO 7
Applied
367
C
Egoism is related to _____ as altruism is related to _____.
a. helping behavior, welfare of others
b. personal welfare, helping behavior
c. personal welfare, welfare of others
d. welfare of others, personal welfare

10.62
d
LO 8
Concept
367
M
Which of the following includes the three characteristics of empathic individuals?
a. feeling sympathetic, perspective taking, welfare of others
b. fantasy, feeling sympathetic, perspective taking
c. welfare of others, fantasy, feeling sympathetic
d. feeling sympathetic, perspective taking, fantasy

10.63
d
LO 8
Concept
367
M
The characteristic of empathy of being able to "put oneself in someone else's shoes" is called
a. feeling sympathetic
b. welfare of others
c. fantasy
d. perspective taking

10.64
c
LO 8
Concept
367
M
The characteristic of empathy of being able to "feel empathy for a fictional character" is called
a. feeling sympathetic
b. welfare of others
c. fantasy
d. perspective taking

10.65   Research indicates that _____ tend to score higher on empathy than _____.
c
LO 8   a. Blacks, Whites
Study   b. Whites, Blacks
368   c. females, males
M   d. males, females

10.66   Davis and colleagues (1994) estimated that 32% of the differences in a measure of empathy was due
a   to _____.
LO 8   a. genetics
Study   b. personality
368   c. social factors
M   d. physiological factors

10.67   Knight and colleagues (1994) predicted that children would donate money if they were high in three
c   characteristics. These characteristics are
LO 8   a. sympathy, affective reasoning, perspective taking
Study   b. money knowledge, sympathy, perspective taking
368   c. affective reasoning, money knowledge, sympathy
C   d. perspective taking, affective reasoning, money knowledge

10.68   Lisa believes she can help the world, and that if she does, she will eventually be rewarded. Lisa is
c   showing characteristics of
LO 9   a. an empathic personality
Applied b. internal locus of control
369   c. an altruistic personality
M   d. an internally motivated personality

10.69   Belief in a just world is characteristic of
a   a. altruistic individuals
LO 9   b. conservative individuals
Concept c. liberal individuals
369   d. individuals who witness emergencies
M

10.70   Which of the following are characteristic of the altruistic personality?
a   a. social responsibility, internal locus of control
LO 9   b. social responsibility, egocentrism
Concept c. internal locus of control, egocentrism
369   d. external locus of control, empathy
M

10.71   Which of the following is NOT characteristic of the altruistic personality?
b   a. empathy
LO 9   b. egocentrism
Concept c. acceptance of social responsibility
369   d. internal locus of control
M

10.72   Which of the following aspects of the altruistic personality indicates that altruism might not be
d   expected to be entirely without reward on the part of the subject?
LO 9   a. high self ratings of empathy
Concept b. internal locus of control
369   c. egocentrism
M   d. belief in a just world

10.73
c
LO 9
Concept
369
C

Which of the following are characteristics of the altruistic personality?
a. egocentrism, internal locus of control, empathy
b. external locus of control, social responsibility, empathy
c. empathy, internal locus of control, social responsibility
d. egocentrism, social responsibility, empathy

10.74
c
LO 10
Concept
370
M

The presence of role models and your emotional state influence
a. the number of emergencies that befall you
b. the magnitude of the emergencies that befall you
c. altruistic behavior
d. overt emotional concern

10.75
a
LO 10
Concept
370
M

Observing other people giving money to someone who is perceived in need
a. makes one more likely to contribute, as the others are like role models
b. makes one more likely to contribute, as the others' actions tap into egocentric feelings
c. makes one less likely to contribute, as the others fulfill perceived need requirements
d. has no influence on one's own behavior

10.76
b
LO 10
Concept
370
M

Strangers helping others can act as role models because
a. anyone can be a role model
b. they provide cues for helpful behavior
c. role models overtly encourage helping behavior
d. strangers do not act as role models; only people who know each other can be role models

10.77
b
LO 10
Applied
371
M

Ralph and Lisa are walking down the street when they see someone helping an old man across the road. On the next block, they see a woman having difficulty in trying to get across the street. Lisa says, "We'd better give her a hand." The person who helped the old man
a. acted as a boost to egocentrism
b. acted as a role model
c. acted as a boost to self-monitoring theories
d. helped increase other directed affect

10.78
c
LO 10
Concept
371
M

Role models are limited to
a. other people
b. other people and/or animals
c. other people, animals and/or animations
d. animals

10.79
d
LO 10
Study
371
M

Experimental results indicate that helpful models
a. have no effect on other bystanders' likelihood of intervening
b. discourage the helping of others
c. make an emergency situation more ambiguous
d. promote helping in others

10.80
d
LO 10
Concept
371
M

All of the following are factors that reduce the likelihood of intervention in a helping situation EXCEPT
a. fear of making a social blunder
b. diffusion of responsibility
c. the presence of bystanders
d. exposure to helpful models

10.81   How does recently observing a male helping a female affect the likelihood of offering to
c   change another female's flat tire?
LO 10   a. no change in helping is produced
Concept b. the male is less likely to help for having observed the earlier incident
371   c. the male is more likely to help for having observed the earlier incident
M   d. the quantity of help is improved, although the frequency of helping is not affected

10.82   In the Sprafkin and colleagues (1975) study, 6 year olds viewed television programs before getting an
a   opportunity to assist puppies in seeming discomfort. The amount of time spent trying to help the
LO 10   animals was greatest for those 6 year olds who had just watched
Study   a. an episode of "Lassie" containing a prosocial, rescue theme
371   b. an episode of "Lassie" without a prosocial theme
C   c. a humorous episode from the "Brady Bunch" series
         d. no television at all

10.83   Shaw and colleagues (1994), in a study using the "wrong number technique", found that
a   a. individuals tended to help an identified heterosexual
LO 10   b. individuals tended to help an identified homosexual
Study   c. individuals helped a heterosexual and homosexual about equally
373   d. female subjects helped more than male subjects
C

10.84   The Shaw and colleagues (1994) study lends support for the idea that people tend to help those
b   a. with whom they interact
LO 10   b. whom they like
Study   c. whom they self assess
373   d. with whom they share ideals
E

10.85   Bornstein (1994), using a meta-analytic technique, investigated the impact of dependency on
a   helping. The results indicated
LO 11   a. that the level of dependency was the primary factor, regardless of similarity
Study   b. that the level of dependency was important, but was influenced by similarity
373   c. that the level of dependency did not matter; similarity was the primary factor
C   d. that dependency and similarity both had an impact, depending upon the helping situation

10.86   Koehler and Willis (1994), investigating the relationship of gender of police officers and citations,
d   found
LO 11   a. police officers tended to give citations to offenders of the opposite gender and warnings to
Study   offenders of the same gender
374   b. male police officers tended to give citations to male offenders and warnings to female offenders
C   c. female police officers tended to give citations to male offenders and warnings to female
             offenders
         d. police officers tended to give citations to offenders of the same gender and warnings to offenders
             of the opposite gender

10.87   The study by Koehler and Willis (1994) indicated that, in some cases, _____ may be an advantage.
b   a. similarity
LO 11   b. dissimilarity
Study   c. dependency
374   d. nondependency
C

10.88
b
LO 11
Concept
375
M

In deciding whether or not to aid someone, victim characteristics are used by potential helpers to generate impressions of
a. reward capacity
b. victim responsibility
c. negative affect
d. general affective state

10.89
c
LO 11
Applied
375
C

An example of helping vs. not helping a victim based on assessment of responsibility is the finding that
a. people in a hurry are more likely to bypass a possible victim
b. a seminary student is more likely to help a prostrate person than the average passerby
c. most people pass by a prostrate person who appears drunk
d. most people are glad to see that a previously successful individual has fallen on hard times

10.90
d
LO 11
Concept
375
M

According to Weiner's model, a person who is deemed responsible for his or her troubles tends to generate feelings of
a. fear
b. empathy
c. negative state relief
d. disgust

10.91
a
LO 12
Concept
375
M

Victim blaming is most often performed by people who use
a. sensitizing defenses
b. repressing defenses
c. motivated defenses
d. empathic defenses

10.92
b
LO 12
Concept
375
M

Thoughts about a threatening event that may or may not happen to you are dealt with by the defenses of
a. empathy and state relief
b. repression and sensitization
c. repression and state relief
d. sensitization and empathy

10.93
c
LO 12
Study
375
C

Bell and colleagues (1994) found that the
a. the more similar a person feels to the female victim, the more the victim is blamed for the attack
b. the more similar a person feels to the male rapist, the less the female victim is blamed for the attack
c. the more similar a person feels to the female victim, the less the victim is blamed for the attack
d. the less similar a person feels to the male rapist, the more the rapist is blamed for the attack

10.94
c
LO 12
Fact
375
M

The sensitization defense against threats is characterized by
a. ignoring the threat
b. repressing the threat
c. worrying and intellectualizing about the threat
d. overestimating the harmful potential of the threat

10.95
d
LO 12
Concept
375
C

Repression-sensitization hypotheses about victim blaming have been demonstrated using
a. responsibility for hate crimes
b. people who are assumed to be responsible for experiencing an emergency
c. empathy reduction by trained crisis counselors
d. rape description

10.96   Victim blaming is most likely to be lessened when the victim is
a   a. someone who is similar to the person doing the blaming
LO 12   b. assumed to be wealthy
Concept   c. assumed to be poor
375   d. assumed to be responsible for being in an emergency
M

10.97   Who is least likely to remember details of a newspaper account of a mugging of a college student?
b   a. a person who blames the victim
LO 12   b. a person who does not blame the victim
Applied   c. a person who empathizes with the victim
375   d. another college student who blames the victim
C

10.98   In thinking about helping a person or persons in a distant country,
d   a. the major choice point interpreting that there is an emergency
LO 13   b. only four of the choice points are relevant
Concept   c. the five choice points are not relevant
376   d. the five choice points remain relevant
M

10.99   An example of how the five step cognitive model applies to long term helping behaviors is when
a   a. an advertisement for a child sponsoring program catches your attention
LO 13   b. you help a person because you were taught to do so as a child
Applied   c. you manage to repress the sight of a victim because you have been through the same experience
376   yourself
C   d. you manage to repress the feelings of guilt about failing to help a victim because you have never
              been in the same emergency

10.100   An example of long term helping behavior as defined in the text is
b   a. participating in a bake sale for charity
LO 13   b. AIDS volunteerism
Applied   c. the U. S. relief operation in Somalia
376   d. volunteering to locate people who need shelter
M

10.101   Varied messages for recruiting long term help are useful because there are
d   a. many types of people who need help
LO 13   b. multiple causes for emergencies
Concept   c. few people who are willing to volunteer
376   d. multiple forms of motivation to perform long term help
M

10.102   Pullium (1993), in an investigation of why people help or do not help AIDS victims, found that
c   people were
LO 13   a. more empathic but less willing to help an AIDS victim who had control over the source of the
Study   disease
377   b. less empathic but more willing to help an AIDS victim who had control over the source of the
C   disease
           c. less empathic and less willing to help an AIDS victim who had control over the source of the
              disease
           d. more empathic and more willing to help an AIDS victim who had control over the source of the
              disease

10.103
b
LO 13
Concept
377
C

Which of the following are motivations for helping AIDS victims?
a. personal values, need to enhance self-esteem, self-confidence
b. desire for personal development, personal values, need to enhance self-esteem
c. self-confidence, need to enhance self-esteem, concern for the community
d. concern for the community, desire for personal development, self-assessment

10.104
a
LO 13
Concept
377
M

The desire for personal growth as it relates to long term helping behavior is a form of
a. motivation to help
b. positive affect influencing the chances of being involved in an emergency
c. helping behavior
d. cognitive processing that increases the chances of helping behavior being offered

10.105
a
LO 13
Study
377
C

Omoto and Snyder (1995) found that individuals who engaged in sustained volunteer work over 2.5 years, seemed to be motivated by
a. need to enhance self-esteem, need to gain understanding, desire for personal development
b. concern for the community, need to enhance self-esteem, self-confidence
c. self-assessment, desire for personal development, personal values
d. self-confidence, personal values, concern for the community

10.106
c
LO 13
Concept
377
M

Volunteerism is most likely to be maintained if the major motivational element is
a. a state
b. empathy
c. self-centered
d. genetically inherited

10.107
d
LO 13
Concept
377
M

Volunteerism motivation can be divided into two major components, which are
a. genetic motives, social motives
b. temporary motives, permanent motives
c. trait motives, state motives
d. selfish motives, selfless motives

10.108
c
LO 14
Concept
378
M

One likely influence on whether or not a person in an emergency will ask for help is
a. how often the emergency occurs
b. how likely the emergency is to occur in the future
c. their (victim's) demographic characteristics
d. how often this victim has been involved in this emergency

10.109
d
LO 14
Concept
378
C

A basic reason that people sometimes do not ask for help in emergencies is that they
a. do not know how to get out of trouble themselves
b. are in a negative state
c. expect potential helpers to be in a negative state
d. do not wish to appear incompetent

10.110
a
LO 14
Concept
378
M

In terms of socioeconomic status, people high in socioeconomic status are
a. most likely to ask for help
b. least likely to ask for help
c. more likely to ask for help that those who are low in socioeconomic status, but less likely to do so than those in the middle
d. less likely to ask for help than those low in socioeconomic status, but more likely to do so than those in the middle

10.111   Immediate influences on whether or not individuals will ask for help include their
b   a. expectations of a recurrence of the emergency
LO 14   b. perceptions about potential helpers' reaction to the request
Concept   c. assessments of the similarity of this emergency to other emergencies
378   d. past experiences helping other people
C

10.112   Nadler (1993) found that individuals with low _____ were perceived most negatively when they
c   asked for help.
LO 14   a. self-esteem
Study   b. self-confidence
378   c. socioeconomic status
M   d. familial relationships

10.113   Asking for help is associated with
c   a. positive relief
LO 15   b. increased self-monitoring
Concept   c. lowered self-esteem
378   d. reduced self-monitoring
M

10.114   In situations where individuals are asking for help, self-esteem is examined as
d   a. a transitional variable
LO 15   b. a dispositional variable
Concept   c. a trait variable
378   d. a situational variable
M

10.115   Liking of a victim for a helper has been found to be moderated by the
b   a. level of self-esteem of the helper
LO 15   b. level of self-esteem of the victim
Concept   c. cognitive ability of the helper
378   d. cognitive ability of the victim
M

10.116   Sibling help is considered more threatening if the sibling is
c   a. male
LO 15   b. older
Concept   c. younger
379   d. in better physical health
M

10.117   Based on the likelihood of a sibling to help, and upon the victim's perceived threat from being
d   helped, the most preferred helper is
LO 15   a. a younger sister
Concept   b. a younger brother
379   c. an older brother
M   d. an older sister

10.118   Fisher and colleagues (1982) found that help that does _____ does _____.
a   a. arouse negative feelings, motivate self-help
LO 15   b. arouse positive feelings, motivate self-help
Study   c. not arouse positive feelings, not motive self-help
379   d. arouse positive feelings, not motivate self-help
C

10.119
c
LO 16
Concept
380
M

A general assumption concerning why people help is that
a. people try to maximize the positive affect
b. people try to minimize the negative affect
c. people try to maximize the positive affect and minimize the negative affect
d. people aren't concerned with the affect, but are concerned with self-protection

10.120
d
LO 16
Concept
381
C

Positive mood increases helping behavior
a. in virtually all situations
b. only if the victim shares the same characteristics as the potential helper
c. only in the presence of others
d. if the behavior does not threaten to destroy the good mood

10.121
c
LO 16
Concept
381
C

If you need help that may prove embarrassing to whoever helps you, you are more likely to be helped by someone
a. in the presence of others
b. in a positive mood
c. in a negative mood
d. who has low empathy

10.122
a
LO 16
Concept
381
M

An example of a situation in which positive mood decreases helping behavior is
a. when helping may be costly
b. when social evaluation may be involved
c. when the victim does not share the potential helper's physical characteristics
d. when the potential helper decides that the victim will not be grateful

10.123
d
LO 16
Concept
381
C

Sometimes people in a positive mood are less likely to accede to requests for help than people in a negative mood because they
a. are more likely to have previously refused to help
b. are less likely to recognize the situation as one where help is required
c. are less likely to share some characteristics of the victim
d. feel more power, including the power to say "NO"

10.124
a
LO 16
Study
381
M

Baron and Thomley (1992) found that
a. helping was more likely to occur when a pleasant smell was present
b. helping was more likely to occur when pleasing lighting was present
c. helping was more likely to occur when smell was neutral
d. helping was more likely to occur when the lighting was neutral

10.125
a
LO 17
Concept
381
M

Empathy among people in a negative mood is stimulated by
a. focusing upon the misfortunes of the victim
b. visible characteristics of the victim
c. focusing upon the positive affect obtained from giving aid
d. thinking of their own negative state

10.126
b
LO 17
Concept
381
M

Helping behavior is many times a function of
a. negative mood
b. empathy
c. positive mood
d. heredity

10.127 c LO 17 Concept 383 M	The empathy-altruism hypothesis suggests that a. people reduce negative affect by helping others b. people increase their own positive affect by minimizing the negative affect of others c. prosocial behavior is motivated solely by the desire to help others d. people increase their own positive affect by minimizing the negative affect of others
10.128 d LO 17 Concept 383 M	A helping situation where the potential helper feels some of the emotion of the victim and wants to help is described by the a. negative state relief hypothesis b. empathic joy hypothesis c. biological theory of altruism d. empathy-altruism hypothesis
10.129 b LO 17 Concept 383 M	If you wanted to influence a person to help another, the empathy-altruism hypothesis would suggest that you a. try to make the victim accept help b. emphasize the similarities between the potential helper and the victim c. emphasize the magnitude of the threat to the victim d. emphasize possibility of rewards for helping
10.130 a LO 17 Concept 383 M	Potential helpers will help a victim rather than leave a situation, even if it is easy to leave, if they have a. empathy for the victim b. been in the same position c. responsibility for the emergency d. witnessed the emergency occurring
10.131 b LO 18 Concept 383 M	The negative state relief model explains why a. people in a bad mood are more likely to request help b. people in a negative mood are likely to give aid to others c. people in a negative mood are less likely to receive help from others d. people in a negative mood need more help on average than people in a positive mood
10.132 c LO 18 Concept 383 M	The finding that people in a negative mood may help others to make themselves feel better is described by the a. empathy-altruism hypothesis b. empathic joy hypothesis c. negative state relief model d. sociocultural model of altruism
10.133 d LO 18 Concept 383 M	The negative state relief model of helping asserts that helping behavior is based on a. identifying with the victim b. empathy c. positive affect derived from the ideal of helping d. the desire to make oneself feel better
10.134 d LO 18 Concept 384 C	The power of the negative state relief model to produce helping behavior is a function of a. the needs of the victim b. the ability of the victim to project his or her needs to another individual c. the intensity of the emergency d. the intensity of negative affect in a potential helper

10.135
b
LO 18
Concept
384
M

Supporters of the negative state relief model of helping say that the empathy-altruism hypothesis is not sufficient to explain helping behavior because
a. feelings of empathy do not increase helping behavior
b. feelings of empathy are confounded by feelings of stress
c. affective state has no impact on helping behavior
d. people are more likely to help others if they are related to them

10.136
c
LO 18
Concept
384
M

The idea that an emergency arouses feelings of sadness that a person is then motivated to alleviate by helping others is contained in the
a. empathy-altruism hypothesis
b. empathic joy hypothesis
c. negative state relief model of helping
d. sociocultural theory of helping

10.137
a
LO 19
Concept
384
M

The empathic joy hypothesis states that helping behavior occurs because
a. people enjoy seeing that another's needs have been met
b. people are sad when they perceive that others are in emergencies
c. we are happiest when we help our kin
d. empathy arouses feelings of positive affect

10.138
b
LO 19
Concept
384
C

The empathy-altruism hypothesis and the empathic joy hypothesis differ in
a. their definitions of empathy
b. their assumptions about selfishness in helping behavior
c. the centrality of empathy in each theory
d. their assumptions about the effects of evolution

10.139
c
LO 19
Study
384
C

Researchers have tested the empathic joy hypothesis against other theories of helping behavior by manipulating
a. the amount of prior information that the helper has about the victim
b. the amount of information that the victim has about the helper
c. the demographic characteristics of the victim
d. feedback conditions about the results of helping

10.140
a
LO 19
Applied
384
M

Ralph helps Lisa carry her groceries up the stairs. Lisa comes by 15 minutes later and says, "Thank you. The frozen food would have melted if you hadn't helped me." Ralph is motivated to help others later. This scenario is most consistent with the
a. empathic joy hypothesis
b. empathy-altruism hypothesis
c. negative state relief model
d. genetic determinism

10.141
c
LO 20
Concept
384
M

According to genetic models, helping behavior is a function of
a. victim characteristics
b. helper characteristics
c. relatedness of victim and helper
d. stress magnitude

10.142
c
LO 20
Concept
384
E

Relatedness encourages helping behavior because related people
a. are more empathetic to one another
b. are less likely to resent help being offered
c. have similar genes
d. like each other more

10.143   The unconscious motivation to pass on as many of one's genes to the next generation as possible
d   is known as
LO 20   a. reproductive egocentrism
Fact   b. chromosomal theory
384   c. empathy altruism
E   d. maximization of fitness

10.144   The unconscious motivating factor in the genetic determinism model of helping is the pressure to
b   a. relieve a negative state
LO 20   b. help those like ourselves
Concept c. raise our positive affect by helping another
384   d. make another feel better
M

10.145   An argument against helping through genetic determinism is that
d   a. we empathize mainly with those who appear different from us
LO 20   b. we empathize mainly with those who appear similar to us, but do not help them more than
Concept   dissimilar people
385   c. we help others who appear to be like ourselves
M   d. we help others like ourselves, but some similarities are not genetically determined

10.146   The most recent conclusion on genetic influences on altruism is that
b   a. altruism is attributable to genetic influences
LO 20   b. there is no prosocial gene, but people are inherently sociable
Concept c. the prosocial gene is only effective part of the time
385   d. altruism cannot be explained through genetic influences
M

10.147   The three basic standards related to prosocial goals that were suggested by Reykowski (1982) are
d   a. hedonism, conformity, perception
LO 20   b. conformity, perception, conceptual reasoning
Study   c. perception, conceptual reasoning, hedonism
386   d. conceptual reasoning, hedonism, conformity
M

10.148   Boehnke and colleagues (1989) found that across the four countries studied, preferences were
b   consistent with
LO 21   a. hedonic standards being most preferred
Study   b. hedonic standards being least preferred
386   c. conformity standards being most preferred
M   d. conformity standards being least preferred

10.149   Boehnke and colleagues (1989) found that across the four countries studied, preferences were
b   consistent with
LO 21   a. self-interest standards being most preferred
Study   b. self-interest standards being least preferred
386   c. conceptual standards being most preferred
M   d. conceptual standards being least preferred

10.150   There seems to be widespread agreement that prosocial behavior is most valued if done purely in
a   response to
LO 21   a. the needs of someone else
Concept b. the needs of oneself
386   c. the needs of relatives
M   d. the needs of friends

CHAPTER 11

Learning Objectives

After studying this chapter, students should be able to:

1. *Discuss the problem of aggression in the world today vs. in the past. Define aggression. Describe Freud's version of "instinct theory," and contrast Freud's view to Lorenz's. Discuss aggression and sociobiology.*

2. *Cite the two reasons that aggression is probably not controlled by the genes. Describe the biochemistry that is linked with aggression against self or others.*

3. *Discuss how testosterone affects female transsexuals. Discuss the interplay of biological and cultural/environmental factors in producing aggression. Describe the drive theories.*

4. *Outline the social learning theory of aggression, and explain what we learn that directs our aggressiveness (three categories).*

5. *Define a "script" and when we appraise and reappraise. Discuss Berkowitz's "negative affect," and the factors that produce aggression or not, according to cognitive theory.*

6. *Outline the Buss technique for studying aggression, and describe the critical difference with Milgram's method. Discuss the controversy over whether the Buss method involves real aggression.*

7. *Understand the logic behind the frustration-aggression hypothesis, as well as the problems with it.*

8. *Describe how we tend to react to provocation. Cite the sources of provocation (Harris), and indicate an unexpected source of violent portrayals on TV. Characterize the laboratory experiments using media presentations to provoke subjects.*

9. *Indicate what is involved in the "static observation" studies. Outline the procedures of the 10 and 20 year follow-up "longitudinal" study by Huesmann and Eron. Discuss the gender difference in the exposure to TV violence-aggression link.*

10. *Discuss Zillmann's "excitation transfer" theory. Tell how cognition influences the effects of residual arousal.*

11. *Consider when sexual arousal decreases aggression and when it increases it. Discuss the factors in Zillmann's "two component" theory of response to erotica. Define sexual jealousy, and describe the sex difference in response to a sexual infidelity.*

12. *Unravel the web of gender-related emotions relating to infidelity as it once was and as modern contraception has made it. Outline how people tend to react when exposed to violence toward women in a sexual context.*

13. *Discuss the effects of pornography and whether rape is a sex act or an act of violence.*

14. *Describe the Type A and Type B personality patterns. Examine Berman and colleague's study about the joint effect on aggression of Type A orientation and testosterone. Contrast Type As and Bs with regard to hostile and instrumental aggression.*

15. *Discuss hostile attributional bias. Describe how Dodge and colleagues demonstrated that this bias predicts real-life bias. List and define the "Big Five."*

16. *Discuss our beliefs about gender differences in aggressiveness and the reality of gender differences. Indicate the situations that interact with gender to influence aggressiveness. State Eagly's "social role" explanation of gender differences in aggressiveness.*

17.   *Explain how testosterone relates to aggressiveness. Indicate Gladue's finding when male and female heterosexuals and homosexuals were tested on testosterone levels and aggressiveness.*

18.   *Define child maltreatment and indicate whether maltreatment as a child absolutely predicts maltreatment of children as an adult. Describe the three classes of variables that relate to child abuse.*

19.   *Describe three factors that programs target. State the facts about workplace violence vs. the myths and discuss some organizational sources of increased aggression at work.*

20.   *Explain the controversy over capital punishment. Outline the conditions under which punishment can be expected to deter aggressiveness.*

21.   *Describe "catharsis" and indicate how it is supposed to reduce aggressiveness. Explain how cognitive processes limit catharsis' effectiveness.*

22.   *Describe how perceived level of control exercised by an attacker influences the effectiveness of his/her excuses. Indicate the way a "cognitive deficit' contributes to aggressiveness.*

23.   *State how models can reduce aggressiveness. List the deficits of the socially unskilled, how they contribute to aggressiveness and how they can be remedied. Describe some responses that are incompatible with aggression (note the Richardson et al. study).*

24.   *Describe cross-cultural studies of violence. Describe Ostermann et al.'s studies of aggressiveness among children in several societies.*

Questions

11.1   Aggression is defined as the
d
LO 1   a. infliction of physical harm upon others
Fact   b. infliction of harm upon others
392   c. desire to inflict harm upon others
M   d. intentional infliction of harm upon others

11.2   Aggression has been studied by social psychologists in particular because it is
a
LO 1   a. a form of social behavior
Concept   b. harmful to many people
392   c. covered in psychological theories
M   d. unlikely that it occurs naturally in humans

11.3   In social psychology, the nature and origins of aggression are primarily addressed by _____, while
b   aspects of others' behavior are examined under _____.
LO 1   a. biological studies, social studies
Concept   b. theoretical perspectives, social determinants
393   c. philosophy, practical conditions
C   d. laboratory experiments, field experiments

11.4   The oldest theory of aggression is
c
LO 1   a. social learning theory
Fact   b. classical conditioning theory
393   c. instinct theory
M   d. behaviorism

11.5   Thanatos describes
d
LO 1   a. how aggression is directed toward others
Fact   b. how individuals learn to be aggressive
393   c. how aggression can be intrinsically rewarding
M   d. an individual instinct for death

11.6   According to Freud, the death instinct relates to aggression because
a
LO 1   a. people learn to direct it against others
Concept   b. death is a form of aggression
393   c. death is common, and people try to avoid it
M   d. of the instinct of self-preservation

11.7   An alternative instinctual theory of aggression to the death wish theory is the
c
LO 1   a. life instinct theory
Concept   b. theory of social learning
393   c. fighting instinct theory
M   d. theory of passion

11.8   The fighting instinct theory of aggression is based on
d
LO 1   a. the apparently innate desire for aggression
Concept   b. the apparently innate desire for domination
393   c. the need for people to express pressures within them
M   d. alleged beneficial aspects of aggression

11.9   According to Lorenz, the fighting instinct benefits humans by
b   a. weeding out the unfit
LO 1   b. spreading the population over a broad area of natural resources
Concept   c. providing lessons in survival for children
393   d. encouraging technological development
M

11.10   Freud held that aggression stems mainly from a _____ instinct, whereas Lorenz held that aggression
d   stems mainly from a _____ instinct.
LO 1   a. life, death
Concept   b. death, life
393   c. fighting, death
M   d. death, fighting

11.11   The sociobiological theory explains aggression through
c   a. the spreading of people over an area of resources
LO 1   b. its beneficial effects on producing hunters
Concept   c. maximizing genetic reproduction
393   d. encouraging technological development
M

11.12   Which of the following theories is not a theory arguing that aggression is inborn or genetically
b   determined?
LO 1   a. sociobiology
Concept   b. social learning theory
394   c. Freudian theory
M   d. Lorenz's theory

11.13   An argument against a universal theory of aggression is the
d   a. lack of need for people to hunt today
LO 2   b. development of non-aggressive technology
Concept   c. recent development of legal inhibitions against widespread aggression
394   d. broad differences in aggression across cultures
M

11.14   The difference between homicide rates across the world indicates that
a   a. social and cultural factors impact upon aggression
LO 2   b. aggression occurs in many varied forms
Concept   c. homicide is not a good measure of aggression
394   d. not all humans are driven by instincts
M

11.15   The gaps in instinctual explanations of aggression indicate that
c   a. biological factors do not play a role in aggression
LO 2   b. culture is the main explanatory cause of aggression
Concept   c. social and cultural factors must play a role in explaining aggression
394   d. some cultures are immune to instinctual drives
M

11.16   Which theories of aggression have been criticized because of their circular nature (questionable
a   logic)?
LO 2   a. instinct theories
Concept   b. drive theories
394   c. social learning theories
C   d. cognitive theories

11.17
c
LO 2
Concept
394
M

An example of a biological influence upon aggression is the
a. similarities in homicide rates across the world
b. differences in homicide rates across the world
c. correlation between reduced levels of serotonin and aggression
d. greater reproduction rate of non-aggressive males in North America

11.18
d
LO 3
Study
395
C

Van Goozen and colleagues (1994), in an investigation of the effect of testosterone on female transsexuals, found that after receiving the hormones, these individuals
a. reported increased levels of overt aggression
b. reported decreased levels of overt aggression
c. reported lower tendencies to become angry
d. reported higher tendencies to become angry

11.19
b
LO 3
Study
395
M

Research evidence suggests that biological processes do not operate alone, but exert their influence
a. in mysterious ways
b. in combination with social and cognitive factors
c. in nonevaluative, but impressive ways
d. in isolation from the social and cognitive factors

11.20
d
LO 3
Concept
395
M

The difference between social and instinctual drive theories of aggression is that social drive theories rely upon
a. internal mechanisms
b. classical conditioning techniques
c. instrumental conditioning techniques
d. an external stimulus to elicit the drive response

11.21
d
LO 3
Concept
395
M

Theories that explain aggression by reference to externally elicited motives to harm or injure others are called
a. sociobiological theories
b. physiological theories
c. Lorenzian theories
d. drive theories

11.22
b
LO 3
Concept
395
M

Drive theories postulate
a. that aggression is determined completely by the genes
b. that external conditions arouse strong internal motives
c. that aggression is practiced because it has been adaptive in the history of the species
d. that internal forces, free of any external influences, determine aggression

11.23
a
LO 3
Fact
396
E

An example of a modern external stimulus that elicits an aggressive drive response is
a. frustration
b. the need to hunt
c. maintenance of health
d. a conditioning mechanism

11.24
c
LO 3
Concept
396
M

Relative to instinctive theories, drive theory is
a. pessimistic
b. indifferent
c. optimistic
d. lacking in support

11.25   Which of the following theories suggests that neither aggression nor the capacity to respond
a   aggressively is innate?
LO 4   a. social learning theory
Concept   b. sociobiology
396   c. thanatos-eros
M   d. cognitive theory

11.26   According to social learning theory, individuals become aggressive through
b   a. release of tension
LO 4   b. direct and vicarious experience of aggression from others
Concept   c. learning that the most satisfying way to reduce frustration is through aggression
396   d. inheritance of "aggressive" genes
M

11.27   Social learning theory assumes
b   a. biology is unimportant in understanding aggression
LO 4   b. humans are born with few if any aggressive responses
Concept   c. humans' behavior is unrelated to that of other animals
396   d. that, unlike other behaviors, aggression is instinctive
M

11.28   In social learning theory, individuals can learn to respond with aggression in terms of
c   a. situations
LO 4   b. situations and actions
Concept   c. situations, actions, and target groups
396   d. situations, actions, target groups, and affective states
C

11.29   Which of the following is among the main learning issues to which social learning theory is
c   addressed?
LO 4   a. the manner in which aggression is extinguished
Concept   b. the specific environmental conditions to which a species has adapted
396   c. the specific situations in which aggression is appropriate
M   d. whether the brain plays a role in learned aggression

11.30   Compared with Freud and Lorenz, social learning theorists are _____ about the control of
c   aggressiveness.
LO 4   a. pessimistic
Concept   b. indifferent
396   c. optimistic
E   d. philosophical

11.31   The statement, "Aggression depends on past experience, reinforcements, thoughts, and perceptions"
d   represents the basic assumption of what theory?
LO 4   a. sociobiological
Concept   b. social adaptation
397   c. social anthropological
C   d. social learning

11.32   The negative feelings you have experienced when you aggressed against someone play a role in the
a   a. cognitive theories of aggression
LO 5   b. Freudian theory of aggression
Concept   c. Jungian theory of aggression
397   d. Newtonian theory of aggression
M

11.33
d
LO 5
Concept
397
M

Which of the following theoretical positions suggests that, if an aversive event occurs and unpleasant feelings result, whether or not aggression occurs depends upon thought processes.
a. Freudian theory
b. social learning theory
c. instinct theory
d. cognitive theory

11.34
a
LO 5
Concept
397
M

One of the cognitive factors that plays a role in whether you aggress or not in a situation is
a. the script you have for behavior in that situation
b. the cognitive elaboration that you have done in that situation
c. the cognitive dissonance you feel in that situation
d. the cognitive evaluation that you have completed in that situation

11.35
a
LO 5
Concept
397
M

Which of the following cognitive factors is NOT one that must be considered when evaluating how a person would act in an aggressive situation?
a. dissonance
b. scripts
c. reappraisal
d. appraisal

11.36
c
LO 5
Applied
397
M

Ralph is walking down the street and bumps into another person. That person calls Ralph a name and then hits him on the shoulder. Before Ralph reacts, he uses the which of the following cognitive factors to influence whether he will react in an aggressive manner?
a. dissonance
b. attribution
c. appraisal
d. elaboration

11.37
b
LO 5
Applied
397
C

Lisa is dressed in formal attire while waiting for a ticket to the opera. While in line, the person behind her shoves her and shouts at her, "Pay attention, move forward." Because of the _____ Lisa has for this situation, Lisa probably will not retaliate against this person.
a. negative affect
b. script
c. associations
d. financial investment

11.38
d
LO 5
Study
397
C

Berkowitz (1994) suggests that unpleasant experiences may generate _____, which in turn might trigger _____.
a. positive affect, withdrawal
b. positive affect, aggressive reactions
c. negative affect, aggressive reactions
d. negative affect, cognitive reappraisal

11.39
d
LO 6
Concept
398
E

In studying aggression, experimenters have to first balance validity of method with
a. generalizability
b. theoretical constraints
c. situations
d. the potential harm to participants

11.40   The classical laboratory method of studying aggression involves
c   a. a situation where the participants have equal opportunity to harm each other
LO 6   b. a situation where the participants think that they have equal opportunity to harm each other, but
Study   really do not
398   c. making participants think that they have the ability to harm others without their actually being
M   able to do so
        d. observation of naturally occurring aggression

11.41   The Buss method for studying aggression relies on
b   a. low intensity shocks to produce compliance
LO 6   b. a person who thinks that he or she will be able to shock another person
Concept c. shocks of progressive intensity to induce compliance
399   d. a person who receives shock from a machine that he or she believes to be operated by another
M   person

11.42   Which of the following is true of the method devised by Buss for studying aggression in the
d   laboratory?
LO 6   a. it measures a subject's blood pressure
Study   b. it accepts the idea that to study aggression realistically, painful shocks must be delivered to the
399   target
M   c. there is little evidence to support the validity of this technique
        d. it allows for the study of aggression without inflicting physical harm on the target

11.43   How have social psychologists solved the problem of studying aggression in the laboratory?
a   a. they have used an aggression machine
LO 6   b. they have accepted the necessity of hurting subjects
Study   c. they have resigned themselves to studying only verbal aggression
399   d. they have abandoned the laboratory study of aggression
M

11.44   What is involved in the modern study of aggression?
a   a. a subject who is supposed to teach by the use of electric shock
LO 6   b. a subject who continually insults a confederate
Concept c. a confederate who continually shocks the subject for wrong answers
399   d. an experimenter who orders the subject to shock a confederate
M

11.45   What are the ways to measure aggression in the modern laboratory study?
c   a. count the number of insults
LO 6   b. measure the subject's blood pressure
Concept c. record the intensity of shocks delivered
399   d. rate the subject's degree of anger
M

11.46   Aggression exhibited through the Buss method of arousal of aggression can be measured through
c   a. the duration of shocks administered to another subject
LO 6   b. the duration of shocks administered to the experimenter
Concept c. the duration of shocks that the subject thinks that he or she is administering to another subject
399   d. the intensity of shocks delivered to the experimenter
C

11.47   The Buss procedure differs from Milgram's obedience studies in that in the Buss procedure,
d   a. the experimenter controls the amount of shock that is administered
LO 6   b. the experimenter controls the amount of perceived shock that is administered
Concept c. the participant is shocked by the confederate, not the other way around
399   d. administration of punishment is left up to the person who is administering the shock
C

11.48
c
LO 6
Concept
400
M

Which of the following serves as validation of the Buss procedure?
a. people actually do deliver shocks to others while under pressure
b. if ordered to do so, most people will lie to another person
c. people with prior violent histories tend to administer higher intensity shock to a victim
d. people with prior violent histories are less responsive to the experimenter's orders

11.49
b
LO 7
Fact
400
M

The frustration-aggression hypothesis holds that
a. frustration is the same concept as aggression
b. frustration always leads to aggression
c. aggression always leads to frustration
d. frustration and aggression must be experienced simultaneously for an aggressive act to occur

11.50
c
LO 7
Fact
400
M

Which of the following is a fundamental assertion of the frustration-aggression hypothesis?
a. aggression is the same emotion as frustration
b. an aggressive experience is always followed by frustration
c. aggression is always preceded by frustration
d. aversive experiences lead to the pairing of aggressive stimuli with negative affect

11.51
d
LO 7
Concept
401
M

Tests of the frustration-aggression hypothesis suggest that
a. aggression is never preceded by frustration
b. frustration is never preceded by aggression
c. frustration does precede aggression
d. aggression can be stimulated by other emotions than frustration

11.52
b
LO 7
Concept
401
M

Frustration is most likely to lead to aggression if it is perceived as
a. uncontrolled
b. illegitimate
c. unexplained
d. uncontrollable

11.53
a
LO 7
Concept
401
E

In order for frustration to produce aggression, the frustration must be
a. unexpected and be viewed as illegitimate
b. expected and be viewed as legitimate
c. weak and be viewed as arbitrary
d. weak and be viewed as legitimate

11.54
c
LO 7
Concept
401
M

The current view of frustration seems to be that
a. frustration always produces some form of aggression
b. frustration is not a factor that produces aggression
c. under some conditions, frustration produces aggression
d. until we find a valid way of producing frustration, most questions will remain unanswered

11.55
d
LO 7
Concept
401
M

A criticism of the original frustration-aggression hypothesis was that it
a. underestimated the strength of the frustration-aggression connection
b. hypothesized too much variety in terms of how people respond to frustration
c. hypothesized too much variety in terms of the conditions that produce aggression
d. overstated the strength of the frustration-aggression connection

11.56
c
LO 7
Applied
401
M

Ralph has just received a low grade on a psychology test, which he attributes to his failure to study his notes or read his text. According to the revised frustration-aggression hypothesis
a. Ralph has an external locus of control
b. the frustration-aggression effect has been overwhelmed by the self-serving bias
c. Ralph is unlikely to have aggressive feelings toward the professor
d. Ralph will feel some aggression tendencies toward his professor

11.57
d
LO 8
Concept
401
M

The framework for studying how aggression stimulates aggression is centered on studies of
a. frustration
b. bias
c. heuristics
d. provocation

11.58
a
LO 8
Study
401
M

According to research, provocation is usually met with
a. retaliation
b. flight
c. frustration
d. thanatos

11.59
c
LO 8
Concept
401
M

Retaliation to provocation is directly influenced by
a. the associationistic network
b. reproductive strategies
c. reciprocity
d. perceived intentionality

11.60
b
LO 8
Concept
402
M

In many cases, aggressive behaviors in retaliation are _____ than the behaviors in provocation.
a. less intense
b. more intense
c. less specific
d. more specific

11.61
c
LO 8
Concept
402
E

Returning aggression or provocation in kind and in magnitude is suggested by the theory of
a. aggressive drive
b. balanced response
c. reciprocity
d. cognition

11.62
a
LO 8
Stidu
402
M

The research of Harris (1993) found which of the following gender differences in anger provocation behaviors?
a. females were angered by someone exhibiting behaviors that were not kind, nurturant, and sensitive to others' feelings
b. males were angered by someone exhibiting behaviors that ignored the feelings of others
c. females were angered by someone exhibiting inefficient behavior
d. males were angered by someone exhibiting dishonesty

11.63
a
LO 8
Concept
402
E

What is the rule that people typically follow when they are provoked?
a. reciprocity
b. "turn the other cheek"
c. flee
d. reason

11.64
b
LO 8
Concept
402
M

Aggression is more likely when a victim of provocation perceives the harm she or he has suffered has been
a. due to clumsiness
b. perpetrated intentionally
c. due to circumstances beyond the perpetrator's control
d. accidently perpetrated

11.65
a
LO 8
Concept
402
M

Assessment of aggression and responses to it are dependent upon
a. attributions about the underlying causes of aggression
b. the chances of increasing reproductive success
c. the outcome of the conflict
d. attributions about locus of control

11.66
b
LO 8
Study
403
M

The general pattern of results of studies of TV violence suggest that
a. the effects of TV are minimal to non-existent
b. media depictions of violence contribute to increased aggression levels in viewers
c. since TV programs generally lack a frustrating conclusion, it cannot be said that they contribute to aggression
d. TV programs often constitute an outlet for aggressive affect

11.67
b
LO 8
Study
403
M

Television violence as an influence on aggression in individuals is explained through
a. instinctual theories of aggression
b. social learning theory
c. sociobiological theories
d. the frustration-aggression hypothesis

11.68
c
LO 8
Study
403
M

The idea that people who have just seen violence are prone to score higher on aggression tests is tested through
a. TV viewing
b. ratings of aggression
c. systematic observation
d. sociobiology

11.69
d
LO 9
Study
403
M

The bulk of research shows that
a. it is impossible to differentiate between children who have been exposed to media violence and those who have not
b. TV cannot be blamed for children's aggression levels because it is impossible to know their aggression levels prior to watching TV
c. media violence is not seen by most children
d. children exposed to media violence exhibit more aggression than those who are not

11.70
a
LO 9
Concept
404
M

The effects of viewing an aggressive event are best determined over
a. the long term
b. the short term
c. a laboratory situation
d. a field experiment

11.71
a
LO 9
Study
404
M

Boys in which condition of a long term field study showed the most aggression?
a. those shown the violent film
b. those shown the nonviolent film
c. those who saw no film
d. those shown the cartoon violence

11.72   In their correlational studies, Eron and colleagues typically
a   a. have classmates or teachers rate aggressiveness of subjects
LO 9   b. involve elaborate laboratory procedures
Study   c. employ electronic devices to record shows that children watch
404   d. are experimental in nature, as opposed to observational
M

11.73   The work of Eron and colleagues in which there are ratings of aggressive content in actual TV shows
b   watched by children includes
LO 9   a. only short-term studies
Study   b. studies done over long periods of time
404   c. studies that measure only the immediate effects of TV violence
M   d. studies that predict what TV shows subjects will be watching 10 years in the future

11.74   Eron and colleagues report that studies entailing initial observations and follow-ups over many years
b   revealed
LO 9   a. only short-term effects of viewing violence on TV
Study   b. a link between viewing violence on TV and aggressiveness
404   c. high aggressiveness only in children who had moderate exposure to violence on TV
M   d. no relationship between exposure to TV violence and aggressiveness

11.75   Research on the relationship between TV violence and aggressiveness has found that
c   a. only males showed increased aggressiveness after watching violence on TV
LO 9   b. only females showed increased aggressiveness after watching violence on TV
Study   c. both males and females showed increased aggressiveness after watching violence on TV
404   d. neither males nor females showed increased aggressiveness after watching violence on TV
M

11.76   According to research, a person who has experienced an arousing event
a   a. can transfer that arousal to another situation
LO 10   b. tends to seek out that situation, or similar situations
Study   c. always reduces the tension through aggression
405   d. experiences collateral frustration
C

11.77   In circumstances where aggressive feeling is a common emotion, previously enhanced arousal
c   a. tends to replace aggression
LO 10   b. is construed as frustration
Concept   c. increases the likelihood of an aggressive display
405   d. is dependent on the amount of aggressive affect felt at the time that arousal is enhanced
M

11.78   Excitation transfer theory is relevant to
d   a. methodological behaviorism
LO 10   b. the spreading of people over resources through aggression
Concept   c. the genetic inheritance of aggressive genes
405   d. the increased feelings of aggression after emotional arousal
C

11.79   Excitation transfer relies upon which of the following assumptions?
b   a. predispositions to aggress are inherited
LO 10   b. arousal dissipates very slowly
Concept   c. emotions are matched with typical behaviors
405   d. arousal often generalizes to aggression
M

11.80
b
LO 10
Concept
405
M

Excitation transfer refers to
a. transferring excitation from one sense to another
b. transferring excitation from one context to subsequent aggression in another context
c. transfer of anger to sexual feelings to a state of profound arousal to subsequent aggression
d. transfer of excitation from one person to another

11.81
c
LO 10
Concept
405
E

Excitation transfer suggests that the conserved aggression from an arousing experience
a. is placed into long term memory
b. can only help for a brief period of time
c. intensifies emotional reactions to an annoying event
d. is unusual in adult humans

11.82
d
LO 10
Applied
405
C

The effects of excitation transfer are most pronounced when people _____ that they are aroused, but _____ the source of arousal.
a. misinterpret, identify
b. are concerned, like
c. do not know, misinterpret
d. realize, misinterpret

11.83
c
LO 10
Study
405
C

Zillmann and Cantor (1976) gave subjects information about the reasons for rudeness on the part of another person before they interacted with this rude person. They were investigating
a. appetite for aggression
b. cognitive reappraisal of events that are emotion-provoking
c. the effect of rudeness on aggression
d. intervening variables that stem from non-cognitive sources

11.84
a
LO 10
Study
405
M

Zillmann and Cantor (1976) gave subjects information about the reasons for rudeness on the part of another person before they interacted with this rude person. They found that
a. mitigating information lowered aggression more than if subjects received no information
b. mitigating information increased aggression more than if subjects received information after the rudeness
c. mitigating information increased aggression more than if subjects received no information
d. mitigating information had no impact on later aggression

11.85
c
LO 10
Study
405
M

Zillmann (1995) describes the negative impact that strong emotional arousal has on the ability to formulate rational plans as
a. cognitive reappraisal
b. cognitive upheaval
c. cognitive deficit
d. cognitive evaluation

11.86
a
LO 10
Concept
405
C

Cognition has an impact on emotion resulting from arousing events through the
a. memory and reappraisal of past emotion arousing events
b. reward/punishment of emotional responses
c. conservation of arousal from past emotion-arousing events
d. use of heuristics

11.87
c
LO 10
Applied
405
C

An example of the effect of cognition on emotion would be the
a. increase in transfer of arousal when individuals begin to think about the effects of the original arousing event
b. use of arousal to stimulate memory of past arousing events
c. failure of excitation transfer to occur when individuals think about the effects of the original arousing event
d. use of memory in interpreting aggression from others

11.88   Excitation transfer affects cognitive processes through
d   a. altering the rewards and punishments surrounding aggressive behavior
LO 10   b. altering the perceptions of rewards and punishments surrounding aggressive behavior
Concept   c. reducing the amount of time necessary for coming to a decision about a response to an arousing
405   event
C   d. impeding our ability to process complex information about others

11.89   _____ sexual arousal tends to _____ aggression
b   a. mild, increase
LO 11   b. mild, reduce
Fact   c. any, not affect
406   d. low, replace
M

11.90   The shape of the function that describes the effects of sexual arousal on aggression is
c   a. a straight line starting with no arousal and increasing with the amount of arousal
LO 11   b. a straight line starting with no arousal and decreasing with the amount of arousal
Applied   c. U-shaped line starting with no arousal
407   d. S-shaped line starting with no arousal
C

11.91   The two factors that influence the relationship between exposure to erotic stimuli and aggression
d   are
LO 11   a. arousal level, past experience
Concept   b. affective state, expectations
407   c. aggressive tendencies, expectations
M   d. arousal level, enhanced affective state

11.92   According to the two-component theory of sexual arousal and aggression, mild sexual arousal
a   reduces aggression because it induces mild arousal and
LO 11   a. strong positive affect
Concept   b. low expectations
407   c. non-aggressive memories
M   d. socially oriented attitudes

11.93   Which of the following must be present if erotic displays are to yield high levels of aggressiveness?
d   a. moderate sexual arousal
LO 11   b. subjects who possess the XYY pattern
Concept   c. anonymity
407   d. negative feelings
M

11.94   Weerth and Kalma (1993), in a study investigating sexual infidelity, found that
c   a. both males and females reacted with a high degree of aggressiveness against their partners
LO 11   b. neither males nor females reacted with a high degree of aggressiveness against their partners
Study   c. females, rather than males, were more likely to react aggressively against their partners
408   d. males, rather than females, were more likely to react aggressively against their partners
C

11.95   In a study by Weerth and Kalma (1993) that investigated the reactions of males and females to sexual
b   infidelity on the part of their partners, the results indicated that
LO 11   a. males were more likely to react with a high degree of aggressiveness
Study   b. males were more likely to react by getting drunk
408   c. females were more likely to react in a passive, unemotional manner
M   d. females were more likely to react by getting drunk

11.96
c
LO 11
Applied
408
C

Ralph has just found out that Lisa, his girlfriend, has been having an affair with another person. Based upon the results of the Weerth and Kalma (1993) study, Ralph will probably
a. go out and physically assault this other person
b. go out and physically assault Lisa
c. go out and get drunk
d. go out and cry on his mother's shoulder

11.97
a
LO 12
Concept
408
M

One explanation for differences in sexual jealousy between male and females regarding sexual infidelity is that
a. females focus on the potential loss of resources necessary for child rearing
b. males focus on the potential loss of resources necessary for child rearing
c. females focus on the potential loss of a sexual partner
d. males focus on the potential loss of a sexual partner

11.98
c
LO 12
Concept
408
C

The advent of effective contraceptive devices has _____ to act aggressively when they discover that their partner is sexually involved with another person.
a. weakened the reasons for females
b. strengthened the reasons for females
c. weakened the reasons for males
d. strengthened the reasons for males

11.99
b
LO 12
Study
409
M

Research suggests that violent pornography
a. is distasteful but harmless
b. promotes violence against women
c. increases negative attitudes toward women, but not behavior
d. provides an outlet for harmful sexual affect

11.100
c
LO 12
Concept
409
M

A primary danger of violent pornography is the development of
a. expectations of aggression from women
b. pleasurable expectations from painful experiences
c. generally calloused attitudes toward women
d. harmless but distasteful attitudes about women

11.101
a
LO 12
Concept
409
M

A behavioral explanation of how violent pornography promotes calloused attitudes about rape is
a. the association of sex and violence
b. the idea that the sex drive and the aggression drive are related
c. the stimulation, through pornographic viewing, of memory of past events where sexual aggression has been rewarded
d. excitation transfer

11.102
a
LO 12
Applied
409
M

Ralph is talking to one of his friends, and this friend says, "You mean you have problems watching violent pornography? I have been watching this kind of stuff for a long time, and it doesn't bother me." This statement indicates which of the following effects?
a. desensitization
b. acquisition of new forms of aggression
c. weakening of inhibitions
d. priming effect

11.103
c
LO 13
Study
410
M

Research suggests that violent pornography
a. is distasteful, but harmless
b. provides an outlet for harmless sexual affect
c. constitutes a very small proportion of available pornographic materials
d. increases negative attitudes toward women, but not behavior

11.104
c
LO 13
Study
410
C

Kutchinsky (1991), in a study investigating the relationship between pornography and rape, found that, in the United States,
a. the incidence of rape increased when pornographic materials became readily available
b. the incidence of rape decreased when pornographic materials became readily available
c. the incidence of both rape and assault increased when pornographic materials became readily available
d. the incidence of both rape and assault increased when pornographic materials became readily available

11.105
c
LO 13
Study
410
M

Kutchinsky (1991) found that the incidence of rape _____ in Denmark, Sweden, and Germany when pornographic materials became readily available.
a. increased
b. decreased
c. stayed the same
d. varied considerably

11.106
b
LO 13
Study
411
M

The results from the research done by Kutchinsky (1991) on the relationship between availability of pornographic materials and incidence of rape suggests that
a. rape is an act of sexual arousal
b. rape is an act of violence
c. depiction of explicit sexual behavior is the primary issue of concern
d. depiction of implicit sexual behavior is the primary issue of concern

11.107
b
LO 14
Applied
412
E

Lisa works at a job taking complaints from callers on a switchboard. Lisa probably has a
a. Type A personality
b. Type B personality
c. Type C personality
d. a passive aggressive personality

11.108
b
LO 14
Concept
412
M

Hormonal influences of testosterone appear to be strongest on
a. people who are easily made to feel guilty
b. Type A males
c. people who are easily made to feel shame
d. Type B males

11.109
c
LO 14
Study
412
M

Research suggests that the influence of testosterone level on aggression is moderated by
a. morphology
b. learning techniques
c. personality variables
d. feelings of shame

11.110
d
LO 14
Concept
412
M

The influence of personality on aggression, independent of hormonal influences, is demonstrated by
a. different responses to the feeling of shame by different people
b. differing attributions about guilt from aggression by different people
c. the influence of testosterone on Type A personalities
d. differences in aggression level between high testosterone Type A and Type B personalities

11.111
d
LO 14
Concept
412
M

Which of the following is a characteristic of Type A personalities?
a. laid back
b. obese
c. procrastination
d. hostile aggressive

11.112
b
LO 14
Concept
412
M

The goal of _____ is to attain a goal, not to injure someone else.
a. hostile aggression
b. instrumental aggression
c. achievement aggression
d. attainment aggression

11.113
a
LO 15
Fact
412
M

A person who interprets ambiguous cues from others as aggressive in nature is said to have a
a. hostile attributional bias
b. Type A personality
c. Type B personality
d. cognitive deficit

11.114
c
LO 15
Study
412
M

Dodge and Coie (1987) suggest that hostile attributional bias exists because
a. aggressive children are more likely than non-aggressive children to respond to aggression with aggression
b. children from Western cultures are most likely to respond to aggression with aggression
c. boys rated as aggressive tend to misinterpret ambiguous cues as aggressive cues
d. Type A personalities are more prone to act aggressively than Type B personalities

11.115
b
LO 15
Study
413
C

Which of the following three individual traits were related to aggression, according to Caprara and colleagues (1994)?
a. irritability, extraversion, rumination
b. irritability, emotional reactivity, rumination
c. extraversion, emotional reactivity, conscientiousness
d. agreeableness, emotional stability, extraversion

11.116
c
LO 15
Study
414
C

Caprara and colleagues (1994) found that several individual traits related to aggression were also related to which of the following two "Big Five" dimensions of personality?
a. extraversion and conscientiousness
b. extraversion and emotional stability
c. agreeableness and emotional stability
d. agreeableness and conscientiousness

11.117
a
LO 16
Study
415
M

Research indicates which of the following circumstances determines the degree of sex difference in aggressiveness?
a. the degree to which the aggression studied is physical
b. just about any circumstance
c. when aggression is optional
d. the age of subjects

11.118
a
LO 16
Concept
415
C

Gender differences tend to shrink or disappear in
a. situations in which provocation is present
b. situations in which provocation is not present
c. situations in which females dominate
d. situations in which males dominate

11.119
b
LO 16
Study
415
M

Research suggests that indirect aggression is more often performed by _____, and direct aggression is more often performed by _____.
a. males, females
b. females, males
c. Type A personalities, Type B personalities
d. Type B personalities, Type A personalities

11.120   The argument that males tend to show more aggression because society expects them to do so
d   is an argument based mainly on
LO 16   a. psychoanalytic interpretation
Concept   b. humanistic interpretation
415   c. developmental interpretation
M   d. social-role interpretation

11.121   Higher testosterone levels contribute to aggression
a   a. in males
LO 17   b. in adults
Concept   c. in aggressive people
415   d. in male children, but not male adults
M

11.122   Testosterone and aggression
d   a. are positively related for everyone
LO 17   b. are negatively related for everyone
Concept   c. are only related in males
416   d. interact with gender
C

11.123   The interaction of gender and testosterone on levels of aggression indicates that
a   a. aggression is not completely based on social learning
LO 17   b. social learning theory provides the best explanation for aggression
Concept   c. aggression is not inherited across generations
416   d. aggression serves a biological purpose
C

11.124   The constancy of self-reported aggression by gender, which is independent of gender roles, provides
c   support for
LO 17   a. social theories of aggression
Concept   b. the adaptiveness of aggression
416   c. biological theories of aggression
C   d. the link between aggression and shame

11.125   The perception that males are driven to be more aggressive than females due to biological factors
a   a. ignores the effects of potential social pressures
LO 17   b. is supported by most research
Concept   c. underlies current aggression theory
416   d. explains the occurrence of Type A personality
M

11.126   Research by Emory (1989), regarding child abuse, indicates that many individuals who abuse children
a   a. appear to be quite normal psychologically
LO 18   b. appear to be seriously deranged individuals
Study   c. appear to have an abusive personality type
417   d. appear to enjoy child abuse
M

11.127   Peterson and Brown (1994) offer a model of three factors responsible for child maltreatment. These
c   factors are
LO 18   a. psychocultural variables, caregiver-based variables, child-based variables
Study   b. psychosocial variables, parent-based variables, child-based variables
417   c. sociocultural variables, caregiver-based variables, child-based variables
C   d. sociopolitical variables, parent-based variables, child-based variables

11.128
c
LO 18
Concept
417
M

Poverty, crowding, isolation, and stress are characteristic of
a. child-based variables of child maltreatment
b. sociocultural variables of child maltreatment
c. caregiver-based variables of child maltreatment
d. psychological variables of child maltreatment

11.129
a
LO 18
Concept
418
M

Characteristics such as high activity level, impulsive, and resistant to discipline make up
a. child-based variables of child maltreatment
b. sociocultural variables of child maltreatment
c. psychocultural variables of child maltreatment
d. caregiver-based variables of child maltreatment

11.130
d
LO 19
Concept
419
M

Several procedures aimed at reducing child maltreatment generally target which of the following list of variables?
a. environment, psychological health, children
b. environment, caregivers, sociological health
c. environment, psychosocial health, parents
d. environment, caregivers, children

11.131
d
LO 19
Concept
419
M

Providing economic assistance and job training would be addressing issues related to the _____ variable of child maltreatment.
a. caregiver
b. child
c. institutional
d. environment

11.132
a
LO 19
Concept
419
M

An instance in which a person kills his or her spouse and one or more child is known as
a. familicide
b. fratricide
c. patricide
d. matricide

11.133
b
LO 19
Concept
420
E

Workplace violence is
a. quite common
b. quite rare
c. usually committed by angry employees harming supervisors
d. usually connected to shrinking resources

11.134
b
LO 19
Concept
420
M

Workplace aggression usually takes the form of
a. overt aggression
b. covert aggression
c. harming the property of another person
d. harming another person

11.135
d
LO 19
Concept
420
C

Covert aggression tends to have which of the following characteristics?
a. direct, physical, active
b. indirect, physical, passive
c. direct, verbal, active
d. indirect, verbal, passive

11.136   Research by Baron and Neuman (in press) indicated that the amount of aggression
c   a. correlated negatively with the magnitude of organizational change
LO 19   b. correlated neutrally with the magnitude of organizational change
Study   c. correlated positively with the magnitude of organizational change
422   d. correlated curvilinearly with the magnitude of organizational change
C

11.137   One of the difficulties regarding capital punishment is answering the question concerning its
a   potential value as
LO 20   a. a deterrent
Concept   b. a motivational factor
423   c. a learning experience for others
M   d. a politically correct approach

11.138   Punishment is often a poor deterrent to aggression because
b   a. punishment only breeds resentment
LO 20   b. the conditions under which it is most effective are rarely met
Concept   c. the learning concepts behind punishment have been shown to be false
423   d. punishment is effective at altering behavior in the short term, but not in the long term
C

11.139   Punishment is more effective as a deterrent to aggression if it is
a   a. prompt
LO 20   b. mild
Concept   c. variable
423   d. impossible to anticipate
E

11.140   In order for punishment to be effective in deterring aggression, it must be
c   a. prompt, certain, strong, random
LO 20   b. prompt, uncertain, strong, random
Concept   c. prompt, certain, strong, justified
424   d. prompt, uncertain, strong, justified
C

11.141   Reduction of aggression through aggressive acts is known as
c   a. social learning
LO 21   b. behavioral reductionism
Fact   c. catharsis
424   d. outlet therapy
E

11.142   The catharsis hypothesis states that
d   a. tension from aggression can only be reduced by time
LO 21   b. punishments for aggression must be indirect if they are to be effective
Concept   c. punishments for aggression must be direct if they are to be effective
424   d. "safe" actions that allow the expression of anger will reduce later aggression
M

11.143   Physically releasing anger through catharsis tends to
b   a. enhance aggression
LO 21   b. temporarily reduce arousal levels
Concept   c. permanently counter arousal feelings
424   d. replace one kind of arousal with another
M

11.144
d
LO 21
Concept
425
M

Theories of catharsis tend to ignore
a. the role of affect in aggression
b. the potential for aggressive cues to reduce aggression
c. biological considerations
d. the impact of cognition upon arousal

11.145
b
LO 21
Concept
425
M

Contrary to popular belief, catharsis
a. results in a reduction of aggression
b. is not very effective
c. results in a deadening of aggression tendencies
d. is correlated with social variables

11.146
a
LO 22
Concept
425
E

The effectiveness of explanations as excuses is greater if they are
a. sincere
b. general
c. short
d. unusual

11.147
b
LO 22
Concept
425
M

Which of the following is most likely to reduce aggressive feelings due to a provocative action?
a. the threat of an immediate aggressive response
b. a sincere, detailed explanation
c. a quick apology
d. the presence of a non-aggressive cue in the background

11.148
b
LO 22
Concept
425
C

An excuse that makes reference to _____ is much more effective.
a. causes within the excuse giver's control
b. causes beyond the excuse giver's control
c. events that conceal the true malicious intent
d. events that are connected to the victim's situation

11.149
c
LO 22
Concept
425
M

Any procedure that assists in _____ may help reduce overt aggression.
a. increasing affective states
b. reducing physiological states
c. reducing cognitive deficit
d. reducing behavioral enhancement

11.150
a
LO 22
Concept
425
M

One way to overcome cognitive deficit is to
a. engage in activities that prevent you from ruminating about your experienced or perceived wrongs
b. engage in activities that assist you in thinking about previous wrongs
c. engage in activities that require physical activity
d. engage in other aggressive activities

11.151
b
LO 23
Concept
426
M

Models can
a. by their behavior, raise but not lower aggression
b. by their behavior, lower aggression
c. by their behavior, lower but not raise aggression
d. influence only people who are highly similar to themselves

11.152   Aggression might be lowered by
a   a. placing nonaggressive models in potentially explosive situations
LO 23   b. placing surveillance devices around places where violence is expected
Concept   c. by the presence of many armed personnel prominently displayed
426   d. by admonishing people to avoid violence for the good of their country
C

11.153   Teaching children social skills is
c   a. helpful in reducing short term aggression only
LO 23   b. helpful in reducing long term aggression only
Concept   c. helpful in reducing aggression
426   d. not helpful in reducing aggression, only in rechannelling it
M

11.154   One cognitively oriented technique for reducing aggression is
d   a. instrumental conditioning
LO 23   b. classical conditioning
Concept   c. neocognitive associationism
426   d. education in social skills
C

11.155   Exposure to humor is effective in reducing aggression because humor and aggression are
c   a. facets of the same emotion
LO 23   b. both coping mechanisms
Concept   c. complementary states
426   d. incompatible emotional states
M

11.156   The "incompatible response" hypothesis says that humor, empathy, or mild sexual arousal will cause
b   angry subjects
LO 23   a. to increase the amount of overt aggression they display
Applied   b. to decrease the amount of overt aggression they display
426   c. to reduce their short term emotional arousal, although overt aggression will increase later
M   d. to displace their aggression to a new target

11.157   Different cultures have different rules about the overt display of aggression and also
d   a. different categories for interpreting frustration
LO 24   b. whether or not aggression is ever adaptive
Fact   c. different forms of social learning
428   d. where it is appropriate to display aggression
M

11.158   Ostermann and colleagues (1994), in their investigation of children and aggression, found that
b   a. African American and Caucasian American children had the lowest rates of aggression
LO 24   b. African American children had the highest rate of aggression
Study   c. Caucasian American children had the highest rate of aggression
428   d. African American had the highest rate in overt aggression, but the lowest rate in covert aggression
C

11.159   In the study by Ostermann and colleagues (1994), it was found that across all cultures, children
d   tended to rate other children as more aggressive than themselves, thereby engaging in
LO 24   a. other-blaming
Study   b. ingroup stereotyping
428   c. cognitive deficit
C   d. self-serving attributional bias

11.160   Research seems to support the idea that
a   a. large cultural differences in aggression appear in young children
LO 24   b. large individual differences in aggression appear in young children
Study   c. large psychological differences in aggression appear in young children
428   d. large physiological differences in aggression appear in young children
C

CHAPTER 12

Learning Objectives

After studying this chapter, students should be able to:

1.   *Examine the text's definition of a group, and know the six key aspects of the definition.*

2.   *List the five reasons people join groups.*

3.   *Describe how the group benefits by having different members fulfill different roles, and indicate how role conflict and constraints imposed by roles can sometimes be detrimental to group functioning.*

4.   *Describe how the prestige of various roles is reflected in status differences, and also indicate how prescriptive and proscriptive norms affect group members' behavior.*

5.   *Define cohesiveness and list factors that contribute to group cohesiveness.*

6.   *Explain how the presence of others affected subjects' ability to produce word associations and to counterargue in Allport's classic research.*

7.   *Explain how Zajonc's drive theory resolves the "puzzle" created by the fact that performance is sometimes improved by an audience and sometimes impaired.*

8.   *Describe research findings regarding the evaluation apprehension hypothesis, indicating which are consistent and which are inconsistent with the hypothesis.*

9.   *Describe research findings that support the distraction-conflict theory.*

10.   *Give examples that illustrate the concept of social loafing.*

11.   *According to the collective effort model, describe the conditions that produce the social loafing effect.*

12.   *Understand the five techniques that can be used to reduce social loafing.*

13.   *Describe how outcomes must be distributed among members of a group in order for a member to perceive that equity exists.*

14.   *Describe the conditions that lead a person to conclude that procedural justice exists, as well as the conditions that lead to the perception of interpersonal justice.*

15.   *Summarize strategies to restore fairness used by persons who feel they've been treated unfairly.*

16.   *Explain how apologies and explanations influence employees' willingness to steal from an employer who cuts their wages.*

17.   *Summarize the four social decision schemes used by groups to make decisions, and indicate when "majority-wins" and "truth-wins" are used.*

18.   *Explain how decision-making groups are affected by straw polls.*

19.   *Describe group polarization and explain this phenomenon in terms of social comparison and the arguments presented during discussion.*

20.   *Define groupthink, and explain how it is related to group cohesiveness, emergent group norms, and collective entrapment.*

21.   *Describe three steps that can be taken to reduce the likelihood of groupthink.*

22.   *Explain why the hoped-for advantage of pooling resources often fails to occur in group discussions.*

23.   *Describe under what two circumstances might groups manage to counter their tendency to ignore unshared information.*

24.   *List key traits that are characteristic of leaders, and how the social situation affects leadership.*

25.   *Describe how leadership style is influenced by each of the following: a) autocratic vs. democratic style; b) directive vs. permissive style; c) task orientation; and d) person orientation.*

26.   *Explain how female and male leaders differ in their leadership styles. Describe circumstances in which female leaders tend to be down-rated compared to male leaders.*

27.   *Describe the relationship between charismatic leaders and their followers, and indicate tactics used by transformational leaders to generate this special kind of relationship.*

28.   *Examine the occurrence of social loafing in individualistic cultures such as the United States in comparison to collectivistic cultures such as Israel and China.*

Questions

12.1   Which of the following factors is NOT a part of defining a group?
c
LO 1   a. that the individuals must have common goals
Concept   b. that the individuals must have a stable relationship
434   c. that there must be three or more individuals involved
M   d. that the individuals must be interdependent

12.2   Which of the following is definitely a group, according to the definition?
d
LO 1   a. the staff of a university
Applied   b. the staff of IBM
435   c. the staff of a door-to-door sales company
C   d. the staff of a McDonald's franchise

12.3   Which of the following is a criterion that must be satisfied for a collection of individuals to be
c   called a group?
LO 1   a. there must be at least three members
Fact   b. the relationship must persist for at least one day
434   c. members must be interdependent
M   d. simply being together at some point in time is sufficient

12.4   The stability component of a group means that
a
LO 1   a. the relationships within a group must be relatively constant over a period of time
Fact   b. individuals have to remain part of the group, although their rolls will change
435   c. the group has to address the same issues all the time to remain in existence
M   d. the group has to adapt to new challenges in order to remain in existence

12.5   If group members are interdependent, it means that
d
LO 1   a. their interactions are structured in some manner
Fact   b. the members must interact with one another
435   c. the relationship must persist over an appreciable period of time
M   d. what happens to one affects what happens to the others

12.6   Individuals sometimes enter groups because
c
LO 2   a. leadership roles are determined by individual differences
Concept   b. leadership roles are determined through external circumstances
435   c. membership can satisfy attentional needs
M   d. roles within groups can change over time

12.7   Which of the following have been found to be advantages of group membership?
a
LO 2   a. security, enhanced task performance
Concept   b. raised job interest, security
435   c. heightened self-focusing, raised job interest
M   d. heightened self-esteem, heightened self-focusing

12.8   Group memberships that become part of the working self-concept contribute to a sense of
d
LO 2   a. self-esteem
Concept   b. self-efficacy
436   c. self-focusing
M   d. social identity

12.9
a
LO 2
Applied
436
M

Ralph has just been invited to join a prestigious social group. Only 12 students per year are accepted into this group. Such acceptance should enhance Ralph's
a. self-concept
b. financial status
c. self-assessment
d. self-monitoring

12.10
d
LO 3
Concept
436
M

Which of the following is NOT one of the three aspects of a group that are most important in determining group influence?
a. roles
b. norms
c. cohesiveness
d. leadership

12.11
d
LO 3
Fact
437
M

The set of behaviors individuals occupying specific positions within a group are expected to perform are known as
a. norms
b. incentives
c. drives
d. roles

12.12
a
LO 3
Concept
436
E

The fact that people in groups become differentiated, performing different functions for the group, is what is implied by the term
a. roles
b. goals
c. group influence
d. norms

12.13
d
LO 3
Concept
436
M

Pressures stemming from the fact that people must play two or more roles simultaneously in a group produce what is known as
a. prescriptive norms
b. proscriptive norms
c. role ambiguity
d. role conflict

12.14
d
LO 3
Concept
436
M

The clarification of responsibility along with constrained freedom are aspects of
a. social facilitation
b. task performance
c. risk taking
d. group roles

12.15
d
LO 4
Fact
436
C

Differentiation of function played within a group is specified by ____; rules about how to and how not to behave are called ____.
a. social decision schemes, roles
b. social decision schemes, norms
c. norms, roles
d. roles, norms

12.16
a
LO 4
Concept
436
M

The differences in relative position or rank of persons in a group, such that some roles carry considerable prestige, are reflections of differences in
a. status
b. norms
c. role ambiguity
d. cohesiveness

12.17   In most groups, differing amounts of prestige attached to different roles are indicative of role
c   a. differentiation
LO 4   b. performance
Concept   c. status
436   d. stability
M

12.18   Group behaviors are generally dictated by
b   a. the path of least resistance
LO 4   b. group norms
Concept   c. the path of least stress
436   d. social facilitation
M

12.19   The rules, either implicit or explicit, established by groups to regulate the behavior of their members
d   are called
LO 4   a. roles
Concept   b. goals
436   c. group influence
E   d. norms

12.20   Rules established by groups that tell members how to behave in various situations are known as
c   a. role prescriptions
LO 4   b. role proscriptions
Concept   c. prescriptive norms
437   d. proscriptive norms
M

12.21   Rules established by groups that tell members how NOT to behave in various situations are known
d   as
LO 4   a. role prescriptions
Concept   b. role proscriptions
437   c. prescriptive norms
M   d. proscriptive norms

12.22   The term that refers to all of the forces, both positive and negative, that cause an individual to
d   remain in a group is
LO 5   a. leadership
Concept   b. norms
438   c. deindividuation
E   d. cohesiveness

12.23   When there is attraction between members, a good match between individuals' needs and the
d   group's goals, and very high costs associated with leaving, the group is said to be
LO 5   a. high in normative power
Concept   b. high in role establishment
438   c. an additive group
M   d. high in cohesiveness

12.24   Generally, a high level of cohesiveness has _____ effects on group performance and _____ the impact
d   that the group has on the individual.
LO 5   a. bad, minimizes
Concept   b. good, minimizes
438   c. bad, maximizes
M   d. good, maximizes

12.25
c
LO 5
Concept
438
M

A group in which members like each other, desire the goals their group is seeking, and feel there is no possible alternative group that could satisfy as well is a group high in
a. status
b. norms
c. cohesiveness
d. proscription

12.26
c
LO 5
Concept
438
C

Liking for other group members because they belong to the group and represent its key features describes
a. cohesive attraction
b. personalized attraction
c. depersonalized attraction
d. individualized attraction

12.27
a
LO 5
Concept
439
C

Cota and colleagues (1995) suggest that cohesiveness involves the two primary dimensions of
a. task-social and individual-group
b. task-relations and personalized-depersonalized
c. task-social and ingroup-outgroup
d. task-relations and personal-social

12.28
b
LO 5
Concept
439
M

External threats tend to increase group
a. leader effectiveness
b. cohesiveness
c. task facilitation
d. social loafing

12.29
c
LO 6
Study
440
M

Allport (1920), in a study involving the generation of arguments against historical passages, found that when participants were in groups their
a. performance was not affected
b. performance was decreased
c. performance was increased
d. performance was decreased at first, then increased after the participants became familiar with the task

12.30
a
LO 6
Study
440
M

In Allport's research, the presence of others
a. increased the number of arguments that participants generated
b. increased the number of resources used in the arguments
c. increased the level of affect associated with the arguments
d. decreased the number of arguments that participants generated

12.31
c
LO 6
Study
441
M

Allport's early research on generation of arguments in the presence or absence of others laid the foundation for the research area of
a. counterarguments
b. cognitive deficits
c. social facilitation
d. cognitive dissonance

12.32
d
LO 6
Concept
441
M

The research area of _____ is interested in the effects that the presence of others has on performance.
a. cognitive dissonance
b. social evaluation
c. social comparison
d. social facilitation

12.33   Why is the term "social facilitation" (as it is currently used) misleading?
a   a. because it refers to decrements as well as to improvement in performance
LO 6   b. because social psychologists still have little idea of why it occurs
Concept c. because such facilitation can be produced by nonsocial as well as social sources
441   d. because many people prefer to work alone rather than with others
C

12.34   The drive theory of social facilitation was offered to explain why
c   a. working conditions affected mean group performance
LO 7   b. groups did well on some tasks but not on others
Concept c. the presence of others sometimes improved performance, and sometimes hindered performance
442   d. social loafing is related to cohesiveness
M

12.35   Which of the following situations is an example of the effects of social facilitation?
d   a. finishing a paper an hour before it is due to be handed in
LO 7   b. a beginner raising the level of her tennis game in front of a crowd
Applied c. helping another to finish a typing task more quickly
442   d. a senior tripping on the approach to the long jump in front of the track team
M

12.36   The foundation of the drive theory of social facilitation is that
d   a. the presence of others increases levels of arousal
LO 7   b. the presence of others improves performance
Concept c. the presence of others decreases performance
442   d. the presence of others can increase or decrease performance
M

12.37   Whether social facilitation helps or hinders performance depends on whether
b   a. many people are watching
LO 7   b. the dominant response is the correct response
Concept c. the task performer knows the watchers
442   d. the task causes positive or negative affect
M

12.38   In which of the following situations is social facilitation most likely to hinder performance?
c   a. exercising on a rowing machine
LO 7   b. riding on a bicycle
Applied c. playing an aria from Mozart on the violin
442   d. racing on a bicycle
M

12.39   Ralph, a novice tennis player, plays worse when others are around. Lisa, an experienced tennis
d   player, plays better when others are around. This effect on Ralph and Lisa is an example of
LO 7   a. group polarization
Applied b. a disjunctive task
442   c. a conjunctive task
M   d. social facilitation

12.40   Choose the best alternative.
b   a. the dominant response tendency in any situation is simply the correct response
LO 7   b. the presence of others will improve performance in situations where the performer's dominant
Concept   response is correct
442   c. the presence of others will improve performance in situations where the performer's dominant
C   response is incorrect
         d. the presence of others will impair performance in situations where the performer's dominant
             response is correct

12.41
b
LO 7
Concept
442
M

Increases in arousal enhance the performance of
a. weak responses
b. dominant responses
c. social responses
d. correct responses

12.42
a
LO 8
Concept
442
M

The theory of evaluation apprehension suggests that
a. social facilitation only occurs when a person thinks that others will evaluate the performance
b. the dominant response is usually the correct response
c. people increase the level of their performance when being observed at simple tasks
d. people increase the level of their performance when being observed at complex tasks

12.43
b
LO 8
Concept
442
M

The idea that a concern over being evaluated by others causes an increase in arousal and so contributes to social facilitation is the
a. distraction-conflict theory
b. evaluation apprehension hypothesis
c. contingency theory
d. drive theory

12.44
b
LO 8
Concept
442
C

Research suggests that
a. self-presentation concern is a better explanation for social facilitation than evaluation apprehension
b. social facilitation can occur without evaluation apprehension
c. evaluation apprehension does not exist
d. social facilitation is the same concept as evaluation apprehension

12.45
c
LO 8
Applied
443
C

According to the evaluation apprehension hypothesis, your tendency to perform dominant responses would be increased if you were
a. alone in a room doing a task
b. with two persons wearing blindfolds who could not possibly judge your performance
c. with two persons who carefully watch your behavior
d. with two persons, regardless of the situation

12.46
a
LO 8
Study
443
M

In a strange but revealing experiment, Zajonc and colleagues (1969) found that roaches are affected by an audience in much the same way as humans. These findings provide evidence against the ____ explanation for social facilitation.
a. evaluation apprehension
b. drive
c. arousal
d. distraction-conflict

12.47
d
LO 9
Concept
444
C

Distraction-conflict theory refers to the conflict between
a. evaluative and non-evaluative observers
b. task cognition attention and task performance attention
c. groups that are task oriented and groups that are relations oriented
d. attention that has to be paid to a task versus attention that has to be paid to an audience

12.48   The distraction-conflict model suggests that
b   a. the conflict between being fair vs. getting as much for oneself as possible produces feelings of
LO 9   inequity
Concept   b. the conflict between attending to the task vs. attending to the audience produces heightened
444   motivation
C   c. the conflict between attending to the task vs. attending to the audience produces poorer
              performance because of the distraction
           d. the conflict between being a risk-taker vs. being cautious produces indecision in a group situation

12.49   Which of the following is NOT an assumption underlying the distraction-conflict explanation of social
c   facilitation?
LO 9   a. organisms have a strong tendency to pay attention to the task at hand
Concept   b. organisms have a strong tendency to pay attention to an audience
444   c. the distraction produced by being in conflict causes the organisms to perform poorly
M   d. the distraction produced by being in conflict leads to increases in the organism's arousal

12.50   Consistent with the distraction-conflict model of social facilitation, it has been found that
d   a. both human and animal subjects show social facilitation effects
LO 9   b. subjects report experiencing distraction when they perform in front of an audience
Concept   c. many nonsocial forms of distraction produce results similar to social forms
444   d. all of the above have been found and are consistent with the model
C

12.51   Which theory is best able to account for social facilitation results among both human and animal
a   subjects?
LO 9   a. distraction-conflict theory
Concept   b. evaluation apprehension hypothesis
444   c. contingency theory
M   d. drive theory

12.52   A task where the output of the task is dependent upon the sum of the group's efforts is called
b   a. a conjunctive task
LO 10   b. an additive task
Fact   c. a pooled task
444   d. a parsimonious task
M

12.53   Assuming that group members are able to coordinate their efforts, one would expect better
c   performance by groups than individuals on
LO 10   a. a conjunctive task
Concept   b. a disjunctive task
444   c. an additive task
M   d. a normative task

12.54   Social loafing refers to
c   a. increased difficulty in completing a difficult task in front of other people
LO 10   b. the fact that some individuals do not care about group performance
Fact   c. the reduced efforts by some individuals in group tasks
444   d. attempts by some group members to obtain a negative outcome for the group
M

12.55   Which of the following is a form of social loafing?
d   a. cheating on a test
LO 10   b. not showing up for a test
Applied   c. not studying for a test
445   d. not contributing to a group study session
M

12.56
c
LO 10
Concept
445
M

Which describes the social loafing phenomenon?
a. when people are doing a task, they work harder when getting paid for it
b. when people are doing a task, they work harder when it is their own project rather than one to which they've been assigned
c. when people work together on a group task, each member exerts less effort than when working alone
d. when people are doing a task, they work harder when being watched

12.57
a
LO 10
Study
445
C

When students were asked to clap or cheer as loudly as they could, the amount of noise generated by each person was greatest when the person was
a. alone
b. in a 2-person group
c. in a 6-person group
d. in any group: the number of coactors did not matter

12.58
c
LO 11
Concept
446
M

An explanation for social loafing according to social impact theory is that as group size increases, each member
a. feels more and more responsible for the task
b. identifies more with the group than with the task
c. feels less and less responsible for the task
d. identifies more with the task than with the group

12.59
b
LO 11
Concept
446
M

The _____ explains social loaf in terms of individual effort and outcome.
a. social impact model
b. collective effort model
c. individual effort model
d. cognitive impact model

12.60
a
LO 11
Concept
446
C

In Karau and Williams' (1993) collective effort model of social loafing, three factors are important in determining whether social loafing occurs or not. These three variables are
a. expectancy, instrumentality, valence
b. expectancy, valence, impact
c. valence, instrumentality, impact
d. instrumentality, impact, expectancy

12.61
d
LO 11
Concept
446
C

One prediction of the _____ of social loafing is that when _____, then performance will be high.
a. social impact model, diffusion is low
b. collective effort model, valence is low
c. cognitive impact model, impact is high
d. collective effort model, expectancy is high

12.62
c
LO 11
Concept
446
C

According to the _____ of social loafing, _____ in groups than alone, therefore social loafing occurs.
a. collective effort model, valence is higher
b. social impact model, expectancy is lower
c. collective effort model, instrumentality is lower
d. cognitive impact model, impact is higher

12.63
b
LO 11
Concept
446
C

According to the CEM, social loafing will be weakest when
a. individuals come from cultures emphasizing group outcomes, and emphasize producing the same outcome over time
b. individuals work in small rather than large groups, and work on intrinsically interesting tasks
c. individuals work in small rather than large groups, and work on extrinsically interesting tasks
d. individuals work with friends, and emphasize producing the same outcome over time

12.64   Social loafing is most likely to occur under conditions
a   a. in which individual contributions cannot be evaluated
LO 11   b. in which respect for others is obvious
Concept   c. in which all coworkers are known fairly well, so individual output is known
447   d. in which leaders are committed to the task
M

12.65   Social loafing usually increases with group size unless
b   a. the group has more than about ten people
LO 12   b. groups norms pressure people to contribute the maximum
Concept   c. it is impossible to measure individual outcomes
447   d. group members perceive equity
M

12.66   Easy identification of the contributions of group members
c   a. increases reward salience
LO 12   b. decreases reward salience
Concept   c. decreases social loafing
447   d. decreases group efficiency
M

12.67   One way to decrease social loafing relies on
d   a. relaxing conformity norms in favor of individually driven ones
LO 12   b. decreasing reward salience
Concept   c. having group members perform disjunctive tasks
448   d. increasing group members commitment to task performance
M

12.68   Which of the following methods is most likely to reduce social loafing in a group?
a   a. increasing the apparent importance of the task
LO 12   b. setting the group an additive task
Concept   c. setting the group a disjunctive task
448   d. setting the group a cooperative task
C

12.69   High group cohesiveness tends to reduce social loafing because in these conditions
b   a. individual contributions are easily identifiable
LO 12   b. group members tend to care more about group outcomes
Concept   c. groups increase performance on disjunctive tasks
448   d. groups increase performance on additive tasks
C

12.70   While perceived social loafing is usually met with negative affect, behavioral reactions often involve
c   a. less attention to the group outcome
LO 12   b. decreased contributions by others
Concept   c. increased contributions by leaders
448   d. forgiveness, based on expectations of future performance
C

12.71   Which of the following can lead to feelings of unfairness in social situations?
a   a. the belief that we have been shortchanged
LO 13   b. the belief that our input is the same as others
Applied   c. the belief that each person's outcome is reflective of his or her contributions
448   d. the belief that we have contributed to the outcome
M

12.72
b
LO 13
Concept
449
M

In order to decide whether a social exchange is fair or not, individuals rely on several different standards. One of these requires that all participants in an exchange receive outcome proportional to their inputs. This standard is known as
a. equality
b. equity
c. relative needs
d. justice

12.73
d
LO 13
Concept
449
M

When persons who have made large contributions receive relatively large outcomes, and those who have made small contributions receive small outcomes, we have
a. inequity
b. equality
c. egocentrism
d. equity

12.74
d
LO 13
Concept
449
M

Which of the following is a statement of the rule of distributive justice?
a. each person in a fair exchange should receive the same outcome
b. each person in a fair exchange should make the same contribution
c. a fair distribution is one in which each person's needs are met
d. each person's outcome in a relationship should reflect his or her contributions

12.75
c
LO 13
Applied
449
C

Ralph and Lisa work for the same company. Ralph has 10 years experience and holds an advanced degree. Lisa just started working for the company and has a bachelor's degree. Ralph has a larger salary than Lisa. What would probably occur?
a. Lisa would experience strong feelings of inequity, since Ralph is paid more than she
b. Ralph would experience strong feelings of guilt, since he is paid more than Lisa
c. Ralph and Lisa might perceive that equity exists, since Ralph seems to deserve more pay than Lisa
d. Lisa may attempt to derogate Ralph as a means of reducing her feelings of inequity

12.76
a
LO 13
Concept
449
M

Which type of inequity bothers us more?
a. underpayment inequity
b. overpayment inequity
c. these two types bother us equally
d. when someone else is the victim, rather than ourselves

12.77
b
LO 14
Concept
449
M

One factor that influences whether or not we perceive fairness is the way the available rewards are distributed, or
a. distributive justice
b. procedural justice
c. interpersonal justice
d. personal justice

12.78
c
LO 14
Concept
450
M

The considerateness and courtesy with which available rewards are distributed plays a part in how we perceive fairness or unfairness. This concept is called
a. procedural justice
b. distributive justice
c. interpersonal justice
d. personal justice

12.79
d
LO 14
Concept
450
M

Procedures that are _____ are generally perceived as fair.
a. based on accurate information, highly sophisticated, and represent the interests of all parties
b. consistent, informal, and informative
c. informal, represent the interests of all parties involved, and are considerate
d. consistent, based on accurate information, and represent the interests of all parties

12.80   Lisa has a question about a grade she received on a psychology test. She goes to speak to the
b   professor about the grade, but the professor's response is, "I don't have time to explain the grade.
LO 14   You got the grade you deserve, and if you don't like it, that's tough!" Lisa would probably
Applied   experience a sense of unfairness due to a violation of one of the factors of
451   a. personal justice
M   b. interpersonal justice
            c. procedural justice
            d. distributive justice

12.81   In a study on the announcement of a smoking ban, Greenberg (1994) found that when the chief
a   executive officer of a company announced the ban in an interpersonally fair manner, the ban
LO 14   a. was more readily accepted by heavy smokers
Study   b. was more readily accepted by nonsmokers
451   c. was not as readily accepted as a straight-forward, direct statement of the ban
C   d. was accepted equally, regardless of smoking level

12.82   In perceptions of fairness, _____ is important.
c   a. interpersonal justice only
LO 14   b. interpersonal and personal justice   ·
Concept   c. distributive justice as well as interpersonal justice
451   d. distributive justice only
M

12.83   The worker who works longer hours in order to justify the increase in pay she received with her
b   recent promotion is using the strategy of _____ in order to eliminate feelings of unfairness.
LO 15   a. altering her outcomes from the situation
Applied   b. altering her contributions to the situation
452   c. changing her perceptions
M   d. withdrawal from the situation

12.84   The most common alteration of outcomes sought by people in an inequitable situation is
a   a. under-rewarded persons seek a larger share of the rewards
LO 15   b. over-rewarded persons seek to reduce their share of the rewards
Concept   c. rewards are justified across several different relationships
452   d. each of the above are equally likely to happen
M

12.85   The text suggests that a fairly drastic strategy for dealing with inequity is
c   a. alteration of contributions to the situation
LO 15   b. alteration of outcomes from a situation
Concept   c. withdrawal from the situation
453   d. alter beliefs or perceptions regarding the situation
M

12.86   Which of the following is not an example of a change in perception that is used to reduce feelings
c   of unfairness?
LO 15   a. people convince themselves that the person exploiting them deserves an extra share of the
Concept   rewards
453   b. people convince themselves that they are actually benefitting from the unfair treatment they
C   receive
            c. people convince themselves that they need to work harder in order to justify their increased
                outcome
            d. people convince themselves that a little suffering is good for them

12.87
b
LO 16
Concept
454
M

One reason (but not justification) that employees might steal from their companies is that such stealing
a. alters their impressions of the company, thereby making the employee feel good
b. alters their outcomes from the company, thereby achieving equity
c. alters their perceptions of themselves as hard workers
d. alters their input in the company, thereby achieving equity

12.88
b
LO 16
Study
454
M

Greenberg (1990) found that in a plant where a pay cut was announced in a limited information, direct, no-nonsense manner
a. theft decreased in the next few months
b. theft increased in the next few months
c. theft increased at first, then decreased in the next few months
d. there were increased resignations in the next few months

12.89
c
LO 16
Study
454
M

In a controlled study of theft in the laboratory, Greenberg (1993) found that participants who received a detailed explanation why there was a cut in pay plus an apology
a. stole no money even though there was ample opportunity to do so
b. stole more money than individuals in the other groups
c. stole less money than individuals in the other groups
d. did not have the opportunity to steal money

12.90
b
LO 16
Study
455
C

One implication of the results of Greenberg's studies on stealing from employers is that employers should
a. be direct but avoid apologies with employees because they need information not emotion
b. be fair to employees because it is difficult to steal from a friend
c. be careful with explanations because the employees are going to steal anyway and they do not need additional justification
d. be careful not to give too much information because such information might provide a justification to steal

12.91
b
LO 17
Fact
456
M

Social decision schemes are
a. formal rules for reaching the best decision possible in a given situation
b. rules that relate the initial distribution of member views to a group's final decision
c. rules indicating precisely how groups shift from an initial view to a final decision
d. techniques used by groups for reaching decisions in the shortest amount of time possible

12.92
d
LO 17
Fact
456
E

The methods by which groups arrive at a decision from varied views are called
a. feedback loops
b. convergent schemes
c. divergence inhibition
d. social decision schemes

12.93
a
LO 17
Applied
456
E

An example of social decision scheme is
a. the election of a class treasurer
b. the appointment of the Attorney-General
c. the succession of a monarch
d. the completion of an in-class exam

12.94
a
LO 17
Concept
456
E

Which is not one of the social decision schemes mentioned in the text?
a. the dominant member rule
b. the truth-wins rule
c. the majority-wins rule
d. the first-shift rule

12.95   The truth-wins rule suggests that the final decision reached by a group will depend on
c   a. whatever position is initially supported by a majority of the members
LO 17   b. the direction of the first shift in opinion shown by any member
Concept   c. the correctness of the decision, with more and more members recognizing "correctness"
456   d. the initial distribution of views among the members
M

12.96   Assume that a person wishes to influence the group decision. Which social decision scheme implies
d   that she should start by supporting a view other than the one she actually favors and quickly changes
LO 17   to the favored position?
Concept   a. the majority-wins rule
456   b. the truth-wins rule
C   c. the social transition scheme
           d. the first-shift rule

12.97   When a correct answer exists, groups often follow the
c   a. majority-wins rule
LO 17   b. first-shift rule
Concept   c. truth-wins rule
456   d. power-wins rule
M

12.98   The majority-wins rule seems best in predicting group decisions in _____ tasks; the truth-wins rule
b   seems best in predicting groups decisions on _____ tasks.
LO 17   a. simultaneous, sequential
Concept   b. judgmental, intellective
456   c. intellective, judgmental
C   d. sequential, simultaneous

12.99   Straw polls can influence group decisions through giving information on
a   a. the distribution of opinions in a group
LO 18   b. other groups' decisions
Concept   c. the type of decision that has to be made
456   d. who is likely to engage in social loafing
M

12.100   What is the impact on group members of conducting a straw poll?
c   a. since straw polls are not binding, group members are not influenced
LO 18   b. group members usually harden their own prior positions when confronted with straw polls
Concept   c. group members usually change toward the position taken by others in straw polls
456   d. the impact of straw polls depends primarily on whether others report their votes sequentially or
C   simultaneously

12.101   A straw poll is likely to unduly shape the outcome of group decisions if the straw poll is conducted
a   a. early in deliberations
LO 18   b. after considerable deliberations
Concept   c. just before the final vote is taken
457   d. when every person has the opportunity to present his or her opinion before voting in the poll
M

12.102   Lisa is a member of a jury that has just retired to the jury room for deliberations. The foreman of
b   the jury suggested that a straw poll be taken at first just to see where everyone is on the issues. Why
LO 18   would Lisa argue against such a poll?
Applied   a. she is disruptive and wants to show her power
457   b. the poll would tend to influence people in their later decisions
M   c. the poll is a waste of time, since the issues have not been discussed
           d. the poll will bring out issues that might not be relevant

12.103
d
LO 19
Concept
457

Group polarization occurs because
a. most people have different opinions from one another
b. most groups tend to have a broad range of opinions
c. people like each other less than is expected
d. group discussion tends to lead to group members becoming more extreme in their positions

12.104
c
LO 19
Concept
457

If individuals are mildly in favor of a course of action prior to a group discussion, the group polarization hypothesis predicts that they will
a. be mildly opposed to the action after discussing their shared views
b. neither favor not oppose the action after discussing their shared views
c. come to favor the action more strongly after discussing their shared views
d. be strongly opposed to the action after discussing their shared views

12.105
d
LO 19
Applied
457
M

When it comes to decisions, Lisa thinks she is bolder than her coworkers. In a recent meeting, she discovered that other workers in the office favored even bolder decisions. As a result, Lisa shifted toward an even bolder position herself. The process underlying this change is
a. groupthink
b. cohesiveness
c. evaluation apprehension
d. social comparison

12.106
a
LO 19
Concept
457
M

Social comparison provides an explanation of group polarization through the common belief of individuals that
a. they are more right than most people
b. the opinions of other people will not affect their own
c. they have to protect their views against those of others
d. groups means do not reflect population means

12.107
b
LO 19
Concept
457
C

Which is NOT an assumption of the social comparison explanation of group polarization?
a. most people assume they hold views that are "better" than other peoples' views
b. people perceive their own initial views to be more moderate than those of "average others"
c. people frequently discover in discussion groups that their views are more moderate than they had initially believed
d. people often shift toward greater extremity in order to establish a favorable position relative to others in the group

12.108
d
LO 19
Concept
458
M

The idea that group polarization is the result of quality and quantity of ideas exchanged in a group is called
a. groupthink
b. social monitoring
c. social comparison
d. persuasive arguments

12.109
b
LO 19
Concept
458
M

When most of the arguments presented during a group discussion favor a particular point of view, the group usually shifts toward this view. This finding is consistent with the _____ view of group polarization.
a. social comparison
b. persuasive arguments
c. self-presentation
d. risky-shift

12.110
a
LO 19
Concept
458
C

With regard to the choice between the social comparison and persuasive arguments explanations for group polarization, the text concludes that
a. social comparison is somewhat more important
b. persuasive arguments is somewhat more important
c. neither view is important
d. both explanations probably play a role, but neither is more important than the other

12.111   Group polarization can be dangerous because it can lead to
c
LO 19   a. groupthink
Concept   b. high levels of negative affect
458   c. risky strategies that have a high chance of failure
M   d. an inability to reach decisions

12.112   When groups display too much cohesiveness in decision making, a common result is
d
LO 20   a. group polarization
Concept   b. failure in negotiations
458   c. authoritarian leadership
M   d. groupthink

12.113   Groupthink occurs when group members are
a
LO 20   a. overconcerned with maintaining consensus
Concept   b. overconcerned with maintaining consistency
459   c. strongly polarized in their individual decision processes
C   d. strongly polarized in the outcome of their group decision

12.114   Groupthink is often maintained by
b
LO 20   a. group polarization tendencies
Concept   b. internal and within group pressure to conform
459   c. weak leadership roles
M   d. poorly defined group roles

12.115   Which is characteristic of groups in which groupthink has developed?
a
LO 20   a. an illusion that the group is unanimous
Concept   b. effective decision-making
459   c. vigorous dissent
M   d. a feeling that the group is morally inferior

12.116   Which of the following is NOT likely to happen in a group experiencing groupthink?
d
LO 20   a. feelings of invulnerability develop
Concept   b. members feel that the group is correct
459   c. pressure toward conformity is correct
E   d. information contrary to the group's current thinking is carefully considered

12.117   The tendency for groups to cling stubbornly to unsuccessful decisions even with the knowledge that
b   they are bad decisions is called
LO 20   a. social comparison
Fact   b. collective entrapment
460   c. social decision scheme
M   d. group polarization

12.118   Kameda and Sugimori (1993), in a study investigating promoting of poor job applicants, found
d   that groups that were originally split and had to make a unanimous decision tended to support their
LO 20   original decision to promote an employee whom they later discovered had done poorly. This result
Study   illustrates
460   a. social comparison
C   b. social decision scheme
          c. group polarization
          d. collective entrapment

12.119
d
LO 21
Concept
460
M

Groupthink can be eliminated or minimized by
a. insulating the group from outside influences
b. decreasing the impartiality of the leader
c. assigning a task to only one subgroup
d. holding "second-chance" meetings

12.120
c
LO 21
Fact
460
C

The textbook has three suggestions for avoiding groupthink. Which is NOT one of these suggestions?
a. promote open inquiry and skepticism among group members
b. have independent groups consider various aspects of the problem
c. avoid necessary dissent in the group so that unanimity can develop
d. arrange second-chance meetings for group members to express lingering thoughts

12.121
c
LO 21
Concept
460
M

The role where one or more group members deliberately provide arguments against the prevailing group opinion is that of the
a. polarization candidate
b. leader
c. devil's advocate
d. mindguard

12.122
b
LO 21
Concept
460
C

What purpose is served by second-chance meetings among group members concerned about the possibility of groupthink?
a. second-chance meetings allow groups to develop unanimously-supported decisions
b. second-chance meetings allow group members to express any lingering doubts
c. second-chance meetings allow group members to internalize their decisions
d. second-chance meetings assure that the support of group members is not merely compliance

12.123
c
LO 22
Concept
461
M

Evidence that information is more likely to be discussed in a group if many people know about it suggests that
a. most people have roughly the same information
b. resources have to be pooled to be effective
c. the pooling of resources in groups is rare
d. resource pooling is a disjunctive phenomenon

12.124
a
LO 22
Concept
461
M

Underlying the pooling of resources notion is the idea that
a. the group's final decision will reflect a blending of the unique skills and knowledge brought to the task by individual members
b. the position taken by the leader will determine how individual members' contributions are blended
c. the group must decide on its social decision scheme before beginning to discuss issues
d. the social transition scheme used will be important in determining the final decision

12.125
b
LO 22
Study
461
M

According to Stasser and Titus (1985), why don't groups engage in unbiased pooling of members' resources?
a. members give undue attention to unshared information
b. members give undue attention to shared information
c. members give undue attention to members with unusual ideas
d. in fact, groups do engage in unbiased pooling of resources

12.126
a
LO 22
Concept
461
C

The advantage of shared information over unshared information in the pooling of resources situation is greater in
a. larger groups
b. smaller groups
c. unstructured discussions
d. groups that boil information down to reflect key issues

12.127   The tendency for group members to discuss shared information and to exclude unshared
c   information is strongest in
LO 22   a. smaller groups given no instructions regarding their discussions
Concept   b. smaller groups that structure their discussions
461   c. larger groups that structure their discussions
C   d. larger groups given no instructions regarding their discussions

12.128   Groups are more likely to discuss all information available, rather than just shared information, if
d   they believe
LO 23   a. that there is no correct solution to a problem
Concept   b. that the task before them is disjunctive in nature
462   c. that the task before them is additive in nature
M   d. that there is a correct solution to the problem

12.129   Under which of the following conditions are groups most likely to discuss all information?
a   a. when trying to estimate the average speed of an American car
LO 23   b. when trying to estimate what is the most beautiful picture in the world
Concept   c. when trying to come up with the person who is most likely to be the next president
462   d. when trying to estimate the most satisfying jobs on the market today
M

12.130   Information is more likely to be shared by all group members if
b   a. pressures for immediate consensus is high
LO 23   b. it is possible to find a correct solution to the problem facing the group
Concept   c. members are inclined to groupthink
462   d. potential agreement is limited
M

12.131   The tendency for information held by most members of a group to exert a stronger influence on the
c   final decision than information not held by most members is called
LO 23   a. group polarization effect
Fact   b. group consensus effect
462   c. common knowledge effect
E   d. persuasive arguments effect

12.132   Leadership is defined as
a   a. the process through which one member influences other members toward certain goals
LO 24   b. the degree of overt authority displayed by a group member
Fact   c. the influence of a non-member over a group
463   d. the degree of overall authority displayed by a group member
M

12.133   The great person theory of leadership suffered a setback when
b   a. people could not agree on a specific set of "great leaders"
LO 24   b. people could not agree on a specific set of leadership traits in "great leaders"
Concept   c. it was found that traits are affected by situations
463   d. it was found that traits are not affected by situations
M

12.134   Leadership motivation is seen in the
c   a. desire to cooperate and form networks
LO 24   b. desire for achievement
Concept   c. desire to exercise authority over others
463   d. desire to integrate large amounts of information
E

12.135
d
LO 24
Concept
464
C

Leadership, like all forms of social behavior, can be understood only in terms of
a. cognitive influences on affect
b. affective influences on cognition
c. social interactions of individuals
d. complex interactions of social situations and individual characteristics

12.136
c
LO 25
Fact
464
E

A leader who invites input and participation in decision making by followers would be classified as
a. a permissive leader
b. a person oriented leader
c. a democratic leader
d. a cooperative leader

12.137
b
LO 25
Fact
464
E

A directive leader is one who
a. permits followers to work in any way they wish
b. directs how followers will work on a task
c. directs how he or she will work on a task
d. allows participation in decision-making

12.138
d
LO 25
Fact
464
C

One model of leadership proposes that there are four basic leadership styles that vary on two dimensions. These two dimensions are
a. democratic-permissive, autocratic-directive
b. autocratic-permissive, democratic-directive
c. autocratic-task oriented, democratic-person oriented
d. autocratic-democratic, directive-permissive

12.139
c
LO 25
Concept
465
M

A leader who focuses on the task completion rather than the social aspects of the group is called
a. a directive leader
b. a democratic leader
c. a task oriented leader
d. a productive leader

12.140
d
LO 26
Study
466
M

Predominate evidence on gender differences among leadership styles suggests that
a. males are more likely to be effective leaders
b. females are more likely to be effective leaders
c. styles of leadership differ according to situations
d. females and males generally do not differ in leadership style

12.141
a
LO 26
Study
466
E

Studies of gender differences in leadership style often contrast concern with task performance with
a. concern with interpersonal relations
b. concern about groupthink
c. concern about social loafing
d. concern about task style

12.142
b
LO 26
Study
466
M

One of the differences in leadership style between males and females is that females appear to be slightly
a. more authoritarian
b. more democratic
c. more confident of their decisions
d. less confident of their decisions

12.143   Female leaders are rated lower than male leaders when
d   a. the evaluators were female and the leadership style was stereotypically masculine
LO 26   b. the evaluators were female and the leadership style was stereotypically feminine
Study   c. the evaluators were male and the leadership style was stereotypically feminine
466   d. the evaluators were male and the leadership style was stereotypically masculine
C

12.144   Components of a charismatic relationship include
b   a. authoritarian tendencies
LO 27   b. enhanced performance by followers
Concept   c. democratic tendencies
467   d. high permissive tendencies
M

12.145   A transformational leader attracts followers with a
d   a. democratic style hiding authoritarian tendencies
LO 27   b. system of highly developed management and task oriented skills
Concept   c. system of social facilitation and relations oriented speech
467   d. vision of a future and a recognizable way of attaining it
C

12.146   Framing as applied to transformational leadership refers to
b   a. naming a goal, and only deviating a small amount from it
LO 27   b. defining a purpose in a meaningful way
Fact   c. a way of gathering support for leadership
467   d. a method of social facilitation for attaining a goal
M

12.147   Which of the following is NOT a necessary characteristic of a transformational leader?
d   a. impression management
LO 27   b. enhanced motivation
Concept   c. possession of framing techniques
468   d. aggressive motivation
C

12.148   Research by Earley (1993) found that social loafing is greatest in _____ cultures as compared to _____
b   cultures.
LO 28   a. collectivistic, individualistic
Study   b. individualistic, collectivistic
469   c. individualistic, culturalistic
C   d. culturalistic, collectivistic

12.149   According to the research by Earley (1993), cultures that emphasized individual accomplishment
a   a. had the highest level of social loafing
LO 28   b. had the lowest level of social loafing
Study   c. had the highest level of employee stealing
469   d. had the lowest level of employee stealing
M

12.150   In Earley's (1993) study of culture and social loafing, it was found that
d   a. social loafing was lower in the U. S. than in China and Israel
LO 28   b. social loafing was higher in Israel than in the U. S. and China
Study   c. social loafing was higher in China than in the U. S. and Israel
470   d. social loafing was lower in China and Israel than in the U. S.
C

CHAPTER 13

Learning Objectives

After studying this chapter, students should be able to:

1.   *Define "forensic psychology" and describe the dimensions of interrogation and accompanying styles.*

2.   *Describe how minimization vs. maximization induces a suspect to confess. Discuss the Kassin and McNall findings regarding the effectiveness of the two techniques with jurors.*

3.   *Give an example of a leading question. Indicate the role of the interrogation setting.*

4.   *List the three typical feelings of the witness during leading questions and say what happens when the typical target of leading questions answers definitely and confidently.*

5.   *Contrast the '90s and '80s crime rates and youth gun death across the two decades. Discuss our belief in "presumed innocence" and whether exposure to media "facts" about a crime affects jurors' dispositions regarding guilt.*

6.   *Indicate the implications of "automatic vigilance" and that the U.S. public is not "sequestered." Give examples of how stereotypes shape our perceptions about who committed heinous crimes.*

7.   *Describe the racial rift in the O.J. trial, and the findings of Page and Gropp in their investigation of pretrial publicity in the O.J. case. Explain how emotions eclipse thinking in such cases.*

8.   *Discuss our perceptions of and the reality about the reliability of eyewitness testimony.*

9.   *Describe Munsterberg's personal experience as an eyewitness. Discuss the accuracy level of "experts" witnessing a staged assault, and the effect of "misleading postevent information" on memory of an event.*

10.   *Describe conditions in which eyewitness' memory remains intact. List the circumstances under which confidence in memory increases and decreases.*

11.   *Discuss the use of hypnosis in court. Explain why a line-up is like an experiment.*

12.   *Tell how to identify an accurate witness based on her/his experience during an identification. Explain how the goal of attorneys in selecting jurors is different from our perception of the ideal.*

13.   *Discuss leading questions and list some sources of bias on the part of judges. Describe Hart's study of judges' non-verbal video-communications conveying their own private opinion concerning guilt.*

14.   *Describe the profile of the likely successful defendant, and when the traits can backfire. Indicate the value of a smile (LaFrance and Hecht), and for whom attractiveness is an asset. Tell how attractiveness affects judges and attorneys.*

15.   *Discuss the interplay of defendant's and victim's attractiveness level (Castellow and colleagues). Examine the observation that African-Americans commit more violent crimes, with special attention to the death penalty.*

16.   *Discuss when a suspect is most suspect, and whether language is a barrier to acquittal. List Adler's suggestions for a better juror system. Contrast competent and incompetent, experienced and inexperienced, authoritarian and lenient, pro- and anti- death penalty and pro- or anti- expert attitudes of jurors.*

17.   *Describe "industrial-organizational psychologists." Contrast attitudes toward jobs and attitudes toward companies. Describe when people tend to report high job satisfaction (JS). List and describe organization factors in JS. Describe the Melamed et al. findings on monotony and JS, and personal factors that relate to JS.*

18.   *Give the reasons why JS relates poorly to work behaviors. Describe the three components of organizational commitment uncovered by Allen and Meyer.*

19.   *Describe what effects of organizational commitment are reflected in "organizational citizenship behavior." Explain "workaholicism." Detail "impression management" during job interviews. List the interview factors Pingitore et al. studied.*

20.   *Discuss how interviewer-expectations become self-fulling prophesies. Discuss tactics that slant "office politics" in one's favor (attend to "office chameleons," "when push comes to shove," "dirty tricks," "hidden agendas" and "human resources").*

21.   *List the "anti-office-politics" countermeasures. Contrast workplace "conflict" and "aggression." Describe the organizational and interpersonal sources of workplace conflict and modes of reacting to conflict. Contrast concern for own vs. others outcomes.*

22.   *Describe three "negotiation" tactics. Explain "incompatibility error" and "Superordinate goals." Describe the questions asked of "expatriate managers" by Guzzo et al. and the answers provided.*

Questions

13.1   The judicial process is examined in
d   a. industrial psychology
LO 1   b. industrial-organizational psychology
Fact   c. forensic psychology
476   d. sociolegal psychology
E

13.2   Williamson (1993), in an investigation of methods of interrogation, proposed that there were the
a   following two dimensions related to questioning a suspect.
LO 1   a. cooperative-confrontational, adversarial-inquisitorial
Study   b. collusive-confrontational, dominant-inquisitorial
478   c. cooperative-collusive, adversarial-dominant
M   d. counseling-confrontational, dominant-collusive

13.3   In looking at the interrogation styles used by British detectives, the majority of them (40%) used a
c   a ____ style, which is characterized as ____.
LO 1   a. businesslike, impatient and emotional
Study   b. counseling, helpful and problem-solving
478   c. collusive, helpful and problem-solving
C   d. dominant, brusque and factual

13.4   The interrogation style that uses an approach described as helpful, ingratiating, paternalistic, and
b   problem-solving is called
LO 1   a. counseling
Fact   b. collusive
478   c. dominant
M   d. businesslike

13.5   One subtle tactic for getting a confession involves exaggerating the strength of the evidence, which
c   is called
LO 2   a. enhancing
Fact   b. elaboration
478   c. maximization
M   d. reverberation

13.6   In addition to being effective in getting a confession, the technique of minimization
c   a. relies on the foot in the door technique
LO 2   b. puts the interrogator in the position of being a hard-sell questioner
Concept   c. avoids legal problems raised by threatening the suspect
479   d. creates an atmosphere of reciprocity
C

13.7   In interrogation, the technique of minimization
c   a. downplays the availability of legal support
LO 2   b. downplays the seriousness of the potential confession
Concept   c. is a less obvious method to elicit compliance
479   d. puts the interrogator in a weak position
M

13.8   Kassin and McNall (1991) found that mock jurors gave higher conviction rates when the confession
c   was obtained by
LO 2   a. force
Study   b. maximization
479   c. minimization
M   d. threat

13.9   What is a "leading question?"
b   a. one that leads the witness away from what was observed
LO 3   b. one that leads the witness to a desired answer
Concept   c. one that leads the questioner astray
479   d. one that misleads the witness as to what the questioner desires
E

13.10   A question that contains cues to what the questioner either wants to hear or is interested in finding
d   out is a
LO 3   a. demand question
Fact   b. "plea for help" question
479   c. "plea for understanding" question
M   d. leading question

13.11   While questioning Lisa about the mugging that occurred outside her apartment, the impatient
c   detective says, "Are you sure you saw a man snatch that woman's purse and run?" This is a
LO 3   a. demand question
Applied   b. "plea for help" question
479   c. leading question
M   d. "plea for understanding" question

13.12   It has been suggested that people are particularly responsive to leading questions in interrogations
b   because
LO 3   a. police officers are adept at asking them
Concept   b. people assume the interrogator has special knowledge
479   c. the stress of the event leads to a desire to get out of the situation as fast as possible
M   d. leading questions generally correspond to the answers that people are prone to give anyway

13.13   When Smith and Ellsworth (1987) presented subjects with a videotape of a bank robbery and then
c   asked them questions about it, what did they find?
LO 3   a. the knowledgeability of the questioner had no effects
Study   b. only answers to unbiased questions were affected by the knowledgeability of the questioner
479   c. only answers to leading questions were affected by the knowledgeability of the questioner
C   d. whether the questions were unbiased or leading had no effect

13.14   Two components that encourage suggestible responses are
a   a. uncertainty, trust
LO 4   b. uncertainty, fear of reprisal
Concept   c. trust, fear of reprisal
479   d. expectations that they should know the answer, low I.Q.
M

13.15   Research indicates three factors encourage compliance with interrogator's suggestions. These three
d   factors are
LO 4   a. fear of reprisal, trust, expectation
Fact   b. uncertainty, trust, fear of reprisal
479   c. fear of reprisal, uncertainty, expectation
M   d. uncertainty, trust, expectation

13.16   When an individual is asked a question by an interrogator, that individual tends
a   a. to provide an answer, even if the individual is not sure
LO 4   b. to provide no answer
Concept   c. to provide a neutral response, such as "I don't know"
479   d. to wait for more information before responding
C

13.17   If an individual gives a tentative answer to an interrogator's question, that individual tends
c   a. to know that the answer was tentative and waits for more information
LO 4   b. to know that the answer was not completely accurate
Concept   c. to believe what he or she said and incorporate it into memory
479   d. to believe what he or she said at that moment, but not incorporate it into memory
M

13.18   The U. S. Bureau of Justice Statistics indicates that gun murders by
a   a. teenage boys are rapidly increasing
LO 5   b. teenage boys are decreasing slightly
Study   c. older males are increasing
480   d. females are increasing
M

13.19   Overall, _____ crime is decreasing while _____ crime is increasing.
a   a. violent, teenage
LO 5   b. teenage, violent
Concept   c. property, violent
481   d. violent, property
M

13.20   Press reports can influence trial outcome by
a   a. influencing public opinion and potential jurors
LO 5   b. influencing jurors during a trial
Concept   c. the perception that reporters are more knowledgeable than the average citizen
481   d. printing false testimony before a verdict is reached
M

13.21   Research indicates that on the whole, the more knowledge people have about a crime, the more
d   a. impartial they are
LO 5   b. reluctant they are to make a judgment
Study   c. likely they are to assume the suspect is innocent
482   d. likely they are to blame the suspect
M

13.22   The tendency to weigh negative information about an individual more heavily than positive
b   information is called
LO 6   a. weighted impression formation
Concept   b. automatic vigilance
482   c. cognitive weighting
M   d. impression weighting

13.23   In comparison to media coverage of trials in the U. S., Canada _____ on media coverage.
b   a. has no restrictions
LO 6   b. imposes severe restrictions
Concept   c. has limited restrictions
482   d. has restrictions for posttrial appeals
M

13.24   A tongue-in-check comment about trials in Canada is that the public is _____.
b   a. fully informed
LO 6   b. sequestered
Concept   c. not invited
482   d. welcome with open arms
M

13.25   Which of the following is an effect of media coverage of crimes?
b   a. they lead people to doubt presumptions of guilt
LO 7   b. they lead to viewing other crimes more harshly
Concept   c. they lead to greater self perceptions of impartiality
483   d. they lead to lower self perceptions of impartiality
M

13.26   The more exposure to pretrial publicity in the Simpson case, the
a   a. greater the perception of guilt
LO 7   b. lower the perception of guilt
Concept   c. greater the cognitive complexity
484   d. lower the cognitive complexity
M

13.27   Page and Gropp (1995) found that _____ was associated with perceptions of guilt of Simpson.
d   a. neither pretrial publicity nor racism
LO 7   b. pretrial publicity, but not racism
Concept   c. racism, but not pretrial publicity
484   d. racism and pretrial publicity
M

13.28   The results of Page and Gropp's (1995) suggest that exposure to pretrial publicity
c   a. affects selective exposure concerning reading positive or negative information
LO 8   b. affects beliefs about a defendant on a cognitive basis, not on an emotional basis
Study   c. affects beliefs about a defendant on an emotional basis, not on a cognitive basis
484   d. has no effect on beliefs, but does have an effect on behavior concerning the defendant
M

13.29   For the approximately 75,000 suspects arrested each year, what is the major source of evidence?
c   a. fingerprints
LO 8   b. DNA "fingerprinting"
Fact   c. eyewitnesses
485   d. confessions
M

13.30   Eyewitnesses are
d   a. invariably accurate
LO 8   b. infrequently wrong
Concept   c. correct or incorrect depending on large individual differences
485   d. frequently wrong
M

13.31   Inaccurate eyewitness identification is
a   a. the single most important reason innocent defendants are convicted
LO 8   b. the single most important reason there are as many hung juries as there are
Concept   c. the single most important reason there are so many mistrials
485   d. the single most important reason there are so many acquittals
M

13.32   Subjects who witnessed the dramatized criminal act in the classic Munsterberg (1907) study
b   a. remembered the details amazingly well
LO 9   b. had many omissions and inaccuracies in their descriptions
Study   c. were unable to recall that anything had happened
486   d. were able to recall details of the incident only under hypnosis
M

13.33
c
LO 9
Study
486
M

In his classic research, Munsterberg (1907) found that
a. while subjects were accurate in their reports of simple laboratory phenomena, eyewitness accounts of a sudden dramatic interaction were quite inaccurate
b. subjects were accurate for both simple laboratory phenomena and the sudden dramatic interaction
c. subjects were quite inaccurate for both simple laboratory phenomena and the sudden dramatic interaction
d. subjects were inaccurate for the simple laboratory phenomena but very accurate for the dramatic interaction

13.34
d
LO 9
Study
487
C

What number of subjects (out of 40 total witnesses) did Munsterberg (1907) find made very accurate eyewitness reports in describing the criminal action that was portrayed in front of them?
a. nearly all
b. approximately half
c. about one quarter
d. only one

13.35
c
LO 9
Study
488
M

Loftus (1992) has suggested that during the interval between the actual event and the presentation of testimony in court, _____ is responsible for distortions of memory of the event.
a. cognitive deficit
b. cognitive overload
c. misleading postevent information
d. inaccurate pretrial acquisition

13.36
a
LO 9
Study
488
C

Loftus (1992) points out that during the time between the event and the presentation of testimony concerning the event
a. it becomes difficult to distinguish what one remembers and what one has subsequently learned
b. it becomes difficult to separate the emotion of the event and the cognition of the event
c. some type of cognitive overload can occur, thereby distorting the testimony
d. some type of emotional overload can occur, thereby distorting the testimony

13.37
c
LO 10
Concept
488
C

What is the relationship between the certainty with which eyewitnesses report what they allegedly observed and accuracy of their accounts?
a. Strong; as the U. S. Supreme Court anticipated, the greater the certainty the greater the accuracy
b. Moderate; certainty was a modest predictor of accuracy
c. Moderate yet qualified; certainty was a modest predictor, but only if the memory hadn't been contaminated
d. Inverse; the greater the certainty, the less the accuracy

13.38
c
LO 10
Concept
488
M

All of the following have some impact on juries exposed to eyewitness testimony, except one. Which one is the exception?
a. witnesses speak confidently
b. witnesses speak without hesitation
c. witnesses have socioeconomic status
d. witnesses provide many details

13.39
b
LO 10
Fact
488
M

If a suspect is carrying a weapon, accuracy of eyewitness testimony
a. increases
b. decreases
c. is not affected
d. depends on the type of weapon

13.40   Accuracy of eyewitness testimony _____ if suspect and the witness belong to different racial groups.
b   a. increases
LO 10   b. decreases
Concept   c. is not affected
488   d. depends on the racial group of the witness
M

13.41   In general, if an eyewitness is a child, the credibility of the witness
b   a. increases
LO 10   b. decreases
Concept   c. is not affected
488   d. is higher than an adult, but not significantly higher
M

13.42   Which one of the following factors does NOT have a role in increasing the credibility of a child as an
c   eyewitness?
LO 10   a. the child is younger rather than older
Concept   b. there is corroboration of the child's account by other witnesses
488   c. the child is a female
C   d. the jurors are women

13.43   One of the problems that Munsterberg (1907) encountered with the use of hypnosis to increase
d   witness accuracy was that
LO 11   a. not all witnesses could be hypnotized
Study   b. not all hypnotists used the same technique, so the level of hypnosis was variable
488   c. the general atmosphere of the crime could be reconstructed, but not the details
C   d. inaccurate details could be suggested under hypnosis and then remembered as accurate

13.44   Orne and colleagues (1984) concluded that unless there was independent corroboration of
b   such a memory, it was dangerous to rely on
LO 11   a. cognitively constructed memory
Study   b. hypnotically refreshed memory
488   c. postevent correlated memory
M   d. introspectively constructed memory

13.45   If a police lineup is analogous to a social psychological experiment, what is the stimulus?
c   a. the police officer
LO 11   b. the eyewitnesses
Applied   c. the suspect
489   d. the lineup itself
M

13.46   If a police lineup is analogous to a social psychological experiment, is it necessary to vary the
a   position of the suspect in the lineup for each witness?
LO 11   a. yes, the order in which stimuli are presented should be randomized
Applied   b. no, in order to maintain consistency and control of conditions, this mixing should not
489   occur
C   c. no, each witness should have the same view as every other witness
            d. yes, for efficiency it is necessary to have a different order each time

13.47   An experiment is to _____ as a police lineup is to _____.
c   a. an independent variable, the eyewitness
LO 11   b. a dependent variable, the suspect
Concept   c. a control group, a blank lineup
489   d. an experimenter, the eyewitness
C

13.48 c LO 11 Concept 489 M	Eyewitness identification in a lineup is improved by a. telling the eyewitness to ignore as much of the context of the crime as possible b. slightly altering the appearance of the suspect, because differences stand out c. allowing the eyewitness to practice with a lineup of innocent volunteers, and then provide feedback d. making the eyewitness choose as quickly as possible
13.49 a LO 11 Applied 489 M	In a blank-lineup control, if a witness selects no one from that lineup, the confidence in the accuracy of that witness a. increases b. decreases c. is not affected d. depends on how many people are in the lineup
13.50 a LO 11 Concept 489 C	It is suggested that practice with a lineup of innocent volunteers aids eyewitness accuracy because a. actually being wrong and knowing the consequences of being wrong improves ability to recall crucial details b. viewing as many similar people as possible improves ability to recall crucial differences c. practice reduces stress level in the eyewitnesses when they engage in the real thing d. practice increases stress in eyewitnesses, but this stress helps them sharpen the memory of the criminal act
13.51 d LO 11 Concept 489 M	Which one of the following is NOT a technique that can be used to improve eyewitness accuracy? a. provide the witness with identification practice b. inform the witness of the seriousness of errors in identification c. after the lineup, inform the witness when there was an incorrect identification d. provide multiple exposures to a lineup including the suspect
13.52 b LO 12 Fact 490 M	The phrase "reinstating the context" refers to a. the accuracy level of individual eyewitnesses b. showing the eyewitness pictures of the crime scene and victim to jog their memories c. altering the context of a crime and asking the eyewitnesses to correct the changes d. the contrary reports of different eyewitnesses
13.53 c LO 12 Study 490 C	Research indicates that, in comparison to a multiple person lineup, one-person show-ups lead to a. more inaccurate identifications b. more accurate identifications c. no difference in inaccurate identifications d. no difference in accurate identifications, but only for male witnesses
13.54 b LO 12 Study 490 C	Dunning and Stern (1994) found that research participants who a. used a deliberate elimination process were more accurate b. used a nonverbal process were more accurate c. used a cognitive elaboration process were more accurate d. used a reproduction grid process were more accurate
13.55 d LO 12 Study 490 M	Dunning and Stern (1994) suggest that a. faces are stored in memory in a verbal pattern rather than a visual pattern b. faces are stored in memory with emotions attached, and are not just cognitions c. faces are stored in memory with cognitions attached, and are not just emotions d. faces are stored in memory in a visual pattern rather than a verbal pattern

13.56   Research has found that lawyers' choices of jurors are
c   a. based on a long set of predictively accurate criteria
LO 12   b. very different from non-lawyers' choices
Study   c. no better than for their clients than inexperienced college students
491   d. arbitrary and irrelevant
M

13.57   Which of the following statements about lawyers and jury choice is true?
d   a. most lawyers use a single criterion for choosing jurors
LO 12   b. most lawyers focus on different characteristics of potential jurors from case to case
Concept   c. most lawyers, as compared to non-lawyers, use a very different set of criteria for picking jurors
491   d. most lawyers use a limited set of criteria for picking jurors
C

13.58   When questioning their own witnesses, lawyers tend to ask _____ questions; when questioning
b   witnesses for the other side, lawyers tend to ask _____ questions.
LO 13   a. leading, unbiased
Applied   b. unbiased, leading
491   c. leading, leading
M   d. unbiased, unbiased

13.59   Asking unbiased questions of witnesses supporting one's case and leading questions of witnesses for
d   the opposing side is a tendency of
LO 13   a. judges
Concept   b. police
491   c. grand juror questioners
E   d. lawyers

13.60   Cross-examining lawyers tend to ask more leading questions of witnesses than examining lawyers.
c   One result is that
LO 13   a. witnesses always answer the way the lawyer wants
Applied   b. witnesses experience more stress from leading questions
491   c. witnesses are perceived as less competent when responding to leading questions
C   d. leading questions elicit more accurate information

13.61   Judges have an important duty to perform, but this duty can lead to bias. What is it?
c   a. they always decide on guilt or innocence
LO 13   b. they always decide on the sentence
Concept   c. they always are able to decide what evidence is admissible
491   d. they always are the ones to clarify evidence presented by witnesses
M

13.62   Which of the following behaviors related to a judge's duties can lead to bias?
d   a. they can decide on guilt or innocence
LO 13   b. they can decide on the sentence
Concept   c. they can clarify evidence presented by witnesses
491   d. they can attack the credibility of a witness when addressing a juror
M

13.63   The actions of the judge (e.g., admitting certain forms of evidence) in a trial often influence the
b   behavior of a jury. The aspect of social cognition that is most strongly related to these actions is
LO 13   a. the availability heuristic
Concept   b. priming
492   c. the representative heuristic
C   d. the adjustment heuristic

13.64
a
LO 13
Study
492
C

Hart (1995), in a study to investigate the judge's unstated opinion on jury decision, found that
a. if a judge had the opinion that the defendant was guilty, the participants were more likely to find the defendant guilty
b. if a judge had the opinion that the defendant was guilty, the participants were more likely to find the defendant innocent
c. if a judge had the opinion that the defendant was innocent, the participants were more likely to find the defendant guilty
d. if a judge had an opinion of guilt or innocence, that opinion did not significant influence the participant's decision

13.65
c
LO 13
Study
492
C

One of the explanations of the results of the Hart (1995) study in which it was found that the opinions of a judge influenced the decisions of mock jurors was that
a. the judge's opinion about guilt or innocence influenced the lawyers' behavior and the types of questions they asked the witnesses which in turn influenced the jurors
b. the judge's opinion about guilt or innocence influenced the witnesses which in turn influenced the jurors
c. the judge's opinion about guilt or innocence influenced the nonverbal behavior of the judge which in turn influenced the jurors
d. the judge's opinion about guilt or innocence influenced what he said to the jurors so that it was very clear what verdict he expected from the jurors

13.66
c
LO 13
Study
493
M

What is the evidence concerning the belief that some judges are "soft on crime" and others are "hanging judges?"
a. most fit the last category
b. most fit the first category
c. most fit into one category or the other category
d. about 75% fit into the first category and about 25% in the last category

13.67
c
LO 14
Concept
493
M

In most cases, you are more likely to be treated better in court if you are an
a. attractive male
b. attractive female
c. attractive person of either gender
d. unattractive person of either gender

13.68
d
LO 14
Applied
493
M

Most lawyers ask their clients to dress well in the courtroom, even if a smart outfit does not really fit the client's usual style. They make this request because
a. good dress is a sign of respect for the process of law
b. good dress is a sign of respect for the judge
c. good dress will be perceived as a sign of respect for the judge and the process of law
d. juries respond more positively to people who are attractive in appearance

13.69
c
LO 14
Study
493
M

According to research by Mazella and Feingold (1994), for most crimes it is to the defendant's advantage to be
a. physically attractive, male, high socioeconomic status
b. physically attractive, male, low socioeconomic status
c. physically attractive, female, high socioeconomic status
d. physically attractive, female, low socioeconomic status

13.70
a
LO 14
Concept
493
M

In a case of swindling, _____ is more likely than a _____ to be found guilty.
a. an attractive person, an unattractive person
b. an unattractive person, an attractive person
c. a female, a male
d. a male, a female

13.71   A ____ is more likely to be found guilty in an assault case because ____.
b   a. male, he is engaging in expected gender-role behavior, and the behavior does not stand out
LO 14   b. female, she is engaging in unacceptable gender-role behavior and the behavior stands out
Concept   c. male, he is more physically powerful and the jury lends more credence to this attribute
493   d. female, she is not as able to defend herself in court as a male
M

13.72   Juries are more likely to find someone guilty if they are
b   a. attractive
LO 14   b. perceived to be acting in an out of role manner
Concept   c. prosecuted with statistical evidence
493   d. aware of their nullification rights
M

13.73   LaFrance and Hecht (1995), in a study designed to investigate the reaction to an accused female's
c   smile, found that
LO 14   a. if the accused smiled, she was found guilty less often
Study   b. if the accused did not smile, she was found guilty more often
493   c. if the accused smiled, she received greater leniency
C   d. if the accused did not smile, received less leniency, but only by male participants

13.74   How does the physical attractiveness of the person on trial affect the decision of the jury?
b   a. it doesn't, as should be the case
LO 14   b. attractive defendants are acquitted more often
Concept   c. attractive defendants are convicted more often
493   d. attractive defendants are acquitted more often, but receive longer sentences when convicted
M

13.75   How does the physical attractiveness of the defendant affect the decision of the jury?
d   a. it doesn't, as should be the case
LO 14   b. attractive defendants are given harsher sentences
Concept   c. attractive defendants are found guilty more often
493   d. attractive defendants are acquitted more often, and receive lighter sentences when found guilty
M

13.76   It seems to be an advantage for defendants to appear attractive to the judge in cases involving
c   a. a judge and a defendant of the same gender
LO 14   b. nullification rights
Concept   c. misdemeanors
494   d. felonies
M

13.77   In sexual harassment cases, plaintiffs are more likely to win their cases if
a   a. they are attractive
LO 15   b. they are unattractive
Concept   c. they are average looking
495   d. physical attractiveness is downplayed
M

13.78   Among sex offenders, who is more likely to be found guilty?
c   a. attractive defender with an attractive plaintiff
LO 15   b. attractive offender with an unattractive plaintiff
Study   c. unattractive offender with an attractive plaintiff
495   d. unattractive offender with an unattractive plaintiff
.C

13.79
b
LO 15
Concept
496
M

What lessens the impact of a subject's attractiveness on jurors?
a. nothing, it always has impact
b. sufficient factual information
c. verbally degrading the subject
d. pleading for jurors to be fair

13.80
d
LO 15
Study
496
C

Moore and colleagues (1994), in a study designed to investigate the effects of attractiveness and character of defendants on juror decisions, found that with both types of information present
a. physical attractiveness influenced decisions
b. physical attractiveness influenced decisions, but only with good character statements
c. character did not influence decisions
d. character did influence decisions, regardless of physical attractiveness

13.81
a
LO 15
Applied
496
C

One possible interpretation of the effect that attractiveness has on juror decisions is that
a. what is beautiful is good
b. what is good is beautiful
c. beauty is only skin deep
d. you can't make a silk purse out of a sow's ear

13.82
b
LO 15
Concept
496
M

How does the race of the person on trial affect the decision of the jury?
a. it doesn't, as should be the case
b. black defendants are more likely to be convicted
c. black defendants are less likely to be convicted
d. black defendants are no more likely than whites to be convicted, but if convicted, are less likely to receive a prison sentence

13.83
a
LO 15
Fact
496
M

Criminals who kill white victims have a(n) _____ percent chance of receiving a death sentence in the U. S.; those who kill a black victim have a(n) _____ percent chance of receiving a death sentence.
a. 11.1, 4.5
b. 4.5, 11.1
c. 11.1, 11.1
d. 4.5, 4.5

13.84
d
LO 16
Concept
496
M

A suspect is most likely to be judged guilty when he or she
a. pleads that social circumstances are the cause
b. denigrates the victim
c. denies being guilty
d. denies accusations that have not been made

13.85
b
LO 16
Concept
496
M

If a defendant cannot speak English and the testimony must be translated, the defendant is
a. less likely to be found guilty
b. more likely to be found guilty
c. equally likely to be found guilty
d. less likely to be found guilty, but if found guilty, will receive a lesser sentence

13.86
a
LO 16
Study
496
M

Adler (1994) makes several suggestions for improving the American jury system. Some of these suggestions are
a. eliminate peremptory challenges, eliminate exemptions for best-educated citizens, allow jurors to take notes
b. eliminate peremptory challenges, limit juror exposure to suspect, limit prior juror experiences
c. limit juror exposure to suspect, allow questions from jurors, eliminate peremptory challenges
d. limit prior juror experience, eliminate exemptions for best-educated citizens, allow questions from jurors

13.87   Research suggests that _____ is one basis for jury incompetence.
c   a. differences in physical stamina
LO 16   b. differences in emotional variability
Study   c. differences in cognitive processing
496   d. differences in physiological functioning
M

13.88   More competent jurors process trial information by
c   a. constructing a schema and then processing all information in light of that schema
LO 16   b. deciding quickly which information will be used in making a decision
Concept   c. constructing alternative schemas and evaluating evidence in light of these alternative
497   constructions
C   d. listening until all the evidence is in and then doing elaborate processing

13.89   Research indicates that the more complex and technical the evidence, the
b   a. greater the confidence in the juror decision
LO 16   b. greater the difficulty jurors have in processing the information
Study   c. better the decision is guilt or innocence
497   d. greater the sophistication of the decision
C

13.90   Ms. James, the defense attorney, is questioning potential jurors for eligibility. One woman responds
a   that she has served on a criminal jury before. Based upon this statement, Ms. James is likely to
LO 16   a. reject the person
Applied   b. accept the person
497   c. ask that the person be permitted to serve as forewoman
M   d. ask her to explain her previous jury duty in detail for the court

13.91   Which of the following does NOT refer to a true juror bias?
a   a. the age of the jurors affects their decisions
LO 16   b. whether the jury is composed of a majority of experienced jurors affects decisions
Fact   c. whether the jurors believe in the death penalty affects their decisions
497   d. some jurors show a leniency bias -- bias in favor of the defendant
C

13.92   A jury that is "pro death" is
b   a. less likely to convict the defendant
LO 16   b. more likely to convict the defendant
Concept   c. ordinarily not used in cases where the death penalty may be involved
497   d. never used in the U. S.
M

13.93   Jurors who _____ are more likely to believe the plaintiff's version.
b   a. do not know about the dynamics of spousal abuse
LO 16   b. know about the dynamics of spousal abuse
Concept   c. know the social status of the victim
497   d. know the social status of the plaintiff
M

13.94   _____ is a psychologist who investigates all aspects of behavior in work settings.
b   a. a social psychologist
LO 17   b. an industrial-organizational
Fact   c. a career psychologist
498   d. an employment psychologist
E

13.95   Attitudes that people hold about their jobs are called
c   a. job dimension
LO 17   b. job commitment
Fact   c. job satisfaction
499   d. job identification
E

13.96   Long-term surveys of people's attitudes toward their jobs indicate that
b   a. most people express quite negative attitudes toward their jobs
LO 17   b. most people report being relatively satisfied with their jobs
Study   c. most people express neutral attitudes -- neither positive nor negative - about their jobs
499   d. job satisfaction has declined significantly over the past 10 years
M

13.97   A possible reason offered by cognitive dissonance theory for the high number of people who report
d   being satisfied with their jobs is
LO 17   a. a job is something a person must do, and this causes feelings of reactance
Concept   b. jobs provide for people's economic necessities
499   c. people would be bored with nothing to keep them busy
M   d. to dislike one's job is inconsistent with the knowledge that remaining in it is a necessity

13.98   Attitudes that people hold about the organization for which they work are called
b   a. company pride
LO 17   b. organizational commitment
Fact   c. organizational pride
499   d. job commitment
M

13.99   Factors that influence whether a person likes or does not like his or her job are divided into
c   a. internal and external factors
LO 17   b. personal and environmental factors
Fact   c. organizational and personal factors
499   d. required and optional factors
M

13.100   Which of the following are NOT organizational factors affecting job satisfaction?
b   a. reward systems
LO 17   b. status
Applied   c. supervisory quality
499   d. degree of allowed employee participation
M

13.101   Melamed and colleagues (1995) suggested that _____ would cause monotony and lower levels of job
a   satisfaction.
LO 17   a. underload
Study   b. overload
499   c. contraload
M   d. equaload

13.102   Melamed and colleagues (1995) found that _____, the lower _____.
b   a. the less the jobs were involving, the sickness-related absences
LO 17   b. the more jobs involved underload and were hectic, the job satisfaction
Study   c. the more jobs were complex, the job satisfaction
500   d. the more jobs were simplified, the sickness-related absences
M

13.103 Jobs that involve underload and are hectic are related to
b a. increased job satisfaction
LO 17 b. decreased job satisfaction
Concept c. neutral job satisfaction
500 d. no change in job satisfaction
M

13.104 Which of the following are NOT personal factors affecting job satisfaction?
d a. status
LO 17 b. seniority
Applied c. optimism
500 d. reward systems
M

13.105 Job satisfaction is _____ related to task performance
b a. strongly
LO 18 b. weakly
Concept c. negatively
501 d. not
E

13.106 Job satisfaction is weakly related to task performance because
a a. there are limits in most jobs to performance variation
LO 18 b. most people have high rates of job satisfaction
Concept c. most people have average rates of job satisfaction
501 d. most people have low rates of job satisfaction
M

13.107 Job satisfaction is more closely linked to _____ than task performance
c a. protecting the organization
LO 18 b. making constructive suggestions
Concept c. organizational performance
501 d. praising the company to outsiders
M

13.108 The correlation between job satisfaction and job turnover is high when
d a. absenteeism is a problem
LO 18 b. many employees are happy with their jobs
Applied c. many employees are unhappy with their jobs
501 d. unemployment is low
M

13.109 A model of organizational commitment developed by Allen and Meyer (1990) contains
d which of the following three components?
LO 18 a. affective component, cognitive component, conative component
Concept b. affective component, cognitive component, normative component
502 c. affective component, continuance component, conative component
C d. affective component, continuance component, normative component

13.110 The _____ of organizational commitment involves _____.
c a. cognitive component, knowledge about the organization
LO 18 b. conative component, behavior toward the organization
Concept c. affective component, emotional attachment to the organization
502 d. dispositional component, internal tendencies toward the organization
C

13.111 The _____ of organizational commitment involves _____.
d
LO 18
Concept
502
C
a. cognitive component, knowledge about the organization
b. conative component, behavior toward the organization
c. dispositional component, internal tendencies toward the organization
d. continuance component, potential cost in leaving the organization

13.112 The _____ of organizational commitment involves _____.
a
LO 18
Concept
502
C
a. normative component, feelings of obligation to stay with the organization
b. conative component, behavior toward the organization
c. cognitive component, knowledge about the organization
d. dispositional component, internal tendencies toward the organization

13.113 Voluntary behaviors by individuals that aid their organizations and that are not related to the formal
b
LO 19
Concept
503
M
job are called
a. brown-nosing
b. organizational citizenship behavior
c. altruistic behavior
d. job participation

13.114 A person who is called a "workaholic" is usually
a
LO 19
Concept
503
M
a. willing to commit large amounts of time to the organization
b. very unhappy at home because of the lack of time for family
c. very unhappy at home because of the continuity of work
d. a person who says he or she has a lot of work to do but is procrastinating

13.115 Research by Romzek (1989) suggested that individuals high in organizational commitment
d
LO 19
Concept
503
C
a. report less enjoyable home lives than individuals low in organizational commitment
b. report the same level of enjoyment of home lives as individuals low in organizational commitment
c. report less enjoyment of job experiences than individuals low in organizational commitment
d. report more enjoyable home lives than individuals low in organizational commitment

13.116 In job interviews, the tactics of _____ are often used.
c
LO 19
Concept
504
M
a. job skills
b. social skills
c. impression management
d. attribution management

13.117 In job interviews, _____ people are often given an advantage over _____ people.
c
LO 19
Concept
504
M
a. sophisticated, unsophisticated
b. fast talking, slow talking
c. attractive, unattractive
d. tall, short

13.118 In job interviews, _____ are often given higher ratings.
a
LO 19
Concept
504
M
a. people who emit high level of nonverbal cues
b. people who dress as if they don't need the job
c. people who ask questions continuously
d. people who act as if they do not need the job

13.119   Pingitore and colleagues (1994), in a study designed to investigate the effects of gender and weight
b   on interview ratings, found
LO 19   a. that males received lower ratings than females
Study   b. that females who were overweight received the lowest ratings
505   c. that males who were overweight received the lowest ratings
C   d. that there was no difference in ratings between overweight and normal weight individuals

13.120   Pingitore and colleagues (1994) found that female raters who were very comfortable with their own
c   bodies and weight were
LO 19   a. relatively generous with their ratings of all individuals
Study   b. no different in their ratings of females than males
505   c. relatively harsh in their ratings of overweight individuals
M   d. no different in their ratings of overweight or normal weight individuals

13.121   Dougherty and colleagues (1994) found that ratings of job applications were _____ by initial ratings.
a   a. strongly influenced
LO 20   b. weakly influenced
Study   c. not influenced in one way or the other
506   d. strongly influenced, but in the opposite direction, as if interviewers were compensating
M

13.122   Dougherty and colleagues (1994) found that interviewers
c   a. tended to behave in a manner to compensate for their initial ratings
LO 20   b. tended to behave in a manner to override their initial ratings
Study   c. tended to behave in a manner to confirm their initial ratings
506   d. tended to behave in a manner to negate their initial ratings
M

13.123   The role of _____ was confirmed by the research of Dougherty and colleagues (1994).
b   a. cognitive deficit
LO 20   b. interviewer expectancy
Study   c. applicant expectancy
506   d. job expectancy
M

13.124   In contrast to applicants who look good on paper, those whose records are unimpressive may
c   a. find themselves facing an interviewer who is apathetic
LO 20   b. find themselves facing an interviewer who is confirming
Concept   c. find themselves facing an interviewer who is adversarial
506   d. find themselves facing an interviewer who is supportive
M

13.125   Lisa went for her first job interview after her first year in college and had very impressive
a   impressive credentials in her application file. The job interviewer was more than likely
LO 20   a. supportive and helpful
Concept   b. adversarial and confrontive
506   c. apathetic and nonsupportive
M   d. sarcastic and attacking

13.126   Which of the following is NOT a list of tactics used in organizational politics?
a   a. hurtful actions, base of complaint, supportive victim
LO 20   b. dirty tricks, base of support, cultivating a good image
Fact   c. cultivating a good image, controlling access to information, dirty tricks
507   d. cultivating a good image, developing a base of support, controlling access to information
C

13.127 An ____ is a person who does or says whatever it takes to build a favorable reputation.
b
LO 20   a. adaptive organizer
Concept b. organizational chameleon
507   c. office manipulator
M   d. organizational mover and shaker

13.128 Individuals who are developing a base of support as a tactic of organizational politics often use ____
c   as their method.
LO 20   a. hidden agenda
Concept b. resource issues
507   c. reciprocity
M   d. information concealing

13.129 Working against other individuals in organizations where cooperation would be beneficial to all is
b   a. known as the Prisoner's Dilemma
LO 21   b. fairly common
Concept c. rare
509   d. due to inequity
M

13.130 According to the text, many of the reported complaints about conflict at work originate with
d   a. performance causes
LO 21   b. marriage problems
Concept c. constitutional problems
509   d. organizational causes
M

13.131 Ambiguity over responsibility is what kind of cause of conflict at work?
a   a. organizational
LO 21   b. personal
Fact   c. disciplinary
509   d. resource oriented
M

13.132 According to recent research, complaints about conflict at work can be attributed in large part to
c   a. organizational factors
LO 21   b. personal factors
Concept c. interpersonal factors
510   d. resource factors
M

13.133 Which one of the following is NOT one of the five patterns of responding to conflict?
d   a. compromise
LO 21   b. collaboration
Concept c. competition
510   d. collusion
M

13.134 The basic patterns of responding to conflict relate to the which of the following two dimensions?
a   a. concern for one's own outcome, concern for others' outcome
LO 21   b. concern for one's own input, concern for others' input
Concept c. concern for one's own equity, concern for others' equity
511   d. concern for one's own inequity, concern for others' inequity
C

13.135   The most likely way to resolve conflict in the workplace is through
c   a. time
LO 22   b. appealing to authority
Concept   c. negotiation
512   d. inherent disciplinary structures
M

13.136   The big lie technique refers to one side in the bargaining process
c   a. claiming that they have an "out"
LO 22   b. claiming that they have other options for getting what they want
Concept   c. claiming that their break-even point is lower than it really is
512   d. pretending to bargain for something that they do not really want
C

13.137   Claiming an "out," the big lie, and extreme initial offers are all examples of
d   a. striking-under behavior
LO 22   b. manipulation within a company
Concept   c. plea bargaining in trials
512   d. bargaining in the workplace
M

13.138   The incompatibility error is associated with
b   a. difficulty in decision making
LO 22   b. the perceptions of at least one side about mutual interests
Concept   c. the problem of people working together who do not like one another
512   d. the suitability of people for certain jobs
C

13.139   Goals that tie two sides together are called
b   a. integrator goals
LO 22   b. superordinate goals
Fact   c. Sherif goals
512   d. operative goals
E

13.140   Guzzo and colleagues (1994), in a study investigating expectations of expatriate managers, found that
c   to the degree that ____ were met, ____ would be high.
LO 22   a. manager expectations, job satisfaction
Study   b. manager commitments, job satisfaction
513   c. manager expectations, organizational commitment
C   d. manager reimbursements, job performance

CHAPTER 14

Learning Objectives

After studying this chapter, students should be able to:

1.   *Define "health psychology." Consider what and how much to drink, and whether we misperceive health dangers. Indicate when inducing fear is best and when a positive message is best.*

2.   *Outline the procedures and results of the Liberman and Chaiken caffeine and breast cancer study. Explain how sensitizers and repressors react differently to messages about breast cancer (Millar and Millar).*

3.   *Consider the smoking rate worldwide, government preventive efforts, attempts to start teens smoking and positive effects of smoking. List five strategies emerging from the De Vries et al. study using the "bogus pipeline" that may lessen smoking among teens.*

4.   *Define stress and name the major work stressors, college student stressors, and commuter stressors. Discuss reasons why stress generates physical illness. Describe "Psychoneuroimmunology" and the causal chain linking stress with secretory immunoglobulin A and illnesses.*

5.   *Contrast reactions to stress and traits of disease-prone personalities vs. the self-healing personalities. Indicate the health-importance of perceived control. Give real-life examples of attempts to obtain or maintain control.*

6.   *Describe how Bandura immunized subjects against stress-produced health-related physiological reactions. Outline the Compas and colleagues two-level stress management program.*

7.   *Describe how Emmons interpreted his findings when he studied high level and low level goals of undergraduates along with their negative emotions and illnesses. Contrast Type As and Bs on physical health indexes.*

8.   *Describe "fitness" and Brown's findings with regard to its health benefits. Indicate why "counterfactual thinking" is harmful. Discuss which is worse, an increase in negative events or a decrease in positive events.*

9.   *Discuss the effect of good smells. Tell why social support helps. List some real-life areas where social support lessen stress. Describe the plight of the support provider and those with a support deficit.*

10.   *Discuss over- and under-attention to physical symptoms. Outline the effects of preexisting anxiety on complaints during illness, Type As' control need and illnesses, as well as the problem of perceived pain in relation to illness.*

11.   *Describe the dangers of self-diagnosis and medication discontinuation. Indicate how self-efficacy plays a role in "being your own physician." Explain when people call the physician and when they self-medicate.*

12.   *Indicate the kinds of people who consult a physician and those who do not. Show how dependency relates to seeking medical advice.*

13.   *Discuss private physician talk, and "doctor interpersonal skills" as related to doctor-patient relations and "framing." Examine sources of distraction as alleviators of threat.*

14.   *Give real-life examples of how increased perceived control boosts coping. Discuss Freudenheim's laser-disk source of control.*

15.   *Define "environmental psychology." Link "technophobia" to environmental fears. Consider ineffective coping with environmental threat. Describe "noise" and when is it most noxious.*

16.   *Consider the devices for eliminating noise. Give real examples of heat, hot tempers, and aggression.*

17.   *Indicate whether heat and aggression are related in straight line fashion or aggression drops off with very hot temperatures.*

18.   *Indicate an appropriate index of pollution's harmful effects. Describe how good smells affect performance.*

19.   *Discuss positive and negative ions and their effects. List real-life ways that we affect our environments.*

20.   *Characterize the "population explosion," and outline the three philosophies of world population growth.*

21.   *Give some sources of greenhouse gases, and explain CFCs. Indicate how we can reduce these gases. Discuss the two major consequences of reducing the rain forests. Relate the Ebola threat to rain forest destruction.*

22.   *Describe the "bone of contention" for an Asian and a European-American doctor debating about treatment of a Korean woman. Indicate the dimensions of cultural difference they considered. Discuss the relevance of collectivism vs. individualism as related to medical care.*

Questions

14.1 Health psychology
c a. is a new field that looks at whether current theories are "philosophically healthy"
LO 1 b. is an ancient field -- the one upon which psychology was founded -- that is concerned with
Fact   opposing domination by the medical community
520 c. is the field that studies the psychological processes affecting the development, prevention, and
M   treatment of physical illness
d. is a new field, started by physicians, that seeks to unite medical and psychology personnel in the
    fight against disease

14.2 Two major obstacles to preventing physical disorders is
a a. our confusion in processing medical information and our reluctance to change our behavior
LO 1 b. our dedication to processing only positive information and our inability to understand the
Concept   connection between the physical and the psychological
520 c. our limitations when dealing with experts and our hesitation to ask appropriate questions
C d. our inability to comprehend medical resources and our inability to modify attitudes and
    cognitions regarding health

14.3 Threatening messages tend to be processed
d a. more quickly than non-threatening messages
LO 1 b. according to heuristics
Concept c. in a way that promotes coping activities
520 d. in a way that reduces the need to change personal behaviors
M

14.4 People are using the _____ regarding the threats to health, and are therefore overestimating these
b threats.
LO 1 a. representative heuristic
Concept b. availability heuristic
522 c. overestimate heuristic
M d. realistic heuristic

14.5 You would probably be surprised to learn that the annual death rate is
c a. the most variable of all measures of health
LO 1 b. a very poor indicator of the health of a country
Concept c. at a record low
522 d. at a record high
M

14.6 Some research indicates that when a health message induces fear, that message is _____ than when
d fear is not induced.
LO 1 a. processed more easily
Study b. processed more quickly
522 c. processed more casually
C d. processed more carefully

14.7 Rothman and colleagues (1993) propose that a _____ is best for _____.
b a. positively framed message, facilitating detection behavior
LO 1 b. positively framed message, facilitating preventative behavior
Study c. negatively framed message, facilitating preventative behavior
522 d. negatively framed message, facilitating collaborative behavior
M

14.8
a
LO 1
Applied
522
M

An example of a message that would facilitate preventative behavior would be
a. "Eat high fiber foods to promote good health"
b. "Avoid colon cancer -- get an exam"
c. "Give yourself a self-exam for breast cancer"
d. "Get a pap smear annually and avoid the pain and suffering associated with uterine cancer"

14.9
b
LO 2
Study
522
C

Liberman and Chaiken (1992) designed a study, using information about caffeine and cancer, to investigate the relationship between
a. the attitudinal framing of a message and the acceptance of that message
b. personal relevance of a message and the acceptance of that message
c. the availability of information and the acceptance of a message
d. the cognitive deficit of an individual and the acceptance of a message

14.10
b
LO 2
Study
522
C

One result of the Liberman and Chaiken (1992) study on the relationship between caffeine and cancer was that if the message was highly relevant for an individual, the message
a. was believed more than by individuals for whom the message was not relevant
b. was believed less than by individuals for whom the message was not relevant
c. was believed the same as by individuals for whom the message was not relevant
d. was believed more than by individuals for whom the message was not relevant, but only in the threatening condition

14.11
c
LO 2
Fact
523
M

A person who tries to deal with threat by thinking about it and gathering information about the threat is using the defense mechanism of
a. repression
b. intellectualization
c. sensitization
d. rationalization

14.12
d
LO 2
Study
523
M

The research of Millar and Millar (1993), on type of message and type of self-focus concerning breast self-examination, found that _____ agreed with messages more if the messages were
a. repressors, emotional with emotional focus or informational with informational focus
b. repressors, emotional with affective focus or informational with cognitive focus
c. sensitizers, emotional with cognitive focus or informational with affective focus
d. sensitizers, emotional with affective focus or informational with cognitive focus

14.13
c
LO 3
Fact
524
E

It is estimated that 3000 _____ start smoking each day.
a. women
b. men
c. teenagers
d. pregnant women

14.14
b
LO 3
Study
524
M

Research suggests a possible causal link between the dramatic increase in smoking by teenage girls and _____.
a. women's rights
b. introduction of cigarette brands for women
c. lack of parental supervision
d. lack of self-esteem

14.15
a
LO 3
Study
525
M

In line with the idea that "smoking makes you feel better," research indicates that seventh graders who express _____ are more likely to use tobacco.
a. low positive affect
b. high positive affect
c. medium positive affect
d. unrelated positive affect

14.16   A study by De Vries (1995) in an attempt to verify self-report measures of smoking, used the _____.
c   a. cognitive enhancement technique
LO 3   b. polygraph technique
Study   c. bogus pipeline technique
526   d. smoke exhaler technique
M

14.17   De Vries (1995) found which of the following three factors influenced students' smoking behavior
d   and intentions to smoke in the future?
LO 3   a. social influence, attitudes and beliefs, self-esteem
Study   b. social norms, social influence, self-concept
526   c. normative pressure, self-concept, social influence
C   d. social influence, attitudes and beliefs, self-efficacy

14.18   Which one of following items is NOT one of the causative factors of teenage smoking that smoking
c   prevention programs should address?
LO 3   a. explain how modeling effects can occur
Applied b. make it explicit than nonsmoking is the norm
527   c. emphasize assertiveness training aimed at resisting peer pressure
C   d. present accurate evidence about the consequences of smoking

14.19   Successful coping behavior results in
b   a. exhaustion and sleep responses
LO 4   b. threat reduction
Concept c. enhanced adrenalin flow
527   d. reduced perceptual capacity
M

14.20   Ralph finds out that he has been fired from his job. One night soon after, Ralph takes an overdose
a   of sleeping pills (and recovers). In psychological terms, the job situation and Ralph's response to
LO 4   it are defined as
Applied a. stress, coping behavior
527   b. trauma, stress response
M   c. environmental stimulus, dispositional stimulus
         d. stress, perceptual dysfunction

14.21   Stresses can influence the likelihood of illness if they are
d   a. physical only
LO 4   b. psychological only
Concept c. physical and psychological at the same time only
527   d. either physical or psychological
M

14.22   Is there a relationship between stressful periods of one's life and the likelihood of illness?
a   a. yes, illness is more likely during periods of stress
LO 4   b. no, illness is less likely during periods of stress
Concept c. yes, illness is less likely during periods of stress
527   d. undecided, adequate research has not yet been done
M

14.23   Multiple negative events increase feelings of stress because of a
b   a. geometric progression
LO 4   b. cumulative effect
Concept c. psychological reaction to repeated exposures
528   d. psycho-physical reaction
M

14.24   The concept of a link between stress reactions and defenses against disease is contained in the field
c   of
LO 4   a. psychiatry
Fact   b. psychomedicine
528   c. psychoneuroimmunology
E   d. neuropsychology

14.25   Exposure to stressful situations causes _____ in health preventive behavior and _____ in the
a   effectiveness of the immune system.
LO 4   a. a decrease, a decrease
Concept b. an increase, an increase
528   c. a decrease, an increase
M   d. an increase, a decrease

14.26   What does the area of psychoneuroimmunology study?
d   a. how our responses to internal events affect internal psychological states that, in turn, shut down
LO 4   the immune system
Concept b. our set of beliefs and expectancies regarding health and the threat of illness
528   c. the various needs that people attempt to satisfy in the work setting
M   d. psychological responses and the immune system

14.27   What did Jemmott and Magloire (1988) find when they measured secretory immunoglobulin A in
b   students' saliva before, during, and after final exams?
LO 4   a. levels of this substance determined exam scores
Study   b. levels of this substance were lowest during the exams
528   c. levels of this substance and exam performance were independent
C   d. levels of this substance were highest during the exams

14.28   Friedman and colleagues (1994) identified which of the following two personalities when it comes
a   to dealing with stress?
LO 5   a. disease-prone and self-healing
Study   b. disease-resistant and self-injurious
528   c. disease-enhancing and self-protective
M   d. disease-habituating and self-enhancement

14.29   A person who responds to a stressful situation with negative behaviors and unhealthy behavior
c   patterns has a
LO 5   a. self-healing personality
Concept b. disease-enhancing personality
528   c. disease-prone personality
M   d. self-effacing personality

14.30   A person who has a low self-esteem and an external locus of control and is neurotic has a
b   a. self-healing personality
LO 5   b. disease-prone personality
Concept c. disease-enhancing personality
528   d. self-effacing personality
M

14.31   A person who has a self-healing personality is described as
a   a. hardy, optimistic, internal locus of control
LO 5   b. hardy, neurotic, external locus of control
Concept c. low self-esteem, neurotic, external locus of control
528   d. hardy, pessimistic, internal locus of control
M

14.32	Depression is more likely to occur when
a	a. events are beyond our control
LO 5	b. events are within our control
Concept	c. failure to control an event is perceived as an internal and unstable flaw
529	d. a positive event occurs unexpectedly
M	

14.33	"Perceived control" refers to
a	a. perceptions of degree of control of one's life
LO 5	b. feelings that others are in control of one's life
Concept	c. feelings that external events are in control of one's life
529	d. the illusion that one is in control of one's life
M	

14.34	Lisa is planning a wedding for her sister. When she got started, the wedding was going to be an
c	intimate, sophisticated affair with parents and friends. As time passed, she found that the wedding
LO 5	got larger and larger, became more expensive, more invitations were sent out, more food was
Applied	ordered, etc. Lisa is now responding to the demands of parents, friends, caterers, decorators, etc.
529	When she started, Lisa was very excited and happy about the wedding. Now, she wishes her sister
M	would elope, or dump her fiance. Lisa is suffering from

a. wedding plans neurosis
b. a perceived lack of control in a negative event
c. a perceived lack of control in a positive event
d. sister planning blues

14.35	In the "ice water" studies of Bandura (1993), participants were given a guided procedure that
b	increased their _____, and then were again exposed to the stressor.
LO 6	a. self-concept
Study	b. self-efficacy
529	c. self-enhancement
M	d. self-aggrandizement

14.36	The "ice water" studies of Bandura (1993), in which he increased the self-efficacy of participants, led
c	to the conclusion that
LO 6	a. uncontrollable stressors impair the central nervous system, but controllable stressors have no
Study	impact on the peripheral nervous system
529	b. controllable stressors impair the immune system, but uncontrollable stressors have no effect
C	c. uncontrollable stressors impair the immune system, but controllable stressor have no effect
	d. controllable stressors impair the central nervous system, but uncontrollable stressors have no
	impact on the peripheral nervous system

14.37	The two level process for coping with stress that is proposed by Compas and colleagues (1991)
b	proposes that the first level of emotional distress is dealt with using _____, and the second level is
LO 6	dealt with using _____.
Study	a. problem-focused coping, emotion-focused coping
530	b. emotion-focused coping, problem-focused coping
C	c. emotion-focused coping, task-focused coping
	d. problem-focused coping, task-focused coping

14.38	Ralph finds out that rising interest rates are going to drive up his interest payments again. He
d	decides to go and play a game of racquetball to take his mind off the problem. This situation is an
LO 6	example of
Applied	a. associative training behavior
530	b. associative coping behavior
M	c. problem-focused coping behavior
	d. emotion-focused coping behavior

14.39   Researchers have found gender differences in coping, with females using _____ and males using
a   _____.
LO 6   a. emotion-focused coping, problem-focused coping
Study   b. problem-focused coping, emotion-focused coping
530   c. affect-focused coping, cognition-focused coping
M   d. cognition-focused coping, affect-focused coping

14.40   Porter and Stone (1995), using married couples as participants, found that there were no gender
c   differences in _____, just gender differences in _____.
LO 6   a. emotion, cognition
Study   b. cognitive deficit, cognitive activity
530   c. coping, problems
M   d. self-efficacy, self-enhancement

14.41   Hardiness is
a   a. perceptions of commitment and of control, and the view that difficult situations are challenges and
LO 7   opportunities
Fact   b. willingness to start and maintain an exercise program
531   c. ability to survive stress
M   d. endurance, strength, and maintaining a good physical condition

14.42   Who is most likely to experience elevated blood pressure and increased risk of heart failure?
d   a. Type Bs
LO 7   b. externals
Concept   c. high self-monitors
531   d. Type As
M

14.43   What is behind the elevated blood pressure and increased risk of heart disease shown by "time
a   urgent" people?
LO 7   a. hostility
Concept   b. over optimism
531   c. external locus of control
M   d. neurotic instability

14.44   Research indicates that _____ is a critical component leading to coronary disease and other health
d   problems. Health psychologists have increasingly used the term _____ to describe these individuals.
LO 7   a. hostility, emotion-focused copers
Study   b. anger, problem-focused copers
531   c. hostility, hostile Type A
M   d. anger, hostile Type B

14.45   Three strategies have been identified to cope with stress and ward off its negative effects on health.
c   These three strategies are
LO 7   a. becoming physically fit, becoming involved in some project, providing comforting contact
Concept   b. becoming physically fit, decreasing negative affect, becoming involved in some project
531   c. becoming physically fit, increasing positive affect, seeking social support
M   d. becoming physically fit, increasing cognitive effort, seeking social support

14.46   Your best friend is exhibiting strong signs of Type A coronary prone behavior. What do you suggest
b   as the best activity to reduce this behavior?
LO 8   a. cognitive distraction
Applied   b. aerobic exercise
531   c. staying still for 10 minutes each day
M   d. more challenging work

14.47
c
LO 8
Fact
531
E

The term used to describe the maintenance of a good physical condition as indicated by one's endurance and strength is
a. hardiness
b. strength
c. fitness
d. wellness

14.48
b
LO 8
Study
532
M

Brown (1991), in a comprehensive study of stress, illness, and fitness, found that individuals who experienced little stress had _____, regardless of their physical fitness.
a. many illnesses
b. few illnesses
c. few, but very severe, illnesses
d. many, but not severe, illnesses

14.49
d
LO 8
Study
532
M

Brown (1991), in a comprehensive study of stress, illness, and fitness, found that individuals who experienced a high level of stress and a high level of physical fitness had _____
a. more severe illnesses
b. more less-severe illnesses
c. more visits to the health center
d. fewer visits to the health center

14.50
b
LO 8
Study
532
M

The research indicates that the best protection against illness is
a. a good string of garlic
b. a combination of fitness and hardiness
c. a high level of fitness
d. a high level of hardiness

14.51
a
LO 8
Concept
532
M

A fairly effective strategy to deal with stress is to discover how to
a. increase the positive affect in ourselves
b. decrease the negative affect in ourselves
c. increase the cognitive activity in ourselves
d. increase the cognitive deficit in ourselves

14.52
c
LO 8
Concept
533
C

One response to an unpleasant event is counterfactual thinking, which involves
a. disregarding countering thoughts, and concentrating on reality
b. thinking positive thoughts, which is counter to what actually happened, which takes away from the negative aspect of the event
c. dwelling on alternative behavior that might have prevented the event, which adds to the negative affect
d. thinking about facts that are counter to what really occurred, which obscures the negative event

14.53
b
LO 8
Study
533
C

Research by Stone and colleagues (1994) indicates that positive events _____ more than negative events _____.
a. contribute to the evaluation, detract from the evaluation
b. enhance the immune system, weaken the immune system
c. change the situation, maintain the situation
d. alter our perceptions, strengthen already held perceptions

14.54
a
LO 8
Study
533
M

Research by Stone and colleagues (1994) found that _____ had a greater adverse effect on health than _____.
a. a decrease in positive events, an increase in negative events
b. a change in environment, a change in social relations
c. an increase in negative events, a decrease in positive events
d. a modification in perception, a modification of emotion

14.55   Baron and Bronfen (1994) introduced pleasant fragrances into a room where participants were
a   working on a stressful task and found that such fragrances resulted in
LO 9   a. a more positive emotional state, and increased performance
Study   b. a more positive emotional state, but not increased performance
533   c. a more negative emotional state, but decreased performance
M   d. a more negative emotional state, and more variable performance

14.56   Social support is an important factor in
c   a. problem focused coping
LO 9   b. psychoneuroimmunological studies
Concept   c. avoiding and recovering from illness
533   d. reducing cognitive distraction
M

14.57   Social support refers to
b   a. providing support for friends and family
LO 9   b. friends and relatives who are available when difficulties occur
Fact   c. the support one receives from governmental entitlement programs
533   d. support of the social system that, in turn, supports the people
M

14.58   Talking about problems is most beneficial when
a   a. it is oriented toward problem solving
LO 9   b. it is oriented toward coping with the accompanying emotional distress
Concept   c. it is a means of catharsis
533   d. the problem can be relatively easily solved
M

14.59   Which of the following is a step in an illness episode?
c   a. accepting that stress is a cause of illness
LO 10   b. choosing an emotion or a problem focused coping strategy
Concept   c. attention to or noticing of symptoms
534   d. reducing the amount of stress in one's life
M

14.60   Individuals who focus on and overestimate the seriousness of every perceived symptom are called
a   a. hypochondriacs
LO 10   b. false positives
Concept   c. complainers
534   d. reactive personalities
M

14.61   Speaking about one's health more when one has been exposed to health related words is an
d   example of
LO 10   a. regulation
Concept   b. self-regulation
534   c. self-concealment
M   d. priming

14.62   Priming effects refer to
b   a. the greater likelihood of some stresses to produce illness
LO 10   b. the greater speed or detail of a response to a stimulus when previously exposed to something
Fact   related to that stimulus
534   c. the increased chance of illness as a result of certain personality dispositions
M   d. initial steps in an illness episode

14.63
b
LO 10
Study
535
M

In a study conducted by Cohen and colleagues (1995), it was found that the ____, the ____.
a. lower a person anxiety level, fewer disease-specific complaints
b. greater a person's anxiety level,   more disease-specific complaints
c. greater a person's anxiety level, fewer disease-specific complaints
d. lower a person's anxiety level, more disease-specific complaints

14.64
c
LO 10
Study
535
M

According to the research of Basso and colleagues (1994) those individuals with ____ reported the greatest number of physical complaints.
a. the highest number of negative events
b. the lowest self-esteem
c. the greatest need for interpersonal control
d. the greatest number of anxiety attacks

14.65
a
LO 10
Concept
535
M

One factor that influences the relationship between pain and physical problems is ____.
a. self-efficacy
b. self-control
c. self-handicapping
d. self-effacement

14.66
c
LO 11
Concept
536
M

A person who relies on common-sense in an initial self-diagnosis
a. will obviously seek out the help of a medical doctor when it is necessary
b. is necessarily making a serious mistake
c. may mistake aches and pains for "old age"
d. rarely makes a misdiagnosis

14.67
c
LO 11
Concept
536
M

In dealing with potential symptoms of illness, most people rely upon
a. medical authorities
b. traditional authority figures
c. "commonsense" self-diagnosis
d. most symptoms of illness go unnoticed

14.68
b
LO 11
Concept
536
M

If a person is taking prescription drugs to control high blood pressure, and then stops taking this medication because he or she "feels OK," that person increases the risk of coronary disease because
a. the medication is habitual
b. hypertension has no symptoms
c. blood pressure can be monitored
d. without the pills, the physiological structure is modified

14.69
a
LO 11
Concept
536
M

If we make an incorrect decision about symptoms, we risk
a. overreacting to a minor symptom or neglecting a major symptom
b. angering the physician
c. countering the effects of medication already being taken
d. diluting the effect of the medical regime already present

14.70
b
LO 11
Concept
537
M

If a self-diagnosis of a symptom indicates that the disorder involves the upper half of the body, the most common response is to
a. seek help from a medical expert
b. avoid help from a medical expert
c. get a partial diagnosis from a medical expert
d. contact an friend for a second opinion

14.71   Professional help is reserved for what kind of problems in what part of the body?
b   a. viral problems in the lower body
LO 11   b. non-viral problems in the lower body
Concept   c. psychological problems of the upper body
537   d. disruptive problems of the upper body
M

14.72   Likelihood of taking one's problem to a physician is positively associated with
a   a. self-monitoring
LO 12   b. self-concealment
Concept   c. self-diagnosis
537   d. priming responses
M

14.73   Bornstein and colleagues (1993) identified _____ as a major determinant of visits to a college health
c   center.
LO 12   a. interpersonal relationships
Study   b. interpersonal hostility
537   c. interpersonal dependency
M   d. interpersonal identification

14.74   Bornstein and colleagues (1993) found that male and female students _____ sought medical help
d   more than male and female students _____ .
LO 12   a. high in anxiety, low in anxiety
Study   b. low in anxiety, high in anxiety
537   c. low in dependency, high in dependency
M   d. high in dependency, low in dependency

14.75   Bornstein and colleagues (1993) found that as the semester progressed, students _____ tended to
c   increase their visits to the health center.
LO 12   a. high in avoidance
Study   b. low in avoidance
537   c. high in dependency
M   d. low in dependency

14.76   What did Roter (1984) suggest that patients do in preparation for a visit to a physician?
c   a. read about their suspected disorder
LO 13   b. get to know the physician; call ahead about the credentials of the physician
Study   c. practice what is to be said and asked
538   d. get ready for medication by anticipating what will be prescribed
M

14.77   Which of the following is critically important to successful physician-patient interaction?
a   a. the physician's communication skills
LO 13   b. the lack of a personality clash
Applied   c. empathy on the part of the patient
539   d. mutual liking
M

14.78   Dr. Abrams is unsure about the nature of a patient's problem. It is most likely to be beneficial to
c   the patient's well-being if
LO 13   a. Dr. Abrams makes an early decision on the nature of the illness
Applied   b. Dr. Abrams is completely truthful with the patient
539   c. Dr. Abrams does not communicate uncertainty to the patient
M   d. Dr. Abrams has a Type B personality

14.79
c
LO 13
Concept
539
M

Indicating that a pregnancy has a 50/50 chance of producing a normal child, rather than saying that it has a 50/50 chance of producing an abnormal child, is an example of
a. hedging probabilities
b. being tactful and reassuring
c. framing
d. optimizing probabilities

14.80
c
LO 13
Concept
539
M

Framing effects are evident in the medical profession through
a. patient coping strategies
b. the rapid increase in availability of medicine to most people
c. the way in which physicians present medical information
d. the rapid increase in the price of medicine for most people

14.81
b
LO 13
Concept
540
M

Simple denial, or thinking of something else
a. is always a bad strategy
b. may backfire if an individual fails to consult a physician when symptoms get worse
c. is usually a good strategy; however, denying pain in the dentist's chair is clearly a bad strategy
d. is especially helpful in coping with a situation in which symptoms get progressively worse

14.82
b
LO 13
Applied
539
M

Avoidance and denial are probably most useful in situations such as when
a. you have minor pain in your mouth
b. you are having a cavity filled
c. you have something in your eye
d. you have a mild pain in your knee

14.83
a
LO 13
Concept
540
E

People report less pain when they are made to feel
a. happy
b. sad
c. angry
d. moody

14.84
b
LO 14
Concept
540
M

For information on a patient's condition to help the patient, it
a. must be vicarious
b. must be accurate
c. must be concrete
d. only has to be accurate or concrete in the mind of the patient

14.85
d
LO 14
Concept
540
M

All of the following except one are true with regard to coping with medical procedures. Which one is the exception?
a. it is helpful for patients to know what is being done to them and why
b. active participation in the treatment is helpful
c. having a roommate who has already completed the procedures a patient will have is helpful
d. believing that passively submitting to medical technology will yield a beneficial outcome is helpful

14.86
a
LO 14
Study
540
M

Research indicates that optimal medical adjustment occurs when threat is _____ and the perception of control has at least _____.
a. high, some basis in reality
b. low, some basis in reality
c. high, no basis in reality
d. low, no basis in reality

14.87
b
LO 14
Study
540
M

The work done by Freudenheim (1992) involves _____ and the patient entering data about a surgery and then making a decision.
a. a four dimension spreadsheet
b. a laser-disk player and computer terminal
c. a cellular phone
d. a multichanneled phone circuit

14.88
b
LO 15
Fact
541
M

Environmental psychology is
a. applying psychological theory to studying problems such as pollution
b. a field dealing with the relationship between the physical world and human behavior
c. applying ecological theory to studying human behavior
d. the study of how the human psyche affects the environment

14.89
b
LO 15
Fact
542
M

Environmental stress
a. is an external stimulus rather than a reaction on our part
b. is our reaction to perceived threats in the world around us
c. is almost always overwhelming, unless there is some psychological intervention
d. has no physiological correlates

14.90
b
LO 15
Fact
542
M

Technophobia is
a. a fear of being without technology
b. fear of living in a technological society
c. hatred of environmentalists and others who oppose technology
d. fear of using technology such as computers

14.91
b
LO 15
Concept
542
E

When one is fearful of being near appliances, telephones, and computers, one is probably suffering from
a. agoraphobia
b. technophobia
c. technosis
d. stress resulting from a lack of information about modern objects

14.92
b
LO 15
Concept
543
M

Which of the following stressors has effects that primarily occur when it is unpredictable?
a. heat
b. noise
c. water pollution
d. high humidity

14.93
b
LO 15
Concept
543
M

Living in a street that has a fire station should be more stressful in general than living on a street with a school because noise from the fire station is
a. longer lasting
b. unpredictable
c. less familiar
d. more familiar

14.94
c
LO 15
Study
543
M

Compared to children who live in relatively quiet environments, children who live in noisy environments
a. are more sensitive to sound
b. have more behavioral problems
c. have lower reading abilities
d. have a worse sense of balance

14.95
d
LO 15
Study
543
M

In the Glass et al. (1973) study of noise and reading skills
a. noise was produced in the lab
b. subjects lived in an orphanage
c. some subjects could control noise level
d. traffic noise was studied

14.96
b
LO 15
Study
543
M

Glass et al. (1973) studied noise and reading skills and found that
a. subjects would could control noise did best
b. subjects on the lower floors did most poorly
c. new arrivals at the orphanage did most poorly
d. there were no differences among conditions

14.97
c
LO 16
Applied
543
M

A device to reduce the room noise elsewhere uses _____ to accomplish its purpose.
a. unpredictable noise
b. predictable loud noise
c. many different sound frequencies
d. the same frequency repeated many times

14.98
a
LO 16
Concept
544
E

In general, criminal violence occurs more frequently as the temperature
a. rises
b. falls
c. stays constant
d. gets closer to the average temperature for the year

14.99
a
LO 16
Study
544
M

A study by Kenrick and McFarlane (1986) found that, in baseball, the higher the temperature,
a. the greater the number of hit batters
b. the greater the number of batters charging the pitcher
c. the fewer the number of runs for each team
d. the greater the number of errors per team

14.100
c
LO 16
Concept
544
M

Which of the following crimes is most likely to become more frequent as temperature rises?
a. burglary
b. car theft
c. rape
d. double parking

14.101
b
LO 16
Concept
544
M

Rape is more likely than car theft to increase in frequency as the temperature rises because
a. rape is a sex crime
b. rape is a violent crime
c. more people are outdoors when the temperature rises
d. people are more likely to be alone when the temperature rises

14.102
b
LO 16
Concept
544
M

Temperature can affect liking of
a. ourselves
b. a stranger
c. relatives
d. a love

14.103   Vrij and colleagues (1994) found that when police officers were asked questions about a portrayed
c   crime, those who had watched the crime under "hot" conditions said that they
LO 16   a. were less likely to fire a shot at the suspect
Study   b. were less likely to engage in apathetic activity with the suspect
545   c. were more likely to fire a shot at the suspect
M   d. were more likely to engage in apathetic activity with the suspect

14.104   More recent studies of the notion "the hotter it is, the more the aggression" showed
c   a. no relationship between the variables
LO 17   b. support for the notion
Concept c. the notion to be true only up to a certain point
545   d. a relationship opposite to the notion
M

14.105   Some researchers (Anderson, 1989) argue that with extremely high temperatures, as temperature
a   goes up ____
LO 17   a. so does aggression, in a straight line relationship
Study   b. aggression drops off, but still stays relatively high
545   c. aggression is eliminated
M   d. aggression changes from direct to indirect

14.106   The name of the model that predicts that as temperatures rise to uncomfortable levels, aggression
c   decreases is the
LO 17   a. negative cognitive avoidance model
Concept b. high temperature avoidance model
545   c. negative affect escape model
M   d. negative aggression model

14.107   Why are some people unconcerned about air pollution?
d   a. they think it is not a problem
LO 18   b. they are simply ignorant
Concept c. they have been victims of propaganda
546   d. they have adapted to pollution and tend not to notice it
M

14.108   An example of an environmental stressor that is associated with negative affect is
a   a. air pollution
LO 18   b. high self-concealment
Concept c. having a job
546   d. high self-monitoring
M

14.109   Which of the following is NOT a form of atmospheric pollution that contributes to negative affect?
b   a. cigarette smoke
LO 18   b. artificial air fresheners
Concept c. exhaust from gasoline engines
546   d. exhaust from diesel engines
M

14.110   In looking at the impact of pleasant smell on task performance, Baron (1990) found that workers
c   who were exposed to the scent of an air freshener
LO 18   a. stayed longer at their work stations
Study   b. set lower goals
546   c. set higher goals
M   d. used less efficient work strategies

14.111   Electrical ions are the result of
c   a. smog
LO 19   b. artificial ventilation systems that generate magnetic aura
Fact   c. molecules splitting apart due to environmental stress
547   d. fiberoptic technology
M

14.112   All of the following except one are behaviors that are affected by ionic atmosphere conditions.
b   Which is the exception?
LO 19   a. increased suicides
Concept   b. increases in certain mental disorders
547   c. increases in industrial accidents
M   d. increases in some types of crime

14.113   A high level of negative ions may increase aggression in
b   a. everyone
LO 19   b. Type As
Concept   c. Type Bs
548   d. nonauthoritarians
M

14.114   Negative ions affect behavior through
d   a. speeding up cognitive processes
LO 19   b. creating positive affect in people
Conceptual   c. slowing down cognitive processes
548   d. adding to the strength of dominant responses
M

14.115   In the Baron (1987) study of the effects of negative ions on attraction
a   a. the effects of the similarity-dissimilarity effect were enhanced by high negative ions
LO 19   b. the effects of the similarity-dissimilarity effect were voided by high negative ions
Study   c. high negative ions led to general rejection of others
548   d. high negative ions led to general acceptance of others
M

14.116   How many people were there 10,000 years ago?
c   a. 4.5 billion
LO 20   b. 150,000
Fact   c. 5,000,000
549   d. 6 billion
E

14.117   By the year 2000, how many people will there be on this planet?
d   a. 4.5 billion
LO 20   b. 150,000,000
Fact   c. 5,000,000
549   d. 6 billion
M

14.118   How many people were on this planet in the year 1800?
d   a. 55 million
LO 20   b. 80 billion
Fact   c. 15.2 million
549   d. 1 billion
M

14.119
b
LO 20
Concept
549
M

Historically, an increase in a nation's population has generally been
a. considered to be dangerous
b. considered to be positive
c. a symptom of declining economy
d. discouraged by religious leaders

14.120
a
LO 20
Concept
549
M

Population growth is presently
a. exponential
b. arithmetic
c. multiplicative
d. stable

14.121
b
LO 20
Concept
549
C

Cornucopians suggest that population growth is beneficial because it
a. helps to weed out those who cannot adjust
b. acts as an incentive to improve production and increase standards of living
c. increases the chances of an individual reproducing, based on an arithmetic progression
d. increases the chances of an individual reproducing, based on a geometric progression

14.122
a
LO 20
Concept
549
M

The view that human resource and ingenuity are sufficient to overcome population pressures is the
a. cornucopian view
b. Malthusian view
c. geometric view
d. theory of natural selection

14.123
d
LO 20
Applied
549
C

In response to the immigration of an extra 50,000 people into Bovinia, the Dairy Institute invents a way to get an extra pint of milk from every cow each day. This situation fits the
a. theory of natural selection
b. concept of survival of the fittest
c. "natural" theory of advancement
d. cornucopian view of the world

14.124
a
LO 20
Concept
549
M

A "natural" way of restoring population equilibrium is
a. famine
b. sterilization
c. the Chinese "one child" law
d. an invention for new ways to increase food production

14.125
a
LO 20
Applied
550
M

The most effective way of controlling population discussed in the text includes governmental employment of
a. strong social conformity pressure
b. education about the rhythm method
c. famine
d. limiting education to certain classes of people

14.126
b
LO 21
Concept
550
M

A major problem with most waste products is that
a. humans recycle today than at any other point in history
b. waste products are presently produced faster than they decay
c. little or no importance is attached to recycling
d. most waste products are non-recyclable

14.127
d
LO 21
Concept
551
M

Recycling behavior often fails to occur because
a. many people are opposed to recycling
b. many people are opposed to the effort involved in recycling
c. many people do not know that recycling is beneficial
d. advice to recycle is not given in a persuasive form

14.128
d
LO 21
Concept
551
M

Does one person's garbage make a difference?
a. no, it is trivial relative to industrial pollution
b. yes, each person produces 1.5 million units of debris during his or her lifetime
c. no, it is too small in amount to make a difference
d. yes, given that everyone is unconcerned about his or her litter, the accumulated litter of all of us creates an environmental problem

14.129
c
LO 21
Concept
551
M

Global warming will cause the sea level to
a. drop due to evaporation
b. drop because water contracts as it heats beyond the freezing point
c. rise due to the melting of the polar ice caps
d. rise because water that evaporates into space will be trapped by the greenhouse effect and fall as rain

14.130
d
LO 21
Fact
551
E

The Republic of Maldives is an example of a nation that will be drastically affected by global warming through
a. increased smog
b. holes in the ozone layer
c. increasingly violent tropical storms
d. the rising sea level

14.131
b
LO 21
Fact
551
M

Which of the following is NOT a gas that traps heat in the atmosphere?
a. carbon dioxide
b. nitrogen
c. methane
d. chlorofluorocarbons

14.132
d
LO 21
Concept
551
M

Carbon dioxide production is primarily associated with
a. the digestive systems of domestic cattle
b. the "exhalation" of plants
c. the slow decay rates of chlorofluorocarbons
d. the burning of fossil fuels such as coal or oil

14.133
c
LO 21
Fact
551
E

The greenhouse gas that is most likely to be reduced the most in the near future is
a. nitrogen
b. carbon dioxide
c. chlorofluorocarbons
d. methane

14.134
a
LO 21
Fact
551
E

Which greenhouse gas is associated with creating holes in the ozone layer?
a. CFCs
b. carbon dioxide
c. methane
d. nitrogen

14.135   The major human behavioral source of carbon dioxide is people's use of
c   a. refrigerants
LO 21   b. rice
Fact   c. oil
551   d. so-called "alternative sources of energy"
M

14.136   A human behavioral source of methane is people's use of
b   a. refrigerants
LO 21   b. rice
Fact   c. oil
551   d. so-called "alternative source of energy"
M

14.137   It is thought that some diseases such as AIDS and Dengue Fever
b   a. will never be curable
LO 21   b. originated with non-human species
Concept   c. may be passed from generation to generation
552   d. are genetically linked to one another
M

14.138   The extinction of the rain forest species may be related to diseases such as Ebola through
c   a. such diseases being transmitted to human being directly from these animals
LO 21   b. the placing of rare animals in zoos
Concept   c. the adaptation of viruses from an extinct host species to human beings
552   d. the relatively safe and efficient means of transport available today that makes it possible to travel
C   to many places before a virus dies naturally

14.139   Human beings may become the targets of viruses that need to adapt to another species because
d   a. viruses adapt more easily to mammalian species than other species
LO 21   b. the proximity of most human beings to one another make it easy for any virus to infect many
Concept   humans
552   c. large scale human migrations are now rare, so a virus will not be exposed to many climates
C   d. human beings are the most likely species to physically replace the newly extinct species

14.140   Nilchaikovit and colleagues (1993) suggest that the basic reasons for different responses to a medical
a   setting are in
LO 22   a. the difference between Eastern and Western concepts of self
Study   b. the difference between Eastern and Western concepts of medicine
554   c. the difference between Eastern and Western concepts of communication
C   d. the difference between Eastern and Western concepts of interpersonal behavior

NOTES

NOTES

NOTES

NOTES

NOTES

NOTES

NOTES

NOTES

NOTES

NOTES

NOTES

NOTES

NOTES